LET'S GO

BARCELONA

RESEARCHERS
SEPH KRAMER
JUSTINE LESCROART

MARY POTTER MANAGING EDITOR
JESSE BARRON RESEARCH MANAGER

EDITORS
COURTNEY A. FISKE
SARA PLANA
RUSSELL FORD RENNIE
CHARLIE E. RIGGS
OLGA I. ZHULINA

CONTENTS

RESEARCHERS

Seph Kramer *Ribera, l'Eixample, Barri Gòtic, Barceloneta, Poble Nou, Palafrugell, Cadaqués, Girona, Serra de Collserola, Sant Andreu, Nou Barris, Sants*

The Lord Byron of Barcelona, a wolf in casanova's clothing, Seph saw his summer through the eyes of a true romantic. And with good reason: his dad proposed to his mom in Barcelona oh so many years ago. In l'Eixample, he found us restaurants with just the right amount of candlelight. When Justine was busy on the nude beaches in Sitges, Seph picked up the slack in Montjuïc and partied like a Barcelonese, dancing until way after sunrise. Seph's favorite board game is a table for two.

Justine Lescroart *Raval, Gràcia, l'Eixample Esquerra, l'Eixample Dreta, Sitges, Tossa, Puigcerdà, Poble Sec, Montjuïc, Sarrià, Horta, Vall d'Hebron, Montserrat*

Oscar Wilde told New York City customs officials, "I have nothing to declare except my genius." Justine had nothing to declare except for a full-blown case of mono, which, incredibly, didn't stop her from finding us the best tapas bars in Gràcia, talking her way into an haute couture runway show, and mastering enough Catalan to order every part of a pig (the choice is yours: botifarra, llom, or xorico?). That, and her genius for sending us copy that makes Oscar look like Danielle Steel.

STAFF WRITERS

Dan Barbero

Sanders Bernstein

Nick Charyk

Meg Popkin

Kyle Bean

Julia Cain

Anna Kendrick

Madeleine Schwartz

CONTRIBUTING WRITER

Caitlin Connolly earned a Bachelor of Arts in Political Science from Barnard College in Manhattan. After a year spent traveling through South America, Asia, Africa and Europe, she is now studying law at Harvard. She hopes to pursue public interest law and to continue learning about the world through its people and their music.

ACKNOWLEDGMENTS

JESSE THANKS: Seph and Justine for all their hard work.

THE EDITORS THANK: First and foremost our lord (Jay-C) and savior (Starbucks, Terry's Chocolate Orange). We also owe gratitude to Barack Obama (peace be upon Him), the Oxford comma, the water cooler, bagel/payday Fridays, the HSA "SummerFun" team for being so inclusive, Rotio (wherefore art thou Rotio?), the real Robinson Crusoe, the Cambridge weather and defective umbrellas, Bolt-Bus, Henry Louis Gates, Jr. (sorry 'bout the phone call), the office blog, gratuitous nudity, the 20-20-20 rule and bananas (no more eye twitches), the Portuguese flag, trips to the beach (ha!), sunbathing recently married Mormon final club alums, non-existent free food in the square, dog-star puns, and last but not least, America. The local time in Tehran is 1:21am. But seriously, the MEs and RMs, our researchers (and all their wisdom on tablecloths and hipsters), LGHQ, HSA, our significant others (future, Canadian, and otherwise), and families (thanks Mom).

Publishing Director
Laura M. Gordon
Editorial Director
Dwight Livingstone Curtis
Publicity and Marketing Director
Vanessa J. Dube
Production and Design Director
Rebecca Lieberman
Cartography Director
Anthony Rotio
Website Director
Lukáš Tóth
Managing Editors
Ashley Laporte, Iya Megre, Mary Potter, Nathaniel Rakich
Technology Project Manager
C. Alexander Tremblay
Director of IT
David Fulton-Howard
Financial Associates
Catherine Humphreville, Jun Li

Managing Editor
Mary Potter
Research Manager
Jesse Barron
Editors
Courtney A. Fiske, Sara Plana, Russell Ford Rennie, Charlie E. Riggs, Olga I. Zhulina
Typesetter
Rebecca Lieberman

President
Daniel Lee
General Manager
Jim McKellar

Our researchers list establishments in order of value from best to worst, honoring our favorites with the Let's Go thumbs-up (☝). Because the best *value* is not always the cheapest *price*, we have incorporated a system of price ranges based on a rough expectation of what you will spend. For **accommodations,** we base our range on the cheapest price for which a single traveler can stay for one night. For **restaurants,** we estimate the average amount one traveler will spend in one sitting. The table below tells you what you'll *typically* find in Barcelona at the corresponding price range, but keep in mind that no system can allow for the quirks of individual establishments.

ACCOMMODATIONS	RANGE	WHAT YOU'RE *LIKELY* TO FIND
❶	under €20	Campgrounds, HI hostels, basic dorm rooms, *albergues* or *refugios*. Expect bunk beds and a communal bath; you may have to provide or rent towels and sheets.
❷	€20-29	Upper-end hostels or lower-end *pensiones*. You may have a private bathroom, or there may be a sink in your room and a communal shower in the hall. Breakfast is often included, or meals may be available cheaply to hostel guests.
❸	€30-37	A small room with a private bath, probably in a budget hotel, *hostal,* or *pensión*. Should have decent amenities, like a phone and TV. Breakfast may be included.
❹	€38-50	Similar to ❸, but should have more amenities or be in a more highly touristed or conveniently located area. Breakfast is often included in the price of your room.
❺	over €50	Large hotels, upscale chains, or government-run luxury *paradores*. If it's a ❺ and it doesn't have the perks or service you're looking for, you've probably paid too much.

FOOD	RANGE	WHAT YOU'RE *LIKELY* TO FIND
❶	under €6	Probably a *kebap* or fast-food stand, *cafetería*, bar, or bakery. Rarely a sit-down meal, unless you're sitting at the bar feasting on free tapas with your drinks.
❷	€6-12	*Bocadillos* (sandwiches), salads, tapas, and some entrees and set *menús*. May be sit-down or take-out, but expect to be served by a waiter or bartender.
❸	€13-17	Typically a sit-down meal. Many set *menús* include a 3-course meal that includes wine and dessert.
❹	€18-25	Entrees are more expensive than ❸, but you're paying for quality service, ambience, and decor. Few restaurants in this range have a dress code, but you'll want to clean yourself up after a day of travel.
❺	over €25	Your meal might cost more than your hostel, but here's hoping it's something fabulous or famous. Just don't plan on wearing flip-flops.

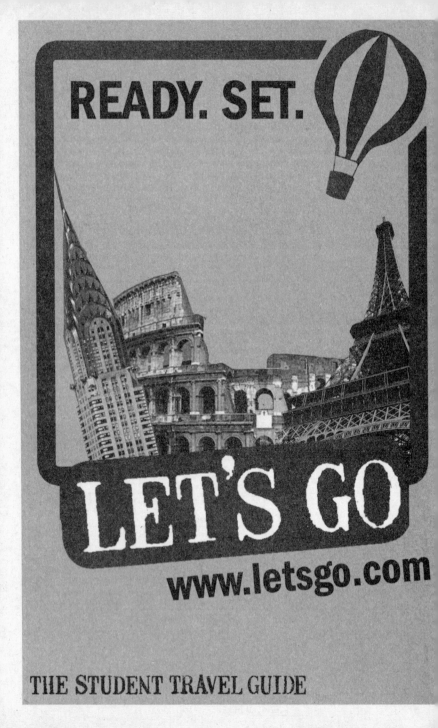

ABOUT LET'S GO

THE STUDENT TRAVEL GUIDE

Let's Go publishes the world's favorite student travel guides, written entirely by Harvard students. Armed with pens, notebooks, and a few changes of clothes stuffed into their backpacks, our student researchers go across continents, through time zones, and above expectations to seek out invaluable travel experiences for our readers. Because we are a completely student-run company, we have a unique perspective on how students travel, where they want to go, and what they're looking to do when they get there. If your dream is to grab a machete and forge through the jungles of Costa Rica, we can take you there. If you'd rather bask in the Riviera sun at a beachside cafe, we'll set you a table. In short, we write for readers who know that there's more to travel than tour buses. To keep up, visit our website, www.letsgo.com, where you can sign up to blog, post photos from your trips, and connect with the Let's Go community.

TRAVELING BEYOND TOURISM

We're on a mission to provide our readers with sharp, fresh coverage packed with socially responsible opportunities to go beyond tourism. Each guide's Beyond Tourism chapter shares ideas about responsible travel, study abroad, and how to give back to the places you visit while on the road. To help you gain a deeper connection with the places you travel, our fearless researchers scour the globe to give you the heads-up on both world-renowned and off-the-beaten-track opportunities. We've also opened our pages to respected writers and scholars to hear their takes on the countries and regions we cover, and asked travelers who have worked, studied, or volunteered abroad to contribute first-person accounts of their experiences.

FIFTY YEARS OF WISDOM

Let's Go has been on the road for 50 years and counting. We've grown a lot since publishing our first 20-page pamphlet to Europe in 1960, but five decades and 54 titles later our witty, candid guides are still researched and written entirely by students on shoestring budgets who know that train strikes, stolen luggage, food poisoning, and marriage proposals are all part of a day's work. This year, for our 50th anniversary, we're publishing 26 titles—including 6 brand new guides—brimming with editorial honesty, a commitment to students, and our irreverent style. Here's to the next 50!

THE LET'S GO COMMUNITY

More than just a travel guide company, Let's Go is a community that reaches from our headquarters in Cambridge, MA all across the globe. Our small staff of dedicated student editors, writers, and tech nerds comes together because of our shared passion for travel and our desire to help other travelers get the most out of their experience. We love it when our readers become part of the Let's Go community as well—when you travel, drop us a postcard (67 Mt. Auburn St., Cambridge, MA 02138, USA), send us an e-mail (feedback@letsgo.com), or sign up on our website (www.letsgo.com) to tell us about your adventures and discoveries.

For more information, updated travel coverage, and news from our researcher team, visit us online at www.letsgo.com.

DISCOVER BARCELONA

Fantastical Barcelona. Spain's most cosmopolitan city welcomes innumerable travelers and expats from the US, South America, and nearly everywhere else. They come for the sun-soaked beaches, the wild clubs, the world-class food, and the legendary art. Picasso came from Barcelona. Gaudí and Miró did, too. Here, a bottle of good champagne is cheaper than a ham sandwich.

Barcelona doesn't speak Spanish. This city is proud of its identity as the capital of Catalunya, which it has been since Classical Antiquity, when walls were laid around the Roman city of Barcino in the third century BC. Until Columbus's voyage made the Atlantic the new Mediterranean, it was a major player in European trade. In Barcelona, pride in the history of the region and the city is as much a part of the culture as the siesta.

People will tell you that the 1992 Olympics were the turning point for Barcelona. Don't believe them. It was the end of the Franco era in 1974 that catapulted Barcelona—and Catalan culture—to the forefront of a new Spain.

The result is a vanguard city squeezed between the blue waters of the Mediterranean and the green Tibidabo hills, flashing with such vibrant colors that you'll see it long after you've closed your eyes.

FACTS AND FIGURES

METRO AREA POPULATION: 1,503,884

AS PERCENT OF SPAIN'S POPULATION: 2.6%

PERCENT OF POPULATION THAT IS NOT ROMAN CATHOLIC: 10%

LENGTH OF LONGEST SAUSAGE IN CATALUNYA: 5200m (World Record)

ANNUAL PER CAPITA PORK CONSUMPTION: 55.78kg

PERCENTAGE OF CATALUNYANS WHO DON'T SPEAK CATALAN: 6.4%

NUMBER OF BARS THAT HAVE ANCIENT ROMAN WALLS: 7

NUMBER OF EXPATS ARRIVING TO SPAIN PER YEAR: More than 250,000

LENGTH OF BARCELONA'S ROMAN NAME: 41 letters ("Colonia Faventia Julia Augusta Paterna Barcino")

NUMBER OF YEARS SINCE CONSTRUCTION BEGAN ON THE SAGRADA FAMÍLIA: 127

NUMBER OF WHITE GEESE IN RESIDENCE: 13 (visit the Cathedral).

LAST TIME SPAIN PLACED IN THE WORLD CUP FINAL FOUR: 1950

PERCENTAGE OF POPULATION THAT CHAIN SMOKES: 25%

AVERAGE ANNUAL RAINFALL: 1000m

NUMBER OF RESIDENTS WHO ARE FAMOUS FOR WALKING AROUND NAKED: 2

WHEN TO GO

Barcelona's Mediterranean climate makes it an excellent destination no matter the season. The tourist season officially runs from the middle of June through late August, when the city is filled to capacity with travelers and the weather is at its most spectacular. During high season, the days are warm and sunny (72°F with sea breezes). January and December are the coldest months of

DISCOVER

winter, when sunset will be early and temperatures hover around 50°F. Be aware that during July and especially August, many native Barceloneses take advantantage of vacations from work and head elsewhere. Those looking for the full Barcelona experience will want to visit during the summer, when warm weather, music and theater festivals, a vibrant street scene, and full-tilt nightlife mayhem draw tourists from all over the world. Just the same, it's not unusual to visit during the autumn or winter to enjoy a quieter city. Cheaper tickets and comparably good weather prevail throughout the spring and early fall. European airline prices spike again around Christmas and New Year's. Keep in mind that August will be the busiest month for the tourist industry, as French and British arrive in droves, bringing the festive atmosphere of late summer and the biggest crowds of the season.

BARCELONA'S NEIGHBORHOODS

The first city built on the site of today's Barcelona was the Roman city of Barcino, whose walls were laid in the AD third century. The Barcino of 1700 years ago is the "Barri Gòtic" of today, a part of the Ciutat Vella, or old city. The Ciutat Vella includes three neighborhoods: the Barri Gòtic, La Ribera, and El Raval. Northeast of Plaça de Catalunya, the newer neighborhoods, L'Eixample and Gràcia, are home to Barcelona's wealthier residents and some of its most famous Modernista architecture. The waterfront includes both Port Vell and the neighborhood of Barceloneta. In the west, the hill of Montjuïc looms over some of Barcelona's more suburban neighborhoods, such as Sants. Most tourist activity is concentrated in the Ciutat Vella and L'Eixample, but those willing to explore will be well rewarded by hidden restaurants, museums, and parks. For more on Barcelona's climate, see the **Appendix, p. 224**.

CIUTAT VELLA

BARRI GÒTIC AND LAS RAMBLAS

Orientation: between Las Ramblas in the west and Via Laietana in the east. The ocean borders the neighborhood to the south and C. Fontanella borders it to the north. Transportation: ⓂCatalunya, L1/3; Liceu, L3; Drassanes, L3; Jaume I, L4. Because of the narrow streets, no buses run through the Barri Gòtic, only on the bordering streets. Buses #14, 38, 59, and 91 traverse Las Ramblas, while buses #17, 19, 40 and 45 come down Via Laietana. Accommodations: see p. 69.

 HANG ON TO YOUR HAT. Pickpocketing is a problem on Las Ramblas. Keep a close eye on your stuff if you want to keep it.

The oldest sections of Barcelona, the Barri Gòtic and Las Ramblas are the tourist centers of the city. Originally settled by the Romans in the third century, and by the Carthaginians before that, the Barri Gòtic is built on the ruins of the Roman city Barcino (named for Bareas, a king of Carthage). Subsequent invasions and inhabitations, by Visigoths, Moors, and Franks, left their mark on the winding streets of the old city. This is a district made for walking, and cars are prohibited from many of its shady stone streets. There are no parks here: keep in mind that in 1200 there was no city surrounding it, only wilderness. A stroll down C. Avinyò is a great way to see some of Barcelona's most treasured architectural landmarks, just meters away from the area's popular bars and restaurants.

DON'T MISS...

SIGHTS AND MUSEUMS: Relax in the tranquil cloister of **La Catedral de la Santa Creu** (p. 110).

FOOD AND DRINK: Falafel at **Maoz** or a picnic from the **Boqueria** are only appropriate (p. 83).

NIGHTLIFE: The bars in the **Plaça Reial** (p. 171) fill early and close late.

LA RIBERA

Orientation: La Ribera is separated from the Barri Gòtic by Via Laietana and is bordered on the east by C. Wellington, on the far side of Parc de la Ciutadella. Often grouped with its northwestern neighbor, Sant Pere, the district extends to Ronda de Sant Pere and southeast to Av. Marqués de l'Argentera and the Estació de Fraça. The most convenient metro stops are Ⓜ Urquinaona, L1/4 and Ⓜ Jaume I, L4. La Ribera is a 15min. walk from Po. de Catalunya. Buses #17 and 19 drive down Via Laietana. Accommodations: see p. 71.

La Ribera has always been a neighborhood for Barcelona's working class, and it has been witness to two of the most formative events in Barcelona's history. In the 18th century, Felipe V demolished much of La Ribera, then the city's commercial hub, to make space for the impressive Ciutadella, the seat of Madrid's proxy control of Barcelona, today a park. Angry that Barcelona had favored his opponent, the Archduke Carlos, as its leader, Felipe V stuffed the wealthy, and therefore powerful, citizens of Barcelona into the Ciutadella's chambers. Luckily, his successors were more lenient on their subjects; most victims were freed, and La Ribera was rejuvenated. Then, in 1888, the former site of Ciutadella became home to the Universal Exposition, and La Ribera served as its launching point, displaying the new flair for *Modernisme* and the simplicity of old Spanish architecture and traditional values. In recent years, the neighborhood has evolved into Barcelona's bohemian nucleus, attracting a young, artsy crowd of locals, a community of expats, and tourists in the know.

DON'T MISS...

SIGHTS AND MUSEUMS: With a great multimedia English tour explaining its every nuance, the **Palau de la Música Catalana** (p. 116) will leave even the most jaded tourist in awe of the excessive beauty of Modernisme. The **Museu Picasso** (p. 143) has a collection of the early and late works by the father of modern art (and a proud sometime Barcelonese).

FOOD AND DRINK: Enjoy tapas and a glass of cava at **Xampanyet** (p. 86), the most renowned tapas bar in La Ribera (which is saying a lot).

NIGHTLIFE: Passeig del Born has some of the hippest, most diverse bars in Barcelona, and a picturesque backdrop for some serious barhopping (p. 174).

EL RAVAL

Orientation: El Raval is the neighborhood to the west of Las Ramblas. It is bordered by Av. Parallel and the Rondas St. Pau, St. Antoni, and Universitat. C. Hospital is the main street that divides the neighborhood into two halves. On the north side, MACBA and more upscale restaurants. On the south side lies the Rambla del Raval, a more bohemian area. Accommodations: see p. 72. Nightlife: see p. 176. The most convenient metro stops are Ⓜ Urquinaona, L1/4 and Jaume I, L4. La Ribera is a 15min. walk from Po. de Catalunya. Buses #17 and 19 drive down Via Laietana.

KEEP YOUR WITS ABOUT YOU. El Raval used to be more dangerous than it is today, but travelers are still advised to exercise caution when walking around at night. Women may want to bar-hop with a friend.

Though each neighborhood of the old city gets as much love from locals as from tourists, El Raval in particular is a hometown favorite. This ethnically diverse and culturally rich neighborhood has a special charm, with small, quirky shops and eateries, welcoming bars, and hidden historical attractions.

El Raval began as a small village outside the Roman walls, it was enveloped by the new city boundaries in the 14th century and has since continued expanding. Raval's importance to Barcelona's international trade gave it the nickname Barrio Chino (Chinatown), not because many Chinese lived there but because Chinese goods so frequently passed through.

The late 19th century was slightly less glorious for Raval, as overcrowding led to a rise in crime, drug use, and prostitution. In the grand scheme of things, this is a small detour for this vibrant neighborhood. The neighborhood formerly known as Chinatown is today too diverse to bear a single designation.

DON'T MISS...

SIGHTS AND MUSEUMS: The **MACBA** (p. 144) does it all: art, videos, food, and a party every Thursday night.

FOOD AND DRINK: Tea under a tent on the Rambla Del Raval, or healthy vegetarian food at Organic, are just two ways to get into the culinary spirit of the Raval.

NIGHTLIFE: Sip absinthe at **Bar Almirall** or **Marsella Bar** (p. 176).

PLAÇA DE CATALUNYA

Orientation: The most important streets in the city emanate from Pl. de Catalunya. The Aerobus airport shuttle drops off newcomers on the Corte Inglés side of the plaça. The city's main tourist office is directly across the street from the store, underground. On this side of the plaça one can also catch the Bus Turístic red route (p. 109), which visits the city's northern areas of interest. Looking out onto the plaça from El Corte Inglés, you'll see the Hard Rock Café side of the plaça on the left. Las Ramblas begins next door. Directly across the plaça from El Corte Inglés is the Triangle shopping center, featuring a FNAC store and the crowded Café Zurich. The line for the Bus Turístic blue route, which hits the southern sights, forms on this side. To the right is the Banco Español de Crédito. Across the street from here is the plaça's underground police station. Ronda Universitat runs in front of the Banco Español. Passeig de Gràcia, with its Modernista architecture and upscale shops, begins between the Banco Español and El Corte Inglés. The Avinguda Portal de l'Angel, a wide pedestrian way, and Carrer Fontanella, which houses a few accommodations, start between El Corte Inglés and the Hard Rock Cafe.

Plaça de Catalunya is of more historical interest than actual interest. When l'Eixample was built, this commercial square was conceived as a link between the old city and the new city, which is to say, a link between narrow streets and wide ones. The size of the plaça deserves attention, because it represents a departure, architecturally, from the small, street-width plaças that predominate in the old quarter. It's commonly observed that Plaça de Catalunya operates on "automobile scale" while Ciutat Vella operates on "human scale."

That said, you won't be able avoid it during your visit. The airport shuttle, a fleet of tourist buses, and almost all city buses pass through here, creating snarling traffic jams at all hours. It is the starting point of Passeig de Gràcia and Las Ramblas and it is full of internet cafes and currency exchanges.

The plaça itself contains little greenery but over 26 fountains and statues. Of these, the most visible is the *Monument a Macià* (1991) by Josep Subirachs, the architect who desgined the controversial Passion Façade of the Sagrada Família (p. 123). Subirach's monument, set on the Ramblas corner of the plaça, appears to be two sets of steps piled precariously on top of one another; the bust of Macià, president of the Generalitat in the 1930s, isn't exactly Notre Dâme, either.

The plaça is the official meeting point for Barcelona's Parliament of Fowls, whose constituents, the pigeons, conduct their business at all hours.

DON'T MISS...

THE BUS up to l'Eixample. You probably won't want to stay in Plaça de Catalunya for much longer than necessary.

L'EIXAMPLE

Orientation: Bound by Gran Via de les Corts Catalanes and Plaça de Catalunya in the south and Travessera de Gràcia in the north. L'Eixample extends east to Carrer de Tarragona and west to the Sagrada Família. Most maps divide l'Eixample into 2 neighborhoods: Esquerra de l'Eixample (left expansion) and La Dreta de l'Eixample (right expansion). We add a 3rd neighborhood, which we call Passeig de Gràcia, as Pg. de Gràcia and its immediate environs have distinctive sights and restaurants that differentiate it from the rest of l'Eixample. Transportation: Metro lines 3, 4, 5, and the FCG trains run through l'Eixample; about half the city buses pass through it, and all Nitbuses originate at Pl. de Catalunya.

Around the turn of the 19th century overcrowding became a problem in the old city. When Madrid refused permission for the destruction of the Roman walls, Barceloneses tore them down in civil disturbances during the late 1850s, paving the way for the construction of l'Eixample ("the expansion" in Catalan), the wealthy neighborhood around Pg. de Gràcia.

L'Eixample is built on an entirely different scale than Ciutat Vella. Its wide avenues and elegant three-story houses were designed for wealthy factory owners and captains of industry who would commute, first by carriage and later by car, into the city center down Pg. de Gràcia. The splendid houses that they commissioned would define Barcelona's Modernisme movement, which Josep Puig i Cadafalch—one of its chief adherents—defined as "a modern art, taking our traditional arts as a basis, adorning it with new material, solving contemporary problems with a national spirit." No visit to Barcelona is complete without a stroll down Pg. de Gràcia, home to many of Gaudí's masterpieces as well as work by major Modernisme architects like Domènech i Montaner and Cadafalch.

You will notice that l'Eixample's streets are not perfect squares. This isn't because the surveyors had one too many glasses of absinthe; in fact, it's because Madrid chose Idlefons Cerdà's plan for octagonal blocks, a clever way to make sure this new neighborhood had wide streets and plenty of space in front of houses.

Gaudí once called his Sagrada Família "a bible for the illiterate." The façades of l'Eixample's Modernisme buildings are a bible for the architecturally curious—surprises and hidden pleasures wait around every octagonal corner.

At night, l'Eixample is the capital of gay nightlife and home to many tapas bars and larger clubs. It used to be that tourists saw the Pg. de Gràcia and Sagrada

Família and then escaped back to the Ciutat Vella. No longer: the l'Eixample of today lives up to its name, "expanding" visitors' experience of Barcelona.

DON'T MISS...

SIGHTS AND MUSEUMS: No trip is complete without a visit to **La Sagrada Família** (p. 123), **La Manzana de la Discòrdia** (p. 121), and **Casa Milà** (p. 120).

FOOD AND DRINK: The Passeig de Gràcia teems with outdoor cafes and is perfect for people-watching. Grab a seat at **Café Torino,** where Gaudí tried his hand at restaurant design.

NIGHTLIFE: Sample "Gay-xample's" famous LGBT nightlife at **Dietrich,** or pick from our other favorite clubs (p. 179).

BARCELONETA

Orientation: Barceloneta is the neighborhood between Port Vell and Port Olímpic, which is another way of saying that it's the beach. Pg. Joan de Borbó, running along the port, is the neighborhood's main drag, while the Pg. Marítim borders the beach area. Public transportation: Ⓜ Barceloneta. Buses #59 and 14 both run down Las Ramblas to the waterfront area. Also accessible by buses #17, 36, 40, 45, 57, and N8. Sights and Museums: see p. 147. Food and Drink: see p. 96. Nightlife: see p. 183. Accommodations: see p. 76.

Barceloneta ("little Barcelona") was born out of necessity. In 1718, La Ribera was butchered to make room for the enormous Ciutadella fortress (p. 117); the transformation of that neighborhood displaced thousands of lower class workers. The rapid construction of workers' barracks in Barceloneta was the solution.

You will notice that all the buildings here are the same height. That's not an accident, but the result of zoning laws aimed at bringing sunlight into every home. Today, the buildings are clean, attractive additions to a neighborhood with a great seaside location and a vibrant, diverse culture.

At one time, Barceloneta's residents were mainly workers in the factories owned by l'Eixample's wealthy residents. Today it's home to the city's sailors, fishermen, and their families.

DON'T MISS...

THE BEACH, THE BEACH, OR THE BEACH (p. 153).

FOOD AND DRINK: Fresh seafood at one of Barceloneta's hidden restaurants.

POBLE NOU AND PORT OLÍMPIC

Orientation: Bound by C. de Marina, Av. Diagonal, the Vila Olímpica, and the ocean. Transportation: Central metro stops Ⓜ Marina, L1; Bogatell, L4; Llacuna, L4; Ciutadella/Vila Olímpic, L4; Poble Nou, L4. Glories, L1, and Selva de Mar, L4, run along the outskirts of the neighborhood. Bus lines include #6, 7, 36, 41, 71, and 92. Accommodations: p. 76. Food and Drink: p. 97. Nightlife: p. 184. Sights and Museums: p. 126.

While industrial Poble Nou fueled Barcelona's economic growth in the 19th century, it enjoyed little of the era's wealth. Until recently, Poble Nou consisted mainly of factories, warehouses, and low-income housing. Auto shops and commercial supply stores still abound, but the major factories were all removed for the 1992 Olympics.

A little history: when Barcelona was granted its Olympic bid in 1986, the privilege presented a two-sided problem. The city had to comfortably house 15,000 athletes while beautifying its long-ignored coastline. Oriol Bohigas, Josep Martorall, David Mackay, and Albert Puig Domènech designed the solution: the Vila Olímpica, a residential area with wide streets, symmetrical apartment buildings, pristine parks, and open-air art pieces. Most social activity in the area takes place in the L-shaped Port Olímpic, home to docked sailboats, more than 20 restaurants, a large casino, and a strip of gaudy nightclubs.

In the wake of this development, old industrial buildings are slowly being converted into more apartments and nightclubs. With the exception of the Olympic areas, the atmosphere in Poble Nou is that of a village: nondescript corner bars abound, and the tree-lined Rambla de Poble Nou is more likely to be filled with chatting grandmothers, small children, and gossiping teens than street artists and tourists. Besides its Olympic structures, Poble Nou's claims to fame are its sparkling city beaches and a raging alternative and hard rock music scene.

MONTJUÏC

Orientation: Montjuïc lies in the southwest corner of the city, bordering the Poble Sec neighborhood. Transportation: The metro has stops on the outskirts of Montjuïc; a few buses run through Montjuïc. ⓂEspanya is best for reaching the MNAC and Poble Espanyol area, while ⓂParal·lel, L2/3, gives you access to the underground funicular, a convenient way to reach the Fundació Miró, Miramar, and the Castell de Montjuïc; it lets you off on Av. Miramar. The funicular runs 9am-10pm. Take bus #50 from Pl. d'Espanya to reach Poble Espanyol and the more distant Montjuïc sights like the Olympic area. Accommodations: p. 76. Food and Drink: p. 97. Nightlife: p. 185.

Montjuïc has been strategically significant since Barcino was Carthaginian, and when you see the city from its crest, you'll understand why. From here, generations of military commanders have surveyed the harbor and defended their city against attacks from the south.

The Laietani collected oysters on Montjuïc before they were subdued by the Romans (p. 41), who erected a temple to Jupiter on its slopes. Since then, dozens of despotic rulers have constructed and modified the Castell de Montjuïc, built atop the ancient Jewish cemetery (hence the name "Montjuïc," which means "Hill of the Jews"). In the 20th century, Franco made the Castell de Montjuïc one of his "interrogation" headquarters; somewhere deep in the recesses of the structure, his *beneméritos* (ironically "the honorable ones") shot Catalunya's former president, Lluís Companys, in 1941, and tortured anarchists, socialists, and other enemies of the Franco regime. The fort was not re-dedicated to the city until 1960.

Since reacquiring the mountain, Barcelona has given Montjuïc a new identity, transforming it from a military stronghold into a vast park by day and playground by night. The park is one of the city's most visited attractions, with a little bit of something for everyone—world-famous art museums and theater, Olympic history and facilities, walking and biking trails, a healthy dose of nightlife, and an awe-inspiring historical cemetery (really).

Montjuïc is an immense park, not a neighborhood, and as such is not the easiest area to navigate. Street signs are scarce. In times of need, a simple map marking particular locations and the curves of major roads is most helpful—check out our maps or pick one up at the Barcelona tourist office (p. 64) or El Corte Inglés (p. 165).

DON'T MISS...

SIGHTS AND MUSEUMS: The **Castell de Montjuïc** (p. 128) offers incredible views of the city and the sea. The **Fundació Miró** (p. 148) will make a Miró fan of anyone.

NIGHTLIFE: If you thought you knew wild and gaudy, may we suggest an evening at **Terrazza** (p. 185) followed by a trip to one of *los afters*?

PORT VELL

Orientation: Port Vell is the L-shaped strip beginning at Plaça d'Antoni Lopez and extending out to Maremagnum.

After moving a congested coastal road underground, the city opened Moll de la Fusta, a wide pedestrian zone that leads to the beaches of Barceloneta and connects the bright Maremagnum and the Moll d'Espanya. Today, the rejuvenated Port Vell—the "Old Port"—is as hedonistic and touristy as Barcelona gets.

ZONA ALTA

Zona Alta is a catch-all term for neighborhoods north and northwest of l'Eixample. It includes the neighborhoods east of the Collserola mountains, Gràcia, and a number of other, smaller neighborhoods. Keep in mind that these areas were once independent towns and have been gradually incorporated into Barcelona; that helps explain their distinctive atmospheres, as well as the eccentric street grid that connects them. Because the village plans are a mix of various pre-19th century designs, the roads that connect their grids are curvy, following the topography of the land rather than the dictates of engineers.

GRÀCIA

Orientation: Gràcia lies past l'Eixample, above Av. Diagonal and C. de Còrsega, and stretches up to the Park Güell. Transportation: Ⓜ Lesseps, L3; Fontana, L3; Diagonal, L3/5; Joanic, L4; or FGC: Gràcia. Buses #24, 25, 28, and N4. Accommodations: p. 77. Sights and Museums: p. 130.

Gràcia is one of Zona Alta's most charming neighborhoods. Originally an independent, largely working-class village, it was incorporated into Barcelona in 1897, much to the protest of its residents. Calls for Gràcian independence continue even today, albeit with less frequency. The area has always had a political streak—consider the names of the Mercat de Llibertat, Pl. de la Revolució, and other important landmarks. After incorporation, the area continued to be a center of left-wing activism and resistance throughout the oppressive Franco regime.

Untouched by tourism until relatively recently, Gràcia retains the local charm that has been sapped from some of Barcelona's more popular sections. The neighborhood packs a surprising number of *Modernista* buildings and parks, international cuisine, and chic shops into a relatively small area, making it a good choice for exploring.

DON'T MISS...

SIGHTS AND MUSEUMS: *Modernista* houses abound in Gràcia, by all of the favorites from l'Eixample and some you've never heard of.

FOOD AND DRINK: The **tapas** places in Gràcia are the real thing; there's a good one on almost every corner. *Patatas bravas*, anyone? (p. 99).

PARC GÜELL: Gaudí's take on the urban playground was bound to be fantastical, but no one could have predicted the ceramic serpent, endless park bench, and melting stonework that make Güell Montjuïc's only rival for outdoor splendor in Barcelona.

VALL D'HEBRON AND HORTA-GUINARDÓ

Orientation: Horta and Vall d'Hebron are past l'Eixample Dreta, in the upper northeastern corner of the city. Transportation: Ⓜ Horta, L5; Vall d'Hebron, L3; Mundet, L3; Montbau, L3. Accommodations: p. 78. Food and Drink: p. 102. Sights and Museums: p. 134.

Horta didn't surrender its status as an independent village until 1904, and its abundance of narrow pedestrian streets and old apartment buildings attest to that small town history. It boasts a few farmhouses and fortresses from the Middle Ages, as well as aristocratic estates dating from the 19th century, when the base of the Collserola mountains was a popular place to build wealthy country homes.

In contrast, the neighboring Vall d'Hebron was built up specifically to serve as one of four main Olympic venues in 1992, housing the centers for cycling, tennis, and archery competitions. The Olympics also gave the neighborhoods the gigantic Velòdrom d'Horta. One non-Olympic attraction is the Jardins del Laberint d'Horta (p. 134).

In general, the area has a nondescript atmosphere perfect for suburbanites but lacking the adventure and excitement sought by many travelers.

NOU BARRIS AND SANT ANDREU

Orientation: Sant Andreu begins at the terminus of Rambla de Prim, considerably northeast of La Sagrada Família, and extends north to Passeig de Santa Coloma. Its northwestern neighbor, Nou Barris, Begins around the intersection of Ronda de Dalt and Via Júlia. Transportation: ⓜVerneda, Sant Andreu, Via Júlia, Trinitat Nova. Sant Andreu: Bus #126. Accommodations: p. 81 and p. 80.

Nou Barris ("Nine Neighborhoods") is a group of 14 (once 9) tiny suburban neighborhoods, and one of the few areas of Barcelona to have recorded a net decrease in population in the latest census. It has the largest population of Roma people (those derogatorily called "gypsies") in Barcelona, and holds the distinction among other neighborhoods of having the Wikipedia page with the most Eastern European language translations.

In high season, Nou Barris may be a good last-resort option for clean, affordable lodging close to non-Spanish ethnic cuisine.

SARRIÀ

Orientation: Sarrià lies at the base of the Collserola mountains and is loosely bordered by Av. Pedralbes and Av. Tibidabo on either side. Divided from l'Eixample and Les Corts by Av. Diagonal; Via Augusta separates it from Gràcia. Transportation: FGC: Bonanova, Tres Torres, Sarrià, and Reina Elisenda. Bus lines include #66, 30, and 34. Accommodations: p. 79. Food and Drink: p. 103. Sights and Museums: p. 136.

Sarrià embodies both meanings of the name Zona Alta ("Uptown")—economic prosperity and altitude. The last neighborhood incorporated into the city (in 1927), Sarrià often falls off the edge of Barcelona maps. Despite its location, the neighborhood is replete with many un-touristed sights and residential splendor. Sarrià is home to some of the city's most coveted apartments, mansions, and chic boutiques, yet the neighborhood's center, Pl. Sarrià, still retains an Old World village feel.

PEDRALBES AND LES CORTS

Orientation: Pedralbes and Les Corts lie above Sants, below the mountains, and west of C. Numància. Transportation: ⓜPalau Reial, L3, or Collblanc, L5. Buses #22, 63, 64, 75, and 114 run through the neighborhood. Accommodations: p. 80. Food and Drink: p. 104. Sights and Museums: p. 138.

Welcome to Pedralbes 90210, home to Barcelona's rich and famous. The name "Pedralbes" comes from a 14th-century monastery (Monestir de Pedrables) that once called the neighborhood home. In the 1950s, the growing University of Barcelona moved most of its academic buildings to the area, but the neighborhood is hardly a "college town," as it remains one of the city's most exclusive residential areas. This part of Zona Alta also has great shopping, particularly along Av. Diagonal.

SANTS

Orientation: Sants occupies the western end of the city, between Gran Via de Carles III and C. Tarragona, the area's border with l'Eixample. Montjuïc borders on the ocean side and Les Corts toward the mountains. Transportation: ⓂSants-Estació, L3/5, and Pl. de Sant, L1/5. Bus lines include #32, 44, 78, and 109, coming mostly from the outskirts of the city. Accommodations: see p. 79. Food and Drink: see p. 106.

The Sants neighborhood began as a resting spot for travelers heading into historic walled Barcelona (the city gates closed shortly after dark). Today, the area still serves as a point of entry for travelers coming through the city's international train station, Estació Barcelona-Sants, but its status as a textile manufacturing zone hardly offers a warm welcome for weary travelers. The busy industrial and commercial area is crammed full of narrow streets, low-level apartment buildings, and plaças. Flooded with locals who do much of their household shopping along C. de Sants, the area attracts few tourists besides those passing through the train station. Sants does have an eclectic display of colorful political graffiti, especially in and around the run-down Parc de l'Espanya Industrial.

COLLSEROLAS AND TIBIDABO

Orientation: The Collserola mountain range, 17km long and 6km wide, marks the western limit of Barcelona, and incorporates the neighborhoods of Tibidabo and Vallvidrera. Transportation: the Tibibus runs from Pl. de Catalunya to Pl. Tibidabo (the very top of the mountain) stopping only once en route (every 30-40min., only when the Parc d'Attracions is open; €2.80). FGC (U7) line runs from Pl. de Catalunya to the Tibidabo stop; it stops at the foot of the peak in Pl. JFK, where C. Balmes turns into the Av. Tibidabo. Sights and Museums: p. 135 and p. 150.

The Collserola mountains hovered between wilderness and civilization for centuries. Fossils found in the park from the Neolithic and Bronze Ages suggest it was home to many long before the Romans set up shop in the area. With the fall of the Roman Empire, Barcelona became vulnerable to the attack of many Germanic tribes, forcing peasants north to defend their territory, which they did, with varying degrees of success, against such unwelcome guests as the Visigoths (AD 415) and Charlemagne's Franks (AD 778; see **Life and Times,** p. 41, for a complete explanation of the decline and fall of the Roman Empire).

For most of the last 1000 years, the area has been home to the agrarian people who built the area's historic chapels and *masias* (traditional Catalan farmhouses). In the last century, the installation of railtracks, trams, and funiculars has made the mountains easily accessible to urban residents.

The man most responsible for the development of Tibidabo and the surrounding slopes was Dr. Salvador Andreu, who in 1899 founded the Tibidabo Society and invested heavily, installing transportation and building hotels, the amusement park, and an extravagant casino (now in ruins). Soon after, much of Barcelona's bourgeoisie rushed to outdo one another in country home construction, and the hillsides are now dotted with outstanding examples of early 20th-century *Modernista* architecture.

DON'T MISS...

THE AMUSEMENT PARK AT TIBIDABO. Thanks to Woody Allen, the secret's out. There's no excuse not to visit (p. 135).

SEASONAL HIGHLIGHTS

For all of Barcelona's idiosyncrasies, the city does share at least one thing with the rest of the country—it knows how to have fun. Festivals abound in this happening city; so be sure to know what will be going on during your visit. For information on all festivals, see p. 154, or call the tourist office ☎ 933 689 700.

SPRING

Día de Sant Jordi, celebrated on April 23, is a favorite day for the lovebirds out there and is similar to North America's Valentine's Day. A festival in honor of one of Barcelona's favorite saints, Jordi, is a time to buy nice things for that special someone. Check out the flower district on Las Ramblas, as it will be selling both books and flowers for this special occasion. **Setimana Santa** (Catholic Holy week; the week leading up to Easter) is a huge festival complete with grand processions; Barcelona natives pour into the streets to celebrate. On May 10-11, Fira de Sant Ponç, a festival dedicated to the patron saint of beekeepers, is celebrated on C. Hospital near Las Ramblas. To satisfy your inner comics nerd, head over to Estació de França for the **International Comics Fair,** which is held each May.

SUMMER

Anything called "Festa Major" will be big, popular, and a lot of fun. Poble Nou, Sants, Gràcia, and Sitges all host these huge summer extravaganzas. **Focs de Sant Joan** is held in Girona on June 24 (p. 208). For those on the life-long quest to find a dancing egg, your journey stops in Barcelona. The **Corpus Cristi** festival occurs in June and includes parades, carnival figures, and of course, the traditional *ou com balla*—the dancing egg. Two music festivals keep the party alive: **Sónar** (mid-June) pumps electronic music and **Festa de la Música** (July 1st) invites anyone and everyone to perform. Theater, dance, music, and movies flood Barcelona's top venues from late June to the end of July during the city-wide Grec Festival. For in-depth coverage of major music and theater festivals, including Sonar and El Grec, see **Entertainment,** p. 153.

AUTUMN

Bring your Catalan flag and other paraphernalia to the **Catalan National Day Festival,** held September 11th. You'll find people dressed in traditional

THE LOCAL STORY

SAINT JORDI AND THE 🐉DRAGON

England isn't the only European country with an anti-dragon tradition. In fact, St. Jordi, as St. George is known in Catalunya, is the hero of a Spanish version of everyone's favorite ride-in-kill-dragon-ride-out love story. In Barcelona, St. Jordi's patron day, April 23, is a *jornada festiva* during which the entire city goes crazy-in-love. It's Valentine's Day with a Cervantes twist: girls give books to the guys and guys give roses to the girls. Most businesses close down and the streets are flooded with lovebirds.

The story of Jordi, as they tell it in Catalunya, takes place in the AD fifth century, on the Barbary Coast, where a fierce dragon terrorized the locals. To appease the hungry monster, fearful locals held regular lotteries whose lucky winners were sacrificed to the dragon.

One day, the King's daughter won the big prize. This didn't go over well with the townspeople, who apparently liked having her around, like a darling royal reality TV star. At any rate, at the very last moment, a handsome, mysterious knight rode up and saved the princess, killing the awful dragon and then disappearing as quickly as he had arrived. All that the princess had to remind her of her hero were a few red roses that blossomed out of the slain dragon's spilled blood. Today, with a minimum of blood and dragons, the festival continues to celebrate the story of St. Jordi with rose-giving and general mushiness.

BEST OF BARCELONA

If you want to catch as many of these sights as possible in one shot, try our walking tours.

10. The Mediterranean. Buy yourself some inexpensive beer (Estrella does the trick), suit up, and try not to get burned. Or let it all hang out on the nude beach.

9. The Cathedral. If you think the Sagrada Família is taking a long time to get built, you ain't seen nothin' yet. Check out St. Eulalia, which took over 200 years to build. Berenguer began it in 1068. A cloister, geese, Roman ruins, and mimes round out the experience (p. 110).

8. Palau de la Música Catalana. And you thought the skylight in your apartment was cool. This is Lluís Domènech i Montaner's 1903 Modernista masterpiece, home to some of the most astonishing glasswork you will ever see. Are those naked women walking out the walls? (p. 116).

7. La Manzana de la Discòrdia. The city block with a Modernist identity crisis, where Modernisme's three most famous sons—Puig i Cadafalch, Domènech i Montaner, and Antoni Gaudí—duked it out to become hometown favorites (p. 121).

6. Fundació Miró. Miró's artistic legacy to his homeland, showcasing his own work and that of up-and-coming Catalan artists (p. 148).

5. Museu de l'Erotica. If you're striking out at Barcelona's famous bars and clubs (p. 171), come here to get your phallus fix (p. 141).

costumes and homes decorated with the flag and shield pattern. Wine-makers and *butifarra* (sausage)-makers pile into Barcelona from the surrounding areas to present their goods during the **Feria de Cuina i Vins de Catalunya;** for one entire fall week, you can taste food and wine relatively cheaply. Late September brings fireworks and devils to town for the **Festa de la Verge de la Mercè,** when *correfocs* (devils) run through the streets, flashing their pitchforks at the residents. To retaliate, people throw buckets of water at the devils. Human towers in the streets are also a common spectacle around this time of year. Come October, Barceloneses trade their pitchforks and buckets for saxophones as the **Festival Internacional de Jazz** comes to town. Jazz is in the streets, in the clubs, and in the air as some of the world's finest musicians come to town. One of the best city-wide parties, the **Festival del Sant Çito,** begins in November.

WINTER

Christmastime is, of course, packed with festivities, although people tend to spend more time with their families than on the streets (except in early evening when the avenues pack shoppers in like sardines). Rather than a huge celebration on Christmas Day, the Spanish tend to have a family dinner on **Nochebuena** (Christmas Eve), the most important holiday of the year. Spaniards hold off on exchanging presents until January 5, the **Epiphany,** the day the Three Kings ride their camels into Spain. The night of January 4th, children put their shoes outside to be filled with gifts and candy by the visiting Kings (a good night for those looking to steal children's footwear). That night, people gather to devour *roscón*, an oval-shaped sweet bread with a small toy baked into it. Whoever finds the toy gets to keep it and is dubbed King or Queen for the year. Speaking of special prizes, *caganer* ("shitter") statues become even more popular during this season; just be careful where you step. As residents prepare for the new year, the price of grapes suddenly skyrockets. Spaniards gather with friends on **New Year's Eve,** and when the clock strikes midnight, people pop a grape into their mouth for each chime, 12 in all, for good luck during the coming year.

In February, join natives in celebrating **Festes de Santa Eulàlia,** a holiday dedicated to Barcelona's first patron saint. The Mayor's office organizes events for the city and arranges the special guest appearances by *mulasses* (dragons) in parades; concerts abound during this time. During **Festa** de San Medir, held in Tibidabo, Barcelona's young and old race to the mountain to be showered with candy by men who ride galloping horses. At the end of the month, residents celebrate their last week of indulgence before Lent with **Carnaval.** The more daring head over to Sitges (p. 197).

SUGGESTED ITINERARIES

THREE DAYS

DAY 1: MODERNISME 101

Head out to the **La Sagrada Família** (p. 123) early in the morning to avoid fighting the crowds; grab some *churros y chocolate* at one of the nearby cafes. From there, make your way to the Pl. de Catalunya (ⓂCatalunya, L1/3) and take the half-day walking tour through l'Eixample, which will take you past the most important Modernista houses, including **Casa Milà** (p. 120) and **La Manzana de la Discòrdia** (p. 121), where you can pick up the Ruta del Modernisme pass that offers discounts on sights all over the city. Take a moment: how cool are the chimneys on Casa Milà? We think so too.

Now catch the #24 bus from the Pg. de Gràcia up to your last Modernist stop of the day: **Parc Güell in Gràcia** (p. 130). Wander through the colonnades, park it on the longest and most crooked bench in the world, and snap a photo with the drooling lizard. You may even catch some live music in one of the shady nooks; follow your ears. At the end of the day (and the beginning of a long night), head down to one of l'Eixample's many trendy bars and clubs (see **Nightlife**, p. 171).

DAY 2: OLD TOWN SUPER-TOURIST

Start out at the **Plaça de Catalunya** (ⓂCatalunya, L1/3) and head towards the water on **Las Ramblas** to see the traditional **Boqueria market** (p. 116), where you can buy pastries or fruit for breakfast (as well as a whole pig's head for lunch and lamb ears for dinner). Check out the various offerings of the different sections of Las Ramblas (did we mention that you can buy an emu?), then head into the **Barri Gòtic** via C. Portaferrissa, which will turn into C.

4. Casa Milà (La Pedrera). Gaudí's finished masterpiece and the best look inside his work and his head (p. 120).

3. Parc Güell. Straight paths? Cropped lawns? Monotonous landscape? Who do you think you're dealing with, Olmstead? This is Gaudí's madcap take on the city park (p. 130). What started as an unfinished housing project (are you noticing a pattern?) is now the wackiest park in the world. Hikes lead to spectacular views: buns of steel not included.

2. Las Ramblas, the central and most colorful street in Barcelona's oldest district, complete with mimes, flowers, and baby turtles (p. 2). Picasso strolled down it every afternoon returning from the studio.

1. La Sagrada Família, Gaudí's unfinished masterpiece, and his tomb (p. 123). Picasso famously wanted to "send Gaudí and the Sagrada Família to hell." It's a good thing Picasso wasn't mayor; today this "bible for the illiterate" is the icon of the city and the world's most-visited construction site.

dels Boters and ends at the **Cathedral** (p. 110). Hang out with the resident geese and peruse the Roman walls.

Then get your Ruta de Modernisme pass ready for your next stop just off the Via Laietana, the **Palau de la Música Catalana** (p. 116) in La Ribera. The guided tour here is well worth your while. Make your way through La Ribera's twisting alleys to the **Museu Picasso** (p. 143). Check out the **galleries** in the labyrinth of streets and stay in the area for tapas (see **Food, p. 83**). Finish up the night by heading back into the Barri Gòtic for the clubs and bars around the Plaça Reial, whose fountain is another Modernista icon (p. 114).

DAY 3: JOAN MIRÓ TONES YOUR GLUTES

Take a quick ride up to Montjuïc from the waterfront on the **Transbordador Aeri cable car,** then head over to the **Fundació Miró** (p. 148) to see the master's paintings and tapestries. Leave yourself enough time to wander the lovely (and hilly) paths of Montjuïc.

Onward! To the **Museu Nacional d'Art de Catalunya** (p. 147). On your way out of the museum, try to catch one of the shows of the **Fonts Luminoses** (p. 128). If you still have energy to party, you can to head back to Poble Espanyol, which transforms from tacky to trendy (and by trendy, we mean total grade-A nightlife madness) after dark (see **Nightlife,** p. 171).

FIVE DAYS

If three days just aren't enough, have another cup of coffee and keep up the pace for another 48 hours.

DAY 4: ON THE WATERFRONT

Start your day with an espresso in one of La Ribera's excellent cafes (see **Food,** p. 83), then suit up and head down Pg. Joan de Borbó to some of the liveliest city beaches anywhere. For lunch, explore the interior of Barceloneta; you'll be rewarded with fresh seafood and cold beer. If you want to escape the afternoon heat, **Parc de la Ciutadella** offers shade, a zoo, and an aquarium (in case you prefer your seawater in a tank).

Tonight, the gaudy clubs of Poble Nou (p. 184) or the relaxing bars of La Ribera (p. 174) beckon you with cold drinks and good music.

DAY 5: DALÍLAND AND EL RAVAL

Get up early: you've got a train to catch, to nearby **Figueras** (see **Daytrips,** p. 214). Spend the morning at the surreal **Teatre-Museu Dalí** (p. 215), the second-most popular museum in Spain, where you can stand on **Dalí's tomb,** listen to rain inside a Cadillac, or watch a room turn into Mae West. You can make it back to Barcelona before sundown and take a rest, since you haven't lived like a true Spaniard until you've had a siesta. This evening, try tapas in Gràcia (see **Food,** p. 99) or a vegetarian feast in El Raval (see **Food,** p. 87).

☑ LET'S GO PICKS

MOST AESTHETICALLY PLEASING BATHROOM EXPERIENCE: Els Quatre Gats (p. 85).

BEST PLACE TO BUY AN EMU AND A SUNFLOWER ON THE SAME BLOCK: Las Ramblas (p. 2).

MOST OBSCENE PHOTO-OP: The giant phallus at Museu de l'Eròtica (p. 141).

BEST PLACE TO GO CRAZY AND UNLEASH YOUR INNER SOCCER FAN, WITHIN THE BOUNDS OF THE LAW: Camp Nou, the home of FC Barcelona (p. 150).

ONLY MUSEUM THAT THROWS A PARTY EVERY THURSDAY NIGHT: The MACBA. Check out Nits de Macba (p. 144).

BEST THING ABOUT CAVA: It tastes like champagne, it looks like champagne, it's served like champagne. So what's the difference? Oh yeah, it's €3 a bottle.

MOST AMAZING GLASSWORK YOU WILL EVER SEE: The colorful dome of the Palau de la Música Catalana (p. 116).

BEST TIME TO SHOOT OFF FIREWORKS ON THE BEACH: During the festival of Sant Joan (p. 154).

ONLY TWO INGREDIENTS IN A CALIMOCHO: Cheap red wine and SPAR-brand cola. Yum. Really.

MOST UNCOORDINATED CITY BLOCK: Stunning Manzana de la Discordia, along Pg. de Gràcia in l'Eixample (p. 121).

BEST ACTIVE CONSTRUCTION SITE: Gaudí's Sagrada Família, more than 80 years old and still not even close to completed (p. 123).

MOST APPROPRIATE BAR FOR YOUR FIRST ABSINTHE: Marsella Bar, the cowboy hangout of El Raval. Be careful: once you've tried just one... (p. 176).

BEST LOCATION FOR A MUSEUM: the park on Montjüic. You haven't seen Miró like this before.

BEST ALL-NIGHT BEACHSIDE HEDONISM: In Sitges, of course (p. 197).

ESSENTIALS

PLANNING YOUR TRIP

ENTRANCE REQUIREMENTS
Passport (p. 18). Required for citizens of Australia, Canada, Ireland, New Zealand, the UK, and the US.
Visa (p. 19). Required only for citizens of Australia, Canada, Ireland, New Zealand, the UK, and the US for stays over 90 days.
Work Permit (p. 19). If you are an EU citizen, you are not required to obtain a work permit to work in Spain. Those outside of the EU, however, must have both a work permit and a visa.

EMBASSIES AND CONSULATES

SPANISH CONSULAR SERVICES ABROAD

Australia: 15 Arkana St., Yarralumla, P.O. Box 9076, Deakin ACT 2600 (☎2 62 73 35 55; fax 73 39 18; www.embaspain.com). **Consulates:** Level 24, St. Martin's Tower, 31 Market St., Sydney, NSW 2000 (☎2 92 61 24 33; fax 83 16 95); 146 Elgin St., Carlton, Melbourne, VIC 3053 (☎3 93 47 19 66; fax 47 73 30).

Canada: 74 Stanley Ave., Ottawa, Ontario K1M 1P4 (☎613-747-2252; fax 744-1224). **Consulates:** 1 Westmount Sq., Ste. 1456, Ave. Wood, Montreal, Quebec H3Z 2P9 (☎514-935-5235; fax 935-4655); 2 Bloor St. E., Ste. 1201, Toronto, Ontario M4W 1A8 (☎416-977-1661; fax 593-4949).

Ireland: 17a Merlyn Park, Ballsbridge, Dublin 4 (☎1 35 3269 1640; fax 269 1854).

UK: 39 Chesham Pl., London SW1X 8SB (☎20 7235 5555; fax 7259 5392). **Consulates:** 20 Draycott Pl., London SW3 2RZ (☎20 7589 8989; fax 581 7888); Ste. 1A, Brookhouse, 70 Spring Gardens, Manchester M2 2BQ (☎16 1236 1262; fax 228 7467); 63 North Castle St., Edinburgh EH2 3LJ (☎220 1843; fax 226 4568).

US: 2375 Pennsylvania Ave. NW, Washington, DC 20037 (☎202-728-2340; fax 833-5670; www.spainemb.org). **Consulates:** 150 E. 58th St., 30th fl., New York, NY 10155 (☎212-355-4080 or 355-4081; fax 644-3751); others in Boston, Chicago, Houston, Los Angeles, Miami, New Orleans, San Juan (PR), and San Francisco.

CONSULAR SERVICES IN SPAIN

Embassies are generally located in Madrid, but there are a few consulates in Barcelona.

Australia: Pl. Gala Placidia, 1-3, 1st fl., 08006 (☎93 490 9013; fax 93 411 0904).
Canada: C. Elisenda de Pinós, 10, 08034 (☎93 204 2700; fax 93 204 2701).
Ireland: Gran Via Carles III, 94, 08028 (☎93 491 5021; fax 93 490 0986).
New Zealand: C. Travessera de Gràcia, 64, 08006 (☎93 209 0399).

UK: Avinguda Diagonal 477, 13, 08036 (☎93 366 6200; fax 93 366 6221).

US: Passeig de la Reina Elisende de Montcada, 23, 08034 (☎93 280 2227).

TOURIST OFFICES

Spain's tourist office operates a comprehensive website at www.tourspain.es. For cool tidbits on Barcelona, visit www.barcelonaturisme.com. The tourist board also has offices abroad in Canada, the US, and the UK.

Canada: 2 Bloor St. W., Ste. 3402, Toronto, ON M4W 3E2 (☎416-961-3131; fax 961-1992; www.tourspain.toronto.on.ca).

UK: PO Box 4009, London W1A 6N (☎207 486 8077; fax 486 8034; www.tourspain.co.uk).

US: 666 5th Ave., 35th fl., New York, NY 10103 (☎212-265-8822; fax 265-8864; www.okspain.org). Additional offices in Chicago (☎312-642-1992), Los Angeles (☎323-658-7188), and Miami (☎305-358-1992).

DOCUMENTS AND FORMALITIES

PASSPORTS

REQUIREMENTS

Citizens of Australia, Canada, Ireland, New Zealand, the UK, and the US need valid passports to enter Spain and to re-enter their home countries. Spain does not allow entrance if the holder's passport expires in under six months; returning home with an expired passport is illegal and may result in a fine. New passports may be obtained at any passport office or at selected post offices and courts of law. Download passport applications from the official website of your country's government or passport office. Any new passport or renewal applications must be filed well in advance of the departure date, though most passport offices offer rush services for a steep fee. Note that "rushed" passports still take up to two weeks to arrive, so make sure to get your act together; the sooner the better.

 ONE EUROPE. The European Union's policy of freedom of movement means that most border controls have been abolished and visa policies harmonized. Under this treaty, formally known as the Schengen Agreement, you're still required to carry a passport (or government-issued ID card for EU citizens) when crossing an internal border, but, once you've been admitted into one country, you're free to travel to other participating states. Most EU states are already members of Schengen (excluding Cyprus), as are Iceland and Norway. The UK and Ireland have opted out of the agreement, but have created their own Common Travel Area, whose regulations match those of Schengen.

For more on how the EU benefits travelers, see **The Euro** (p. 20) and **Customs in the EU** (p. 20).

PASSPORT MAINTENANCE

Photocopy the page of your passport with your photo, visas, traveler's check serial numbers, and any other important documents. Carry one set of copies in a safe place, apart from the originals, and leave another set at home.

If you lose your passport, immediately notify the local police and your home country's nearest embassy or consulate. To expedite its replacement, you must show ID and proof of citizenship; it also helps to know all information previously recorded in the passport. In some cases, a replacement may take weeks to process, and it may be valid only for a limited time. Any visas stamped in your old passport will be lost forever. In an emergency, ask for immediate temporary traveling papers that will permit you to re-enter your home country.

VISAS, INVITATIONS, AND WORK PERMITS

VISAS

A visa is not required of EU citizens for travel in Spain. Citizens of Australia, Canada, New Zealand, and the US do not need a visa for stays of up to 90 days, but this three-month period begins upon entry into any of the countries that belong to the EU's **freedom of movement** zone. For more information, see **One Europe** (p. 18). Those staying longer than 90 days may apply for a visa in person at a local embassy or consulate. A visa costs US$100 for US citizens and US$90 for EU citizens, and if granted, allows the holder to spend the requested amount of time in Spain. Double-check entrance requirements at the nearest embassy or consulate of Spain (see p. 17) for up-to-date information before departure. US citizens can also consult http://travel.state.gov.

For information on the **student visa** and the **work permit,** see Beyond Tourism (p. 53).

WORK PERMITS

Admittance to a country as a traveler does not include the right to work, which is authorized only by a work permit. For more information, see the **Beyond Tourism** chapter (p. 53).

IDENTIFICATION

When you travel, always carry at least two forms of identification on your person, including a photo ID. A passport and a driver's license will usually suffice. Never carry all of your IDs together; instead, split them up in case of theft or loss and keep photocopies in your luggage and at home.

STUDENT, TEACHER, AND YOUTH IDENTIFICATION

The **International Student Identity Card (ISIC),** the most widely accepted form of student ID, provides discounts on some sights, accommodations, food, and transportation, access to a 24hr. emergency help line, and insurance benefits for US cardholders. Applicants must be full-time secondary or post-secondary school students at least 12 years old. Because of the proliferation of fake ISICs, some services (particularly airlines) require additional proof of student identity. For travelers who are under 26 years old but are not students, the **International Youth Travel Card (IYTC)** offers many of the same benefits as the ISIC. These identity cards cost US$22 and are valid for one year from the date of issue. To learn more about them, visit www.myisic.com. Many student travel agencies issue the cards; for a list of issuing agencies or more information, see the **International Student Travel Confederation (ISTC)** website (www.istc.org).

The **International Student Exchange Card (ISE Card)** is a similar card available to students, faculty, and children aged 12 to 26. It provides discounts, medical benefits, access to a 24hr. emergency help line, and the ability to purchase student airfares. The card costs US$25; visit www.isecard.com for more info.

ESSENTIALS

ESSENTIALS

CUSTOMS

Upon entering Spain, you must declare certain items from abroad and pay a duty on the value of those articles if they exceed the allowance established by Spain's customs service. Upon returning home, you must likewise declare all articles acquired abroad and pay a duty on the value of articles in excess of your home country's allowance. Jot down a list of any valuables brought from home and register them with customs before traveling abroad. It's a good idea to keep receipts for all goods acquired abroad.

CUSTOMS IN THE EU. As well as freedom of movement of people, travelers in the European Union can also take advantage of the freedom of movement of goods. This means that there are no customs controls at internal EU borders and travelers are free to transport whatever legal substances they like as long as it is for their own personal (non-commercial) use.

MONEY

CURRENCY AND EXCHANGE

The currency chart below is based on August 2009 exchange rates between local currency and Australian dollars (AUS$), Canadian dollars (CDN$), New Zealand dollars (NZ$), British pounds (UK£), and US dollars (US$). Check the currency converter on websites like www.xe.com or www.bloomberg.com for the latest exchange rates.

EURO (€)		
AUS$1 = €0.58		1€ = AUS$1.72
CDN$1 = €0.65		1€ = CDN$1.55
NZ$1 = €0.47		1€ = NZ$2.14
UK£1 = €1.18		1€ = UK£0.85
US$1 = €0.70		1€ = US$1.44

When changing money abroad, try to go only to banks or *casas de cambio* that have at most a 5% margin between their buy and sell prices. Since you lose money with every transaction, it makes sense to convert large sums at one time. It's wise to bring enough foreign currency to last for at least 24-72hr. As a general rule, it's cheaper to convert money in Spain than at home.

If you use traveler's checks or bills, carry some in small denominations (the equivalent of US$50 or less) for times when you are forced to exchange money at poor rates, but bring a range of denominations since charges may be applied per check cashed. Store your money in a variety of forms; ideally, at any given time you will be carrying some cash, some traveler's checks, and an ATM or credit card. All travelers should also consider carrying some US dollars (about US$50), which are often preferred by local tellers.

THE EURO. As of January 1, 2009, the official currency of 16 members of the European Union—Austria, Belgium, Cyprus, Finland, France, Germany, Greece, Ireland, Italy, Luxembourg, Malta, the Netherlands, Portugal, Slovakia, Slovenia, and Spain—has become the euro. Currency exchanges across the eurozone are obliged to exchange money at the official, fixed rate (below) and at no commission (though they may still charge a small service fee). Also, euro-denominated traveler's checks allow you to pay for goods and services across the eurozone at an official rate and commission-free.

TRAVELER'S CHECKS

Traveler's checks are one of the safest and most convenient means of carrying funds. **American Express** and **Visa** are the best-recognized brands. Many banks and agencies sell them for a small commission. Check issuers provide refunds if the checks are lost or stolen, and many provide additional services, such as toll-free refund hotlines abroad, emergency message services, and assistance with lost and stolen credit cards or passports. Traveler's checks are readily accepted by most Spanish businesses. Ask about refund hotlines and refund centers when purchasing checks. **Remember: always carry emergency cash.**

American Express: Checks available with commission at AmEx offices and select banks (www.americanexpress.com). AmEx cardholders can also purchase checks by phone (☎+1-800-528-4800). Cheques for Two can be signed by either of two people traveling together. For purchase locations or more information, contact AmEx's service centers: in Australia ☎+61 2 9271 8666, in Canada and the US +1-800-528-4800, in New Zealand +64 9 583 8300, in the UK +44 1273 571 600, and in Spain +34 902 375 637.

Visa: Checks available at banks worldwide. For the location of the nearest office, call the Visa Travelers Cheque Global Refund and Assistance Center: in the UK ☎+44 800 895 078, in the US +1-800-227-6811; elsewhere, call the UK collect at +44 2079 378 091. Visa also offers TravelMoney, a prepaid debit card that can be reloaded online or by phone. For more information on Visa travel services, see http://usa.visa.com/personal/using_visa/travel_with_visa.html.

CREDIT, DEBIT, AND ATM CARDS

Where they are accepted, credit cards often offer superior exchange rates—up to 5% better than the retail rate used by banks and other currency-exchange establishments. Credit cards may also offer services such as insurance or emergency help and are sometimes required to reserve hotel rooms or rental cars. **MasterCard** (a.k.a. EuroCard in Europe) and **Visa** are the most frequently accepted; **American Express** cards work at some ATMs and major airports.

The use of ATM cards is widespread in Spain. Depending on the system that your bank uses, you can most likely access your personal bank account from abroad. ATMs get the same wholesale exchange rate as credit cards, but there is often a limit on the amount of money you can withdraw per day (usually around US$500). There is also typically a surcharge of US$1-5 per withdrawal, so it pays to be efficient.

Debit cards are as convenient as credit cards but withdraw money directly from the holder's checking account. A debit card can be used wherever its associated credit card company (usually MasterCard or Visa) is accepted.

The two major international money networks are **MasterCard/Maestro/Cirrus** (for ATM locations call ☎+1-800-424-7787 or visit www.mastercard.com) and **Visa/PLUS** (for ATM locations visit http://visa.via.infonow.net/locator/global/). Most ATMs charge a transaction fee that is paid to the bank that owns the ATM. It is a good idea to contact your bank or credit-card company before going abroad; frequent charges in a foreign country can sometimes be dubbed "suspicious activity" and prompt a fraud alert, which will freeze your account.

ESSENTIALS

> **PINS AND ATMS.** To use a cash or credit card to withdraw money from a cash machine (ATM) in Europe, you must have a four-digit Personal Identification Number (PIN). If your PIN is longer than four digits, ask your bank whether you can just use the first four or whether you'll need a new one. Credit cards don't usually come with PINs, so, if you intend to hit up ATMs in Europe with a credit card to get cash advances, call your credit card company before leaving to request one.
>
> Travelers with alphabetic rather than numerical PINs may also be thrown off by the absence of letters on European cash machines. Here are the corresponding numbers to use: 1 = QZ; 2 = ABC; 3 = DEF; 4 = GHI; 5 = JKL; 6 = MNO; 7 = PRS; 8 = TUV; 9 = WXY. Note that if you mistakenly punch the wrong code into the machine multiple (often three) times, it can swallow your card for good.

GETTING MONEY FROM HOME

If you run out of money while traveling, the easiest and cheapest solution is to have someone back home make a deposit to your bank account. Otherwise, consider one of the following options.

WIRING MONEY

It is possible to arrange a **bank money transfer,** which means asking a bank back home to wire money to a bank in Spain. This is the cheapest way to transfer cash, but it's also the slowest, usually taking several days or more. Note that some banks may only release your funds in local currency, potentially sticking you with a poor exchange rate; inquire about this in advance. Money transfer services like **Western Union** are faster and more convenient than bank transfers—but also much pricier. Western Union has many locations worldwide. To find one, visit www.westernunion.com or call the appropriate number: in Australia ☎1 800 173 833; in Canada and the US 800-325-6000; in the UK 0800 735 1815; or in Spain 900 98 32 73. To wire money using a credit card, in Canada and the US call ☎800-CALL-CASH, in the UK 0800 833 833.

US STATE DEPARTMENT (US CITIZENS ONLY)

In serious emergencies only, the US State Department will forward money within hours to the nearest consular office, which will then disburse it according to instructions for a US$30 fee. If you wish to use this service, you must contact the Overseas Citizens Services division of the US State Department (☎+1-202-501-4444, from US 888-407-4747).

COSTS

The cost of your trip will vary considerably depending on where you visit, how you travel, and where you stay. The most significant expenses will probably be your round-trip (return) airfare to Barcelona (see **Getting to Barcelona: By Plane,** p. 27) and a railpass or bus pass.

To give you a general idea, a bare-bones day in Barcelona (camping or sleeping in hostels/guesthouses, buying food at supermarkets) would cost about US$60- 70 (€40-50); a slightly more comfortable day (sleeping in hostels/guesthouses and the occasional budget hotel, eating one meal per day at a restaurant, going out at night) would cost US$70-100 (€50-70); and, for a luxurious day, the sky's the limit. Don't forget to factor in emergency reserve funds (at least US$200) when planning how much money you'll need.

Some simple ways to save money include looking for free entertainment, splitting accommodation and food costs with trustworthy fellow travelers, and buying food in supermarkets rather than eating out. Bring a **sleepsack** (folding a large sheet in half length-wise and sewing the seam will work) to avoid charges for linens in hostels and do your **laundry** in the sink (unless you're explicitly prohibited from doing so). Museums often have days once a month or once a week when admission is free; plan accordingly. For getting around quickly, **bikes** are the most economical option. Drinking at bars and clubs quickly becomes expensive. It's cheaper to buy alcohol at a supermarket and imbibe before going out. That said, don't go overboard. Though staying within your budget is important, don't do so at the expense of your health or safety.

TIPPING AND BARGAINING

Tipping is not widespread in Spain. In restaurants, all prices include a service charge. Satisfied customers occasionally toss in some spare change and while purely optional, tipping is becoming the norm in restaurants and other places that cater to tourists. Many people give train, airport, and hotel porters €1 per bag while taxi drivers sometimes get 5-10%. Bargaining is common at flea markets and with street vendors.

TAXES

Non-European tourists who pay for goods and services in foreign currency are exempt in certain cases from a 7-8% **value added tax**, or *el impuesto sobre el valor añadido* (IVA). The prices listed in *Let's Go* include IVA unless otherwise mentioned. Retail goods bear a much higher 16% IVA, although listed prices are usually inclusive. Non-EU citizens who have stayed in the EU fewer than 180 days can claim back the tax paid on purchases at the airport. Ask the shop where you have made the purchase to supply you with a tax return form, though stores will often provide them only for purchases of more than €50-100. The minimum amount of purchase eligible for VAT refund is €91.

SAFETY AND HEALTH

GENERAL ADVICE

In any type of crisis, the most important thing to do is **stay calm.** Your country's embassy abroad (p. 17) is usually your best resource in an emergency; registering with that embassy upon arrival in the country is a good idea. The government offices listed in the **Travel Advisories** box (p. 24) can provide information on the services they offer their citizens in case of emergencies abroad.

LOCAL LAWS AND POLICE

You should feel comfortable approaching the police, although few officers speak English. There are three types of Spanish police: the **Policía Nacional** wear blue or black uniforms and white shirts; they handle criminal investigations (including theft), guard government buildings, and protect dignitaries. The **Policía Local** wear blue uniforms, deal with local issues, and report to the mayor or town hall in each municipality. The **Guardia Civil** wear olive green uniforms and are responsible for many issues relevant to travelers including customs, crowd control, and national security. Also, in the unlikely event that you should find yourself behind bars, contact your embassy, although they often cannot do much to assist you beyond finding you legal counsel.

DRUGS AND ALCOHOL

Recreational drugs are illegal in Spain and police take these laws seriously. Spain has a legal minimum drinking age of 16.

SPECIFIC CONCERNS

TERRORISM

Basque terrorism concerns all travelers in Spain due to the activities of a militant wing of Basque separatists, the Euskadi Ta Askatasuna (**ETA;** Basque Homeland and Freedom). In March 2006, ETA declared a permanent cease-fire that officially ended in June 2007. ETA's attacks are typically targeted and are not considered random terrorist acts. Spain's troubles with terrorism do not end with domestic groups, however. The March 11, 2004 train bombings in Madrid were linked to **al-Qaeda,** and in June 2008, Spanish police arrested eight men in Barcelona, Pamplona, and Castellón under suspicion of involvement with an Algerian terrorist group linked to al-Qaeda. (See **Current Events** for more information.)

The box below lists offices to contact and websites to visit to get the most updated list of your government's travel advisories.

TRAVEL ADVISORIES. The following government offices provide travel information and advisories by telephone, by fax, or via the web:

Australian Department of Foreign Affairs and Trade: ☎+61 2 6261 1111; www.dfat.gov.au.

Canadian Department of Foreign Affairs and International Trade (DFAIT): ☎+1-800-267-8376; www.dfait-maeci.gc.ca.

New Zealand Ministry of Foreign Affairs: ☎+64 4 439 8000; www.mfat.govt.nz.

United Kingdom Foreign and Commonwealth Office: ☎+44 20 7008 1500; www.fco.gov.uk.

US Department of State: ☎+1-888-407-4747, 202-501-4444 from abroad; http://travel.state.gov.

PERSONAL SAFETY

EXPLORING AND TRAVELING

To avoid unwanted attention, try to blend in as much as possible. Respecting local customs (in many cases, dressing more conservatively than you would at home) may ward off would-be hecklers. Familiarize yourself with your surroundings before setting out and carry yourself with confidence. Check maps in shops and restaurants rather than on the street. If you are traveling alone, be sure someone at home knows your itinerary and **never tell anyone you meet that you're by yourself.** When walking at night, stick to busy, well-lit streets and avoid dark alleyways. If you ever feel uncomfortable, leave the area as quickly and directly as you can. There is no sure-fire way to avoid all the threatening situations that you might encounter while traveling, but a good **self-defense course** will give you concrete ways to react to unwanted advances. **Impact and Prepare** (www.prepareinc.com) and **Model Mugging** (www.modelmugging.org) can refer you to self-defense courses in Australia, Canada, Switzerland, and the US.

POSSESSIONS AND VALUABLES

Never leave your belongings unattended. Bring your own padlock for hostel lockers and don't ever store valuables in a locker. Be particularly careful on **buses** and **trains;** horror stories abound about determined thieves who wait for travelers to fall asleep. Carry your bag or purse in front of you where you can see it. When traveling with others, sleep in alternate shifts.

There are a few steps you can take to minimize the financial risk associated with traveling. First, **bring as little with you as possible.** Second, buy a few combination **padlocks** to secure your belongings either in your pack or in a hostel or train-station locker. Third, **carry as little cash as possible.** Keep your traveler's checks and ATM/credit cards in a **money belt**—not a "fanny pack," trendsetter—along with your passport and ID cards. Fourth, **keep a small cash reserve separate from your primary stash.** This should be about US$50 (US dollars or euro are best) sewn into or stored in the depths of your pack, along with your traveler's check numbers and photocopies of your important documents.

In large cities like Barcelona, **con artists** often work in groups and may involve children in their schemes. Beware of certain classics: sob stories that require money, rolls of bills "found" on the street, mustard spilled (or saliva spit) onto your shoulder to distract you while they snatch your bag. **Never let your passport or your bags out of your sight.** Beware of **pickpockets** in city crowds, especially on public transportation.

If you will be traveling with electronic devices, such as a laptop computer or MP3 player, check whether your homeowner's insurance covers loss, theft, or damage when you travel. If not, you might consider purchasing a separate, low-cost insurance policy. **Safeware** (☎+1-800-800-1492; www.safeware.com) specializes in covering computers and charges US$90 for 90-day comprehensive international travel coverage up to US$4000.

PRE-DEPARTURE HEALTH

In your passport, write the names of any people you wish to be contacted in case of a medical emergency and list any allergies or medical conditions. Matching a prescription to a foreign equivalent is not always easy, safe, or possible, so, if you take **prescription drugs**, carry up-to-date prescriptions or a statement from your doctor stating the medications' trade names, manufacturers, chemical names, and dosages. While traveling, be sure to keep all medication with you in your carry-on luggage. The names in Spain for common drugs are similar to their English names: *aspirina*, *ibuprofen*, and *acetaminofén*.

IMMUNIZATIONS AND PRECAUTIONS

Travelers should make sure that the following vaccines are up to date: MMR (for measles, mumps, and rubella); DTaP or Td (for diphtheria, tetanus, and pertussis); IPV (for polio); Hib (for *Haemophilus influenzae* B); and HepB (for Hepatitis B).

USEFUL ORGANIZATIONS AND PUBLICATIONS

The American **Centers for Disease Control and Prevention** (**CDC;** ☎+1-800-CDC-INFO/232-4636; www.cdc.gov/travel) maintains an international travelers' hotline and an informative website. Consult the appropriate government agency of your home country for consular information sheets on health, entry requirements, and other issues for various countries (see the listings in the box on **Travel Advisories,** p. 24). For quick information on health and other travel warnings, call the **Overseas Citizens Services** (☎+1-202-647-5225) or contact a passport agency, embassy, or consulate abroad. For information on medical evacuation services and travel insurance firms, see the US government's website at http://travel.state.gov/travel/abroad_health.html or the **British Foreign and Commonwealth Office** (www.fco.gov.uk). For general health information, contact the **American Red Cross** (☎+1-202-303-5000; www.redcross.org).

STAYING HEALTHY

ONCE IN BARCELONA

ENVIRONMENTAL HAZARDS

Heat exhaustion and dehydration: Summer temperatures in Spain can reach a scorching 36˚C/97˚F. Heat exhaustion leads to nausea, excessive thirst, headaches, and dizziness. Avoid it by drinking plenty of fluids, eating salty foods (e.g., crackers), avoiding excessive caffeine and alcohol, and wearing sunscreen.

OTHER HEALTH CONCERNS

MEDICAL CARE ON THE ROAD

The public health-care system in Spain is very reliable; in case of emergency, seek out the *urgencias* (emergency) section of the nearest hospital. For smaller concerns, private clinics have shorter waits. Expect to pay cash up front (though most travel insurance will pick up the tab later, so request a receipt) and bring your passport along with alternative forms of identification. *Farmacias* in Spain are also very helpful. At least one *farmacia* is open 24hr. in each Spanish town. Look for a flashing green cross. Spanish pharmacies are not the place to find cheap summer flip-flops or greeting cards, but they do sell contraceptives as well as generic and prescription drugs, and pharmacists can answer simple medical questions or help you find a doctor.

If you are concerned about obtaining medical assistance while traveling, you may wish to employ special support services. The **International Association for Medical Assistance to Travelers** (**IAMAT;** US ☎+1-716-754-4883, Canada +1-416-652-0137; www.iamat.org) has free membership, lists English-speaking doctors worldwide, and offers details on immunization requirements and sanitation. For those whose insurance doesn't apply abroad, you can purchase additional coverage.

Those with medical conditions (such as diabetes, allergies to antibiotics, epilepsy, or heart conditions) may want to obtain a **MedicAlert** membership (US$40 per year), which includes, among other things, a stainless-steel ID tag and a

24hr. collect-call number. Contact the MedicAlert Foundation International (from US ☎888-633-4298, outside US +1-209-668-3333; www.medicalert.org).

WOMEN'S HEALTH

Tampons, pads, and contraceptive devices are widely available in Barcelona, though your favorite brand may not be stocked—bring extras of anything you can't live without. At the time of printing, abortion is illegal in Spain, except in the first trimester for health reasons or in the case of rape. For sexual health information in Spain, contact the **Federación de Planificación Familiar de España (FPFE)**, C. Ponce de Leon 8, 28010 Madrid (www.fpfe.org).

GETTING TO BARCELONA

BY PLANE

When it comes to airfare, a little effort can save you a bundle. The key is to hunt around, be flexible, and ask about discounts. Students, seniors, and those under 26 should never have to pay full price for a ticket.

AIRFARES

Airfares to Spain peak between May and August (except if flying from New Zealand, in which case the peak and downtimes are switched); holidays are also expensive. The cheapest times to travel are spring and fall. Midweek (M-Th morning) round-trip flights run cheaper than weekend flights, but they are generally more crowded and less likely to permit frequent-flier upgrades. Not fixing a return date ("open return") or arriving in and departing from different cities ("open-jaw") can be pricier than round-trip flights. Patching one-way flights together is the most expensive way to travel.

If Barcelona is only one stop on a more extensive globe-hop, consider a round-the-world (RTW) ticket. Tickets usually include at least five stops and are valid for about a year; prices range US$3000-8000. Try the airline consortiums **Oneworld** (www.oneworld.com), **Skyteam** (www.skyteam.com), and **Star Alliance** (www.staralliance.com).

Fares for round-trip flights to Barcelona from the US or Canadian east coast cost US$900-1800 in the high season, US$400-800 in the low season (Oct.-Mar.); from the US or Canadian west coast US$700-1300/500-800; from the UK, UK£60-300/60-124; from Australia AUS$3130-4010/1720-2400; from New Zealand NZ$3300-4500/3600-6000.

BUDGET AND STUDENT TRAVEL AGENCIES

While knowledgeable agents specializing in flights to Spain or Barcelona can make your life easy, they may not spend the time to find you the lowest possible fare—they get paid on commission. Travelers holding ISICs and IYTCs (p. 19) qualify for big discounts from student travel agencies.

The Adventure Travel Company, 124 MacDougal St., New York City, NY 10021, USA (☎+1-212-674-2887; www.theadventuretravelcompany.com). Offices across Canada and the US including New York City, San Diego, San Francisco, and Seattle.

STA Travel, 2871 Broadway, New York City, NY 10025, USA (24hr. reservations and info ☎+1-800-781-4040; www.statravel.com). A student and youth travel organization with offices worldwide, including US offices in Los Angeles, New York City, Seattle, Washington, DC, and a number of other college towns. Ticket booking, travel insurance, railpasses, and more. Walk-in offices are located throughout Australia (☎+61 134 782), New Zealand (☎+0800 474 400), and the UK (☎+44 8712 230 0040).

> ✈ **FLIGHT PLANNING ON THE INTERNET.** The internet may be the budget traveler's dream when it comes to finding and booking bargain fares, but the array of options can be overwhelming. Many airline sites offer special last-minute deals on the web.
>
> **STA** (www.statravel.com) and **StudentUniverse** (www.studentuniverse.com) provide quotes on student tickets, while **Orbitz** (www.orbitz.com), **Expedia** (www.expedia.com), and **Travelocity** (www.travelocity.com) offer full travel services. **Priceline** (www.priceline.com) lets you specify a price and obligates you to buy any ticket that meets or beats it; **Hotwire** (www.hotwire.com) offers bargain fares but won't reveal the airline or flight times until you buy. Other sites that compile deals include www.bestfares.com, www.flights.com, www.lowestfare.com, www.onetravel.com, and www.travelzoo.com.
>
> **Cheapflights** (www.cheapflights.co.uk) is a useful search engine for finding—you guessed it—cheap flights. **Booking Buddy** (www.bookingbuddy.com), **Kayak** (www.kayak.com), and **SideStep** (www.sidestep.com) are online tools that let you enter your trip information and search multiple sites at once. Let's Go does not endorse any of these websites. As always, be cautious and research companies before you hand over your credit card number.

COMMERCIAL AIRLINES

TRAVELING FROM NORTH AMERICA

Crossing the pond? Standard commercial carriers like **American** (☎+1-800-433-7300; www.aa.com), **United** (☎+1-800-538-2929; www.ual.com), and **Northwest** (☎+1-800-225-2525; www.nwa.com) will probably offer the most convenient flights, but they may not be the cheapest. Check **Air France** (☎+1-800-237-2747; www.airfrance.us), **Alitalia** (☎+1-800-223-5730; www.alitaliausa.com), **British Airways** (☎+1-800-247-9297; www.britishairways.com), and **Lufthansa** (☎+1-800-399-5838; www.lufthansa.com) for cheap tickets from destinations throughout the US to all over Europe. You might find an even better deal on one of the following airlines, if any of their limited departure points is convenient for you.

Aer Lingus: ☎+1-800-474-7424; www.aerlingus.ie. Affordable flights to Barcelona from Boston, Chicago, Orlando, New York City, San Francisco, and Washington D.C.

Finnair: ☎+358 600 140 140; www.finnair.com. Cheap round-trips from New York City and Sydney to Barcelona; connections also available throughout Europe.

Icelandair: ☎+1-800-223-5500; www.icelandair.com. Departs from Boston and Seattle with stopovers in Iceland.

TRAVELING FROM IRELAND AND THE UK

KLM: ☎+44 8712 227 474; www.klmuk.com. Cheap tickets to Barcelona from London, Dublin, and elsewhere (UK£200).

TRAVELING FROM AUSTRALIA AND NEW ZEALAND

Qantas Air: Australia ☎+61 13 13 13, New Zealand ☎+64 800 808 767; www.qantas.com.au. Flights from Australia and New Zealand to Barcelona (AUS$2500).

Singapore Air: Australia ☎+61 13 10 11, from New Zealand ☎800 808 909; www.singaporeair.com. Flies from Auckland, Christchurch, Melbourne, Perth, and Sydney to Barcelona (AUS$2075).

BUDGET AIRLINES

For travelers who don't place a premium on convenience, we recommend ▧**budget airlines** as the best way to jet around Europe. Travelers can often snag these tickets for illogically low prices (i.e., less than the price of a meal in the airport food court), but you get what you pay for: namely, minimalist service and no frills. In addition, many budget airlines fly out of smaller regional airports several kilometers out of town. You'll have to buy shuttle tickets to reach the airports of many of these airlines, so plan on adding an hour or so to your travel time. After round-trip shuttle tickets and fees for services that might come standard on other airlines, that €1 sale fare can suddenly jump to €20-100. Still, it's possible save money even if you live outside the continent by hopping a cheap flight to anywhere in Europe and using budget airlines to reach your final destination. Prices vary dramatically; shop around, book months ahead, and stay flexible to nab the best fares. For a more detailed list of these airlines by country, check out www.whichbudget.com.

bmibaby: from the UK ☎9111 545 454, elsewhere +44 870 126 6726; www.bmibaby.com. Departures from throughout the UK. Manchester to Barcelona, (UK£100).

easyJet: ☎+44 871 244 2366; www.easyjet.com. London to Barcelona (UK£120).

Ryanair: from Ireland ☎0818 30 30 30, UK 0871 246 0000; www.ryanair.com. From Dublin, Glasgow, Liverpool, London, and Shannon to Barcelona (UK£180).

SkyEurope: from the UK ☎0906 680 0065, elsewhere +352 27 00 27 28; www.skyeurope.com. Destinations in 19 countries around Europe. Vienna to Barcelona (€120).

GETTING AROUND BARCELONA

BY PUBLIC TRANSPORTATION

Barcelona's public transportation (info ☎010) is quick and cheap. If you plan to use public transportation extensively, there are several Autoritat del Transport Metropolità (ATM; www.atm.cat) *abonos* (passes) available, which work interchangeably for the Metro, bus, and urban lines of the FGC commuter trains, RENFE Cercanías, Trams, and Nitbus. The **T-10 pass** (€7.70) is valid for 10 rides and saves you nearly 50% off single tickets. The **T-Dia pass** (€5.80) is good for a full day of unlimited travel, and the **T-mes** (€48) is good for a month. If you just plan to use the Metro and daytime buses, there are 2-5 day passes at **Transports Metropolitans de Barcelona** (**TMB;** ☎933 18 70 74; www.tmb.net; 2 days €11, 5 days €24). These will save you money if you plan to ride the Metro more than three times per day.

Metro: (☎932 98 70 00; www.tmb.net). Vending machines and ticket windows sell passes. Red diamonds with the white letter "M" mark stations. Hold on to your ticket—

C.OH-NO-YOU-DIDN'T

Spain has notoriously been one of Europe's worst offenders in terms of pollution, but recent studies show that Barcelona has led the way in cutting greenhouse gas emissions. Motivated as much by the economic downturn as by environmental concerns, 68.9% of Barceloneses say that they have been using cars less (compared to 65% in Madrid and 66% throughout Spain). This figure is especially impressive because Barceloneses already tend to walk and use public transportation more than their *madrileño* counterparts.

Credit is due in part to Barcelona's prompt and reliable metro system as well as to the expansive and practical Bicing program, which allows citizens who pay a monthly fee to collect a bike at one of the hundreds of stations across the city for periods of two hours at a time. Other signs of ecological improvement in Barcelona include a growing recycling program, which succeeded in increasing recycling rates in Barcelona by 28 percent from 2007 to 2008.

But it's best not to count the chickens before they come home to roost (or whatever the expression is). Emissions are still well above those called for by the Kyoto agreement in 2002, and challenges like water go unsolved, as fisherman haul up plastic and toxic mud instead of fish from the nearby coasts.

riding without one can incur a €40 fine. Trains run M-Th, Su, and holidays 5am-midnight, F 5am-2am, Sa non-stop service. Extended holiday hours. €1.40 per *senzill/sencillo* (1-way ticket). Switching lines may involve a considerable walk.

Ferrocarrils de la Generalitat de Catalunya (FGC): (☎932 05 15 15; www.fgc.es). Commuter trains to local destinations with main stations at Pl. de Catalunya and Pl. d'Espanya. Note that some destinations within the city (parts of Gràcia and beyond) require taking the FGC. Blue symbols resembling 2 interlocking "V"s mark Metro connections. The commuter line costs the same as the Metro (€1.40) as far as Tibidabo. After that, rates go up by zone: Zone 2 €2.10, Zone 3 €2.90, etc. Metro passes are valid on FGC trains. Info office at the Pl. de Catalunya station open M-F 7am-9pm.

RENFE Cercanías (Rodalies): (☎902 24 02 02; www.renfe.es/cercanias). The C2 Nord to the **airport** (Zone 4; €2.80) is particularly useful. Destinations include **Blanes** (C1, Zone 6; €4.40) and **Sitges** (C2 Sud, Zone 4; €2.80). Main connections at Sants and Pg. de Gràcia, marked by either the RENFE double arrows or a funny-looking red circle with a backwards C.

Buses: Go almost anywhere, usually from 5am-10pm (many leave for the last round at 9:30pm). Most stops have maps, and you can easily figure out which bus to take. Many run on natural gas. Most buses come in central locations every 10-15min. €1.40.

Nitbus: (www.emt-amb.cat/links/cat/cnitbus.htm). 18 different lines run every 20-30min. 10:30pm-4:30am, depending on the line; a few run until 5:30am. All buses depart from around Pl. de Catalunya, stop in front of most club complexes, and work their way through Ciutat Vella and the Zona Alta. Maps are available at *estancos* (tobacco shops), at some bus stops, online, and in Metro stations.

Bus Turístic: Hop-on, hop-off tours of the city. Passes sold for 1-2 days (€21, €27).

BY TAXI

About 11,000 taxis swarm the city. A *"lliure"* or *"libre"* sign or a green light on the roof means vacant; yellow means occupied. On weekend nights, you may wait up to 30min. for a ride; long lines form at popular spots like the Port Olímpic. To call a cab, try **RadioTaxi033** (☎933 033 033; www.radiotaxi033.com; AmEx/MC/V) or **Servi Taxi** (☎933 30 03 00). **Taxi Amic** has wheelchair-accessible vehicles. (☎934 20 80 88).

BY CAR

Let's Go recommends that travelers rely on public transportation in Barcelona; but if Barcelona is one stop on an epic roadtrip, cars will offer speed, freedom, and access to the countryside. Although a single traveler won't save by renting a car, four usually will. If you can't decide between train and car travel, you may benefit from a combination of the two; Rail Europe and other railpass vendors offer rail-and-drive packages. The following rental agencies are available in Barcelona, call ahead to verify license and insurance procedure:

Avis, C. Corcega, 293-295 (☎932 37 56 80; www.avis.es). Open M-F 8am-9pm, Sa 8am-8pm, Su 8am-1pm. Branches at **airport** (☎932 98 36 00; open daily 7am-12:30am) and **Estació Sants,** Pl. dels Països Catalans, s/n. (☎933 30 41 93; open M-F 7:30am-11:30pm, Sa 8am-9pm, Su 9am-9pm).

Budget (☎932 98 36 00; www.budget.es), in the airport. Open M-Sa 7am-12:30am, Su 7am-midnight.

Cooltra, Pg. Joan de Borbo, 80-84 (☎93 221 40 70; www.cooltra.com). Ⓜ Barceloneta. Mopeds from €32 per day between 9:30am-8:30pm, €42 per 24hr., and €290 per month. Open daily from June to mid-Sept. 9am-8:30pm, from mid-Sept. to May 10am-8pm.

Europcar, Pl. Països Catalanes, s/n (☎902 10 50 55; www.europcar.es), near Sants. Open M-F 7am-12am, Sa-Su 8am-11pm. Branch at the airport (☎902 10 50 55). Open 24hr.

Hertz, Av. Diagonal, 3 (☎933 56 11 39; www.hertz.es). Ⓜ Mareseme Fòrum. Open M-Sa 10am-10pm. Branch at the airport (☎932 98 36 37; open daily 7am-midnight) and by **Estació Sants,** C. Viriat, 45 (☎934 19 61 56; open M-F 8am-9:30pm, Sa-Su 8am-2:30pm).

BY MOPED AND MOTORCYCLE

Mopeds and motorized bikes don't use much gas, can be put on trains, and are a good compromise between costly car travel and the limited range on foot. However, they're uncomfortable for long distances, dangerous in the rain, and unpredictable on rough roads. Always wear a helmet and never ride with a backpack. If you've never ridden a moped before, a twisting road is not the place to start. Expect to pay about US$20-35 per day without insurance; try auto repair shops and remember to bargain. Motorcycles are more expensive and normally require a license, but they are better for long distances. Before renting, ask if the price includes tax and insurance, or else you may be hit with an unexpected fee. Avoid handing your passport over as a deposit; if you have an accident or mechanical failure, you may not get it back until you cover all repairs. Pay ahead of time instead.

BY BIKE

Budget Bikes (☎933 04 18 85; www.budgetbikes.eu), C. Marquès de Barberà, 15 (Ⓜ Liceu); C. General Castaños, 6 (Ⓜ Barceloneta); C. Estruc, 38 (Ⓜ Pl. Catalunya). €6 per 2hr., €16 per day, €26 per 2 days, each extra day after that €7. Themed tours €22-28. Open daily 10am-8pm.

Barcelona Bici, Mirador de Colom. (☎932 85 38 32). €4.50 per hr., €11 per 4hr., €15 per 8 hr., €21 per 2 days, €56per week. Open daily 10-8pm.

THE HIDDEN DEAL

FAT TIRES BIKE TOURS

If you miss the feeling of the wind in your hair, if you're trying to stay fit while traveling, or if you're only in Barcelona for a few days but want to see as much of the city as possible, consider renting a bike from Fat Tire Bike Tours. Although the company offers more expensive guided tours, it also allows you to rent a bike for up to three hours for only €7—at €2.33 per hour, that's a steal. You can keep the bike for up to six hours for €10, or more than 6 hours for €15. The bikes are large and comfortable, with wide handlebars friendly to casual bikers, three speeds, comfortable seats, and bells.

While the circuitous streets of the Barri Gòtic may test your reflexes, most of Barcelona is bike-friendly; in areas where there are not designated bike lanes, just hop in with normal traffic. From the Barri Gòtic, it's a quick 15min. ride to the beach. Bike paths lead all the way from the beach to the Sagrada Família.

Fat Tires, C. Escudellers, 48, is open March 1-December 15 10am-7pm. It's located in the Barri Gòtic, near Las Ramblas. You can find out everything you need to know about Fat Tires (and some useful tips about the Barcelona metro system, too) at www. fattirebiketoursbarcelona.com.

Fat Tire, C. Escudellers, 48 (☎933 01 36 12; www.fattirebiketoursbarcelona.com). €6 for 2hr., €10 for 2-4hr., €15 for 1 day, €25 for 2 days. Open daily from Mar. to mid-Dec. 10am-8pm. Famous bike tours include a break at the beach (€22 includes bike rental). Meet in Pl. St. Jaume. Tours from mid-Apr. to Oct. at 11am and 4pm, from Feb. to mid-Apr. and Nov. to mid-Dec. at 11am.

BY FOOT

Some of Europe's grandest scenery can only be seen on foot. *Let's Go* features many daytrips, but native inhabitants, hostel proprietors, and fellow travelers are the best source for tips. In cities like Barcelona, **walking** is both economical and efficient.

KEEPING IN TOUCH

BY EMAIL AND INTERNET

Email and internet are easy to access in Barcelona. Although in some places it's possible to forge a remote link with your home server, in most cases this is a much slower (and thus more expensive) option than taking advantage of free **web-based email accounts** (e.g., **www.gmail.com**). **Internet cafes** are listed in the **Practical Information** section. For lists of additional cybercafes in Barcelona, check out www.cybercaptive.com.

> **WARY WI-FI.** Wireless hot spots make internet access possible in public and remote places. Unfortunately, they also pose **security risks.** Hot spots are public, open networks that use unencrypted, unsecured connections. They are susceptible to hacks and "packet sniffing"—the theft of passwords and other private information. To prevent problems, disable "ad hoc" mode, turn off file sharing and network discovery, encrypt your email, turn on your firewall, beware of phony networks, and watch for over-the-shoulder creeps.

BY TELEPHONE

CALLING HOME FROM BARCELONA

Prepaid phone cards are a common and relatively inexpensive means of calling abroad. Each one comes with a Personal Identification Number (PIN) and a toll-free access number. To purchase prepaid phone cards, check online for the best rates; www.callingcards.com is a good place to start. Online providers generally send your access number and PIN via email, with no actual "card" involved. Another option is to purchase a **calling card,** linked to a major national telecommunications service in your home country. Calls are billed collect or to your account.

PLACING INTERNATIONAL CALLS. To call Spain from home or to call home from Spain, dial:
1. The **international dialing prefix.** To call from **Australia,** dial ☎0011; **Canada** or the **US,** ☎011; **Ireland, New Zealand,** or the **UK,** ☎00; **Spain,** ☎00.
2. The **country code** of the country you want to call. To call **Australia,** dial ☎61; **Canada** or the **US,** ☎1; **Ireland,** ☎353; **New Zealand,** ☎64; the **UK,** ☎44; **Spain,** ☎34.
3. The **city/area code.** For Barcelona, the city code is ☎93.
4. The **local number.**

Placing a collect call through an international operator can be expensive but may be necessary in case of an emergency. You can frequently call collect without even possessing a company's calling card just by calling its access number and following the instructions.

CALLING WITHIN BARCELONA

The simplest way to call within the country is to use a coin-operated phone. Prepaid phone cards (available at newspaper kiosks and tobacco stores) usually save time and money in the long run. Phone rates typically tend to be highest in the morning, lower in the evening, and lowest on Sundays and at night.

CELLULAR PHONES

Spain, like much of the developed world, is relaxed when it comes to technology; you won't have to worry about being unable to communicate with friends and family efficiently. Many travelers find that the availability and usefulness of cell phones in Spain make them well worth the cost.

The international standard for cell phones is **Global System for Mobile Communication (GSM).** To make and receive calls in Spain, you will need a GSM-compatible phone and a **SIM (Subscriber Identity Module) card,** a country-specific, thumbnail-size chip that gives you a local phone number and plugs you into the local network. Many SIM cards are prepaid, and incoming calls are frequently free. You can buy additional cards or vouchers (usually available at convenience stores) to "top up" your phone. For more information on GSM phones, check out www.telestial.com. Companies like **Cellular Abroad** (www.cellularabroad.com) rent cell phones that work in destinations around the world.

TIP

GSM PHONES. Just having a GSM phone doesn't mean you're necessarily good to go when you travel abroad. The majority of GSM phones sold in the US operate on a different frequency (1900) than international phones (900/1800) and will not work abroad. Tri-band phones work on all three frequencies (900/1800/1900) and will operate through most of the world. Additionally, some GSM phones are SIM-locked and will only accept SIM cards from a single carrier. You'll need a SIM-unlocked phone to use a SIM card from a local carrier when you travel.

BY MAIL

SENDING MAIL HOME FROM BARCELONA

Airmail is the best way to send mail home from Barcelona. Write "airmail," *"par avion,"* *"por avión,"* or *"via aerea"* on the front. **Surface mail** is by far the cheapest and slowest way to send mail. It takes one to two months to cross the Atlantic and one to three to cross the Pacific—good for heavy items you won't need for a while, like souvenirs that you've acquired along the way.

SENDING MAIL TO BARCELONA

To ensure timely delivery, mark envelopes "airmail," *"par avion,"* or *"por avión."* In addition to the standard postage system whose rates are listed below, **Federal Express** (☎+1-800-463-3339; www.fedex.com) handles express mail services from most countries to Spain. Sending a postcard or a letter (up to 20g) within Spain costs €0.32.

There are several ways to arrange pickup of letters sent to you while you are abroad. Mail can be sent reliably via **Poste Restante** (General Delivery; **Lista de Correos** in Spanish) to almost any city or town in Spain with a post office. Address Poste Restante letters like so:

Pablo PICASSO
Lista de Correos
Barcelona, España

The mail will go to a special desk in the central post office, unless you specify a post office by street address or postal code. It's best to use the largest post office, since mail may be sent there regardless. It is usually safer and quicker, though more expensive, to send mail express or registered. Bring your passport (or other photo ID) for pickup; there may be a small fee. If the clerks insist that there is nothing for you, ask them to check under your first name as well.

ACCOMMODATIONS

HOSTELS

Many hostels are laid out dorm-style, often with large single-sex rooms and bunk beds, although private rooms that sleep from two to four are becoming more common. They sometimes have kitchens and utensils for your use, breakfast and other meals, storage areas, laundry facilities, internet, transportation to airports, and bike or moped rentals. However, there can be drawbacks: some hostels impose a maximum stay, close during certain daytime "lockout" hours, have a curfew, don't accept reservations, or, less frequently, require that you do chores. In Barcelona, a dorm bed in a hostel will average around €20-30 and a private room around €30-35, per day.

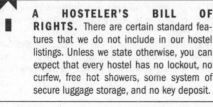

A HOSTELER'S BILL OF RIGHTS. There are certain standard features that we do not include in our hostel listings. Unless we state otherwise, you can expect that every hostel has no lockout, no curfew, free hot showers, some system of secure luggage storage, and no key deposit.

HOSTELLING INTERNATIONAL

Joining the youth hostel association in your own country (listed below) automatically grants you membership privileges in **Hostelling International (HI)**, a federation of national hosteling associations. Non-HI members may be allowed to stay in some hostels, but they will have to pay extra to do so. HI hostels are scattered throughout Barcelona and are typically less expensive than private hostels. HI's umbrella organization's website (www.hihostels.com), which lists the web addresses and phone numbers of all national associations, can be a great place to begin researching hosteling in a specific region.

OTHER TYPES OF ACCOMMODATIONS

HOTELS, GUESTHOUSES, AND PENSIONS

Hotel singles in Barcelona cost about €78 per night, doubles €105. If you make **reservations** in writing, indicate your night of arrival and the number of nights you plan to stay. The hotel will send you a confirmation and may request payment for the first night.

BED AND BREAKFASTS (B&BS)

For a cozy alternative to impersonal hotel rooms, B&Bs (private homes with rooms available to travelers) range from acceptable to sublime. Rooms in

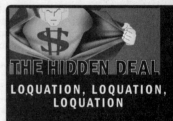

THE HIDDEN DEAL

LOQUATION, LOQUATION, LOQUATION

Accommodations are plentiful in Barcelona, but finding one for the right price often means sacrificing privacy, space, and luxury. One of the best ways to find better housing on the cheap is to search online for apartments and rooms being rented out. Barcelona's best site for this kind of search is **www.loquo.com,** a Craigslist-like website dedicated exclusively to Spain. It has hundreds of listings for both short-term and long-term rentals as well as shared and private apartments. Rooms go for as low as €20 per person per night, or €120 per week, which often less than what you'd be paying in the cheapest of hostels. Plus, you don't have to share a room or bathroom with 6-10 strangers, and you're likely to get more comforts and amenities, like your own fridge, kitchen, Wi-Fi, and laundry machines.

It can be tricky to secure a room online before arriving in Barcelona, without having the chance to see the apartment or place a deposit. It may be wise to book at least your first night or two in Barcelona at a hostel to allow time for details to be sorted out (especially with long-term rentals). But finding an apartment can ultimately save money and provide added comfort, leaving you more cash and energy to enjoy all that Barcelona has to offer.

B&Bs generally cost €40-80 for a single and €100-120 for a double in Barcelona. Many websites provide listings for B&Bs; check out **Bed & Breakfast Inns Online** (www.bbonline.com), **BedandBreakfast.com** (www.bedandbreakfast.com), or **BNBFinder.com** (www.bnbfinder.com).

LONG-TERM ACCOMMODATIONS

Travelers planning to stay in Barcelona for extended periods of time may find it most cost-effective to rent an apartment. A basic one-bedroom (or studio) apartment will range €800-1300 per month. Besides the rent itself, prospective tenants usually are also required to front a security deposit (frequently one month's rent) and the last month's rent.

For more long-term accommodation information, check out **craigslist Barcelona** at www.barcelona.es.craigslist.es. Students searching for a place to crash for a while may also find useful the **Barcelona Housing Service for Students** (www.bcn-housing-students.com).

SPECIFIC CONCERNS

SUSTAINABLE TRAVEL

Ecotourism, a rising trend in sustainable travel, focuses on the conservation of natural habitats—mainly, on how to use them to build up the economy without exploitation or overdevelopment. If you suddenly get the urge to explore beyond Barcelona, definitely consider **Ecotourism Maka** (☎+34 93 112 16 75; www.makaecotourism.com). Explore the natural beauty of Catalonia with incredible outdoor activities like trekking, kayaking, and scuba diving.

> **ECOTOURISM RESOURCES.** For more information on environmentally responsible tourism, contact one of the organizations below:
> **Conservation International,** 2011 Crystal Dr., Ste. 500, Arlington, VA 22202, USA (☎+1-800-429-5660 or 703-341-2400; www.conservation.org).
> **International Ecotourism Society,** 1301 Clifton St. NW, Ste. 200, Washington, DC 20009, USA (☎+1-202-506-5033; www.ecotourism.org).

TRAVELING ALONE

Traveling alone can be extremely beneficial, providing a sense of independence and a greater opportunity to connect with locals. On the other hand, solo travelers are more vulnerable to harassment and theft. For more on how to stay safe when traveling alone, see **Exploring and Traveling,** p. 24.

WOMEN TRAVELERS

Women exploring on their own inevitably face some additional safety concerns. Single women can consider staying in hostels that offer single rooms that lock from the inside or in religious organizations with single-sex rooms. It's a good idea to stick to centrally located accommodations and to avoid solitary late-night treks or metro rides. Always carry extra cash for a phone call, bus, or taxi. **Hitchhiking** is never safe for lone women or even for two women traveling together. Look as if you know where you're going and approach older women or couples for directions if you're lost or feeling uncomfortable in your surroundings. Generally, the less you look like a tourist, the better off you'll be. Dress conservatively, especially in rural areas. Wearing a conspicuous **wedding band** sometimes helps to prevent unwanted advances.

Your best answer to verbal harassment is no answer at all; feigning deafness, sitting motionless, and staring straight ahead at nothing in particular will usually do the trick. The extremely persistent can sometimes be dissuaded by a firm, loud, and very public "Go away!" (¡*Véte!* in Spanish). Don't hesitate to seek out a police officer or a passerby if you are being harassed. Memorize the local emergency numbers and consider carrying a whistle on your keychain. A self-defense course will both prepare you for a potential attack and raise your level of awareness of your surroundings (see **Personal Safety,** p. 24).

GLBT TRAVELERS

In Spain, attitudes toward homosexuality have evolved significantly past the traditional stance of intolerance. Barcelona in particular is well-known for its history of openness toward homosexuality, going back to the Franco regime. During his rule, a prominent gay scene emerged in the area, challenging the illegality of such behavior at the time. A prominent international gay and lesbian film festival takes place every year in the city and Barcelona is right next door to Sitges, a beach destination popular with the gay community. Despite all this, discrimination is still a problem, especially in small, rural regions of Spain, given the country's strong Catholic roots.

For more information on traveling in Spain and elsewhere, check out the organization below.

International Lesbian and Gay Association (ILGA), 17 Rue de la Charité, 1210 Brussels, Belgium (☎+32 2 502 2471; www.ilga.org). Provides political information, such as homosexuality laws of individual countries.

ADDITIONAL GLBT RESOURCES
Damron Men's Travel Guide, Damron Women's Traveller, Damron Accommodations Guide, Damron City Guide, and *Damron Women's Traveller.* Published annually by Damron Travel Guides. For info, call ☎+1-415-255-0404 or visit www.damron.com.
Spartacus International Gay Guide 2009, by Bruno Gmunder Verlag.

TRAVELERS WITH DISABILITIES

Wheelchair accessibility varies widely. Travelers can be sure to find access in modern and big city museums, but elsewhere, wheelchair access is far from given. Travelers with disabilities (*inhabilidades* in Spanish) should inform airlines and hotels of their disabilities when making reservations, as some time may be needed to prepare special accommodations. Call ahead to restaurants, museums, and other facilities to find out wheelchair accessibility. Guide-dog owners: inquire as to the quarantine policies of each destination country.

Rail is probably the most convenient form of transportation for disabled travelers in Europe: many stations have ramps, and some trains have wheelchair lifts, special seating areas, and specially equipped toilets. All Eurostar, some InterCity (IC), and some EuroCity (EC) trains are wheelchair-accessible. For those who wish to rent cars, some major car-rental agencies (e.g., Hertz) offer hand-controlled vehicles. The following organizations will have useful advice for travelers with disabilities:

The Guided Tour, Inc., 7900 Old York Rd., Ste. 111B, Elkins Park, PA 19027, USA (☎+1-800-783-5841; www.guidedtour.com). Organizes travel programs for persons with developmental and physical challenges in Spain.

Mobility International USA (MIUSA), 132 E. Broadway, Ste. 343, Eugene, OR 97401, USA (☎+1-541-343-1284; www.miusa.org). Provides a variety of books and other publications containing information for travelers with disabilities.

MINORITY TRAVELERS

Spain is increasingly cosmopolitan due to immigration and tourism. The infrequent incidents of racism are rarely violent or threatening. However, after the arrest of Moroccans for the terrorist attack of **March 11,** travelers who appear to be of Middle Eastern descent may face some discrimination.

DIETARY CONCERNS

Spain can be a particularly tricky place to visit as a strict vegetarian; meat or fish are featured in most popular dishes. Markets are a good choice, and Barcelona has over 40 strictly vegetarian restaurants. Be careful, however, as many servers may interpret a "vegetarian" order to mean "with tuna or chicken instead of ham." The travel section of **The Vegetarian Resource Group** (www.vrg.org/travel) has a comprehensive list of organizations and websites geared toward helping vegetarians and vegans travel abroad. Vegetarians have countless web resources at their disposal: try www.vegdining.com, www.happycow.net, www.vegeats.com/restaurants and www.vegetariansabroad.com.

Travelers who keep **kosher** may want to take a peek at the worldwide kosher restaurant database to find kosher eateries around Barcelona (http://shamash.org/kosher). If you are very strict in your observance, it wouldn't be a bad idea to prepare your own food on the road. Travelers looking for **halal** restaurants may find www.zabihah.com a useful resource.

LET'S GO ONLINE. Plan your next trip on our newly redesigned website, **www.letsgo.com.** It features the latest travel info on your favorite destinations as well as tons of interactive features: make your own itinerary, read blogs from our trusty Researchers, browse our photo library, watch exclusive videos, check out our newsletter, find travel deals, and buy new guides. We're always updating and adding new features, so check back often!

Rock on, Catalan

Catalunya is at the center of a perpetual love triangle, torn between historical ties to Spain and a fierce desire for independence. Centuries of foreign rule and a location on the Mediterranean Sea near the border with France have forged a singular regional identity. After WWII, Catalunya faced cultural extinction under Franco's oppression, but today the Catalan identity flourishes. Like a troubadour in medieval times, the music of the region literally sings the tale of the hard-fought struggle to preserve a unique heritage.

Ironically, the very force that threatened to eradicate Catalan traditions served to catalyze the movement that would preserve them. Under Franco, all cultural activities were subject to censorship or forbidden on political and moral grounds. Franco was a militant nationalist, mandating Spanish as the sole official language and suppressing other native languages like Galician or Catalan. In the 1960s, a group of musicians conceived an ingenious method of rebellion. The Nova Cançó movement (Catalan for "New Song") paired Catalan lyrics with popular music. Following the success of the first Catalan group, El Setze Jutges, similar efforts began in other marginalized territories of Northern Spain including Galicia, Castile, and the Basque Country. Nova Cançó artists such as Raimon, Lluis Llach, and Joan Manuel Serrat remain popular today.

Franco's death in 1975 ushered in a period of democracy and openness. Deprived of the catalyzing force of oppression, the Nova Cançó movement lost momentum. In the late 1980s, the government of Catalunya began to offer grants to rock bands singing in Catalan. Though the original rebellious motivation behind Nova Cançó no longer inspired Catalan musicians, money worked as an effective lubricant for the gears of creativity. The early 90's witnessed the birth of a Catalan Rock movement that encompassed diverse musical styles connected by the use of Catalan lyrics. Today, Catalan Rock is sung by popular and commercially viable groups that include Lax'n Busto, Els Pets, Sau, and Sopa de Cabra.

As Catalan Rock flourished, the forces of globalization reinforced the individuality of Catalan identity while expanding regional music in a new direction. The 1992 Barcelona Olympic Games revitalized Catalunya, leaving behind an international imprint. From out of the melting pot sprung Manu Chao, a French-born singer of Spanish heritage who is emblematic of the Barcelona he inhabits. Influenced by the singer's own world travels, the music of Manu Chao is a bewildering yet seductive combination of Spanish, French, Catalan, Portuguese, Arabic, and

> **" ...what began as a means of expressing longing for Catalan national identity has matured into a bona fide scene."**

English. With inspiring lyrics about love, immigration, street culture, and leftist politics, Manu Chao is a musical activist in the tradition of the Nova Cançó protest singers.

Catalan music is a potent force in 21st century popular culture. During the run of Operación Triunfo, a televised singing competition in the vein of American Idol, several contestants performed and released albums with Catalan lyrics. With the arrival of Catalan indie bands and hip-hop groups, what began solely as a means of expressing longing for Catalan national identity has matured into a bona fide scene. Now world audiences of any musical taste can appreciate the proud and resilient sound of the Catalan soul.

LIFE AND TIMES

Barcelona, currently the second-largest city in Spain and the capital of the autonomous, nationalist region of Catalunya, has a history that stretches back over two millennia. One popular myth traces its foundation to Hercules, which would make Barcelona even older than Rome itself. Other legends link its foundation to settlement by the Laietani in both Barkeno and Laie, which would later combine to create Barcelona. The city's name has an uncertain history, though most scholars attribute it to the Carthaginian king **Bareas,** who took Barcelona during the Second Punic War in 218 BC. Bareas's conquest marks the foundation of the city we know as Barcelona.

WHEN IN BARCELONA, DO AS THE ROMANS DO: OCCUPY. In an effort to subdue Carthage, the Romans ripped through the Iberian Peninsula in the third century BC, conquering the Laietani along the way. In honor of Emperor Augustus's rule, the Romans gave Barcelona a new name: Colonia Faventia Julia Augusta Paterna Barcino (Latin for "brevity is the soul of wit"). **Barcino,** as Roman Barcelona came to be known, now lies mostly underneath the modern day Barri Gòtic, or Gothic Quarter, whose architecture pays homage to Barcelona's evolution under the Romans. During Classical Antiquity, Barcelona shared Catalunya's spotlight with two smaller cities: Tarragona and Zaragoza.

Over the course of Roman rule, due to threats by Germanic tribes that began around AD 250, the city's fortifications were substantially improved (and in fact can still be seen today). The Romans would gradually but drastically alter the region over the centuries, introducing their style of architecture, roads, irrigation techniques, and cuisine. Romans also gave Catalunya Latin, which would combine with southern France's Langue d'Oc ("language of yes") to give Barcelona an important piece of its national identity, the Catalan language.

The first Christian communities also appeared during the Roman period, though under Diocletian those communities would be persecuted at the start of the AD fourth century. **Saint Cucuphas,** of African origin, as well as **Saint Eulalia** would be made martyrs of Barcino. **The Edict of Milan** in AD 313, however, declared Christianity the official religion, a move which would reverberate through the region of the Empire for over a century, even after Rome's decline.

ROME'S DESTRUCTION: RAMPAGING INVADERS AND BARCELONA. A slew of Germanic tribes swept over the Western Roman region of Iberia in the early fifth century, and **Ataulf of the Visigoths** won the keys to the kingdom, establishing his court at Barcino in 414 and beginning an era of revival. Barcino became an important center for the Visigoths, but by 711, Moorish forces arrived in Iberia and quickly took control of the city. Unlike Tarragona, which was devastated due to its resistance and which never truly recovered, Barcelona maintained its integrity by surrendering peacefully. The newly dubbed Barshiluna flourished under Moorish rule for almost a century and suffered relatively little change for its trouble: though its cathedral was converted to a mosque, the local government allowed Christianity to continue until the city was liberated in 801 by Charlemagne's Son, **Louis the Pious.** Under the Franks, the local government reinstated Christianity despite the Islamic Moors' continued control over most of Spain.

LOCAL LEGEND

THE FOUNDING OF BARCELONA

As with all old things, no one is really sure how Barcelona got started. One popular, somewhat mythic explanation is that the city was founded by the legendary demi-god Hercules around 1200 BC (over 400 years before the founding of Rome). The story goes that as Hercules was accompanying Jason and the Argonauts in search of the Golden Fleece, one of the fleet's nine boats was shipwrecked on a Mediterranean shore. Hercules was sent out to track it down, and found the shipwrecked crew not only alive and well but also completely enamored with the land they had stumbled upon. Hence, a city was founded, taking the name Barca Nona (ninth ship).

Another, slightly less fantastical story posits that the city was founded around 230 BC by Hamilcar Barca, father of the famous Carthaginian commander Hannibal, and himself a prominent general in the first Punic War between Carthage and Rome. He is known to have made several conquests in Spain, especially in the south, although the exact range and extent of his influence is unclear. This account, at least, provides a more plausible origin for Barcelona's ancient name Barcino, which could have been easily derived from the name of the general who supposedly founded the city.

Whatever the truth may be, Hercules, along with other questionably linked figures like Columbus, stands as one of Barcelona's many adopted heroes.

CATALUNYA IN THE MIDDLE AGES. The Frankish governments installed counts of the Carolingian line in Barcelona, notably **Guifré el Pilós** (Wilfred the Hairy), who was chosen by Charles the Bald in AD 874. (Charles, for his part, was inaugurated by Anthony the Bewiggèd.) He spent his life defending the monarch but also increasing the power of Catalunya as an independent, or at least autonomous, region.

The Moors attempted to recapture the city in AD 985. Wilfred's descendent, **Count Borrell,** asked the Frankish king for aid but was ignored. Under Borrell's leadership, despite a lack of military might, Catalunya defeated the Moors in 989. Barcelona and Catalunya remained attached to the Carolingian dynasty until 1258.

Barcelona became one of the wealthiest ports in the region at the turn of the millennium under the guidance of four counts with the same name: **Ramón Berenguer.** The marriage of the fourth Ramón Berenguer to Petronella of Aragon in 1137 would expand the region's sphere of influence into neighboring Aragon, adding to holdings gained with the third's marriage to a Provençale Princess from France. The nation of Catalunya expanded further under **Jaume I** (JA-oh-may; 1213-76) to include Valencia and the Balearic Islands.

BARCELONA GOES SPANISH. In 1469, the marriage of the Catholic Monarchs **Fernando d'Aragon** and **Isabel de Castilla** joined Castilla and Aragon. An alliance between Aragon and Catalunya meant that Fernando inherited the port of Barcelona in 1479. In 1478, the **Inquisition** began to torture and kill the region's Jews, while the Moors were expelled once and for all in 1492. The Mediterranean trade that had once been so lucrative for the city no longer flourished due to a new focus on the Americas. Banned from New World trade, Catalunya faced crippling economic recession.

The insanity continued when **Juana la Loca** (Juana the Mad) married into the Hapsburg Dynasty and when her son, **Carlos I** (1516-56) took control of a vast Eastern European hodgepodge. Spain entered a Golden Age, but marginalized Barcelona languished, left barren both economically and culturally. Much of Spain's greatest art and literature comes from this **Siglo de Oro,** which lasted from 1492 to the mid-17th century. While the rest of Spain produced painters, Barcelona and Catalunya bred rebels. In 1640, as war raged between Spain and France, rebellious Barcelona sided with the enemy. The conflict became known as the **Guerra dels Segadors** (The Reapers' War; later the name of the Catalan national anthem). A truce between France and Spain in 1652 kept Barcelona and most of Catalunya under Spanish rule.

A SHOT OF BOURBON, A SPANISH SUCCESSION. Following **Carlos II's** death without an heir, Europe found itself with a chance to choose Spain's next ruler. Unfortunately, there were many unqualified candidates. Catalunya, bitter at the betrayal almost a century earlier during the Guerra dels Segadors chose to back Charles of Austria instead of the Bourbon Kingdom's Philip V during the ensuing war of Spanish Succession (1701-13).

It turned out Catalunya had backed the wrong horse once again, and Philip V was crowned King of Spain with the **Treaty of Utrecht.** Felipe was swift to recommence Spain's venerable pastime, banging the iron fist on Catalunya. In this case, it was punishment for Catalunya's treachery during the War of Spanish Succession. He forbid the use of Catalan and left a strong military presence in the region, particularly around Barcelona, as a reminder not to cross the Bourbons.

Felipe V's successors lifted these harsh measures and instead focused on rebuilding infrastructure such as canals, roads, towns, and industry. Carlos III lifted the ban on American trade in 1778, which led to an economic boom.

In 1808, Napoleon invaded Spain, menaced the Catalan state, and even attempted to sway it through promises of independence. Having had the nationalist tendencies beaten out of them for the time being, Barcelona showed rare solidarity with Spain and helped expel the French in 1814.

By the early 18th century, the Industrial Revolution had strengthened Barcelona and renewed the calls for freedom common to most nationalist rhetoric. This was merely aided by the slow loss of Spain's empire abroad under Fernando VII as Latin America attained independence. Inspired by the liberal Spanish constitution (ratified in 1812), democratic tendencies took hold and parliamentary liberalism took root following Fernando's death in 1833. Nationalist fervor dominated Catalan politics until the 1920s, when the rise of dictatorship ended Spain's First Republic.

MODERNISME AND ANARCHISM. As Barcelona's population grew, the old city began to operate above capacity. Madrid forbade the destruction of the Roman walls, but Barceloneses ignored this edict and toppled the walls themselves: the era of expansion had arrived.

Repression ended and the city grew. This growth fostered the **Renaixença** (Renaissance), one of Catalan's most prolific artistic ages, in the late 19th and early 20th centuries. The **Modernisme** movement in architecture could only have grown up in the midst of the Catalan nationalism of the early 20th century. The movement attempted to combine Catalan folk culture—a distinctive blend of Greek, southern French, and Spanish styles—with contemporary ideals of efficiency, comfort, and aesthetic splendor. Modernisme became a symbol of the Renaixença that helped strengthen the nationalist movement, which in turn helped spur a resurgence of the Catalan language.

In 1888, under the guidance of liberal mayor Francese de Paula Rius Taulet, Barcelona hosted the Universal Exposition, which gave Catalunya a chance to show off Modernisme and introduce Catalan culture to the world. The Ciutadella, built by Felipe V to serve as a reminder of Bourbon oppression, served as the site for the event. The building's renovation was itself a representation of Barcelona's rejuvenation and recent artistic developments.

The end of the 19th century saw the rise of anarchy in Barcelona, especially among the impoverished working class upon which the industrial boom relied. The 1890s were rocked by a series of bombings. Most notably, the 1893 bombing of the Liceu Opera house served as a reminder of the desire to destroy the wealthy and the system of centralized authority. True anarchy reigned in 1909 during the **Setmana Trágica** (Tragic Week), when protests against the imperialist war with Morocco drew Socialist and Anarchist revolts that turned into organized strikes and riots; over 100 buildings and 100 citizens were immolated.

KINGS AND FASCISTS. The outbreak of WWI brought new waves of rural workers into Barcelona and merely fanned the flames of previous revolts; this led to the rise of Castilian **Miguel Primo de Rivera,** who shut down parliament and established a dictatorship in 1923 with King Alfonso XIII's blessing. His reign, though repressive, was nothing compared to the dictatorship to come. In 1931, the monarch retired, which gave rise to the short-lived **Second Republic** (1931-36).

As a result of the growing military dissatisfaction with the Republic, the fascist **Falange Español** party came to power, and General Francisco Franco wrenched the helm of the regime away from the idealistic republic with a three-year Civil War. While Barcelona served as the republican capital from 1937 until the end of the war, it eventually succumbed to bombings, starvation, executions, and disease. The Republic surrendered in 1939.

Franco violently repressed Catalunya and Catalan culture. In fact, the repression suffered by most Catalans under Franco is essential to understanding their national character (Catalunya sees itself as a nation). Until Franco's death in 1975, speaking Catalan was illegal. Barcelona was the target of economic redistribution, which stripped it of much of its wealth. The city did continue to protest: in 1960, **Jordi Pujol,** the future leader of Catalunya, sang the national anthem in front of Franco; the deed landed him three years in jail. In 1975, Franco's death gave way to more moderate elements and the parliamentary government was restored.

CONTEMPORARY CATALUNYA: THE RESURGANCE OF AUTONOMY. In the post-Franco years, Barcelona has become one of Spain's wealthiest cities. Jordi Pujol, a pariah under Frano's rule, now controls the Generalitat (the regional government), and Barcelona's current mayor is socialist **Jordi Hereu i Boher.**

PEOPLE AND CULTURE

RELIGION

The **Roman Catholic Church** has prevailed in Spain since 1492, and the plethora of churches of varying architectural traditions in the city of Barcelona stand as a testament to the power of the faith in the past. Barcelona itself was elevated to Archdiocese status in 1964 by Pope Paul VI. Yet, decreasing numbers of parish priests and low church attendance by the majority of Catholics are just two indications of Spain's increasing secularism. While Moorish influence in Catalunya was not as significant as in Andalucía, significant Muslim populations also flourish today, alongside notable Evangelical and Buddhist populations.

CUISINE

Barcelona's best cuisine is often found in its bars and private homes—not in its fanciest restaurants. Locals often opt for tapas barhopping in lieu of a formal meal. Often, breakfast is split into two meals: a light first breakfast (*el desayuno*) and a heavier second breakfast in the late morning or early afternoon. The main meal of the day, *la comida*, comes at mid-afternoon, a bit later than

LIFE AND TIMES

traditional lunch, while *la cena*, supper, will often be something light like a sandwich, served much later than in North America. In Barcelona, the Roman triumvirate of olives, grapes, and wheat prevail, alongside seafood, veal, grilled poultry, and pasta. Catalunya is at the forefront of the culinary avant garde and in recent years, its restaurants have racked up the Michelin stars.

Typical tapas fare includes *allioli* (a sauce of garlic and olive oil used to grill meat), *embotits* (types of pork sausages), and *escudella* (a Middle Eastern influenced dish containing chick peas, potatoes, and vegetables). In the realm of drinks, the *vino de la casa* (house wine) is usually the way to go: it tends to be both economical and delicious. That said, Barcelona is the center and largest consumer of Catalunya's wine industry, so be sure to splurge now and then on the sparkling Cava (first made in 1851), which is unique to the region. To order a draught beer, ask for *un tubo*. Often beer and wine are used in mixed drinks, such as the mixture of Coca-Cola and cheap red wine known as *calimocho*, which is as much a part of festival days as the fireworks.

CUSTOMS AND ETIQUETTE

Barceloneses tend to downplay their Spanish identity and instead celebrate Catalan culture. Insulting the Catalan language or Catalan customs is a severe offense.

Be aware that shorts and short skirts are not common in most parts of Spain and are considered disrespectful in places of worship. Wearing these and other especially revealing clothing away from the beaches may garner unwanted attention. Women with bare shoulders should carry a shawl to tour churches and monasteries.

The people of Spain are very polite, so it's a good idea to be as formal as possible in first encounters. Be sure to address people you meet in Spain as Señor (Mr.), Señora (Mrs.), or Señorita (Ms.). Even on first encounters, women kiss on both cheeks to greet one another, as do men and women. Two men usually shake hands.

LANGUAGE

While the official language of Spain is Castellano (Spanish), **Català** (Catalan) is spoken widely throughout Catalunya and is the co-official language of the region. 95% of the population of the city understand Catalan, and though most Barceloneses are bilingual, Catalan is always preferred over Spanish.

Catalan's precise evolution is difficult to pinpoint. Language historians vacillate between classifying it as a Gallo-Romantic language (due to its Latin origins) or an Ibero-Romance language (due to the give and take with Castillian that has brought the two languages closer). There is a safe distance between between Spanish and Catalan, however; don't expect to waltz into Barcelona fluent in Spanish and leave with Catalan under your belt.

THE ARTS

VISUAL ARTS

BARCELONA'S PREMATURE GOLDEN AGE. The first golden age of Catalan painting took place in the late Middle Ages. Its most significant paintings were frescoes that decorated churches and libraries. Fourteenth-century **Ferrer Bassa** is the most renowned painter of the period; his frescoes can be seen in the Monestir de Pedralbes. Works from this period by artists such as **Jaume Huguet**, a Gothic maker of altarpieces, and Flemish-influenced **Bartolomé Bermejo**, are on display in the Museu Nacional d'Art de Catalunya (p. 147). Huguet also has an important work in the Museu d'Història de Catalunya.

Catalan painting experienced a relative lull under the Hapsburgs until the 1800s, when Impressionist-inspired **Mariano Fortuny** started to gain recognition. His paintings, a mélange of experimentation with "oriental" themes and loose brush work, were often commissioned to memorialize battles and campaigns such as the Spanish-Moroccan War. His appearance reenergized Catalan art and began a long line of talented painters that would emerge in the 19th and 20th centuries.

THE SECOND CATALAN RENAISSANCE. One of Barcelona's foremost modern artists was **Ramon Casas** (1866-1932), illustrator of the popular literary magazine *Pèl i Ploma*, hot commodity in the advertising industry, and painter extraordinaire. His contemporary, **Santiago Rusiñol** (1861-1931), was another significant figure on the Barcelona Modernist scene. The novel use of color in his representations of nature influenced Picasso himself. The other major Spanish Modernist was **Salvador Dalí** (1904-89), whose home you can visit in Port Lligat (p. 217), and whose paintings are on display at museums throughout Barcelona. The guy was such an innovator that he lined his waterfront bedroom with mirrors angled toward the east in order to be "the first Spaniard in the world to see the sun rise." Think about it. Morning was Dalí's favorite time. "Each morning when I awake," he famously said, "I experience again a supreme pleasure—that of being Salvador Dalí."

At the same time that Rusiñol was exploring decadent painting, Surrealism was busy entering the world of the subconscious through various portals: childhood, dreams, and madness among them. While this movement began in Paris, Barcelona produced some of the most innovative and best-known artists of the movement. Painter and sculptor **Joan Miró** (1893-1983) painted a series of child-like and often cryptic squiggles that became a powerful statement against the authoritarian society of the post-Civil War years.

BARCELONA IN THE ABSTRACT. It is hard to imagine an artist who has had as profound an effect upon 20th-century painting as Andalucían **Pablo Ruíz Picasso** (1881-1973). As a child prodigy, Picasso headed for Barcelona, then a hothouse of Modernista architecture and political activism. Bouncing back and forth between Barcelona and Paris, Picasso inaugurated his **Blue Period,** which was characterized by somber depictions of society's outcasts. His permanent move to Paris in 1904 initiated his **Rose Period,** during which he probed into the curiously engrossing lives of clowns and acrobats. This thematic and stylistic evolution led Picasso through his own revolutionary style.

Along with his French colleague Georges Braque, Picasso founded **Cubism,** a method of painting objects simultaneously from multiple perspectives. Cubism evolved slowly, but the first Cubist painting is commonly recognized as *Les Demoiselles d'Avignon* (1907).

His most famous work, the mural *Guernica* (1937), depicts the brutal bombing of a Basque town by Nazi planes who were in cahoots with Fascist forces during the Spanish Civil War. A vehement protest against violence and fascism, *Guernica* now resides in the Centro de Arte Reina Sofía in Madrid. Barcelona's Museu Picasso (p. 143) offers a commendable chronological spread of Picasso's work.

Under the Franco regime, Catalan art was vigorously suppressed. But since the dictator's death in 1975, a new generation of artists has begun to thrive. Catalan **Antoni Tàpies** constructs definition-defying works out of unusual and unorthodox materials most commonly referred to as trash. Tàpies is a founding member of the self-proclaimed "Abstract Generation," which sponsored the magazine *Dau al Set*, whose other members included graphic designer and plastic artist (and fellow Barcelonan) Joan Brossa. Tàpies work is commonly interpreted as an expression of urban alienation and decay in the wake of Franco's oppression. The Fundació Tàpies (p. 146) is his shrine.

ARCHITECTURE

As a reflection of its distinct political and social history, Barcelona lacks the "typically" Spanish, Moorish-influenced style prevalent throughout the rest of Catalunya. Instead, as a result of the *Modernisme* movement, the city boasts some of the world's most innovative architecture. Surviving Roman and Medieval structures only add to Barcelona's vibrant aesthetic.

ROMAN EVOLUTION. The numerous Roman ruins that sprinkle the Spanish countryside testify to six centuries of Empire. While Barcelona holds a few Roman reminders (in the form of columns, walls, and sewers), the ruins in Tarragona are much more extensive. Ruins of the squared Roman wall that used to surround the city can be seen in Barcelona's Barri Gòtic.

Little architecture remains from the Visigoths, who inhabited the area from AD 415 until the eighth century. Until the 12th century, the **Romanesque** style, a predecessor to the Gothic, prevailed in Iberia. The Romanesque style is characterized by its extreme simplicity and use of semi-circular arches and load-bearing vaults. North of the city, in Ripoll, **Santa Maria de Ripoll** is a striking example of Romanesque architecture.

GOING MEDIEVAL: BARCELONA'S ORNATE LEAP FORWARD. Evolving from such Romanesque architectural efforts, the Spanish **Gothic** brought experimentation with pointed arches, flying buttresses, slender walls, airy spaces, and stained glass. Catalan architects developed their own style by employing internal wall supports rather than external buttresses and favoring a more plain and simple aesthetic. Using materials such as iron and stone, they created huge facades protecting beautiful gardens inside. **Santa Maria del Mar** and **Santa Maria del Pi** (p. 113) are two churches that exemplify this style.

New World riches inspired the **Plateresque** ("in the manner of a silver-smith") style, a flashy extreme of Gothic that transformed wealthy Andalucía. Before the style could take Barcelona by storm, late 16th-century Italian Renaissance innovations in perspective and symmetry had already arrived to sober up the Plateresque.

During the 17th and 18th centuries, the **Baroque** came to Spain in the form of Gothic renovations. The movement is responsible for the the the **Palau Dalmases,** a palace that adopts the harsh lines of the Catalan Gothic lines while incorporating the Baroque extravagance.

BARCELONA'S ART NOUVEAU. At the turn of the century, **Modernisme** quickly became a symbolic and creative outlet for Catalunya's increasing political autonomy (p. 43). While Modernisme was not limited to Barcelona (similar movements took place in France and Germany), the Catalan version has a unique flavor. The movement exploded onto the architecture scene at the **1888 Universal Exposition** and stayed on top through the first decade of the 20th century.

NO WORK, ALL PLAY

THE SOUNDS OF BARCELONA

A pass for one of these music festivals may put a dent in your wallet, but it will guarantee you three nights of nonstop partying amid thousands of fellow music-lovers, with the soundtrack provided by dozens of the best acts around.

Primavera Sound: Since 2002, this festival has been attracting indie up-and-comers as well as esteemed veterans. Collaboration with Pitchfork and All Tomorrow's Parties ensures the participation of the latest and hippest bands. Primavera Sound 2009 hosted 171 acts (including Neil Young, Sonic Youth, Yo La Tengo, Phoenix, Vivian Girls—we could go on forever). It drew over 80,000 guests over the course of three days, on a complex of six stages at Parc del Forum. In 2010 it will take place May 17th-19th. Ticket prices are not yet set, but in 2009, three-day tickets went for €155, one-day tickets for €70.

Sónar: This festival reigns as Barcelona's biggest musical event of the year and rivals Dia de Sant Joan for the title of biggest party of the summer. Each year, over the course of three days on the third weekend of June, Sónar showcases many of the world's renowned and cutting-edge artists in electronic music. On Friday and Saturday, late night performances by world-class DJ's keep the party going until well past 5am. In 2010 it will take place June 18-20. In 2009 a full pass cost €140, single daytime pass €30, and single night €48.

Antoni Gaudí i Comet, known simply as **Gaudí**, was the most famous of the Modernisme architects. Gaudí gave Barcelona its two biggest tourist attractions: **La Casa Milà** (p. 120) and **La Sagrada Família** (p. 123). Part of Gaudí's genius is his understanding of the space and vision of the finished project—even if that project takes 100 years to complete. Gaudí created such other marvels as **Casa Batlló** (p. 121) and **Park Güell** (p. 130). Other Modernists include **Lluís Domènech i Montaner** and **Josep Puig i Cadafalch.** As the director of Barcelona's School of Architecture, **Domènech** was in the position to influence generations of Catalan architects. At the Universal Exposition of 1888 he presented his **Castell de Tres Dragones** (Castle of Three Dragons), which, designed as a restaurant for the Exposition, officially kicked off the movement. His most renowned works are the **Hospital de la Santa Creu i Sant Pau** (p. 66) and the **Palau de la Música Catalana** (p. 116). **Cadafalch** is the youngest of Barcelona' major Modernist architects. His works are clearly influenced by Gothic architecture; his most well-known building is **Casa Amatller** (p. 122).

Noucentisme—a movement which covered all spheres of visual arts—is often overshadowed by other movements; indeed the movement pales in comparison to its Modernist counterpart. A reaction to the disorder brought by Modernisme and World War I, Noucentisme is a Neoclassical revival that focused on order and simplicity. For examples of this movement, check out the **Museu Arqueològic** (p. 149), which was built for the 1929 International Exposition, and the **Estació França.**

RECONSTRUCTION. After the Civil War destroyed Spain's economy and Franco seized, growth and development of Barcelona's once prospering architectural innovations ground to a halt. Few noteworthy architectural developments occurred during this era. Franco did sponsor the building of the university, although construction stopped a few years later due to a lack of funding. The building of **Camp Nou** (p. 162), Barcelona's soccer stadium, was funded by Barceloneses themselves.

In the modern era, Barcelona has reversed the trend. Mayor **Pasqual Maragall** (who served 1982-97) became a key player in this endeavor; after managing to secure the **1992 Summer Olympics** for the city, he brought modern high rises to Barcelona's beachfront property and turned the waterfront into Nightlife Central.

LITERATURE

Catalan literature was born in the Middle Ages with the Homilies d'Organyà, religious writings from the 12th century. Lyric poetry and epic romance novels would evolve in the centuries that followed, but it was with Romantic Nationalism in the 19th century that Barcelona's literary tradition really took off. The movement was a reaction to imperial rule in art and politics that attempted to re-orient the European Romantic tradition to represent the Catalan language.

Catalan Modernisme also flourished in Barcelona's literary realm in the hands of **Santiago Rusiñol** and **Joan Maragall.** The movement itself was a combination of Romanticism and more decadent themes that led to its division into the darker **Bohèmia Negra** movement and the more aesthetic **Bohèmia Rosa** movement. **Carles Riba** and **Josep Carner,** poets of the Noucentisme movement, led a rebellion against the Moderniste movement with a genre of Neoclassicism that elevated the beauty and perfection of language as the goal of Catalan literature.

Under Franco, the majority of Catalan literature was forbidden, though some notable authors including **Mercè Rodoreda,** author of the acclaimed *The Time of the Doves* (1962) published. Rodoreda's complex, psychological novels, which explored such subjects as the Spanish Civil War, served as a sort of Catalan revival of the Symbolist tradition. Contemporary authors, such as **Quim Monzo,** explore fiction with an acute awareness of pop culture and an ironic tone.

SUGGESTED READING

CARLOS RUIZ ZAFÓN. *The Shadow of the Wind.* Follows a young boy in post-Civil War Spain who seeks out the story of the author of a novel called *The Shadow of the Wind.*

COLM TÓIBÍN. *Homage to Barcelona.* Lots of people were in Barcelona right after the Franco regime fell, but none of them could have written about it as lucidly or incisively as Irish journalist and novelist Colm Tóibín.

MANUEL MONTALBÁN. *Southern Seas.* By another native son. Follows detective Pepe Carvalho, a famous recurring character. The book won the 1979 Planeta Award, and Montalbán is a Raymond Chandler Prize winner.

GEORGE ORWELL. *Homage to Catalonia.* The personal accounts of George Orwell's travels through Catalonia during the Spanish Civil War.

MUSIC

Near the turn of the 20th century, both folk music and a Catalan classical tradition began to develop in Catalunya. Catalan musicians greatly contributed to the classical guitar tradition. **Francisco Tarrega,** after joining a gang of gypsies in his youth, would go on to lay the foundations for much of the 20th-century classical guitar repertoire, and his tour across Europe paved the way for its recognition as a recital instrument. One generation younger, Miguel Solés became well known for his arrangements of folk music for the guitar.

Catalan folk music has been around since the late 19th century, when *musica de cobla* (played by an 11-piece band) accompanied the Sardana. Near the end of Franco's rule, the **Nova Cançó,** a musical movement made up of singer-songwriters such as Barcelona's Joan Manuel Serrat, protested the regime's oppression. In the post-Franco years, rock and roll has become popular, and nationalist musicians have put their own stamp on it with the **Rock Català** scene. Fusion music also gained popularity after the success of the French band **Manu Chao** and local acts such as Barcelona's **Cheb Balowski** and **Ojos de Brujo.**

FILM

Catalan cinema approaches worldwide trends in a local way. Its first major director, **Ignatio F. Iquino,** became well-known for his adaptation of so-called Spaghetti Westerns in the early 20th century. (Iquino's were known affectionately as "Paella Westerns.")

In the 1960s, the **Barcelona School of Film** (Escuela de Barcelona) came into existence. It was guided by such experimental filmmakers as Barcelonese **Jaime Camino** and his contemporary **Vincente Aranada.** Arranda was a socially-oriented master of melodrama whose films, such as *Fata Morgana* (*Left-Handed Fate;* 1965), typified the school. Josep Maria Forn championed Catalan film in the post-Franco years, founding the Institut de Cinema Català in 1975. He became the president of the Catalonian Film Directors College in 1994.

BARCELONA ON SCREEN

VICKY CRISTINA BARCELONA (2008). Directed by Woody Allen, this romantic comedy follows two friends who travel to Barcelona and fall for the same man, only to find out that his ex-wife, played by Penelope Cruz, could take him from both of them. Visitors to the Fundació Antoni Tàpies will recognize the library.

L'AUBERGE ESPAGNOLE (2002). Coming-of-age story about a 20-something French student who moves into an apartment with six others from across Europe to study in the ERASMUS Programme. Xavier came to Spain to learn Spanish; instead he encounters roommate mishaps, wild Barcelona nights, girl trouble, and a city that speaks Catalan.

EN CONSTRUCCIÓN (2001). This documentary follows the construction of a building in Barcelona's Chinese district, painting a stark picture of day-to-day life in the city.

BARCELONA (1994). A salesman working in Barcelona is visited by his cousin, an American naval officer, and the two are taken on a comedic jaunt through the city.

IF THEY TELL YOU I FELL (SI TE DIECEN QUE CAÍ; 1989). This drama uses flashbacks in the style of the disjointed, open-ended narratives of Catalan children, using them to narrate the story of a young man who falls in love with a prostitute.

Perhaps Catalunya's most famous director, **Ventura Pons Sala** has been a celebrated veteran of international film festivals since his first film, *Ocaña, an Intermittent Portrait*, was selected at Cannes in 1978. He has also adapted the texts of many Catalan writers, including Quim Monzó's *What It's All About*. Barcelona's **Juan Bigas Luna,** instead of literally celebrating Catalan's culture and unique artistic tradition, took an interest in conceptual art and produced significant amounts of avant-garde film, such as his viral short film *Collar de Moscas* (2001). Other contemporary directors include: Carlos Atanes, whose *Codex Atanicus* (2008) is a set of bizarre short films reminiscent of Luna's traditions; Joel Joan, whose accomplishments span theater, film, and television; and Jaime Rosales, whose 2007 film *La Soledad* garnered the Goya Awards for Best Director and Best Film.

SPORTS

BARCELONA'S FIGHTING CULTURE. The national spectacle of *la corrida* (bullfighting) derives from earlier Roman and Moorish practices, but its modern form dates to around 1726. A bullfight has three stages: first, *picadores* (lancers on horseback) pierce the bull's neck muscles to lower his head for the kill. Next, assistants on foot thrust *banderillas* (decorated darts) into the bull's back to provoke him. Finally, the matador has 10 minutes to kill his opponent with a sword between the shoulder blades, executing artful passes with confidence and grace while daring the bull closer with agility and nerve. If the matador shows special skill and daring, the audience waves white *pañuelos* (handkerchiefs), imploring the bullfight's president to award the matador the fight's most coveted prize, the ears of the slain bull.

The techniques of the modern matador were refined around 1914 by **Juan Belmonte,** considered one of the greatest *matadores* of all time. Yet bullfighting, like all blood sports, has had its critics: Barcelona, along with the rest of Catalunya, banned bullfighting in 2006.

FÚTBOL FANATICISM. In Barcelona, as in much of the rest of Europe, *fútbol* (soccer to most Americans) is king of sports. In addition to being represented by the national team of Spain, currently the number 2 ranked team in the world and two-time UEFA European Football Championship winners, Barcelona has its own football culture. The city's team, FC Barcelona (*Barça*, to fans), is the current champion of the UEFA Champions League Cup, an annual competition between Europe's top clubs. This followed an impressive victory over British powerhouse Manchester United and made Barça the first Spanish team to win a treble: three top trophies in a single season (La Liga Cup, Copa del Rey, and the Champions Cup).

Their grudge match against another local team, RCD Espanyol, occurs twice each Liga season, though Barcelona has a commanding head to head lead over the years that **El Derbi Barcelones** has been held, winning 83 times to Espanyol's 33. Their prowess is matched closely by the loyalty and ferocity of their fans, the *culers* (literally "ass people": a reference to the fact that passersby at their old stadium, Les Corts, could see the backsides of those sitting in the highest rows of the stadium). Roughly 25% of the entire country counts themselves among Barça's fans, and they come out in force during games, truly representing their motto, *"més que un club"* (more than a club). Today, FC Barça features such superstars as Argentine Lionel Messi and Frenchman Thierry Henry.

THE LOCAL STORY

CLEATS AND CULTURE

Every year, rival soccer clubs Real Madrid and FC Barcelona face of in what has become known as *E Clásico*. On these two days of the year, the bars become even more crowded than usual for a socce match and *El Segadors*, the Cata lan anthem, can be heard ringing throughout the streets. While the game is nearly always importan in determining who will come ou "at the top of the table," its impor tance goes much deeper than the standings in *La Liga*.

El Clásico began in 1929 when Barça lost the inaugura matchup 2-1 (they got revenge ir the rubber with a 1-0 match shut out) and has been played twice a year since. The teams have always been the best in the league, bu the game really began to take or meaning during decades unde Franco. The dictator repressed Catalan culture, forbidding the use of the language and banning all sorts of local traditions. Yet, he couldn't ban FC Barcelona from taking the pitch.

And it was on the pitch tha *Barceloneses* found a sense o pride. In the biannual games against Real Madrid (Franco's heavily funded favorite), they gave expression to their love o the region and their hatred o the cruel regime. FC Barcelona became not just a representative of their region, but an ambas sador of progressive politics. The "beautiful game" is more than jus a game. In Barcelona, the cultur is in the cleats.

BEYOND TOURISM

A PHILOSOPHY FOR TRAVELERS

HIGHLIGHTS OF BARCELONA

FEAST for **free** at the **Pueblo Ingles,** where English is currency (p. 60).

SPEAK **Catalan** like a true Barcelonese with the **Generalitat** (p. 58).

SWEAT as you make the desert bloom with **Sunseed Desert Technology** (p. 56).

As a tourist, you are always a foreigner. Sure, hostel-hopping and sight-seeing can be great fun, but connecting with a foreign country through studying, volunteering, or working can extend your travels beyond tourist traps. We don't like to brag, but this is what's different about a Let's Go traveler. Instead of feeling like a stranger in a strange land, you can understand Barcelona like a local. Instead of being that tourist asking for directions, you can be the one who gives them (and correctly!). All the while, you get the satisfaction of leaving Barcelona in better shape than you found it. It's not wishful thinking—it's Beyond Tourism.

As a **volunteer** in Barcelona or elsewhere in Catalunya, you will have the chance to participate in a wide range of projects. Whether you are looking to work with children, advocate for the environment, or get involved in local politics, this chapter is chock-full of ideas to help get you started.

Study abroad combines the comfort of academic structure and English-speaking friends with the exhilaration of travel and immersion in a foreign culture. Thousands of students descend on Spain every year to take advantage of its broad array of study abroad programs. Barcelona offers language programs to suit everyone from the novice linguist to the master orator. If you're a college student, your local study-abroad office is often the best place to start.

Working abroad is very cool and very complicated. Now that the European countries have teamed up to form the EU, non-Europeans trying to find work in Barcelona must compete with locals and with every unemployed European if they hope to land a job. And then there's the catch-22 familiar to anyone who's every tried to get a work visa; you need a job for a visa and a visa for a job. Spain's high unemployment rate can make it difficult to find a job or obtain a work visa. But take heart: English speakers are always in high demand as teachers, au pairs, or workers in beach towns outside the city. In order to work abroad, you must meet the legal requirements for either short-term or long-term work (see **Working, p. 58**).

SHARE YOUR EXPERIENCE. Have you had a particularly enjoyable volunteer, study, or work experience that you'd like to share with other travelers? A particularly horrible experience you need to warn us about? Post it! www.letsgo.com.

BEYOND TOURISM

VOLUNTEERING

Volunteering can be a powerful and fulfilling experience, especially when combined with the thrill of traveling in a new place. Barcelona's volunteer options range from the mundane (municipal noise ordinance fundraising, anybody?) to the urgent (immigrants' rights, poverty, women's rights, and GLBT advocacy, to name just a few).

Most people who volunteer do so on a short-term basis at organizations that make use of drop-in or once-a-week volunteers. The best way to find opportunities that match your interests and schedule may be to check with local or national volunteer centers. In Spain, contact the **Plataforma del Voluntariado de España,** C. Fuentes, 10, Madrid (☎902 12 05 12) in order to best match your interests to local needs. The **Fediració Catalana de Voluntariat Social,** Grassot, 3, 3er. (☎933 14 19 00) maintains the website **www.federacio.net/en,** which provides information to volunteers interested in social justice issues. The website links to **www.voluntaris.cat,** where you can find a part-time volunteer opportunity based on your availability and area of interest.

Those looking for longer, more intensive volunteer opportunities usually choose to go through a parent organization that takes care of logistical details and often provides a group environment and support system—for a fee. There are two main types of organizations—religious and secular—although there are rarely restrictions on participation in either. Websites like **www.volunteerabroad.com, www.servenet.org,** and **www.idealist.org** allow you to search for volunteer openings both in your country and abroad. The following listings are just a starting point; local opportunities are endless.

> **I HAVE TO PAY TO VOLUNTEER?** Many volunteers are surprised to learn that some organizations require large fees or "donations," but don't go calling them scams just yet. While such fees may seem ridiculous at first, they often keep the organization afloat, covering airfare, room, board, and administrative expenses for the volunteers. (Other organizations must rely on private donations and government subsidies.) If you're concerned about how a program spends its fees, request an annual report or finance account. A reputable organization won't refuse to inform you of how volunteer money is spent. Pay-to-volunteer programs might be a good idea for young travelers who are looking for more support and structure (such as pre-arranged transportation and housing) or anyone who would rather not deal with the uncertainty of creating a volunteer experience from scratch.

SOCIAL JUSTICE

Here's your chance to work toward goals of justice and equality. A diverse network of social organizations addresses all manner of problems, from homelessness to domestic abuse to human rights. Volunteering for social justice in Barcelona can help you better understand the global scope of these issues and immerse you in a foreign environment with a community of like-minded individuals. The following organizations can help you begin your search.

Equanimal, Apdo. 14454, 28080, Madrid (☎902 10 29 45; www.equanimal.org). Works for animal rights, including the abolition of bullfighting, through educational efforts. Volunteers can participate in demonstrations, distribute pamphlets, and organize events.

Fundación Triángulo, C. Eloy Gonzalo, 25, 28010, Madrid (☎915 93 05 40; www.fundaciontrangulo.es). Combats discrimination and promotes equality for gay, lesbian, bisexual, and transgendered people in Spain and around the world. Also sponsors a GLBT film festival in Madrid. Volunteers can help with outreach or legal efforts.

Stop SIDA, C. Muntaner, 121, Entresuelo 1 (☎902 10 69 27; www.stopsida.org). A member of the federation Coordinadora GaiLesbiana, Stop SIDA helps combat the spread of AIDS by raising awareness about the disease's prevention and offering support services.

IMMIGRATION

Today, Spain absorbs more immigrants than any other country in the European Union. Over the past decade, the number of immigrants has risen from two percent of the Spanish population to more than 10 percent, changing the face of Spanish cities and making the turn-of-the-century economic boom possible. Though popular images suggest a flood of immigrants crossing the Strait of Gibraltar from Morocco, in reality only about 20 percent of Spain's immigrants come from Africa. The vast majority emigrate from Europe and Latin America.

ARSIS, C. General Weyler, 257, 08912 (☎902 88 86 07; www.arsis.org). Opportunities to tutor underprivileged children, work in a women's center, or run food and clothing drives for recent immigrants.

Comisión Española de Ayuda al Refugiado (CEAR), Avda. General Perón 32, 2° dcha 28020, Madrid (☎915 98 05 35; www.cear.es). Aims to protect the right to asylum with branches in Barcelona, Bilbao, Madrid, Sevilla, and Valencia. Work in outreach, legal assistance, translation, and human rights.

Federació Catalana de Voluntariat Social, C. Grassot, 2, 3er, 08025 (☎933 14 19 00; www.federacio.net). Umbrella organization of Catalan social service organizations. Volunteers can assist with projects to achieve better standards of living and equality for immigrants in the region.

SOS Racisme, C. Hospital, 49, 08001 Barcelona (☎934 12 00 34; www.sosracisme. org). Volunteers strive to combat racism and achieve equal rights for non-citizens and migrant workers in Spain and Portugal.

ENVIRONMENTAL WORK

Development, abuse of natural resources, and rampant tourism all threaten the land and water of Spain. Many tourists already make an effort to choose the most environmentally-friendly travel possible, whether by using public transit or reducing their local consumption, but some go even further. If you're looking to extend your trip to Spain beyond Barcelona and to get involved in environmental clean-up and conservation, start by checking out the organizations listed below.

Ecoforest, Apdo. 29, Coin 29100, Málaga (☎661 07 99 50; www.ecoforest.org). Fruit farm and vegan community in southern Spain that uses environmental education to develop a sustainable lifestyle for residents. Visitors are welcome to stay, contributing €5-15 per day towards operating costs.

Sunseed Desert Technology, Apdo. 9, 04270, Sorbas, Almería (☎950 52 57 70; www.sunseed.org.uk). Researches methods of preventing desertification in the driest regions of Spain. Volunteers come for a mimimum of 2 weeks for a part-time position, or stay on with a full time residency. Costs range from €91-165 per week, room and board included. Student discounts available.

World Wide Opportunites on Organic Farms (WWOOF), Yainz 33, Casa 14, Cereceda, Cantabria (☎902 01 08 14; www.wwoof.es). Connects members with organic farms in Spain and Portugal, which offer work in exchange for food and board. Membership to the Spanish national organization costs €20 per year.

WORKCAMPS

The word workcamp doesn't summon sunny beaches and cold beer, sure, but, rest assured, it's not what you think. European workcamps, civil service organizations that offer free room and board to young volunteers, abound in Spain. Spanish workcamps usually consist of around 25 to 30 volunteers who work together to help children, tackle environmental issues, teach, or restore historical sites. At night, workcamp participants put down the tools of their trade for drinks, guitars, and some of the most intimate international camaraderie to be found anywhere. An excellent clearinghouse for Catalan workcamps is **COCAT** (www.cocat.org/en/workcamps-in-cat.php), which helps volunteers to network and find workcamps that fit their interests.

UMBRELLA ORGANIZATIONS

The possibilities for meaningful volunteer work in Spain are endless. The following volunteer agencies can help find a volunteer opportunity that excites you and speaks to your talents.

Service Civil International, 5505 Walnut Level Road, Crozet, VA 22932, USA (☎+1-206-350-6585; www.sci-ivs.org). Organizes a huge variety of short- and long-term work camps in Spain. All overseas camps cost $235, which includes simple shared housing and communal meals.

Volunteers for Peace, 1034 Tiffany Road, Belmont, VT 05730, USA (☎+1-801-259-2759; www.vfp.org). Organizes 2- to 3-week group projects in Spain that focus on a wide range of social and environmental issues. Average project cost $300.

STUDYING

Study-abroad programs range from basic language and culture courses to university-level classes for college credit. In order to choose a program that best fits your needs, research as much as you can before making your decision—determine costs and duration as well as what kind of students participate in the program and what sorts of accommodations are provided. Many American universities and student travel organizations, provide international programs for undergraduates.

VISA INFORMATION. Most foreigners planning to study in Spain must obtain a student visa, but those studying for fewer than three months in Spain need only a passport. Visa applications for study in Spain can be completed in your home country at the nearest Spanish consulate (listed under **Consular Services Abroad,** p. 17). Obtaining a visa can be an arduous process; the consulate will often require you to apply in person and provide loads of paperwork (letter verifying enrollment, medical certificate, proof of health insurance, etc.) before they process your application. They are also likely to charge a processing fee of around $100. To study for longer than 90 days, you must obtain a student residency card (student visa) once you arrive in Spain.

UNIVERSITIES

Most university-level study-abroad programs are conducted in the Spanish or Catalan, although some programs offer classes in English. Savvy linguists may find it cheaper to enroll directly in a university abroad, although getting college credit may be more difficult. You can also search **www.studyabroad.com** for various semester- or summer-abroad programs that meet your criteria, including your desired location and focus of study.

AMERICAN PROGRAMS

American Institute for Foreign Study (AIFS), College Division, River Plaza, 9 W. Broad St., Stamford, CT 06902, USA (☎+1-800-727-2437; www.aifsabroad.com). Organizes programs for high school and college study in universities in Spain. Offers study-abroad opportunities in Barcelona in the summer.

Council on International Educational Exchange (CIEE), 300 Fore St., Portland, ME 04101, USA (☎+1-207-553-4000 or 800-40-STUDY/407-8839; www.ciee.org). One of the most comprehensive resources for work, academic, and internship programs around the world.

International Association for the Exchange of Students for Technical Experience (**IAESTE;** www.iaeste.org). IAESTE runs several branches across Spain. Chances are that your home country has a local office where you can apply for hands-on technical internships abroad. You must be a college student studying science, technology, or engineering. Cost-of-living allowance is provided.

School for International Training (SIT) Study Abroad, 1 Kipling Rd., P.O. Box 676, Brattleboro, VT 05302, USA (☎+1-888-272-7881 or 802-258-3212; www.sit.edu/studyabroad). Semester-long programs in Spain run approximately US$23,000-24,000. SIT also runs **The Experiment in International Living** (☎+1-800-345-2929; www.usexperiment.org), 3- to 5-week summer programs that offer high-school students cross-cultural homestays, community service, ecological adventure, and language training in Spain (US$5,300-6,800).

SPANISH AND CATALAN PROGRAMS

The European Union sponsors programs encouraging study abroad opportunities within Europe, and Spain has not missed the train. In less than a decade the number of foreign students in Barcelona has doubled. The **Organismo**

Autónomo de Programas Educativos Europeos (www.oapee.es) provides information on Spanish study programs.

Generalitat de Catalunya, C. de Mallorca, 272 (93 272 31 00). The Secretaria de Política Lingüística runs a program called the Consorci per a la Normalització Lingüística, which offers a 45hr. introductory course for just €36. A serious course with a nationalistic bent, this course is perhaps your best hope for learning Catalan when you visit.

Olé Languages, Av. Mistral, 14-16 (93 185 15 18; info@olelanguages.com). There are many language schools in Barcelona that cater to American tourists. They tend to charge around €135 per week and mix conversation with straight grammar instruction.

LANGUAGE SCHOOLS

Enrolling at a language school has two major perks: a slightly less rigorous course load and the promise that you'll learn exactly what those kids in Cadaqués are calling you under their breath. There is a great variety of language schools—independently run, affiliated with a larger university, local, international—but one thing is constant: they rarely offer college credit. Their programs are best for younger high-school students who might not feel comfortable in a university program. Some worthwhile organizations include:

Amerispan Study Abroad, 1334 Walnut St, 6th Floor, Philadelphia, PA 19107, USA (☎+1-215-751-1100; www.amerispan.com). Offers Spanish language programs that often include homestays.

Enforex, Alberto Aguilera, 26, 28015 Madrid (☎915 943 776; www.enforex.com). Offers 20 Spanish programs in Spain, ranging from 1 week to a year in duration. Opportunities in 12 Spanish cities, including Barcelona, Granada, Madrid, and Sevilla.

Eurocentres, 56 Eccleston Sq., London SW1V 1PH, UK (☎+44 20 7963 8450; www.eurocentres.com). Language programs for beginning to advanced students with homestays in Barcelona and Valencia.

Language Immersion Institute, State University of New York at New Paltz, 1 Hawk Dr., New Paltz, NY 12561, USA (☎+1-845-257-3500; www.newpaltz.edu/lii). Short, intensive summer language courses. Program fees are around US$1000 for a 2-week course.

OTHER PROGRAMS

Associació per a Defensa i L'Estudi de la Natura (ADENC), Ca l'Estruch, C. Sant Isidre, 08208 Sabadell (☎937 17 18 87; www.adenc.org). Catalan conservation group offering short ecotourism courses on such topics as bird-watching and landscape photography.

Taller Flamenco School, C. Peral, 49, E-41002 Sevilla (☎954 56 42 34; www.tallerflamenco.com). Offers courses in flamenco dance (€180-240 per week) and guitar (€225 per week) at varying levels of difficulty.

WORKING

As with volunteering, work opportunities tend to fall into two categories. Some travelers want long-term jobs that allow them to integrate into a community, while others seek out short-term jobs to finance the next leg of their travels. The most common form of long-term work in Spain is teaching English, while short-term employment is centered on the tourist industry, whether it's bartending or giving tours of sherry *bodegas*. **Transitions Abroad** (www.transitionsabroad.com) also offers updated online listings for work over any time span.

> **MORE VISA INFORMATION.** Travelers from within the European Union can work without a permit in Spain, but those from outside the EU need a work permit. Obtaining a work permit requires extensive documentation, often including a passport, police background check, and medical records. The cost of a permit varies. Contact your nearest consulate (p. 17) for a complete list of requirements.

LONG-TERM WORK

If you're planning on spending a substantial amount of time (more than three months) working in Spain, search for a job well in advance. International placement agencies are often the easiest way to find employment abroad, especially for those interested in teaching. Although they are often only available to college students, **internships** are a good way to ease into working abroad. Many find the internship experience is well worth it, despite low pay (if you're lucky enough to be paid at all). Be wary of advertisements for companies claiming to be able get you a job abroad for a fee—often the same listings are available online or in newspapers. Keep in mind that EU candidates will have priority in almost all cases. If you don't have a special skill or are not willing to work for free, your best bet is to network; in Barcelona the expat community is driven by references, conversations, and tips over beer. Common jobs for expats include hotel work, teaching skills (guitar, computer programming, etc.), DJ-ing (you have to be a good DJ), flyering for clubs and venues, bartending, and waiting tables. You'll never get jobs like these by handing out your resumés; you have to do it by socializing. Minimum wage is the norm for foreign workers in the restaurant and bar industries. Some reputable organizations that can help you land a job overseas include:

Council on International Educational Exchange (CIEE), 300 Fore St., Portland, ME 04101, USA (☎+1-207-553-4000 or 800-40-STUDY/407-8839; www.ciee.org). They assist with both studying and teaching abroad. Be sure to visit the website; tucked among study-abroad listings, you'll find resources for international internships.

Career Journal (www.careerjournaleurope.com). The Wall Street Journal publishes this online journal listing thousands of jobs throughout Europe. There are both short- and long-term as well as part- and full-time jobs.

Escape Artist (www.escapeartist.com/jobs/overseas1). Offers information on living abroad, including job listings for Spain.

EURES (www.europa.eu.int/eures). EU agency providing job listings and opportunities across Europe, including Spain and Portugal.

Expat Exchange (www.expatexchange.com). Provides message boards where individuals seeking employment in Spain can advertise.

Instituto Hemingway, C. Bailén, 5, Bilbao (944 167 901; www.institutohemingway.com/practica.htm). Connects applicants with internships in Arts, archaeology, interior design, and many other fields.

Trabajos (www.trabajos.com). Job listings for all regions of Spain.

TEACHING ENGLISH

As an English speaker, you have the chance to contribute your skills (your skills being your ability to speak fluent English) while forming lasting relationships with students and·a community. In almost all cases, you must have at least a bachelor's degree to be a full-fledged teacher, although college undergraduates can often get summer positions teaching or tutoring.

Many schools require teachers to have a **Teaching English as a Foreign Language (TEFL)** certificate. You may still be able to find a teaching job without one, but certified teachers often find higher-paying jobs. Teachers in public schools will likely work in both English and the local language, but private schools usually hire native English speakers for English-immersion classrooms where no Spanish is spoken. Placement agencies or university fellowship programs are the best resources for finding teaching jobs. The alternative is to contact schools directly or to try your luck once you arrive in Spain. In the latter case, the best time to look is several weeks before the start of the school year. The following organizations are extremely helpful in placing teachers in Spain.

International Schools Services (ISS), 15 Roszel Rd., P.O. Box 5910, Princeton, NJ 08543, USA (☎+1-609-452-0990; www.iss.edu). Hires teachers for more than 200 overseas schools. Candidates should have teaching experience and a bachelor's degree. 2-year commitment is the norm.

Pueblo Ingles, Rafael Calvo 18, 4A, Madrid (913 913 400 www.morethanenglish.com/puebloingles/index.asp). When Spain's business elite wants to learn English by spending a week eating 3-course meals in a Medieval resort teeming with interesting native English speakers, they head to Pueblo Ingles. In exchange for pledging to speak only English for a week, you will be housed and fed in Valdelavilla (outside of Soria) or one of PI's other locations along with a number of Spanish speakers for a week of total indulgence and language exchange. Apply online.

Teach Abroad (www.teach.studyabroad.com). This database lists job openings for prospective English teachers.

TESOL-Spain (www.tesol-spain.org). Non-profit association of English teachers in Spain. Website lists job openings.

TEFL Job Placement (www.tefljobplacement.com). Places teachers in countries across the world. Requirements and durations vary.

AU PAIR WORK

Au pairs are typically women aged 18-27 who work as live-in nannies, caring for children and doing light housework in foreign countries in exchange for room, board, and a small spending allowance or stipend. One perk of the job is that it allows you to get to know Spain without the costs of traveling. An au pair can expect to make €50 or more per week. Drawbacks, however, can include mediocre pay and long hours. Much of the au pair experience depends on your relationship with the family with which you are placed. The agencies below are a good starting point.

Childcare International, Trafalgar House, Grenville Pl., London NW7 3SA, UK (☎+44 20 8906 3116; www.childint.co.uk).

InterExchange, 161 6th Ave., New York City, NY 10013, USA (☎+1-212-924-0446 or 800-AU-PAIRS/287-2477; www.interexchange.org).

International Au Pair Association (IAPA), Store Kongensgade 40 H, DK-1264 Copenhagen K, DK (☎+453 317 0066; www.iapa.org). Nonprofit organization that connects to smaller au pair agencies in many nations, including Spain.

Instituto Hemingway, C. Bailén, 5, Bilbao (944 167 901; www.institutohemingway.com/aupair.htm). A private company that helps young women find families looking for au pairs. Must be 18-30, speak Spanish, and have previous experience with children.

SHORT-TERM WORK

Many travelers try their hand at odd jobs for a few weeks at a time to help pay for another month or two of touring the world. Obtaining a work permit, however, is a long, bureaucratic process, and requires proof of employment (read: a signed contract). It is illegal for non-EU citizens to work in Spain or Portugal without this work permit. Many establishments hire travelers under-the-table, particularly in seasonal resort areas. These jobs may include bartending, waiting tables, or promoting bars and clubs. Another popular option is to work several hours a day at a hostel in exchange for free or discounted accommodations. Most often, these short-term jobs are found by word of mouth or by expressing interest to the owner of a hostel or restaurant. You can also try www.Loquo.es (a sort of Spanish Craigslist) or Barcelona's newspapers, **El Periòdico** (www.elperiodico.es) and **La Vanguardia** (www.lavanguardia.es). Due to high turnover in the tourism industry, many places are eager for help, even if it is only temporary. Let's Go does not recommend working illegally.

Intern Jobs (www.internjobs.com). Lists not only internships, but also many ideal short-term jobs like camp counseling and bartending.

Transitions Abroad (www.transitionsabroad.com). Lists organizations in Spain that hire short-term workers and provides links to articles about working abroad.

FURTHER READING ON BEYOND TOURISM

Alternatives to the Peace Corps: A Guide of Global Volunteer Opportunities, edited by Paul Backhurst. Food First, 2005.

The Back Door Guide to Short-Term Job Adventures: Internships, Summer Jobs, Seasonal Work, Volunteer Vacations, and Transitions Abroad, by Michael Landes. Ten Speed Press, 2005.

Green Volunteers: The World Guide to Voluntary Work in Nature Conservation, by Fabio Ausenda. Universe, 2009.

How to Get a Job in Europe, by Cheryl Matherly and Robert Sanborn. Planning Communications, 2003.

How to Live Your Dream of Volunteering Overseas, by Joseph Collins, Stefano DeZerega, and Zahara Heckscher. Penguin Books, 2001.

International Job Finder: Where the Jobs Are Worldwide, by Daniel Lauber and Kraig Rice. Planning Communications, 2002.

Live and Work Abroad: A Guide for Modern Nomads, by Huw Francis and Michelyne Callan. Vacation Work Publications, 2001.

Volunteer Vacations: Short-Term Adventures That Will Benefit You and Others, by Doug Cutchins, Anne Geissinger, and Bill McMillon. Chicago Review Press, 2009.

Work Abroad: The Complete Guide to Finding a Job Overseas, edited by Clayton A. Hubbs. Transitions Abroad, 2002.

Work Your Way Around the World, by Susan Griffith. Vacation Work Publications, 2008.

BEYOND TOURISM

PRACTICAL INFORMATION

Barcelona's layout is easy to visualize if you imagine yourself perched on Columbus's head at the **Monument a Colom** (on Pg. de Colom, along the shore), viewing the city with the sea at your back. From the harbor, the city slopes upward to the mountains. From the Columbus monument, **La Rambla,** the main thoroughfare, runs up to **Plaça de Catalunya** (ⓂCatalunya), the city center. The heavily touristed historic neighborhood, **Ciutat Vella,** is anchored by La Rambla and encompasses the Barri Gòtic, La Ribera, and El Raval. The **Barri Gòtic** is east of La Rambla (to the right, with your back to the sea), enclosed on the other side by **Via Laietana.** East of Via Laietana lies the maze-like neighborhood of **La Ribera,** bordered by Parc de la Ciutadella and Estació de França. To the west of La Rambla is **El Raval,**Barcelona's most multicultural neighborhood, with a growing number of museums and hip bars.

Beyond La Ribera—farther east, outside Ciutat Vella and curving out into the water—are **Poble Nou** and **Port Olímpic,**which boast the two tallest buildings in Barcelona, not to mention an assortment of discotecas and restaurants on the beach. To the west, beyond El Raval, rises **Montjuïc,** a hill crammed with sprawling gardens, museums, the 1992 Olympic grounds, and a fortress. Directly behind your perch on the Monument a Colom is the **Port Vell** (Old Port) development, where a wavy bridge leads to the ultra-modern (and tourist-packed) shopping and entertainment complexes **Moll d'Espanya** and **Maremagnum.**North of Ciutat Vella is upscale**l'Eixample,** a gridded neighborhood created during the expansion of the 1860s that sprawls from Pl. de Catalunya toward the mountains. **Gran Via de les Corts Catalanes** defines its lower edge, and the **Passeig de Gràcia,** l'Eixample's main tree- and boutique-lined avenue, bisects this chic neighborhood. **Avinguda Diagonal,** the expansion's largest non-gridded street, marks the border between l'Eixample and the **Zona Alta** ("Uptown"), which includes Pedralbes, Gràcia, and other older neighborhoods in the foothills. The peak of **Tibidabo,** the northwest border of the city, offers the most comprehensive view of Barcelona.

TOURIST AND FINANCIAL SERVICES

CURRENCY EXCHANGE

ATMs give the best rates. The very best are those marked **Telebanco;** they report the exchange rate on the receipt and on-screen instead of leaving you guessing. Banks are your next best option. Banks are generally open Monday-Friday 8:30am-2pm. La Rambla has many exchange stations open late, but the rates are not as good and they charge a commission.

American Express: La Rambla, 74 (☎933 42 73 11). ⓂLiceu. Open M-F 9am-11pm, Sa 11am-9pm.

TOURIST OFFICES AND TOURS

Aeroport del Prat de Llobregat, terminals A and B. Info and last-minute accommodation booking. Open daily 9am-9pm.

Estació Barcelona-Sants, Pl. Països Catalans. (☎902 240 202) ⓂSants-Estació. Info and last-minute accommodation booking. Open June 24-Sept. 24 daily 8am-8pm; Sept. 25-June 23 M-F 8am-8pm, Sa-Su 8am-2pm.

Institut de Cultura de Barcelona (ICUB), Palau de la Virreina, La Rambla, 99 (☎933 16 10 00; www.bcn.cat/cultura). Info office open daily 10am-8pm.

Oficina de Turisme de Catalunya, Pg. de Gràcia, 107 (☎932 38 80 91; www.gencat.es/ probert). ⓂDiagonal. Open M-Sa 10am-7pm, Su 10am-2pm.

Plaça de Catalunya, Pl. de Catalunya, 17S, underground on the bottom left-hand corner facing south (toward La Rambla). ⓂCatalunya. The main office, along with Pl. de Sant Jaume, has free maps, brochures on sights and transportation, booking service for last-minute accommodations, a gift shop, money exchange, and a box office (Caixa de Catalunya). Open daily 9am-9pm.

Plaça de Sant Jaume, C. Ciutat, 2. ⓂJaume I. Open M-F 9am-8pm, Sa 10am-8pm, Su and holidays 10am-2pm.

Tourist Office Representatives booths dot the city in the summer. Open daily July-Sept.; hours vary; many have shorter hours in winter.

Tours: In addition to the Bus Turístic (p. 109), the Pl. de Catalunya tourist office offers 2hr. **walking tours** of the Barri Gòtic daily at 10am (English) and Sa at noon (Catalan and Spanish). Group size limited; buy tickets in advance. (Info ☎932 85 38 32. €12, ages 4-12 €5.) 2hr. **Picasso tour** (☎932 85 38 32) of Barcelona Tu, Th, Sa, 4pm (English) and Sa at 4pm (Spanish or Catalan with pre-booking). €18, ages 4-12 €7, includes entrance to the **Museu Picasso.** 2hr. *Modernisme* tour through L'Eixample's Quadrat d'Or F-Sa 4pm (English) and Sa 4pm (Catalan and Spanish). €12, ages 4-12 €5. Self-guided tours of Gothic, Romanesque, *Modernista,* and Contemporary Barcelona available; pick up pamphlets with maps at the tourist office. **Bike tours** abound; see **Bike Rental** (p. 31). **Barcelona Segway Glides** offers 2hr. tours ("glides") for €60, Mar.-Nov. M-F 10am and 5pm, Dec.-Feb. 11am. Call for reservations. (☎678 77 73 71; www.barcelonasegwayglides.com. Cash only.)

LOCAL SERVICES

GLBT RESOURCES

Pick up the official **LGBT tourist guide** at tourist office in Pl. de Catalunya, 17S, which includes a section on LGBT bars, clubs, publications, and more. Barcelona's gay neighborhood is called L'Eixample or, colloquially, **Gaixample.** **GAYBARCELONA** (www.gaybarcelona.net) and **Infogai** (www.colectiugai.org) are useful websites in Catalan. Another such resource is the **Associació de Famílies Lésbianes**

i Gais, Carrer Verdaguer i Callís, 10 (☎645 31 88 60; www.familieslg.org). Some info on the web site of **Barcelona Pride** (www.pridebarcelona.org/en) is seasonal, but the site is useful year-round in identifying gay-friendly businesses.

Antinous, C. Josep Anselm Clavé, 6 (☎933 01 90 70; antinouslibros.com). ⓂDrassanes. Specializes in gay and lesbian books and films. Decent selection in English. Open M-F 10:30am-2pm and 5-8:30pm, Sa noon-2pm and 5-8:30pm. AmEx/MC/V.

Cómplices, C. Cervantes, 4 (☎934 12 72 83; www.libreriacomplices.com). ⓂLiceu. A small gay-friendly bookstore with books in English and Spanish and an adequate selection of films. Also provides a map of Barcelona's gay bars and discotecas. Open M-F 10:30am-8pm, Sa noon-8pm. AmEx/MC/V.

LAUNDROMATS

Lavamax, C. Junta de Comerç, 14, in El Raval (☎933 01 59 32). Wash €5 for 8kg. Dry €1 per 8min. Self-service open daily 9:30am-9pm. Drop-off service M-F 9:30am-1:30pm and 5-9pm, Sa 9:30am-1:30pm.

Lavomatic, Pl. Joaquim Xirau, 1, a block off La Rambla and 1 block below C. Escudellers. Branch at C. Consolat del Mar, 43-45 (☎932 68 47 68), 1 block north of Pg. Colon and 2 blocks off Via Laietana. Wash €4.80. Dry €0.90 per 5min. Both open M-Sa 9am-9pm.

Orange Laundry, Pl. del Sol, 11-12 (☎934 15 03 61). Wash €4. Dry €4. Open 7am-11pm.

Wash@Net, C. les Carretes, 56, in El Raval (☎934 42 29 15). Wash €4-6. Dry €1 per 10min. Internet €1 per hr. Open 10am-11pm.

LIBRARIES

Visit **www.bcn.es/biblioteques** for info on Barcelona's libraries.

Biblioteca Barceloneta-La Fraternitat, C. Comte de Santa Clara, 8-10 (☎932 25 35 74), 2 blocks from the beach in Port Vell. Open M 4-9pm, Tu 10am-2pm, W 4-9pm, Th 10am-9pm, F 4-9pm.

Biblioteca Francesca Bonnemaison, C. Sant Pere més Baix, 7 (☎932 68 73 60). ⓂUrquinaona. Walk toward the water, then turn left past the Palau de Música Catalana and C. Sant Pere més Alt. Open M-Tu 4-9pm, W 10am-9pm, Th-F 10am-2pm and 4-9pm, Sa 10am-2pm.

Biblioteca Sant Pau-Santa Creu, C. Hospital, 56 (☎933 02 07 97), in El Raval 1 block up C. Hospital from Las Ramblas. ⓂLiceu. Open M-Tu 3:30-8:30pm, W-Th 10am-2pm, F 3:30-8:30pm.

THE BIG SPLURGE

HI. THIS IS BARCELONA

Jordan Susselman is a born tour guide. He speaks Catalan, is chummy with the locals, and knows everything there is to know about the city's past and present. That's why his "Hi. This is Barcelona" tours are one of our favorite ways to see the city.

"Hi. This is Barcelona" offers "atypical tourism"; the company prides itself on designing small, personalized tours that take you off the beaten track, without missing out on the major sights. Love *Modernista* architecture? Check out the Modernist Fantasy Tour, a three- to eight-hour tour by foot, bicycle, and Metro. More into food? Try Tapas Like a Local, a four-hour gastronomic adventure. Whatever your passion, however quirky, Jordan and his team are always ready to create a tour that matches your interests. As you follow your guide through circuitous streets, he'll regale you with sometimes gory, sometimes romantic stories of the city's history along with some entertaining tales of his own.

You'll come out of a "Hi. This is Barcelona" tour with an intimate knowledge of Barcelona's history, a good idea of the hippest places to drink or dance at night, and even dinner reservations (if you so desire).

Advance reservations are a must. 6-person tours €35 per student; 4-person tours €40-45 per student. For more info, check out www.hithisisbarcelona.com.

LUGGAGE STORAGE

El Prat Airport. €5 per day.

Estació Barcelona-Sants, Ⓜ️Sants-Estació. Lockers €4.50 per day. Open daily 5:30am-11pm.

Estació Nord, Ⓜ️Arc de Triomf. Lockers €3.50-5 per day, 90-day limit.

EMERGENCY SERVICES

EMERGENCY PHONE NUMBERS

Local police: ☎092.

Medical Emergency: ☎061.

National police: ☎091.

Tourist Police: La Rambla, 43 (☎932 56 24 30). Ⓜ️Liceu. Multilingual officers. This is where to go if you've been pickpocketed. Open 24hr.

HOSPITALS

Hospital Clínic i Provincal, C. Villarroel, 170 (☎932 27 54 00). Ⓜ️Hospital Clínic. Main entrance at C. Roselló and C. Casanova.

Hospital General de la Vall d'Hebron (☎932 74 61 00). Ⓜ️Vall d'Hebron.

Hospital del Mar, Pg. Marítim, 25-29 (☎932 48 30 00), before Port Olímpic. Ⓜ️Ciutadella or Vila Olímpica.

Hospital de la Santa Creu i Sant Pau (☎932 91 90 00; emergency ☎91 91 91). Ⓜ️Hospital de Sant Pau.

PHARMACIES

Late-Night Pharmacy: Rotates. Check any pharmacy window for the nearest on duty, contact the police, or call **Información de Farmacias de Guardia** (☎93 481 00 60).

COMMUNICATIONS

INTERNET ACCESS

Bcnet (Internet Gallery Café), C. Barra de Ferro, 3 (☎932 68 15 07; www.bornet-bcn.com), down the street from the Museu Picasso. Ⓜ️Jaume I. €1 for 15min; €3 per hr.; 10hr. ticket €19. Open M-F 10am-11pm, Sa-Su noon-11pm.

Easy Internet Café, La Rambla, 31 (☎933 01 7507; www.easyinternetcafe.com). Ⓜ️Liceu. Fairly reasonable prices and over 200 terminals in a bright, modern center. €2.10 per hr., min. €2. 1-day unlimited pass €7; 1 week €15; 1 month €30. Open 8am-2:30am. Branch at Ronda Universitat, 35. Ⓜ️Catalunya. €2 per hour; 1-day pass €3; 1 week €7; 1 month €15. Open daily 8am-2:30am.

Navegaweb, La Rambla, 88-94 (☎933 17 90 26; navegabarcelona@terra.es). Ⓜ️Liceu. Good rates for international calls ($0.20 per min. to USA). Internet €2 per hr. Open M-Th 9am-midnight, F 9am-1am, Sa 9am-2am, Su 9am-midnight.

POSTAL SERVICES

Pl. d'Antoni López (☎902 197 197). ⓂJaume I or Barceloneta. Fax and **Lista de Correos.** Open M-F 8:30am-9:30pm, Su noon-10pm. Dozens of branches; consult www.correos.es. **Postal Code:** 08001.

TELEPHONES

Buy phone cards at tobacco stores and newsstands; the lowest denomination is usually €6, which promises 45min. of international calling, though rates sometimes require you to use all your minutes in a single call. A much better option is to use **Locotorios** (international call centers), which dot the streets on either side of La Rambla. Purchase cell phones in **El Corte Inglés** in Pl. Catalunya (pre-pay phones with SIM card from €29).

PRACTICAL INFORMATION

ACCOMMODATIONS

While accommodations in Barcelona are easy to spot, finding an affordable bed or room can be more difficult. During one of the busier months (June-Sept. or Dec.), wandering up and down La Rambla looking for a place can be a recipe for anxiety and frustration. If you want to stay in a touristy area, reserve weeks ahead. Consider staying outside heavily trafficked Ciutat Vella; there are plenty of hostels in the Zona Alta, particularly in Gràcia, that have more vacancies. For the best rooms, l'Eixample has good deals and is also quiet at night. La Ribera and El Raval are smart alternatives to the hectic Barri Gòtic; they're just as close to the action and often cheaper. There are some less reputable parts of El Raval on the side streets farther from La Rambla, so choose wisely.

ALTERNATIVE ACCOMMODATIONS. Barcelona is not a cheap city, and a decent hostel will cost at least €23 a night. Those passing through for only a short time, and carrying no valuables, sometimes turn to another option: the so-called "illegal hostels" that offer rooms at significantly reduced prices (€15-18). Backpackers looking to stay illegally sometimes ask around at Travel Bar (C. Boqueria, 27). Illegal hostels can be dangerous and unpredictable, and Let's Go does not recommend them.

CAMPING

A handful of sites lie in the outskirts of the city, accessible by intercity buses (20-45min.; €1.50). The **Associació de Càmpings de Barcelona,** Gran Via de les Corts Catalanes, 608 (☎934 12 59 55; www.campingsbcn.com), has more info. A good choice is **Càmping Tres Estrellas ❶,** Autovía de Castelldefells, km 13.2. Take bus L95 (€1.40) from Pl. de Catalunya to the stop just 300m from the campsite, 13km south. (☎936 33 06 37; www.camping3estrellas.com. €6-8 per person. 2-person tents €7.50-9; cars €7.50-9. BBQ, pool, ATM, supermarket, and internet available. Open from mid-Mar. 15 to mid-Oct. MC/V.)

BARRI GÒTIC AND LAS RAMBLAS

LOWER BARRI GÒTIC

The following hostels lie between C. Ferran and the water. Backpackers flock here to be close to the late-night revelry at the popular, heavily touristed La Rambla. The cheapest accommodations tend to be cramped.

- **Hostal Levante,** Baixada de San Miquel, 2 (☎933 17 95 65; www.hostallevante.com). ⓂLiceu. New rooms are large and tasteful, with light wood furnishings, exceptionally clean bathrooms, A/C, and fans; some have balconies. Ask for a newly renovated room. Apartments have kitchens, living rooms, and washing machines. Internet €1 per hr. Singles €35, with bath 45; doubles from €55/€65; 4-person apartments €30 per person. Credit card number required with reservation. MC/V. ❸
- **Pensión Mariluz,** C. Palau, 4 (☎933 17 34 63; www.pensionmariluz.com), 3rd fl. ⓂLiceu or Jaume I. Gorgeous renovations turned this hostel into a warm, bright space around a classy old courtyard. Shared bathrooms are clean but a bit cramped. Offers

short-term apartments nearby. A/C. Locker, sheets, and towels included. Free Wi-Fi in common area. Dorms €15-24; singles €30-41; doubles €40-60; triples €48-72; quads €65-90, with bath €94. MC/V. ❷

Hostal Fernando, C. Ferran, 31 (☎933 01 79 93; www.hfernando.com). Ⓜ Liceu. Clean rooms with a little more attention and care than most places in this price range. Dorms with A/C and lockers. Common kitchen with dining room and TV on 3rd fl. Private rooms have TV and bath. Towels €1.50. Internet €1 per 30min. Free Wi-Fi. Dorms €20-24; singles €45-55; doubles €65-77; triples €75-90. MC/V. ❷

Kabul Youth Hostel, Pl. Reial, 17 (☎933 18 51 90; www.kabul.es). Ⓜ Liceu. Legendary among backpackers—it's hosted nearly a million since its establishment in 1985. Rooms with balconies overlooking Pl. Reial available by request. Lounge and terrace. Breakfast and dinner included. Linens €2. Free Wi-Fi. Computers provided with 20min. of free use per day. Check-out 11am. Reservations available only on website with credit card. Dorms €20-30. MC/V. ❷

Pensión Canadiense, Bajada de San Miguel, 1 (☎933 01 74 61). Ⓜ Liceu, L3. Across the street from Hostal Levante. Spacious rooms with a slightly more romantic vibe than other hostels in the area. All rooms have bathrooms, A/C, and balconies. Free Wi-Fi. Doubles €68-75; triples €98-10. Discounts for stays over 5 nights. MC/V. ❺

Quartier Gothic, C. Avinyó, 42 (☎933 18 79 45; www.hotelquartiergothic.com). Attractive hostel in a bustling location. Dating back to 1859, it is the oldest Tuscanstyle building in Barcelona. Large and comfortable common room. Rooms have TVs, fans, safes, and high ceilings. Free Wi-Fi. High-season singles €29; doubles €46, with bath €63; triples €63/€84. Cash only. ❷

Pensión Bienestar, C. Quintana, 3 (☎933 18 72 83; www.pensionbienestar.com). Ⓜ Liceu, L3. A left off C. Ferrán coming from Las Ramblas. The building on this small sidestreet may not look the most inviting, but inside you'll find plant-adorned hallways and a friendly staff. Rooms and shared bathrooms are clean and spacious. Singles €18-22; doubles €33-40, with bath €40-50. Cash only. ❶

Hostal Benidorm, La Rambla, 37 (☎933 02 20 54; www.hostalbenidorm.com). Ⓜ Drassanes or Liceu. Clean, plain rooms in one of the best values on La Rambla. Each room comes with phone, A/C, and balcony overlooking the street. Free Wi-Fi. Reception 24hr. Singles €40-50; doubles €60-69; triples €80-95; quads €100-110. MC/V. ❹

California Hotel, C. Rauric, 14 (☎933 17 77 66; www.hotelcalifornia.bcn.com). Ⓜ Liceu, L3. Comfortable, classic rooms all with TVs, full baths, and A/C. Prices are high, but reasonable in light of the location and quality. Breakfast included; no pink champagne on ice. Singles €45-55; doubles €60-85; triples €85-100. AmEx/MC/V. ❹

Hostal Marmo, C. Gignàs, 25 (☎933 10 59 70). Ⓜ Jaume I, L4. A right off Via Laietana from the Metro. Simple rooms in an old building with tiled floors and a multitude of plants. All rooms have balconies. Singles €20; doubles €40. ❶

UPPER BARRI GÒTIC

This section of the Barri Gòtic is between C. Fontanella and C. Ferran, and accommodations are closer to Pl. Catalunya and L'Eixample and a little farther from the rougher lower section of the neighborhood. Portal de l'Àngel, a chic pedestrian avenue, runs through the middle and is busy during the day but, unlike Las Ramblas, quiets down at night. Rooms are pricier here, though it may be worth it for a retreat from the continuous late-night revelry of lower Barri Gòtic.

Hostal Maldà, C. Pi, 5 (☎933 17 30 02). ⓂLiceu. Enter the small shopping center and follow the signs upstairs. Clean, no-frills rooms that would cost twice as much money at other places. All rooms have shared bath. Call for reservations. Singles €15; doubles €30; triples with shower €45. Cash only. ❶

Hostal-Residència Rembrandt, C. de la Portaferrissa, 23 (☎933 18 10 11; www.hostalrembrandt.com). ⓂLiceu. Range of unique rooms. The cheapest are fairly standard but some have large baths, patios, and sitting areas. Breakfast €5. Reception 9am-11pm. Reservations require credit card or €50 deposit. Singles with shower around €30, with bath €40; doubles €50/65; triples €75/85. MC/V. ❷

Hostal Campi, C. Canuda, 4 (☎933 01 35 45; www.hostalcampi.com). Central location, warmly decorated rooms, and helpful staff. Most rooms have balconies, some have TVs. Internet €1 per hr. Singles €32; doubles €55, with bath €65; triples €75/85. Prices rise in high season. MC/V. ❸

Pensión Hostal Paris, C. del Cardenal Casañas, 4 (☎993 301 37 85). ⓂLiceu. Basic, clean bedrooms but an exceptional common room with lavish gilt-framed paintings and a balcony overlooking La Rambla. Free Wi-Fi. Must pay one night with reservation. Singles €30; doubles €55, with bath 65; triples €85. MC/V. ❷

Hostal Residència Lausanne, Av. Portal de l'Àngel, 24 (☎933 02 11 39; www.hostal-residencialausanne.com). ⓂCatalunya. Up 2 fl. at the back of the entrance foyer. White walls, ornate marble staircase, and a lounge overlooking the busy Av. Portal de l'Àngel. Free internet and Wi-Fi. Doubles €54, with bath €64; triples €75-85. MC/V. ❹

Hostal Santa Anna, C. Santa Anna, 23 (☎933 01 22 46). ⓂCatalunya. Small but pretty rooms. Affordable rates given proximity to Pl. Catalunya. Doubles €50, with bath €60; triples €60. Cash only. ❹

Hostal Fontanella, Via Laietana, 71 (☎933 17 59 43; www.hostalfontanella.com). ⓂJaume I, Urquinaona. Tiled floors, hallway curtains, and peacock-feathers lend this hotel an old-fashioned charm. All rooms have TVs and many have balconies. Singles €44, with bath €54; doubles 64/86; triples 102/120. AmEx/MC/V. ❹

Hotel Toledano/Hostal Residència Capitol, La Rambla, 138 (☎933 01 08 72; www.hoteltoledano.com). ⓂCatalunya. A hostal/hotel duo. Wide range of rooms with equally wide price range. All come with cable TVs and phones; outer rooms with balconies, interior with A/C. Free internet access in lobby; free Wi-Fi everywhere. Hotel singles €39, with bath 44; doubles €60-72; triples €95; quads €112. Hostel singles €33; doubles €49, with shower €57; triples €69/€78; quads €84/€93. AmEx/MC/V. ❸

LA RIBERA

Fewer tourist attractions in La Ribera means fewer tourist accommodations. Still, the neighborhood is worth a look if you want a quieter, more authentic alternative.

🏨 **Gothic Point Youth Hostel,** C. dels Vigatans, 5 (☎932 68 78 08; www.gothicpoint.com). ⓂJaume I. Jungle-gym rooms with A/C. Most beds come with curtains and personal lockers. Highly social, with lots of events, including a weekly DJ jam and free concerts. Rooftop terrace and colorful lounge area with TV. Breakfast included. Lockers €3. Linens €2. Free internet. Refrigerator and kitchen access. Dorms €24. €1 credit card fee per night. AmEx/MC/V. ❶

Hostal de Ribagorza, C. de Trafalgar, 39 (☎933 19 19 68; www.hostalribagorza.com). ⓂUrquinaona. Ornate *Modernista* building with attractive rooms, homey decorations, and colorfully tiled floors. TV and A/C. Doubles €45-60; triples €60-75. MC/V. ❹

Pension Ciudadela, C. del Comerç, 33 (☎933 19 62 03; www.pension-ciudadela.com). ⓂBarceloneta. Climb 3 flights of stairs to this small hostel with big, brightly painted rooms. Rooms have TV and balcony; most have A/C. Doubles €50, with bath €56; triples from €66. MC/V. ❹

Hostal Nuevo Colón, Av. del Marquès de l'Argentera, 19 (☎933 19 50 77; www.hostal-nuevocolon.com). ⓂBarceloneta. A modest *hostal* trapped in a gorgeous hotel's body. 26 modern rooms with balconies. Common area and TV. Reservations recommended. Singles €35, with bath €49; doubles €47/67; triples €67/87; quads with bath €87. 3- to 6-person apartments with bunk-beds and kitchenettes €90-155 per day. MC/V. ❸

Hostal Orleans, Av. del Marquès de l'Argentera, 13 (☎933 19 73 82; www.hostalorleans.com). ⓂBarceloneta. Follow Pg. de Joan de Borbó and turn right on Av. del Marqués de l'Argentera. Attractive rooms and a comfortable lounge. Internet €1 per 30min. Doubles €60-65; triples €75. AmEx/MC/V. ❺

Hostal Bresus, C. Sant Pere Més Alt, 61 (☎932 68 22 62). ⓂArc de Triomf. Follow C. de Trafalgar, left on C. de Mendez Nuñez, right on C. Sant Pere Més Alt. Spacious rooms with TV, A/C, and balconies. Singles €40, with bath €50; doubles €40-65. Cash only. ❹

Hotel Triunfo, Pg. de Picasso, 22 (☎933 10 40 85; atriumhotels.com). ⓂJaume I. Go west on C. de la Princesa and turn right on Pg. de Picasso. Sleek, modern rooms, each equipped with a private bathroom and TV. Doubles €70-80. MC/V. ❺

Pension Port-Bou, C. del Comerç, 29 (☎933 19 23 67). ⓂBarceloneta. Follow Pg. de Joan de Borbó, turn right on Av. del Marqués de l'Argentera, and make a left onto C. del Comerc. Simple, spotless rooms do the job. Singles €40; doubles €45, with bath €55. Cash only. ❹

EL RAVAL

Let's Go's favorite area of El Raval, by far, is the neighborhood around **Carrer Dr. Dou** and **Carrer Elisabets**—these student-dominated streets boast healthy restaurants and good shopping. (Even further toward ⓂUniversitat, on C. Pelai, you'll find a number of chain stores, but these have less character and higher prices than the shops on C. Elisabet.) The lower part of El Raval is split roughly in half vertically by las Ramblas del Raval. The area between las Ramblas del Raval and Las Ramblas (ⓂLiceu) is well-traveled and feels perhaps deceptively safe (there are pickpockets aplenty here). Be careful on the far side of Las Ramblas del Raval, as streets can be eerily deserted late at night.

▥ Hotel Peninsular, C. de Sant Pau, 34 (☎934 12 36 99; www.hpeninsular.com). ⓂLiceu. This *Modernista* building has 78 rooms with green doors, phones, and A/C around a beautiful 4-story interior courtyard festooned with hanging plants. Breakfast included. Safety deposit boxes €2 per day with €20 deposit. Free internet and Wi-Fi. Check-out 11am. Singles €55; doubles €78; triples €95; quads €120; quints €140. MC/V. ❺

Barcelona Mar Youth Hostel, C. de Sant Pau, 80 (☎933 24 85 30; www.barcelonamar.es). ⓂParal·lel. This hostel hosts Spanish cooking classes (€18), a tapas-and-flamenco-night (€22), a pub crawl that includes cover and 1 drink per bar (€15), a free walking tour, and more. Shared bathrooms with separate rooms for toilets and new shower curtains. 125 dorm-style beds and ocean-themed decor. Breakfast and lockers included. Linens €2.50, towels €2.50; both €3.50. Self-service laundry €4.50. Free internet and Wi-Fi. 6- to 16-bed dorms in summer €26, in winter €16-19; Doubles €46-58, F-Sa add €2 per person. AmEx/MC/V. ❷

Ideal Youth Hostel, C. la Unió, 12 (☎933 42 61 77; www.idealhostel.com), off Las Ramblas, on the street next to the Gran Teatre Liceu. ⓂLiceu, L3. Located just a block off of Las Ramblas, this hostel feels like the most chic garage you'll ever step into. Entirely concrete 1st floor includes a mural, kitchen, and lounge space. 4- to 10-bed dorms are some of the best deals in the city. Vending machines. Linens €2.50. Laundry €4. Free internet and Wi-Fi. 4-bed dorms €23, 10-bed €20; private room with bath €30. ❶

Hostal Gat Xino, C. L'Hospital, 155 (☎933 24 88 33; www.gatrooms.com). ⓂLiceu. 2nd location at C. Joaquin Costa, 44 (☎934 81 66 70). This posh hostel's minimalist rooms are done up in black, white, and lime green and come with plasma TVs, phone, A/C, and bath. Breakfast room feels new, and rooftop terrace has a shady trellis, low wooden furniture, and brand-new-looking lounge pillows that encourage laziness. Singles €47, with bath €50; doubles €66/70. MC/V. ❹

Center Ramblas (HI), C. de l'Hospital, 63 (☎934 12 40 69; www.center-ramblas.com). ⓂLiceu. Young staff and 200 cheap beds in 4- to 10-bed dormitories. The ambience leaves something to be desired but feels well-kept and is in a great student district. Breakfast included. Lockers €2 per use. Linens included. Towels €2. Laundry €5. Free internet and Wi-Fi. Dorms in summer €24, in winter €17-21. MC/V. ❶

Hostal Ramos, C. L'Hospital, 36, (☎933 02 07 23). ⓂLiceu. This hostel has nicely carpeted hallways and 32 particularly clean rooms with windows that open either onto balconies or a peaceful interior courtyard. Rooms have TV, phone, and hairdryer. Internet in a *sala de estar* and Wi-Fi. The one suite has a small sitting area, a large bathroom with a hot tub, and a large outdoor terrace. Singles €55, in low season €35; doubles €72/45; suite €125. MC/V. ❹

Pension Mare Nostrum, C. St. Pau, 2, (☎933 18 53 40; www.hostalmarenostrum.com). ⓂLiceu. This welcoming hostel has a pleasant breakfast room that overlooks las Ramblas. All rooms have TV, phone, and A/C. Pets allowed. Breakfast included. Wi-Fi available. Doubles €50, with bath €55; quads with bath €95. Discounts available online. MC/V. ❹

chic&basic, C. Tallers, 82 (☎933 02 51 83; www.chicandbasic.com) ⓂUniversitat, L1/2. Take the C. Pelai exit, turn left at the end of the block, and then left again at the pharmacy. This uber-modern hostel boasts a breakfast space with dandelion-meets-disco-ball glass chandeliers and clear plastic barstools. All rooms have plasma TVs, A/C, and bath; some have balconies. Internet and Wi-Fi. Singles €50-59; doubles €65-80. AmEx/MC/V. ❺

L'EIXAMPLE

In this posh neighborhood, expect lodgings to be elegant, well appointed, and a bit pricier. That said, travelers on a budget will still find plenty of places to stay. Besides, it may be worth the extra euro to live among the multitude of nearby *Modernista* masterpieces.

AROUND PASSEIG DE GRÀCIA

By day, these accommodations lie securely within a busy stream of sight-seers and professionals. By night, the wide streets are much quieter than those of the Ciutat Vella.

🏛 **Sant Jordi Hostel Aragó,** C. Aragó, 268 (☎932 15 67 43; www.santjordihostels.com). ⓂPasseig de Gràcia. Walk 3 blocks up Pg. de Gràcia and make a left on C. Arago; it's on the left. Crash in this recently renovated hostel's sleek and homey common room and recuperate from a long day. They'll plan your night out for you if you so desire. Board games, DVDs, lockers, sheets, towels, TV, use of guitar all free. Laundry €5. Breakfast €3.

Kitchen. Laundry €5. Internet and Wi-Fi. Parties and bar crawls organized regularly; call ahead. 4-bed dorms €14-17; 6-bed dorms €13-25. ❶

Somnio Hostel, C. Diputació 251. (☎932 72 53 08, www.somniohostels.com) ⓂPg. de Gràcia. Chic, clean, and neatly arranged rooms just blocks from Pl. de Catalunya. A/C throughout, free internet and Wi-Fi, TV in common area. Drinks available at the front desk. Breakfast €5. Single-sex dorms, complete with sheets and locker €25; singles €42; doubles €77, with bath €85. MC/V. ❷

Hostal Residència Oliva, Pg. de Gràcia, 32, 4th fl. (☎934 88 01 62; www.hostaloliva.com). ⓂPg. de Gràcia. Classy ambience—wooden bureaus, mirrors, and a light marble floor. Fragrant bouquets of flowers in the hallways are perhaps to be expected from a hostel that has been in operation since 1931. Rooms have TV, A/C, and Wi-Fi. Singles €38; doubles €66, with bath €85. Cash only. ❹

Hostal Qué Tal, C. Mallorca, 290 (☎934 59 23 66; www.quetalbarcelona.com), near C. Bruc. ⓂPg. de Gràcia or Verdaguer. Plants, both potted and painted, adorn the hallways of this *hostal.* Warm decorations make the spacious rooms feel cozy. Free internet. Singles €45; doubles €55-65, with bath €75-80. MC/V. ❺

BCN Hostal Central, Ronda Universitat, 11, 1st fl. (☎933 02 24 20; www.hostalcentral. net). ⓂUniversitat. Don't complain if the elevator to this *Modernista* building seems small or outdated; it's protected by the city and can't be replaced. Some rooms with balconies and inviting nooks. Free internet. Reception 24hr. Singles with shared bath €25-45; doubles €30-45, with bath €50-70; triples €65-75; quads €85-90. MC/V. ❹

Centric Point, Pg. de Gràcia, 33 (☎932 31 20 45; www.equity-point.com). ⓂPg. de Gràcia. The bunked bedrooms may be sparse, but this large hostel is no bore, offering 2 bars, a terrace, and a rec room with TV, computers, Wii, and foosball to a host of young travelers. Breakfast included. Free lockers; bring a padlock. Linens €2. Free Wi-Fi. Wheelchair-accessible. 4- and 8- bed dorms €21-30; doubles €48-57. MC/V. ❸

Axel Hotel, C. Aribau, 33 (☎933 23 93 93; www.axelhotels.com). ⓂUniversitat. Colorful, stylish, and plush rooms at this hotel catering to gay clientele. All guests have access to a pool, jacuzzi, and sauna. Room €70-250; book well in advance for lower rates. AmEx/MC/V. ❺

Hostal San Remo, Ausiàs Marc, 19 (☎933 02 19 89; www.hostalsanremo.com). ⓂUrquinaona. 8 quaint rooms have TV and A/C; half have terraces, and some have stained-glass windows. Free internet. Reserve early. Singles with bath €42; doubles €62; triples €75. Reduced prices Jan.-Feb. and Nov. Cash only. ❸

Backpackers House BCN, Gran Via, 602 (☎933 17 01 49; www.backpackershousebcn. com). ⓂUniversitat. Affordable lodgings with colorful common areas should be satisfactory to all but the pickiest of travelers. Room comes with breakfast, locker, linens, safe, Wi-Fi, and kitchen access. Towels €2. 4- and 8-bed dorms €17-25; doubles €45-55. ❷

L'EIXAMPLE DRETA

In L'Eixample Dreta, it's best to find accommodations near a metro stop. The zone to the right of the Sagrada Família is Barcelona's auto-shop district: you may find the number of restaurant and nightlife options here lacking. That said, **Barcelona Urbany Hostel** and **Sant Jordi's Apt. Sagrada Família** are gems and only a quick metro ride from downtown bars and clubs. In short, stay here, but memorize this schedule: trains run until midnight on weekdays, until 2am on Fridays, and continuously on Saturdays.

■ **Barcelona Urbany Hostel,** Av. Meridiana, 97 (☎932 45 84 14; www.barcelonaurbany. com). ⓂClot. Walk down Av. Meridiana. This sleek and modern hostel is perfect for those searching for a social experience. Large dining room, kitchen, and a terrace bar. Beer and sangria €1. Sa nights 8:30pm, the hostel serves paella (€2). Regular free walking tours. Access to new gym with swimming pool (next door) included. Towels €2. Free Wi-Fi. 8-room dorms €12-23; 6-room €14-25; 4-room €16-28; singles €50-82; doubles €25-41. MC/V. ❶

■ **Sant Jordi Hostels: Apt. Sagrada Família,** C. Freser, 5 (☎934 46 05 17; www.santjordihostels.com). ⓂHospital St. Pau. Walk down C. de Cartagena or C. del Dos de Maig until you reach C. Rossello. This street almost immediately forks; the upper street is C. Freser and the hostel is right at the fork. This 110-bed hostel is made up of 2- and 3-room apartments, each with a single room, a double room, and a 4-bed room (all individually locked) with a shared kitchen, bath, and free washing machine. Clean wood floors and balconies. Common room with TV and movie collection. Nightly excursions to bars and clubs. Towels €1. Free internet and Wi-Fi. Reception 8am-2am. 4-bed dorms €16-28 per person; singles €20-38; doubles €18-32 per person. MC/V. ❷

Hostal Gimon, C. Mallorca, 537 (☎934 55 44 32; gimon105@hotmail.com). ⓂEncants. Walk up C. del Dos de Maig and make a right on C. Mallorca. The 18 private rooms at Hostal Gimon are calm and tidy. TV. Reception 24hr. Singles €30; doubles €45, with bath €50; triples €65. ❷

Graffiti Hostal, C. Arago, 527 (☎932 65 09 74; graffiti.hostel@gmail.com). ⓂClot. Walk down Av. Meridiana to C. Arago and make a right. The *hostal* looks like an apartment from the street; look for the buzzer. The establishment's appearance lives up to its name. That said, it's not far from the Sagrada Família and the price is right. BYO padlock for lockers. Linens €2. Towels €1. Internet and Wi-Fi. Rooms €15-20. MC/V. ❶

L'EIXAMPLE ESQUERRA

L'Eixample, the spacious neighborhood known for its open, tree-lined avenues and significant gay population, is a great place to stay in a four- or five-star hotel. Translation: there are not many budget hotels, hostels, or *pensiones* in this peaceful, largely residential neighborhood. Also, long blocks make for long walks—if you do decide to stay here, be aware that it may take you awhile to get to dinner.

■ **Hostal Residencia Neutral, Rambla de Catalunya,** 42 (☎934 87 63 90). ⓂPasseig de Gràcia. Walk up the Passeig de Gràcia to the Carrer del Consell de Cent. Cozy upholstered chairs and mosaic tile floors make the antique but well-kept rooms feel immediately like home. The location can't be beat. Each room comes with TV, fan, and Wi-Fi; some have balconies that open onto La Rambla de Catalunya. Breakfast €8. Singles with shower €35; doubles with shower €60, with bath €65. MC/V. ❸

Pensión Aribau, C. Aribau, 37, 1st fl. (☎934 53 11 06; www.hostalaribau.com). ⓂPg. de Gràcia. Most of the hostel's 11 rooms have TVs and A/C. Ask for one with a balcony overlooking a terrace. Reserve at least 1 month ahead in summer. Singles and doubles €55, with bath €65; triples €70/80. AmEx/MC/V. ❹

Hostal Eden, C. Balmes, 55 (☎934 52 66 20; hostaleden@hotmail.com). ⓂPg. de Gràcia. From the Metro, walk down C. Aragó past Rambla de Catalunya to C. Balmes and turn left. Modern, well-kept rooms are equipped with TVs, lockboxes, and fans; most have large baths. Free internet and Wi-Fi. Singles €25-30, with bath €35-45; doubles €35-45/50-60. AmEx/MC/V. ❷

Pensión Cliper, C. Rosselló, 195 (☎932 18 21 88). ⓂDiagonal. Follow C. Rosselló for 3½ blocks. *Pensión* in Modernista building boasts large, antique rooms with high ceilings that have seen (much) better days. A step down from other listings in terms of quality. Also a step down in terms of price. Your call. €15-20 per person, €40 with shower. ❶

BARCELONETA

Lodging is not Barceloneta's forte, and rooms, especially cheap ones, are hard to come by. Hostels can be found in the area around ⓂBarceloneta, L4.

Pensión Francia, C. Rera Palau, 4 (☎933 19 03 76). ⓂBarceloneta, L4. Head right toward Pl. Palau, cross Pl. Palau, and turn right onto Av. Marqués de l'Argentera; C. Rera Palau is the 2nd left. Comfortable, airy rooms with balconies and TVs. The spotless shared bathrooms. Easy access to Barceloneta, La Ribera, and the Estació de França. Doubles with shower €50, with full bath €60; triples €65. MC/V. ❹

Hostal del Mar, Pl. del Palau, 19 (☎ 902 22 22 70; www.gargallo-hotels.com). ⓂBarceloneta, L4. From the station, head up the street away from the water toward Pl. de Palau, turn left and cross the plaça in front of the palace; it will be on the other side of the plaça. A popular, comfortable hostel. Singles €24; doubles €43, with shower €48, with full bath €58; triples €55/65/72; quads €71/85/85. MC/V. ❷

Pensión Palacio, Pg. Isabel II, 10 (☎933 19 36 09; www.pensionpalacio.com). ⓂBarceloneta. Cheerful, brightly colored rooms at some of the lowest prices around. Towels €1. Free internet. Singles €20-25; doubles €40-50; triples €60-75, with bath €75-90, quads €80-100/€100-120. MC/V with 7% fee. ❷

Sea Point, Pl. del Mar 1-4 (☎932 24 70 75; www.equity-point.com). ⓂBarceloneta. Follow Pg. Joan de Borbó until Pl. del Mar and enter the hostel through the cafe on the right side of the building. Not quite as sharp-looking as the other Barcelona equity-point hostels, but offers unbeatable beach access, just steps away from Platja Sant Sebastian. Kitchen access. Breakfast included. Extra linens, blankets, and towels €2 each. Free internet. Dorm-style beds in low season €15-20, in high season €21-25. MC/V. ❷

POBLE NOU

Poble Nou is dominated by a slew of fancy hotels. Cheap accommodations are scarce, and even the most affordable hotels are pricey. Those who are set on staying close to the beaches in this neighborhood but don't want to spend upwards of €200 per night might do better by searching online for apartments available to rent by the day or week.

Hostal Poblenou, C. Taulat, 30 (☎932 21 26 01; www.hostalpoblenou.com). ⓂPoblenou. Walking down Bilbao (toward the sea), take a right on Taulat and continue until just past Rambla de Poblenou. Luxurious B&B complete with fluffy beds, giant bathrooms, and a quaint terrace for morning meals. Free Wi-Fi. Doubles €60-90. MC/V. ❺

Hotel Pere IV, C. Pallars, 128-130 (☎933 20 96 50; www.salleshotels.com). ⓂBogatell. Go north 1 block on C. Zamora and take a right on C. Pallars. One of the more affordable of the many giant hotels in Poblenou. Pere still boasts plenty of perks: heated indoor pool, sauna, and ornate, comfortable rooms. Doubles €75-220. AmEx/MC/V. ❺

MONTJUÏC AND POBLE SEC

Poble Sec is first and foremost a residential, working-class neighborhood that is conveniently located near everything else. Las Ramblas, El Raval, and the beach are a fifteen-minute walk from here; hopping on the green (L3) line makes the trip even shorter. Montjuïc is a five-minute uphill walk (or a quick funicular ride) away. Because of this great location, many new hostels, *pensiones* and hotels have sprung up here, eager to capture your tourist euro. Among apartment buildings and warehouses, a dusting of bars and clubs cater to the locals who live here permanently and the tourists who pass through. Though not as glitzy as some parts of town, Poble Sec might be just the authentic, down-home Barcelona that you've been searching for.

Hello BCN, C. Lafont, 8-10 (☎934 42 83 92; www.hellobcnhostel.com). Ⓜ Paral·lel. You'll never want to say goodbye to this new and brightly colored hostel that knows what backpackers want and delivers. Spacious common area/bar with TV. Walking and bar tours available. Board games, gym, kitchen, breakfast, lockers, and linens all free. Laundry, internet, and Wi-Fi available. 4- to 6-bed dorms €17-24; doubles €30-35. AmEx/MC/V. ❶

Melon District Residencia and Hostel, Av. Paral·lel, 101 (☎933 29 96 67; www.melondistrict.com). Ⓜ Paral·lel. Walk up Av. Paral·lel. This new, spotless dormitory, while mostly occupied by university students, also has 19 rooms (all with bath) that it rents out to travelers. Gym and swimming pool, kitchen, luggage storage, linens, and towels all free. Laundry, internet, and Wi-Fi available. Singles €45 per night or €672 per month. ❹

Pension Pier, C. Lafont 1-3 (☎933 29 89 91; www.hostalapolo.com). Ⓜ Paral·lel. Pension Pier is located 1 fl. above the Hostal Apolo; the 2 establishments share a building and an owner. Don't be scared off by the building's dilapidated facade; the hostel and its rooms have ample natural light and are clean and tranquil. Request a room that has been recently renovated. Rooms with TV and A/C. Singles €20, with bath €25; doubles €40/45. ❶

Hostal BCN Port Barcelona, Av. Paral·lel, 15 (☎933 24 95 00; www.hostalbcnport.com). Ⓜ Drassanes or Paral·lel. Walk down Avinguda Paral·lel towards the ocean. This hostel (which feels like a hotel) is in a somewhat grimy area, but makes up for it by being meticulously clean. Its 32 rooms come with phone, TV, bath, hair dryer, security box, and A/C. Some have Wi-Fi, also available at reception. Breakfast €7. Wheelchair-accessible. Singles €40-50, with bath €60-74; doubles €55-65/74-84. MC/V. ❹

Hostal BCN, C. Roser, 40 (☎934 42 50 75; www.barcelonahostal.com). Ⓜ Paral·lel. The hostel's 63 hokey but tidy rooms (think orange bedspreads and landscape prints) juxtapose with a newly renovated breakfast and living space. Rooms with TV and A/C. Breakfast €5. Singles €36; doubles €59. AmEx/MC/V. ❸

GRÀCIA

Gràcia is quickly growing in popularity, so it's best to reserve ahead, particularly in the high season (June through mid-September). Many hostels in Gràcia are on the second or third floor of an apartment building; just look for the buzzer on the ground floor, and the receptionist will ring you in.

Pensión Norma, C. Gran de Gràcia, 87 (☎932 37 44 78). ⓂFontana. Meticulously kept rooms with sinks and wardrobes. The spacious shared bath is clean with speckled tile floors. Free Wi-Fi. Singles €27-32; doubles €38-47, with bath €55-60. MC/V. ❷

Hostal Lesseps, C. Gran de Gràcia, 239 (☎932 18 44 34; www.hostallesseps.com). ⓂLesseps. 16 spotless rooms, each with a high ceiling, classy velvet walls, small desk, TV, and bath. A/C €5. Cats and dogs allowed. Free internet and Wi-Fi. Singles €40; doubles €65; triples €75; quads €90. MC/V. ❹

Pensión San Medín, C. Gran de Gràcia, 125 (☎932 17 30 68; www.sanmedin.com). ⓂFontana. Walking into this hostel is a psychedelic experience: the wallpaper has pink metallic floral swirls. 12 rooms with tiled sinks, TVs, and fans; some have balconies.

Free Wi-Fi. Singles €30-38, with bath €39-48; doubles €45-60/€55-72. Special offers sometimes posted online. MC/V. ❸

Albergue Mare de Déu de Montserrat (HI), Pg. Mare de Déu del Coll, 41-51 (☎934 83 83 63; www.xanascat.cat), beyond Parc Güell. Buses #15, 28, and 92 stop across the street. From ⓂVallcarca, L3, walk up Av. República d'Argentina and take the stairs right before C. de Gomis (they're not far) to cross the bridge at C. Viaducte de Vallcarca; signs point the way up the hill. This huge government-sponsored hostel is gorgeous, complete with private grounds, stained-glass windows, and Alhambra-style tile work. Far from the city center, but the silver lining is a hilltop view of Barcelona and the chance to meet backpackers from all around the world. Multiple common spaces and restaurant. Breakfast included; lunch €7.50. Dinner €3-9. Laundry €4.50. Internet €0.90 per 30min. 6-night max. stay. Check-in 10am-3pm and 4:30-11pm. Check-out 10am. Midnight curfew, but doors open every 30min. Reservations suggested. Dorms €16-26. MC/V. ❶

Hostal Valls, C. Laforja, 82 (☎932 09 69 97). FGC: Muntaner. Walk 4 blocks downhill on C. Muntaner and turn left on C. Laforja. Though this hostel is not close to Gràcia's nightlife scene, the building compensates with Neoclassical Doric columns and Greek statues. Several large common spaces, including a TV lounge. Wi-Fi. Reservations suggested. Singles €40; doubles €45-70. MC/V. ❹

Alberg i Residència La Ciutat, C. L'Alegre de Dalt, 66 (☎932 13 03 00; www.laciutat. com). ⓂJoanic. Follow C. Escorial for 5 blocks, then cross to C. L'Alegre de Dalt. This hostel also serves as a dorm for Spanish students in Gràcia. The 4- to 10-bed rooms look like they were once brightly painted. Lounge area with TV and kitchen. Each private room has TV, phone, and bath (but no shower). A/C. Breakfast included. Linens €1.80. Laundry €5.40. Free internet and Wi-Fi. Reception 24hr. Dorms €17-20; singles €35-50; doubles €52-60. MC/V. ❶

Aparthotel Silver, C. Bretón de los Herreros, 26 (☎932 18 91 00; www.hotelsilver. com). From ⓂFontana, walk 1 block downhill on C. Gran de Gràcia and turn right on C. Breton de los Herreros; the hotel is on the right. Catering to short-term tourists and long-term residents, Aparthotel Silver has 49 rooms, each with bath, TV, phone, A/C, and cleverly-concealed kitchenettes. The restaurant-bar has a terrace with a small fountain and tables. Wi-Fi €12 for 24hr. Free internet in lobby. Wheelchair-accessible. Singles €80-120; doubles €85-150. MC/V. ❺

VALL D'HEBRON AND HORTA-GUINARDÓ

If you ever end up playing the game, "If you could take one thing to Vall d'Hebron and Horta-Guinardó, what would it be?" don't hesitate to answer: a car. Okay, so it's not a real game. Just bring a car. These largely residential neighborhoods high in the hills above downtown Barcelona are leafy and pleasant, but getting around by foot up here can be exhausting. That said, student athletes who are traveling and trying to stay in shape might find Vall d'Hebron's fields, combined with Horta's hills, just what they've been searching for.

Hostal Ballestero, C. Manuel Sancho, 2 (☎933 49 50 53; www.hostalballestero.com). ⓂFabra i Puig. Walk up Pg. Fabra i Puig and make a right onto C. Manuel Sancho. This cute, 2-star hostel is conveniently located near a metro stop and isn't far up the hill. Each of its 26 tidy rooms comes with a desk, TV, A/C, and bath. Free Internet. Singles €40; doubles €65. ❶

Edelweiss Hostal, C. Aguilar, 54 (☎933 57 52 80; www.edelweissyouthhostel.com). Catch the #39 bus from Pl. Catalunya or just outside ⓂHorta; there's a stop just above the hostel. Sports sky-blue walls, which is appropriate, considering that it's airy, clean, and perched above the city. Incredible views of Horta-Guinardó. Tidy dorm-style rooms.

Showers close 11:30pm-5am for cleaning. Linens €2. Towels €2. Laundry €3. Free Wi-Fi. 8-bed and 10-bed dorms €15-25; 6-bed and 4-bed dorms €18-26. MC/V. ❷

Agora BCN, Pg. dels Castanyers, 21 (☎931 66 90 00; www.agorabcn.com). ⓜMuncet. Walk up Pg. de la Vall d'Hebron and make a left onto Pg. dels Castanyers, which is just before the Velodrom. (Agora is behind the Velodrom.) This 220-room student residence and hostel has a large patio with wicker chairs and a spacious common room. Each room comes with bath, linens, towels, and A/C. Rooms are cleaned once a week; extra cleanings €2. "Superior" rooms have TV but cost more. Breakfast included. ½-board and full-board optional. Laundry €5. Billiards €1. Internet and Wi-Fi available in lounge area. Singles €40-53; doubles €50-77; triples €70-77. ❹

SARRIÀ

Sarrià is a beautiful neighborhood of private residences with manicured gardens. Walking its shaded streets, or lounging in one of its parks, provides welcome respite from the noisy, occasionally grim city center. The area is relatively inaccessible by Metro and has few budget accommodations. If you do stay out here, it's best to do so with a friend—prices will be slightly lower when you're sharing a room, and with few other tourists around, you may want the company.

Residencia Universitaria Torre Girona, Pg. dels Til.lers, 19 (☎933 90 43 00; www.resa.es). ⓜPalau Reial. Walk up C. Fernando Primo de Rivera, cross Pg. de Manuel Girona, and continue up Pg. de Til.lers. This student dormitory, when it has vacancies, doubles as a hostel—and a particularly nice one. 78 individual rooms and 28 double rooms have baths, kitchens, A/C, phones, TVs, and internet. Gym. Breakfast included. Linens included. Laundry available. Reception 24hr. Singles €45-50; doubles €80-85. MC/V. ❶

Hotel Bonanova, C. Capita Arenas, 51 (☎932 04 09 00; www.hotelbonanovapark.com). ⓜMaria Christina. Light yellow walls, clean rooms and furniture upholstered in classy striped fabric. It's also near to 2 beautiful parks (see **Sights,** p. 136). For those looking to stay in Sarrià and willing to spend the cash, Bonanova has 60 luxury rooms with bathtubs, hairdryers, A/C, telephones, internet, TVs, and minibars. Large breakfast buffet included. Reception 24hr. Singles €97; doubles €127. ❺

SANTS

The neighborhood around Sants-Estació is a bit removed from the heart of the city, but there are plenty of safe lodgings for late-night arrivals, and the area is well connected by Metro to Pl. de Catalunya and Las Ramblas. Be forewarned: though good-value accommodations exist in Sants, there are many hotels and hostels which offer rooms that would cost significantly less elsewhere in the city.

▨ Hostal Sofia, Av. Roma, 1-3 (☎934 19 50 40; www.hostalsofia.es). ⓜSants Estació. Directly across from the front of the station; cross C. Numància on the left and look up for the blue sign. A sunlit hostel with clean, well-priced rooms, some with A/C. Singles €35; doubles €50, with bath €60; triples €60/70. Prices vary by season. MC/V. ❸

Hostal Residencia Sans, C. Antoni de Campany, 82 (☎933 31 37 00). ⓜSants Estació. Leave the station from the back and follow C. Antoni across C. Sants; look for the large vertical yellow sign on the left as you cross the *plaça*. 7 floors of clean, comfortable rooms with A/C overlooking Pl. de Sants. Internet €1 per 30min. Wheelchair-accessible. Singles €33; with bath €38; doubles, €44/51; triples €54/64. MC/V. ❷

Hostel One, C. Casteràs, 9 (☎933 32 41 92). ⓂBadal or Pl. de Sants. Helpful, English-speaking staff and cheerful rooms with wooden bunks. Rooftop terrace and common room with TV, DVDs, kitchen and pool table (€1 per game). Locker, towels, and sheets included. Wash and dry €5. Free internet; Wi-Fi in lobby. 2- to 6-bed dorms €20-38 depending on season and size of room. MC/V. ❷

Hostal Béjar, C. Béjar, 36-38 (☎933 25 59 53). ⓂSants Estació. Exit the front of the station to the right onto C. Rector Triado. Take the 1st left onto C. Mallorca and then a right on C. Béjar. Clean rooms and a welcoming lounge with TV tucked away in an unassuming brick building. Doubles and triples have A/C. 3-night min. stay for apartments. Singles €30; doubles €45, with bath, €55; triples €65. 2-person apartments with kitchen €100; each additional person €10. MC/V. ❸

PEDRALBES AND LES CORTS

Les Corts has a number of nice hotels where rooms run €100-200. For the student traveler, however, there are only two budget options, listed below. Its manageable size, clean and less-touristy streets, and convenient location on the green (L3) line are the neighborhood's advantages. Travelers anticipating wild nights out, however, will be happier staying somewhere more central.

Hostal Sant Jordi Les Corts, Taquígraf Garriga, 7 (☎934 19 09 14; www.santjordi-hostels.com/apt-les-corts). ⓂLes Corts. Walk up C. de Joan Guell and make a right onto Taquígraf Garriga. More house than hostel, it has 6 rooms with a total of 20 beds upstairs. Downstairs, you'll find a living room with TV and couches, a kitchen, and an outdoor patio with a BBQ. Neat and welcoming, the hostel is just the place to stay for those prone to homesicknesses; you're sure to meet at least the owners and probably the other guests as well. Linens and towels included. Wi-Fi. Bikes €7 per day. Reception 10am-8pm; guests can let themselves in later at night. High-season beds €31-37; low season beds €10-12. MC/V. ❸

Hostal Pere Tarres, C. Numancia, 149-151 (☎934 10 23 09; www.peretarres.org/alberg). ⓂMaria Christina. Walk 5min. down Av. Diagonal and make a right on C. Numancia; the building is on the right. This hostel understands a Eurotripper's wants and it delivers. The lobby is industrial (think linoleum floors, plastic tables, and vending machines) but fun—travelers pack in around tables to swap stories and study maps. 240 beds with shared baths, kitchens, and A/C. Ping Pong tables and board games. Breakfast included. Laundry. Linens and towels included. Free internet. Singles €45-50; doubles €80-85. MC/V. ❹

SANT ANDREU

This is another suburban neighborhood; there aren't too many places to stay.

Guest House Sant Andreu, C. Gran de Sant Andreu, 343 (☎616 86 02 07). ⓂSant Andreu. Go up Pg. Torres i Bages, go left on C. Joan Torras, and take the 2nd right onto C. Gran de Sant Andreu. This house-turned-hostel has warm, colorful decor and a cozy common room with a kitchen, shared bath, and TV. Most rooms have A/C. Free Wi-Fi. Credit card required for reservations. 4-bed dorm €20-24; singles €30. MC/V. ❷

Hotel NH La Maquinista, C. Sao Paulo, 33-37 (☎932 74 53 70; www.nh-hotels.com). ⓂSant Andreu. Follow C. de Joan Torras over the traintracks. Take a left on C. Ferran Junoy and a right on C. Sao Paulo. A luxury hotel. Immaculate rooms with light wood furnishings, cushy beds, TVs, and A/C. Breakfast buffet €11. Doubles €67-84. Rates vary by season. AmEx/MC/V. ❺

NOU BARRIS

You're in the 'burbs, kid. There's not much to choose from, but down-town can fill up in high season.

Edelweiss Youth Hostel, C. Aguilar, 54 (☎933 57 52 80; www.edelweissyouthhostel.com). ⓜMaragall. Walk up Maragall and take a left on C. d'Amicar, the first right on C. Dalmau Creixell, and left on C. de l'Arc de St. Martí. Head right on C. St. Martí de Porres, continue on C. Alt de Pedrell, and go left on C. Aguilar. Getting up here can be a hike, but this newly established hilltop hostel (inaugurated 2006) rewards guests with fantastic views of Barcelona from the terrace and even several of the rooms. Communal kitchen available. Free lockers; €5 deposit for lock. Linens and towels €2 each. Free internet and Wi-Fi. Reception 24hr. 6- and 8-bed dorms €20-23. MC/V. ❶

Hostal Ballestero, C. Manuel Sancho, 2 (☎933 49 50 53; www.hostalballestero.com). ⓜFabra i Puig. Walk west on Pg. Fabra i Puig 1½ from Av. Meridiana and take a right on C. Manuel Sancho. The reception area might resemble the DMV, but the owner is friendly and offers well-kept rooms with clean, private bathrooms, TVs, and A/C. Free internet in lounge. Singles €40; doubles €65. ❹

Hotel Ibis Barcelona Meridiana, Pg. Andreu Nin, 9 (☎932 76 83 10; www.ibishotel.com). ⓜFabra i Puig. Follow Av. Rio de Janeiro and take a right on Pg. Andreu Nin. 14 floors of comfortable, plush rooms with satellite TV and A/C. Breakfast €9. Wi-Fi €5 per day. Doubles €79-99. AmEx/MC/V. ❺

FOOD

Barcelona offers every kind of food and ambience imaginable. Whether Basque, Chinese, Indian, or American, restaurants here will exceed your culinary expectations. However, beware of touristy restaurants offering "traditional" dishes—good authentic food can be hard to find. Our best advice is to look to the Catalan option: *fideuà* unseats *paella*, *cava* champagne complements every meal, and *crema catalana* satisfies the local sweet tooth. Barcelona's tapas (sometimes called *pintxos*) bars, concentrated in La Ribera and Gràcia, often serve *montaditos*, thick slices of bread topped with all sorts of delectables from sausage to *tortilla* (omelette) to anchovies. Hopping from one tapas bar to another can be a fun, social, and often cheap way to pass the evening. Most tapas bars are self-serve and standing room only. Plates in hand, ravenous customers help themselves to the toothpick-skewered goodies that line the bars. The bartender calculates the bill by tallying up the toothpicks on the way out, and then it's on to another bar. Though vegetarian options in general have never been easier to find, vegetarians consult the extensive *Guía del Ocio*(€1) at newsstands for a list of available options.

BARRI GÒTIC AND LAS RAMBLAS

Barcelona's nucleus contains all types of eateries. Classic Catalan cuisine is juxtaposed with fast-food options and every species of bar imaginable. Choose carefully; anything along La Rambla is likely to be overpriced.

LAS RAMBLAS

Escribà, Las Ramblas, 83 (☎933 01 60 27). ⓂLiceu, L3 Gran Via, 546 (☎93 454 75 35) ⓂUrgell. This small, classy cafe is a gem, having been remodeled by Ros i Guell in 1902 back when it was a pasta shop known as Casa Figueras. Acquired by the Escribà family, it now offers cakes and sweets as exquisite as the ceramic exterior. Outside seating is available. Coffee €1.50. Pastries €1-4. Open daily 8:30am-9pm. ❶

Café de l'Opera, Las Ramblas, 74 (☎933 17 75 85; cafeoperabcn.com). ⓂLiceu, L3. Once an 18th-century inn and then a 19th-century chocolate shop. In 1929, this Barcelona institution adopted its current name, and was soon reincarnated as a post-opera tradition. Today the cafe retains the same upscale ambience while offering well-priced drinks and tapas. Hot chocolate €2. Churros €1.40. Tapas €2-5. Salads and cheeses €2-10. Open daily 8:30am-2:30am. MC/V over €20. ❷

LOWER BARRI GÒTIC

▨ **Les Quinze Nits,** Pl. Reial, 6 (☎933 17 30 75; www.lesquinzenits.com). ⓂLiceu. Popular restaurant with lines halfway through the plaça every night; arrive early for excellent Catalan cuisine at unusually low prices. Sit in the classy interior or eat outside for no extra charge and keep an eye on your fellow tourists in Pl. Reial. Starters €4-7. Entrees €6-11. Wine €3. Sangria €4.70. Open daily 1-3:45pm and 8:30-11:30pm. AmEx/MC/V. ❷

▨ **L'Antic Bocoi del Gòtic,** Baixada de Viladecols, 3 (☎933 10 50 67; www.bocoi.net). ⓂJaume I. Excellent salads (€7.20-9.20), *coques de recapte* (open-faced toasted sandwiches; €9), and cheese platters (€13-19) feature *jamón ibérico* and local produce. Look for the 1st-century Roman wall inside. Open M-Sa 8:30pm-midnight. Reserve in advance. AmEx/D/MC/V. ❸

Arc Café, C. Carabassa, 19 (☎933 02 52 04; www.arccafe.com). ⓜDrassanes. This secluded, handsome cafe serves curries (€9.50-12) and salads (€4-7). Entrees €8-17. *Menú del mediodía* €9.60. Breakfast until 1pm. Thai dinner menu Th-F. Open M-Th 10am-1am, F 10am-3am, Sa 11am-3am, Su 11am1am. MC/V. ❸

Juicy Jones, C. Cardenal Casañas, 7 (☎93 302 43 30; reservations 60 620 49 06). ⓜLiceu, L3. A vegan's haven, Juicy Jones is a refreshing touch of the psychedelic, with wildly decorated walls and a long bar spilling over with fresh fruit. The creative vegan *menú* (€8.50) features Spanish and Indian inspired dishes (after 1pm). They offer a full juice bar with every conceivable mixture of fresh juices and soy milkshakes (€3-5). Open daily 12:30pm-12am. Kitchen closes at 11:30pm. Cash only. ❷

Vegetalia, Escudellers, 54 (☎933 17 33 31; www.vegetalia.es). ⓜDrassanes. Laid-back establishment with hardcore veggie, protein, and organic options based on tofu, seitan, and tempeh, with 7 veggie burgers (€3.50 alone, €7.20 combo meal) that even meat-eaters can't resist. Also a small natural foods store in the back. Entrees €7-9. *Menú* €10. Open M-F and Su 1:30-11pm, F-Sa 12:30pm-midnight. AmEx/MC/V. ❷

Venus Delicatessen, C. Avinyó, 25 (☎93 301 15 85). ⓜLiceu, L3. Take a right off C. Ferran coming from Las Ramblas. With a black-and-white tiled floor and rotating exhibitions of local art on the stucco walls, this popular Mediterranean cafe fits in well with the funky scene on C. Avinyó right by Pl. Trippy. Unique and refreshing salads like the *ensalada erótica* (tuna, asparagus, and yogurt sauce) or *ensalada afrodita* (avocado, fruit, cheese, and mint). Coffee, wine, and pastries €3.50-4. Vegetarian dishes €8-10. Salads €6-8. *Menú* €10. Open M-Sa noon-midnight. Cash only. ❷

Maoz Vegetarian, C. Ferran, 13 and La Rambla, 95 (☎653 84 76 53; www.maozveg.com). If you don't have enough time, money, or room in your stomach for another enormous 3-course *menú*, this place is your best friend. Excellent, quick, and cheap falafel (€3.80-5.20) and fries (€2.20) served until late. Pile on sweet peppers, tahini, tabouleh, chickpeas, and hot sauce to taste. Open daily 11am-3am. MC/V. ❶

Irati, C. Cardenal Casañas, 17 (☎93 302 30 84; www.gruposagardi.com). ⓜLiceu, L3. Basque restaurant that attracts droves of hungry tapas-seekers. Once you've gorged on the *montaditos* offered on the long bar, the leftover toothpicks will cost you €1.80 apiece. Bartenders also pour Basque *sidra* (cider; €1.70) with the bottle high above your glass. Starters €10-16. Entrees €18-26. Open daily 11am-12:30am. AmEx/MC/V. ❹

El Salón, C. l'Hostal d'en Sol, 6-8 (☎93 315 21 59). ⓜJaume I, L4. Follow Via Laietana toward the water, turn right on C. d'Angel Baixeras and then right on tiny C. l'Hostal d'en Sol; it's on the left. This mellow bar-bistro is perfect for unwinding after a day spent jostling fellow tourists. Sit on the terrace, nestled against a large section of 1st-century Roman wall, and feast on plates of bruschetta, risotto, chicken, pork, or fish (€13-16). Groups may call ahead to arrange lunch or Sunday meals. Open M-Sa 8:30pm-midnight. AmEx/MC/V. ❸

Los Caracoles, C.Escudellers, 14 (☎933 01 20 41; www.loscaracoles.es). ⓜDrassanes. Bustling restaurant with Old World charm has been serving its specialty, *caracoles* (snails; €11), since 1835. Tasty chickens roasting in the window €17. ½-rabbit €16. Open daily 1:15pm-midnight. AmEx/MC/V. ❸

Frankfurt, Pl. Sant Jaume, 2. ⓜJaume I, L4 between Pl. de Sant Jaume and Pl. de Sant Miquel. May not look like much, but frugal locals and broke travelers line up day and night for the sausages and hot sandwiches (€2.60-4). As cheap and quick a meal as you're likely to find with this much local flavor. Open M-Sa 11:30am-4:30pm and 6-11pm, Su and holidays 6-11pm. MC/V. ❶

Bell Amic, C. Gignàs, 25 (☎93 315 12 59). ⓜJaume I, L4. Right off Via Laietana coming from the Metro. Small, cozy, and unpretentious bistro serves classic dishes and executes them well. Perfect for a date. Entrees €13-16. Dinner *menú* €12. Open M 8:30-11:30pm, W-Su 12:30-4:30pm and 8:30-11:30pm. ❸

UPPER BARRI GÒTIC

Attic, La Rambla, 120 (☎933 02 48 66; www.angrup.com). ⓂLiceu. This chic restaurant promises high-class food at manageable prices. The modern, orange interior will feel like a refuge from touristy La Rambla. Mediterranean fusion cuisine, including fish (€10-14), meat (€8-15), and their specialty, ox burger (€11). Open daily 1-4:30pm and 7pm-12:30am. AmEx/MC/V. ❸

Xaloc, C. de la Palla, 13-17 (☎933 01 19 90). ⓂLiceu. Classy local favorite. A clean look complements the butcher counter where pig legs hang from the ceiling. Expect simple plates with high-quality ingredients. Tapas €3-7. *Cocas* €4-6. Open M-F 9am-midnight, Sa-Su 10am-midnight. AmEx/MC/V. ❷

The Bagel Shop, C. Canuda, 25 (☎93 302 41 61). ⓂCatalunya, L3. Walk down La Rambla and take the 1st left, and then bear right onto C. Canuda; it's on the left in Pl. Vila de Madrid. Bagels are rare in Spain, but here you'll find a diverse selection (€1, toasted €0.15 more) and a variety of spreads, from cream cheese to mango chutney. Good place to go for a tasty, inexpensive lunch with plenty of vegetarian options. Bagel sandwiches €4-6. Open M-Sa 9:30am-9:30pm, Su 11am-4pm. MC/V. ❶

Restaurante Self Naturista, C. Santa Anna, 11-17 (☎93 318 26 84). ⓂCatalunya, L4, on the left on C. Santa Anna off Las Ramblas. A self-service vegetarian cafeteria with a line of famished locals and an enormous selection of entrees (€3.30-€6.30) and desserts (€2-4). Lunch *menú* (3 dishes and a dessert) €8.80. Open M-Sa 11:30am-10pm. MC/V. ❶

Els 4 Gats, C. Montsió, 3 (☎933 02 41 40; www.4gats.com). ⓂCatalunya. Literally "the four cats," *els 4 gats* is actually a Catalan expression meaning "just a few guys," an ironically diminutive name considering the cafe's prestigious clientele. An old *Modernista* hangout of Picasso's with lots of Bohemian character; he loved it so much he created a personalized menu. The building itself was designed by Puig i Cadafalch in 1897. These days the restaurant tends to attract more tourists than artistic geniuses, but it's worth having one nice meal here. Food is expensive—entrees €12-20. M-F lunch *menú* 1-4pm (€13) is the best deal and comes with epic desserts; try the *crema catalana.* Live piano daily 9pm-1am. Open daily 10am-1am. AmEx/MC/V. ❹

Čaj Chai, Sant Domenic del Call, 12 (☎933 01 95 92). ⓂJaume I, L4. With quality teas from around the globe, a mosaic-covered interior, and a clever assortment of mismatched chairs and sofas, this tea house attracts a pensive, international crowd, poetry notebooks in hand. Pronounced "chai chai." Tea €2-4. Small pastries €1-2. Open Tu-Su 10:30-10pm. Cash only. ❶

La Colmena, Pl. de l'Àngel, 12 (☎933 15 13 56). ⓂJaume I. A busy dessert shop appropriately named "the Beehive" offering everything from bon-bons to fruit tarts to meringues. The chocolate and whiskey tartlet (€2) is a particularly indulgent treat. Small pastries €1-3. Open daily 9am-9pm. AmEx/MC/V. ❶

Betawi, C. Montsió, 6 (☎934 12 62 64; www.restaurantbetawi.com). ⓂCatalunya, L3. Take the 2nd left off Portal de l'Angel coming from the Metro; it's across the street from Els Quatre Gats. A peaceful, delicately decorated Indonesian restaurant serving quality food in small portions. *Menú* €12. Entrees €9-14. Open M 1-4pm, Tu-Sa 1-4pm and 8-11pm. AmEx/MC/V. ❷

Govinda, Pl. Vila de Madrid, 4 (☎933 18 77 29; www.amalteaygovinda.com). ⓂCatalunya, L3. Just to the right off Las Ramblas on C. Canuda. A mural of a flute-playing Krishna greets happy vegetarians and vegans. A true product of globalization: vegetarian Indian food served just a few feet away from a row of 2000-year-old Roman tombs in one of the world's most pork-crazed countries. Serves *thali* (traditional Indian "sampler" meals with a variety of dishes on one platter; €18-22) as well as spring rolls, crepes, rice, Indian bread, fruit lassis (yogurt shakes), and more. M-F *menú* €9.50. Entrees €8-10. Open daily 1-4pm, for dinner Tu-Sa 8-11:45pm. AmEx/MC/V. ❷

F
O
O
D

LA RIBERA

The eclectic gourmet restaurants of La Ribera cater to a young crowd. The neighborhood is home to a relatively high concentration of Asian restaurants, tapas bars, and wineries.

La Llavor dels Origens, C. d'Enric Granados, 9 (☎934 53 11 20; www.lallavordelsorigens.com); C. de la Vidrieria, 6-8 (☎933 10 75 31); Pg. del Born, 4 (☎932 95 66 90); and C. de Ramón y Cajal, 12 (☎932 13 60 31). A hip dining room with a new-school twist. Delectable entrees include beef-stuffed onion (€6.40) and rabbit with chocolate and almonds (€6.40). Soups, meat dishes, and some vegetarian dishes €4.30-7. Open daily 12:30pm-1am. AmEx/MC/V. ❷

Petra, C. dels Sombrerers, 13 (☎933 19 99 99). ⓂJaume I. Some of the best food in the area at shockingly low prices. Clever decor—stained-glass windows, menus printed on wine glasses, and light fixtures made from silverware—give the place a charming bohemian feel. Try the duck with brie and apple or the rigatoni with *foie gras* sauce and peach. Salads and pasta €5. Entrees €8. Open Tu-Th 1:30-4pm and 9-11:30pm, F-Sa 1:30-4pm and 9pm-midnight, Su 1:30-4pm. MC/V. ❷

El Pebre Blau, C. dels Banys Vells, 21 (☎933 19 13 08). ⓂJaume I. A *nouveau gourmet* restaurant serving Mediterranean and Middle Eastern fusion dishes under starry lanterns. Throw in a cheeky menu (available in English) and an attentive waitstaff for the win. Most dishes €10-18. Open daily 8pm-midnight. Reserve ahead, especially for weekend. MC/V. ❸

El Xampanyet, C. de Montcada, 22 (☎933 19 70 03). ⓂJaume I. Near the Museu Picasso. Crowds spill onto the street, drinks in hand. The house special *xampanyet* (wine; €1.10) is served with *pa amb tomàquet* (bread with tomato) and anchovies (€4.20) or *jamon cerrano* (€1.50). Over 25 varieties of *cava*. *Sidra* (cider; €1.80). Bottles from €8. Open Sept.-July Tu-Sa noon-3:30pm and 7-11pm, Su noon-3:30pm. MC/V. ❷

La Pizza del Born, Pg. del Born, 22 (☎933 10 62 46). ⓂJaume I. The best of Argentine thick-crust pizza meets the best of Spain, with toppings like artichokes, jam *serrano,* and goat cheese. Lunch *menú* (€3.90) is 2 slices and a drink. Slices €1.80. Open M-Th and Su noon-1am, F-Sa noon-2am. Cash only. ❶

Tèxtil Cafè, Pl. Montcada, 12-14 (☎932 68 25 98; www.textilcafe.com). ⓂJaume I. A terrace cafe nestled in an old stone courtyard. Mediterranean salads (€7.50), tapas (€5.30), and a good vegetarian selection. Live jazz Su 9-11pm (cover €5). Lunch *menú* €11; dinner €18. Entrees €8.50-11. Wheelchair-accessible. Open from mid-Mar. to Nov. Tu-Th and Su 10am-midnight, F-Sa 10am-1am; from Nov to mid-Mar. Tu-W 10am-8:30pm, Th and Su 10am-midnight, F-Sa 10am-1am. MC/V. ❷

Va de Vi, C. dels Banys Vells, 16 (☎933 19 29 00). ⓂJaume I. An inconspicuous but romantic spot for tapas and drinks in a candlelit 16th-century stone tavern. Choose from over 300 varieties of wine and *cava* (€1.90-7.70). Wide selection of cheeses €4.60-20. Tapas €1-19. Wheelchair-accessible. Open M-Th 7pm-1am, F-Sa 8pm-3am. Cash only. ❶

Bodega La Tinaja, C. d'Esparteria, 9 (☎933 10 22 50). ⓂJaume I. Walk down C. de la Princessa, make a right on C. de Montcada, take it to C. d'Esparteria, and make a left. Vaulted ceilings and stone walls hung with pots and pans, barrels of wine, and fresh flowers make this *bodega* rustic and charming, if slightly touristy. Serves Iberian comfort foods like ham-and-cheese plates and paella. Entrees €12-30. Occasionally hosts live flamenco guitar. Open M-Sa 8pm-midnight. AmEx/MC/V. ❸

Bubo, C. Caputxes 10 (☎932 68 72 24). ⓂJaume I. This artisanal sweet shop sells brightly colored, jewel-like chocolates, pastries, *petit fours,* and macaroons. Small sweets have big names: try the "light lychee cream and brilliance of strawberry and raspberry à la vanilla" or the "candied sunflower seeds with *fleur de salt,* candied orange-peel, and a sable coat of dark chocolate." Most sweets €1. Open M 4-10pm, Tu-Th 11am-10pm, F-Sa 10am-1am, Su 10am-10pm. MC/V. ❶

Gades Fondues, C. l'Esparteria, 10 (☎933 10 44 55; www.gadesfondues.com). ⓜJaume I. Walk down C. de la Princessa, make a right on C. de Montcada, take it to C. d'Esparteria, and make a left. Wearing your lederhosen and not sure what to do next? At Gades, you'll find salads, carpaccio, and over 15 different fondues, including a cava and truffle cheese and melted-chocolate desert. The pots of melted cheese are served with chunks of bread or crudites such as small pickles and pickled onions. Exposed brick walls, vaulted ceilings, and geometric modern lights. Fondues €12 per person. Open M-Th 8:30pm-12:30am, F-Sa 8:30pm-1:30am. AmEx/MC/V. ❷

El Rovell, C. de l'Aregenteria, 6 (☎932 69 04 58; www.elrovelldelborn.com). ⓜJaume I. Walk down C. de l'Aregenteria. "Rovell" is the Catalan word for the yolk of an egg. Accordingly, while this restaurant serves tapas, bruschetta, grilled meat and more, its emphasis is on egg specials. Wine buckets hang at the end of the venue's tall, wood tables. Eclectic and fun. Try the salmon tartar and lettuce with anchovy vinaigrette (€7.50). Entrees €6-12. Open daily 1-4pm and 7pm-midnight. AmEx/MC/V. ❷

Lonja de Tapas, Plaça de les Olles, 6 (☎933 10 78 45; www.cellerdelaribera.com). Walk down C. de la Princessa, make a right on C. de Montcada, and another right on C. del Bonaire. This 2-tier restaurant has exposed brick walls, sleek black tables, and a long menu of fancy tapas. Try the deep fried camembert with red fruits sauce (€3.60) and the grilled oyster mushrooms with Catalan sausage and garlic dressing (€4.60). Tapas €3.60-13. Open M-Th noon-midnight, F-Sa noon-1am, Su midnight-1am. AmEx/MC/V. ❸

Euskal Etxea, Pl. Montcada, 1-3 (☎93 310 22 00; www.euskaletxeak.org). ⓜJaume 1. This standing-room-only bar greets its many patrons with sharp decor and offers a little more elbow room than the competition. Vast array of tapas (€1.80). Beer from €1.90. Wine from €2.20. Sit-down restaurant in the back serves Basque food. Restaurant open daily 1-4pm and 8pm-midnight. Bar open M-F 10am-12:30am, Sa-Su 10am-1am. MC/V. ❷

Golfo de Bizkaia, C. de la Vidrieria, 12 (☎933 19 24 31; www.golfodebizkaia.com). ⓜJaume I. Routinely packed with young revelers, this tapas bar serves a large spread at good prices. Tapas €1.50. Beer €1.90. Open daily 7pm-1am. MC/V. ❶

Habana Vieja, C. dels Banys Vells (☎932 68 25 04). ⓜJaume 1. Cuban music, cuisine, and mixed drinks reign in this lively restaurant and bar. Most rice and meat dishes (€6-15) are meant to be shared. Mojitos €6. Open M-Th and Su 1:30-3:30pm and 7:30-10:30pm, F-Sa 1:30-3:30pm and 7:30pm-midnight. MC/V. ❷

Cafe del Born, Pl. Comercial, 10 (☎932 68 32 72). ⓜJaume I. Walk up C. de la Princesa and turn right onto Pl. Comercial. This spacious cafe is great for an early morning coffee (€1.30) or midday *entrepà* (sandwich; €1.80-5.50) as you read the paper and recover from the night before. Free Wi-Fi. Wheelchair-accessible. Open M-Th and Su 8am-1am, F-Sa 8am-3am. MC/V. ❶

Nou Cellar, C. de la Princesa, 16 (☎933 10 47 73). ⓜJaume I. Half a block up C. de la Princesa. This old-fashioned restaurant serves simple, hearty *català* cuisine. Meat and fish entrees €10-14. Open daily 10:30am-11:30pm. MC/V. ❸

EL RAVAL

Authentic Catalan mainstays (found mostly on the side of El Raval farthest from Las Ramblas) and trendy fusion spots sit next to Middle Eastern restaurants and a growing number of student- and vegetarian-friendly juice/smoothie bars. There are several wholesome, tasty, self-service vegetarian eateries clustered around **Carrer Dr. Dou.** Near the MACBA, you'll find a few upscale restaurants catering to museum-goers.

FOOD

Organic, C. Junta de Comerç, 11 (☎933 01 09 02; www.antoniaorganickitchen.com). This vegan-friendly eatery provides wholesome, healthy dishes—starting with the filtered water used to prepare the food. Vegan salad bar and lunch *menú* (M-F €10, Sa-Su €14) served under candlelight and exposed ceiling. Salad bar regulars include cheese-and-mushroom *croquetas* and cucumbers and yogurt. Dinner served a la carte. 2nd location in La Boqueria market also has a *menú* and *bocadillos;* takeout only. Open daily 12:30pm-midnight. MC/V. ❷

Rita Rouge, Pl. Gardunya (☎934 81 36 86; ritarouge@ritablue.com). Ⓜ Liceu. 2nd branch **Rita Blue,** Pl. Sant Augustí, 3 (☎933 42 40 86; www.ritablue.com). Savor a healthy, delicious, and high-quality lunch *menú* (€11; weekends €14) full of creative offerings and vegetarian choices on a shady, black-and-red terrace just behind La Boqueria, or come at night for a mixed drink (€6-8) on zebra-striped cushions or in the glittery bar's red and silver bucket seats. Entrees (€9.50-22) include chicken tandoori with yogurt and *basmati* rice. Salads and wok dishes €6-12. Open M-Sa noon-2am, Su 6pm-2am. ❸

Kasparo, Pl. Vicenç Martorell (☎933 02 20 72). Ⓜ Catalunya. Walk down Las Ramblas, make a left on C. Elisabets, and a first right onto C. de les Ramelleres. The plaça is on the right, and the restaurant is in the far right corner. Alternatively, walk down C. de Pelai and make a left onto C. de les Ramelleres. The plaça is 3min. down, on the left. Kasparo capitalizes on—and helps to create—the bustling atmosphere of the Raval plaça. Almost all of Kasparo's seating is outdoors; pull up a metal table under the building's vaulted overhang and people-watch to your heart's content. Perfect for an early-evening drink or a late-night *cortado*—but be warned, you might get comfortable and end up staying for dinner too. Luckily dishes (€5-8) include fresh soups, salads, and pasta, with some vegetarian options. Open daily 9am-midnight. Cash only. ❷

Restaurante Can Lluís, C. Cera, 49, and Reina Amalia, 1, (☎934 41 11 87). Ⓜ Sant Antoni, L2. From the metro, head down Ronda S. Pau and take the 2nd left on C. Cera. For over 100 years, Can Lluís has been a defining force in Barcelona's cuisine—and politics. On Jan. 26, 1946, a grenade set off in the restaurant killed the owner and his son. Later, under Franco, artists used Can Lluís as a gathering place. Eschewing trendiness, the menu is filled with traditional Catalan favorites prepared home-style and always bursting with flavor, including succulent lamb ribs (€9.80), grilled squid (€10), and fresh grilled asparagus (€5.40). Dinner *menús* (20-35) include wine. Entrees €6-20. Open M-Sa 1:30-4pm and 8:30-11:30pm. MC/V. ❸

Mendizabal, Junta de Comerç, 2. Try the *zumo del día* (juice of the day) at this colorful student favorite, right near the school of fine arts. Need something to wash down all that juice? No problem: beer is cheap (€2.50), as are the *bocadillos* (*serrano* ham, brie, tomato; €3.50), freshly grilled behind the counter. Crayola-colored patio furniture beneath umbrellas in the plaça across the street. Open daily 8am-12:30am. Cash only. ❶

Shalimar, C. Carme, 71 (☎933 29 34 96). From Ⓜ Catalunya, L1/3, right on C. Carme. Indian and Pakistani cuisines make their peace at inexpensive prices. Walls sport blue-and-white tilework. Chicken, lamb, and seafood curries €6.50-9. Chicken tandoori €6.50. Open M and W-Su 1-4pm and 8pm-midnight, Tu 8pm-midnight. ❷

Hello Sushi, C. Junta de Comerç, 14 (☎934 12 08 30; www.hello-sushi.com). Ⓜ Universitat. Zen red-and-blue decor and small tea area with floor cushions. Lunch *menú* €9; dinner *menú* €15. Entrees €15-25. Open Tu-Sa 12:30-4:30pm and 8:30pm-12:30am, Su 8:30pm-12:30am. Reservations required F-Su nights. AmEx/MC/V. ❺

Madame Jasmine, Rbla. del Raval, 22. Eclectic decorations, a spirited staff, and an array of wonderfully mismatched chairs overlook Fernando Botero's fat cat sculpture in the middle of Rambla de Raval. Delicious *bocadillos* (€5.50) and salads (€7). Mixed drinks €6. Open M-F 5:30pm-2:30am, Sa-Su 1:30pm-2:30am. Kitchen open daily 1pm-midnight. ❷

FOOD

Juicy Jones, C. Hospital, 74 (☎934 43 90 82; www.juicyjones.com). ⓂLiceu. Walk down C. L'Hospital. JJ is a DIY vegetarian juicebar where everything's made by hand, from the murals and graffiti on the walls to the menus on the tables. Offerings include a lunch *menù* (€8.50), *thalis* (mixed plates of Indian dishes), salads (€4.50-5.30), guacamole (€3.80), the house cookie (€1), and Pear-Celery-Lime juice (mixed juices with three fruits, €3.45; add spices like ginger for €0.50). Open daily 1-11:30pm. MC/V. ❷

Ultramarinos Bar, C. Sant Pau, 126 (☎635 14 47 26; www.ultramarinosbar.com). ⓂParal-lel. Walk down C. Sant Pau; the bar is on the left. By day, Ultramarinos serves up Iberian ham, cheese, and *pa amb tomaquet* (bread with tomato) as well as other traditional Catalan dishes. Showcases local artists' canvases. By night, the 2-tier bar has a DJ and a small but committed crowd of regulars. Entrees €5-10. Mixed drinks €5-7. Open daily 6pm-3am. Cash only. ❷

Elisabets, C. Elisabets, 2-4 (☎933 17 58 26). ⓂLiceu. Walk up Las Ramblas and make a left onto C. Elisabets. This welcoming, smoky old-school bar serves tapas (€1-8) and home-cooked dishes like lasagna to a young clientele. Popular during the day, but really buzzes on weekend nights. Lunch *menù* €8.50. Entrees €6-12. Open M-Th 8am-midnight, F-Sa until 2am. Cash only. ❷

Original Pizza-Bar, C. Joaquim Costa, 47 (☎933 17 20 89). ⓂUniversitat. Walk down Ronda de Sant Antoni and make a right on C. Joaquim Costa. This pizzeria has colorful red, orange, and black walls and serves greasy, delicious, and cheap slices, perhaps best enjoyed late at night. Try the eggplant, goat cheese and walnut pizza, or the ham-and-chili. Slices €2. *Empanadas* €2.90. Open daily 1pm-2am, F-Sa 1pm-3am. Cash only. ❶

Bar Invisible/Pizza Ravalo, Pl. d'Emili Vendrell, 1 (☎934 42 01 00), at the intersection of C. Joaquin Costa and C. del Peu de la Creu. ⓂLiceu. Walk up Las Ramblas and make a left onto C. del Carme. When you hit C. Joaquin Costa, make a right. The bar is on the left, just after the intersection. This bar is easy to miss, but a delight to find. Set back from C. del Peu de la Creu and obscured by shrubs in large terra-cotta pots, the burgundy-walled venue offers delicious mixed drinks. Try the specialty (cava, pineapple juice, peach, and cassis; €5). Pastas and pizzas €7.50-13. Be bold and try the "surprise" pizza (€13). Open daily 6pm-midnight. MC/V. ❷

Chelo, Pl. Vicenç Martorell (☎933 18 55 01). ⓂCatalunya. Walk down C. de Pelai and make a left onto C. de les Ramelleres. The plaça is about 3min. down, on the left. The beautifully stenciled plants and flowers on this restaurant's walls reflect its attention to detail and commitment to natural ingredients. Chelo has open-air seating on a popular plaça and serves excellent smoothies, milkshakes, and pastries (€3-6). Open 10am-midnight. Cash only. ❶

Cafe d'Annunzio, Pl. Vicenç Martorell (☎933 02 40 95). ⓂCatalunya. Walk down C. de Pelai and make a left onto C. de les Ramelleres. The plaça is about 3min. down, on the left. The decapitated heads of Greek statues stare at you from this cheerful eatery's red walls. Inside, 1 table is cozily tucked below the low-hanging ceiling in a sunken recess. The majority of the seating, however, is out in Pl. Vicenç Martorell—enjoy a full breakfast (rare in Barcelona) of coffee, eggs, ham, juice, and toast here for just €6. Entrees €6-12. Open 9:30am-1am. MC/V. ❷

Cafeterium, C. Tallers, 76 (☎667 64 01 11; www.cafetarium.com). ⓂUniversitat. Walk down C. Tallers. This all-purpose cafeteria/restaurant/*cerveceria* has streamlined white tables by day and caramel-colored lighting by night. Tasty, elegantly presented dishes and a relaxing ambience explain why the venue is nearly always full. Tapas €3-12. Sandwiches €2-5. Happy hour 6pm-midnight; beer €1. Open M-Sa 8am-11:30pm. MC/V. ❷

Narin, C. Tallers, 80 (☎933 01 90 04). ⓂUniversitat. Walk down C. Tallers. This shawarma restaurant sets itself apart from a thousand other similar venues with fresh ingredients, fiery sauces, and a dining room with elaborately tiled walls and pine wood tables. You might even

FOOD

consider eating here sober. Hummus plate €3.40. Shawarma with chicken €3.90. Falafel combo plate €7. Open M-Th and Su 11am-2am, F-Sa 11am-3am. Cash only. ❶

L'Antic Forn, C. Pintor Fortuny, 28 (☎933 04 25 18; www.lanticforn.com). From ⓂCatalunya, C. Pintor Fortuny is 5min. down Las Ramblas. From ⓂLiceu, it's 5min. up Las Ramblas. It's rare to find lace curtains, white tablecloths, and gourmet dishes at prices this affordable. Try the risotto with shrimp and parmesan cheese (€6.50) or the grilled lamb chops with garlic salsa (€7.80). Selection of pizzas. Entrees €5.50-16. Open 9am-5pm and 8pm-midnight. MC/V. ❸

En Ville, C. Doctor Dou, 14 (☎933 02 84 67; www.envillebarcelona.es). From ⓂCatalunya, C. Pintor Fortuny is 5min. down Las Ramblas. From ⓂLiceu, it's 5min. up Las Ramblas. Make a right onto C. Doctor Dou; the restaurant is on the right. Although this restaurant is indoors, its terra-cotta floors, mirrored walls, and floral bouqets make it feel like an upscale, outdoor patio. Live music Tu and W nights after 9pm. Try the octopus carpaccio with arugula and citrus (€9.70) or the duck with polenta and caramelized apples (€15). Open M 1-4pm, Tu-Sa 1-4:30pm and 8pm-midnight. AmEx/MC/V. ❸

Tallers 76, C. Tallers, 76 (☎933 18 89 93; www.tallers76.com). ⓂUniversitat. Walk down C. Tallers. This new restaurant serves Valencian-influenced tapas, sandwiches, paella, and a few meat dishes in a geometric, purple space with excellent natural lighting. Start with the tapa of paella (€5.50) and follow it up with a smoked salmon, fresh cheese, and lettuce sandwich (€4.80). Entrees €5-11. Open M-Su 9am-11:30pm. AmEx/MC/V. ❷

Olivia, C. Pintor Fortuny, 22 (☎933 18 63 80). From ⓂCatalunya, C. Pintor Fortuny is 5min. down Las Ramblas. From ⓂLiceu, it's 5min. up Las Ramblas. This white-walled cafe has light wood booths and an organic menu. Savor a perfect cup of coffee and a slice of carrot or apple cake (€3.50-4.50). Tranquil and newspaper-friendly. Open M-Sa 9am-9pm. MC/V. ❶

DosTrece, C. Carme, 40 (☎933 01 73 06; www.dostrece.net). ⓂCatalunya. This restaurant-bar's mosaic bar and high-backed, red leather barstools give it a retro diner feel. American/Mediterranean/Middle Eastern cuisine. Downstairs lounge has Moroccan accents. Lunch menú M-Th €10.50, F-Sa €12. Entrees €6-17. Wi-Fi. Kitchen open daily noon-midnight; bar open Th-Su until 3am. AmEx/MC/V. ❸

Mamacafé, C. Doctor Dou, 10 (☎933 01 29 40), right off C. Pintor Fortuny. ⓂCatalunya, L1/3. A great place to find healthy, fresh options (some vegetarian) with an exotic twist. Try the ravioli with brie, candied onion, and tomato jam (€9.90) or the crunchy chicken with plump sweet corn and olive pesto (€12). Bright, geometric designs make for an atmosphere that is casual without being shabby, and artsy without being pretentious. Lunch menú M-F €9.60, Sa €13. Open M-Sa 1-4pm, F and Sa 8pm-midnight. AmEx/MC/V. ❷

Silenus, C. Angels, 8 (☎933 02 26 80). From ⓂCatalunya, L1/3, a right off C. Carme. As much art gallery as restaurant, the softly elegant Silenus is the place to go for gourmet food and soft conversation (date night, anybody?). The menu, memorably titled "A Short Treatise on the Passions of Flavors," includes duck and a venison hamburger (€12) as well as the exotic *filete de kangoo* (yes: kangaroo) in raspberry sauce (€17). Lunch menú changes daily (€6-14); the artwork changes 3 times per year. Open M-Th 11am-11:30pm, F 11am-midnight, Sa 1pm-midnight. AmEx/MC/V. ❸

Restaurante Biocenter, C. del Pintor Fortuny, 25 (☎933 01 45 83; www.restaurante-biocenter.es). From ⓂCatalunya, L1/3, right on C. del Pintor Fortuny. See-through white wooden shelves and white canvas curtains turn what would otherwise be a sizeable restaurant into a linked chain of intimate, lamp-lit spaces. Organic and vegan options (self-service buffet at lunch, table service at dinner). Try the organic "bio wine" (€2.25), or sip on a "hot chickory drink" (we're not sure what it is either; €2.50). Lunch menu M-F €9.75, Sa €11.75. MC/V. ❷

Papitu, Placa Sant Galdric (www.ravalero.com). ⓂLiceu. A cheerful, yellow-walled food stall with a long chalkboard menu outside. *Boquiera*-fresh tapas like *gambas a la plan-*

cha (€5). Patrons can sit at patio tables among large oak barrels topped with vases of carnations. Beer (€2.50) and wine served. Open daily 9am-1am. Cash only. ❶

Carmelitas, C. Carme, 42 (☎93 412 46 84; www.carmelitas.biz and www.carmelitasgallery.com). From ⓜCatalunya, L1/3, right on C. Carme. Sunshine brightens the simple and stylish interior of this new, airy restaurant during the day; a red light (not that kind) illuminates it at night. Menu items are scrawled on the windows and mirrors in chalk. For lunch, there are entrees of fresh fish straight from the nearby *Boqueria* market (rotating appetizers and entrees €4-14). At night, snacks include artichoke chips (€2.70) and the excellent *calamares a la plancha* (squid strips; €8.50). If you had to lay off your personal sommelier, don't worry; dotted lines on the menu connect dishes with suggested wine pairings. Vegetarian options. Open M-Th and Su 10am-midnight, F-Sa 10am-2am. Reservations recommended Th-Sa. AmEx/MC/V. ❷

Pla dels Àngels, C. Ferlandina, 23 (☎933 49 40 47). ⓜUniversitat. The inspired decor of this colorful, inexpensive eatery befits its proximity to the contemporary art museum. Creative, healthy dishes and a large vegetarian selection served on the terrace. Entrees €5-8. Open daily 1:30-4pm and 9-11:30pm. MC/V. ❷

L'EIXAMPLE

With sidewalk cafes serving everything from fusion to traditional Catalan cuisine, wandering in l'Eixample easily induces rumbling stomachs, especially during a long day of shopping. These upper neighborhoods are full of good places to spend a long dinner (especially l'Eixample Esquerra), but the restaurants are scattered around and interspersed with plenty of nondescript corner bars serving the endless apartment buildings in the area. If you want to sample one of l'Eixample's trendy, high-quality restaurants, pick one ahead of time and put the blinders on as you walk past all the others. Be sure to make reservations on weekends and be prepared to pay a lot for the food and atmosphere.

AROUND PASSEIG DE GRÀCIA

Pg. de Gràcia is lined with nearly as many tapas bars and cafes as it is with shops and *Modernista* structures. Most are tourist-oriented, have sidewalk tables, and are on the expensive side. Eating outside is especially pricey; many establishments charge up to 15% extra. On the weekends, this neighborhood is a good choice for late-night food, as many places stay open until 2am. Sweet (and savory) deals on *bocadillos* and tapas are found on every corner.

🔲 **La Rita,** C. Aragó, 279 (☎934 87 23 76; www.laritarestaurant.com). A killer afternoon lunch *menú* has made Rita a local favorite for a cheap but quality midday meal. Bright red awnings draw crowds to enjoy everything from gazpacho to salmon carpaccio in orange-and-dill sauce. Lines frequently extend out the door; reservations recommended. *Menú* M-F €9. Entrees €6-10. Open daily 1-3:45pm and 8:30-11:30pm. AmEx/MC/V. ❷

🔲 **Taktika Berri,** C. Valencia, 169 (☎934 53 47 59). ⓜUniversitat. Walk up C. d'Aribau and make a left onto C. Valencia. Many consider this Basque restaurant the best one in Barcelona. While you can always eat *pintxos* (skewered tapas) such as *monteditos* (small sandwiches) at the bar, you won't get a table unless you call weeks in advance. Entrees like battered cheek and cod omelette are delicious, but not cheap—expect to pay €35 for a full meal, whether of tapas or entrees. Good selection of Basque wines. Open M-F 1-4pm and 8:30-11pm, Sa 1-4pm. AmEx/MC/V. ❺

Kirin, C. Aragó, 231 (☎934 88 29 19) Rda. Universitat 20 (☎93318769). All-you-can-eat sushi, edamame, and other Asian delicacies roll by on a conveyor belt for you to choose from. While you're at it, grab some raw seafood and vegetables and have them grilled on the spot. Weekday lunch buffet €9.70. Dinner and weekend buffet €14, children €5.50. Open daily 1-4pm and 8pm-midnight. MC/V. ❷

Acalia, C. Rosselló, 197 (☎932 37 05 15). Sparkling French restaurant with an ambience as light and airy as its crepes (€4-7). Lunch *menú* €12. Dinner *menú* €16. Open Tu-Sa 1-4:30pm and 8:30-11:30pm. AmEx/MC/V. ❹

Thai Gardens, C. Diputació, 273 (☎93 487 98 98; www.thaigardensgroup.com). ⓂCatalunya, L1/3/5. The extravagant decor, complete with a wooden bridge entrance, lush greenery, and colorful silk pillows, makes for a romantic meal. Call ahead to reserve a traditional *kantok* table (cushions on the ground). If all you want is some Thai food, order take-out at reduced prices. Entrees €14-18. Dinner *menú* €31. Wheelchair-accessible. Open daily 1-4pm and 8-11:30pm. AmEx/MC/V. ❸

Txapela (Euskal Taberna), Pg. de Gràcia, 8-10 (☎93 412 02 89 www.angrup.com). ⓂCatalunya, L1/3/5. Decide between delicious offerings like eggplant with goat cheese or anchovy with mozzarella and cherry tomato. Tapas €1.40-2. Wheelchair-accessible. Open M-Th 8am-1:30am, F-Su 10am-2am. Tapas served starting at noon. ❶

Menjar Enrotllat, C. Valldonzella 33 (☎654 17 01 74). ⓂUniversitat. Take Ronda Sant Antoni away from Pl. Universitat and take the 2nd left onto Valldonzella. Small, futuristic-looking joint boasts healthy and diverse food on the cheap. Maki from €1.50. Pasta €3.50. Lunch *menú* from €5. Open M-Sa 1-5pm and 8pm-midnight. Cash only. ❶

El Japones, Passatge de la Concepció, 2 (☎93 487 25 92; www.grupotragaluz.com), 2nd location at C. Princesa, 35. ⓂPg. de Gràcia, L2/3/4. Just off of Pg. de Gràcia. Serving all the Japanese cooking you could want: from tempura and skewers to noodles and sushi. Stylish red interior will leave you feeling chic as you fill your stomach with (and empty your wallet for) these tasty plates. Entrees €3.50-13. Wheelchair-accessible. Open M-W and Su 1:30-4pm and 8:30pm-midnight, Th-Sa 1:30-4pm and 8:30pm-1am. No reservations accepted. AmEx/MC/V. ❷

El Ultimo Agave, C. Aragó, 193 (☎934 54 93 43). ⓂUniversitat. Walk up C. d'Aribau and make a left onto C. Arago. This popular Mexican restaurant, which shares its name with a brand of tequila, serves dishes like tacos with marinated pork, pineapple, onion, and coriander (€11). Try the special, *El Ultimo Agave* ("something better than fajitas"; €14). A real cantina: boisterous, fun, and often standing room only. Reservations are a must on weekends. Open daily 7pm-3am. MC/V. ❸

52, Valldonzella, 52. ⓂUniversitat, L1/2. Take Ronda Sant Antoni away from Pl. Universitat and take the 2nd left onto Valldonzella. Learn directly from the students and have a late bite at this funky, orange-lit eatery. Order one of the healthy Asian-Mexican-Catalan fusion concoctions and wash it down with a beer (€1.5o). Tapas €4.10-7.10. Wheelchair-accessible. Open daily 7:30pm-1am, kitchen open 9pm-midnight. Cash only. ❷

Madrid-Barcelona (Pa Amb Tomàquet), C. Aragó, 282 (☎932 15 70 27). ⓂPg. de Gràcia, L2/3/4. At the intersection of Pg. de Gràcia. Named for the railroad line that used to run here, this classy lunchtime hotspot attracts legions of native businessmen and shoppers. Waiters ladle soup and rice at your table straight from the stove. The classic Catalan dishes are tasty. Entrees €7-15. Wheelchair-accessible. Open daily 1-4pm and 8:30-11:30pm. AmEx/MC/V. ❸

Mauri, Rambla de Catalunya, 102 (☎93 215 10 20). ⓂDiagonal, L3/5. This *pastisseria* (pastry and sweet shop) has been turning out delicate sweets, mouth-watering bonbons, and gourmet *bocadillos* (€1.80-3) since 1929. Come to buy delectable gifts, have lunch in the delicatessen-style restaurant (lunch *menú;* €13), or simply to drool at the cake displays. A second location (☎932 15 81 46) across the street specializes in candy and gift baskets. Open M-F 8am-9pm, Sa 9am-9pm, Su and holidays 9am-3pm. MC/V. ❶

Cervecería Catalana, C. Mallorca, 236 (☎93 216 03 68). ⓂPg. de Gràcia, L2/3/4. All-in-one Catalan bar: they've got *flautas* (€3-7), tapas (€3-12), seafood, salads, burgers, and beers (€2.50). Crowded, noisy, friendly; you'll feel as at home as the locals who fill the place. Wheelchair-accessible. Open daily 8am-1am. AmEx/MC/V. ❷

Tapas 24, C. Diputació, 269 (☎934 88 09 77; www.carlesabellan.com). ⓂPg. de Grà-cia. Chef Carles Abellan, formerly of the legendary El Bulli, offers tapas at this less expensive alternative to his acclaimed Comerç 24. Sit at the pearl white bar if it's not too crowded and have a glass of wine (from €3) with your plate of *patatas bravas*. Tapas €2.50-8. *Raciones* €9-12. Open daily 8am-midnight. MC/V. ❷

Cata 1.81, C. Valencia, 181 (☎933 23 68 18; cata181@hotmail.com). ⓂUniversitat. Walk up C. d'Aribau and make a left onto C. Valencia. This classy, modern wine bar has stainless-steel benches with orange seat cushions and matches its drinks with market-fresh food. Try a glass of cava (€2.50-3.50) and the black spaghetti with chicken and prawns (€6.60), or opt for bottles of high-end wine. Open M-F 1pm-midnight, Sa 1pm-1am. AmEx/MC/V. ❷

El Raim, C. Muntaner, 75 (☎934 53 59 53). ⓂUniversitat. Wak to the left down C. Gran Via de les Corts Catalans. Make a right onto C. Muntaner and walk for 3 blocks; the cafe is on the left. Looking for the authentic Barcelona? This local cafe serves immensely satisfy-ing yet inexpensive tapas like chicken leg with stewed plum and stuffed eggplant (€2-3). Salads €3.90. Combination plates €5.10-9.10. Open M-Sa 9am-1am. MC/V. ❷

O'Peixe, C. Aragó, 199 (☎934 53 12 24; www.opeixe.es). ⓂUniversitat. Walk up C. d'Aribau. Make a left onto C. Aragó. This bar-restaurant has white-washed walls hung with a few nautical prints. O'Peixe's specialty is seafood: try the crawfish, the mussels, or the grilled shrimp. Entrees €8-15. Night *menù* €12. Open M-Sa 9am-11pm. MC/V. ❸

Yamamoto, C. Aragó, 197 (☎934 51 87 02). ⓂUniversitat. Walk up C. d'Aribau and make a left onto C. Aragó. This self-serve Japanese restaurant is a convenient place to refuel with a wok of tempura. Befriend the fish in the restaurant's tank while you eat their relatives. Lunch buffet €8.50. Dinner buffet €13. Open daily 1-4pm and 8:30pm-midnight. MC/V. ❸

Indochine, C. Muntaner, 82 (☎934 51 17 96; www.indochinelyleap.com). ⓂUniversitat. Walk to the left down C. Gran Via de les Corts Catalans and make a right onto C. Muntaner; the restaurant is 3 blocks up on the right. The warped wooden bar stools at this Asian fusion restaurant are striking works of art—they fit in nicely with the restaurant's black decor and abstract floral arrangements. A good choice for a special occasion. Try the Tom Yun, or a curry. Entrees €15-25. Open daily 1-4pm and 8pm-midnight. AmEx/MC/V. ❹

Han In Restaurante Coreano, C. Aribau, 32 (☎934 54 05 63; www.haninjung.com). ⓂUniversitat. Walk up C. Aribau. Brick walls, wooden tables, and a TV in the background give this Korean restaurant a hotel lobby feel. Try the soy omelette (€7.50) or the grilled pork ribs korean-style (€14). Entrees €6.50-13. Open noon-4pm and 8:30pm-midnight. MC/V. ❸

Face to Face, C. de Provença, 277 (☎932 72 66 00). ⓂDiagonal. This colorful cafe offers cheap sandwiches with typical combinations of meat, cheese, and *pâté* (€1.70-5.50). Grab your midday *bocadillo* underneath a Gaudí-esque lizard on the ceiling. Wheelchair-accessible. Open M-F 7am-1am, Sa 7am-3pm. MC/V. ❶

L'EIXAMPLE DRETA

▨ **Laie Llibreria Cafe,** C. Pau Claris, 85 (☎933 18 17 39; www.laie.es/cafe/PauClaris_prin_es.php). ⓂUrquinaona, L1/4. Additional locations at Marques de Camillas 6-8 (☎934 76 86 69) and Montcada 15-23 (☎932 68 43 92). An ultra-hip lunch spot for more than just bookworms. Cheap, fresh, and plentiful all-you-can-eat Catalan buffet lunch (M-F €14, Sa-Su €17) in an open, bamboo-draped room. Grab a praline cappuccino (€2.50) at the bar on the way out. Vegetarian options available. Internet €1 per 15min. Open M-F 9am-1am, Sa 10am-1am. AmEx/MC/V. ❸

F O O D

La Muscleria, C. Mallorca, 290 (☎934 58 98 44; www.muscleria.com), on the corner with C. Bruc. ⓂVerdaguer, L4/5. In this bustling basement, you'll get a whole pot of mussels to yourself with fries on the side. The crustaceans come in any size, shape, and flavor (try "white wine") and are culled from Catalunya, France, Galicia, and The Netherlands. Entrees with fries from €9.50. Salads €7. *Cocas* €8. Reservations recommended F-Sa. Open M-Sa 1-4pm and 8:30-11:30pm, Su 1-4pm. MC/V. ❷

Can Cargol, C. València, 324 (☎934 58 96 31; www.cancargol.es), on the corner with C. Bruc. ⓂGirona, L4. Extremely popular—and thus noisy—Catalan restaurant with make-your-own *pan con tomate,* charcoal-grilled meats, and lots of snail options. *Platos del dia* €5-6. Reservations recommended F-Su. Open 1:30-4pm and 8:30pm-midnight. ❷

Blue Mandalay Café, C. Provença, 330 (☎93 458 60 17; www.mandalaycafe.net), between C. Roger de Llúria and C. Bruc. ⓂVerdaguer, L4/5. Exotic pan-Asian cuisine, including gourmet dim sum, Vietnamese noodles, seared fish, delicate meat, and elegant salads, served in a room so draped in color and sultanesque luxury (you can eat on a bed!) that it's been featured in books on interior design. F-Sa night trapeze artist around 11pm. Variable extra cover charge for show (around €2.50). Wheelchair-accessible. Entrees €9-13. Open Tu-Sa 8:30pm-midnight. AmEx/MC/V. ❷

Wok & Bol, C. Diputació, 294 (☎ 933 02 76 75), between C. Roger de Llúria and C. Bruc. ⓂGirona, L4. An elegant, colorful Chinese restaurant serving dim sum (€5-8 per small dish) and Peking duck (€18 per person) in addition to more common dishes like chow mein and veggie stir-fry (€6-8). Reservations recommended. Open M-Sa 1:30-3:30pm and 9:15-11:30pm. ❸

El Rodizio Grill, C. Consell de Cent, 403 (☎932 65 51 12), right next to ⓂGirona, L4. All-you-can-eat Brazilian and Mediterranean buffet *à la churrascaria:* grilled shish-kebab-style chicken, salmon, and cod. Cold dishes include sushi, pasta, and salads. M-F lunch *menù* €19. Sa-Su lunch and dinner menù €21. Includes 1 drink and coffee. Rich desserts €3.30-5.50. Open M-Th 1-4pm and 9pm-midnight, F-Sa 1-4pm and 9pm-1am, Su 1-4pm. ❹

Campechano, C. València, 286 (☎932 15 62 33; campechanobarcelona.com), just to the right of Pg. de Gràcia when you're coming from Pl. de Catalunya. ⓂCatalunya, L1/3. This restaurant goes all out to recreate the atmosphere of a 1940s *merendero* (barbecue—picnic area) on the Barcelona mountainside, from a few real trees and a painted forest wall to train signs marking your progress "toward the mountain." Picnic tables make it perfect for large groups. Choose your favorite meat or poultry from their extensive list. French fries, salads, and a few other dishes serve as sides. *Menú* €10. Salads €4-6. Entrees €6-15. Open M 8am-2pm, Tu-Sa 8am-2am. ❸

A-Tipic, C. Bruc, 79 (☎932 15 51 06), between C. Aragó and C. Consell de Cent. ⓂGirona, L4. A lunchtime gem for vegetarians. A simple buffet (€10) that tastes more like home than a cafeteria, served in a relaxing blue and yellow dining room. Excellent choice of salad, rice, pasta, and veggie calzones. Open Sept.-July M-F 1-4pm. MC/V. ❷

Cafe Parc Belmont, C. Lepant, 256 (☎932 31 13 58). ⓂSagrada Família. Walk downhill on C. Lepant. It's on the left. This tapas bar gets it right; it has both a better atmosphere (bright orange walls decorated with framed, old-fashioned photographs) and better food than most similar venues. Large, delicious salads €4-6. Tapas €1-8. Open M-Sa 9am-11pm. Closed Su. ❷

Frida's Restaurante Mexicana, C. Bruc, 115 (☎934 57 54 09). ⓂPasseig de Gràcia. Walk down C. Arago until you hit C. Bruc; make a left. This fun, piñata-decorated restaurant is well up the block on the left. Your go-to for "real Mexican" (not Tex-Mex) from tacos (€1.90) to *pozole* (€7). Lunch *menú* €11, ½-*menú* €6.90. Margaritas €5-6. Open M-Tu 1-4pm, W-Sa 8:30am-2am, closed Su. ❷

Llibreria Cafe La Xocolatada, C. Buenos Aires, 44 (☎934 05 06 81). ⓂHospital Ciutat. Walk up C. Villaroel until you hit C. Buenos Aires; make a right. Not to be confused with

Laie Libreria cafe, this adorable, intimate, mom-and-pop bookstore has a small coffee counter in the back. *Cortado* €1.20. All the books displayed are available for sale. Open M-F 10am-5pm, Sa-Su noon-4pm. ❶

El Trencadis, C. Sant Antoni Maria Clare, 163-165 (☎934 56 74 22; www.eltrencadis.com). ⓂHospital Sant Pau. Walk down C. de la Industria and make a right on C. de Cartagena; it's at the intersection with Sant Antoni Maria Clare. Avoid the many touristy restaurants on Av. de Gaudí and come here instead. You won't hear much English here—but you will see locals eating fresh tapas and filling lunch *menú* (€9.90). Kitchen open noon-midnight. Open 7am-2am. ❷

Raco Ecologic, C. Bruc, 86 (☎934 67 86 86). ⓂPasseig de Gràcia. Walk down C. Arago until you hit C. Bruc; make a left. This small eco-friendly restaurant has bright green walls adorned with pictures of plants and a green-friendly menu, too. The lunch *menú* (€10) includes 1 Mediterranean option, 1 vegetarian option, and 1 macrobiotic option (a "must try"). Salads €4.60-4.90. Open M-F 7am-5pm. ❷

Cullera de Boix, C. Ronda de St. Pere, 24 (☎932 68 13 36; www.culleradeboix.com), between C. Bruc and Pl. Urquinaona. ⓂUrquinaona, L1/4. With metal chairs, light wood tables, and sleek cylindrical lamps, this restaurant could easily be in Manhattan. Fresh and varied tapas (€3.30-11) include brie served with tomato. Entrees €13-20. Weekend reservations recommended. Open M-Th and Su 1-4pm and 8-11pm, F-Sa 1-4pm and 8-11:30pm. AmEx/MC/V. ❸

L'EIXAMPLE ESQUERRA

Look around. Are you in l'Eixample Esquerra? On a corner? Chances are, you're only inches from a tapas bar, and probably a really good one. If you're looking to *picar* ("snack;" literally, "bite"), walk until one jumps out at you and then eat your fill of *croquetas* and *patatas bravas*. Those with heartier appetites will need heavier wallets—very little in l'Eixample comes cheap. If you do decide to hit up a nicer restaurant, your euro will be well spent.

▨ **Cerveceria Catalana,** C. Mallorca, 236 (☎932 16 03 68). ⓂPg. de Gràcia, L2/3/4. If you want *the* Spanish experience, with locals to keep you company, head here. Noisy, friendly, energetic: the buzz of this restaurant-bar will make you want to return night after night. Pitchers of sangria and creative and fresh tapas €3-12. Wheelchair-accessible. Open daily 7:30am-1:30am. AmEx/MC/V. ❷

▨ **Racó d'en Baltá,** C. Aribau, 125 (☎934 53 10 44; www.racodenbalta.com). ⓂHospital Clínic. Founded in 1900, this restaurant serves innovative Mediterranean dishes like fried camembert with blueberry sauce (€8.70) and veal sirloin with Bernaise (€18). Entrees €9-17. Lunch *menù* €11. Open M-Th 9am-11:30pm, Th-Sa 9am-3am. MC/V. ❸

La Flauta, C. Aribau, 23 (☎933 23 70 38). ⓂPg. de Gràcia, L2/3/4. 2nd branch at C. Balmes, 164-166 (☎934 15 51 86). The House specialties are hot or cold *flautas* (skinny, crusty bread sandwiches stuffed with veggies, cheeses, and meats; ½ €3.90-6.90, whole €5-8). Plenty of vegetarian options and a large selection of fresh *tapas del día*. Weekday lunch *menù* €10.50. Dishes €3-15. Open M-Sa 7am-1:30am. MC/V. ❷

Cafe Chapultepec, C. Comte Borrell, 152 (☎934 51 92 85; www.cafechapultepec.com). ⓂUrgell. Walk down Gran Via de les Corts Catalans to C. Comte Borrell and make a right. It's at the end of the 1st block, on the right. This Mexican cafe has Rubik's Cube-like tile floors and everything your Southwestern American heart may be longing for: *enchiladas verdes* or *rojas* (€5.90), pitchers of margaritas (€15), and even pancakes with maple syrup (€3.80). Open M-F 10am-4:30pm and 7-11pm, Sa 12:30-4:30pm and 7-11pm, Su 12:30-4:30pm. MC/V. ❷

La Pulpería, Consell de Cent, 329 (☎934 87 53 98; www.restaurantelapulperia.com). ⓂPasseig de Gràcia. Walk up Passeig de Gràcia to the Consell de Cent and make a left.

The restaurant is on the right. This fun, classy establishment (think chalkboard menus and a bronze bar) serves a wide variety of Galician tapas and *raciones*, including *el pulpo* (octopus). Plates €4.30-13. Kitchen closes at midnight. Open M-W and Su noon-4pm and 8-midnight, Th-F noon-2am, Sa noon-4pm and 8pm-1am. AmEx/MC/V. ❷

Ginza, C. Provença, 205 (☎934 51 71 93), between Balmes and Enric Granados. ⓜDiagonal, L3. Bamboo-filled restaurant serves delectable but affordable Japanese food. Eat in or take out. Sushi €5-15. Weekday 4 course lunch *menù* €8. Dinner and weekend *menù* €11. Wheelchair-accessible. Open M-Sa 1-4pm and 8pm-midnight, Su 1-4pm. D/MC/V. ❸

La Provença, C. Provença, 242 (☎933 23 23 67; www.laprovenza.com). ⓜDiagonal, L3. Enter through a French hall adorned with fresh flowers into a quiet banquet room with chandeliers. Specialties include baked sea urchin (€13) and batter-fried lamb brains (€11) as well as less adventurous French dishes (carpaccio; €11). Entrees €6-20. Dress well; you're not *chez les ch'tis.* Reservations recommended, especially on weekends. Open daily 1:30-3:30pm and 9-11:30pm. AmEx/MC/V. ❸

Cafe Lateral, C. Valencia, 206 (☎934 53 10 34; www.cafelateral.es). ⓜPasseig de Gràcia. Walk 1 street up to C. Valencia, then 4 blocks toward C. Aribau. This new restaurant has chic, dark-wood decor offset by eggshell benches and classy vases. *Platos del dia* €7.90. Lunch *menù* (€12) mixes traditional Catalan fare and haute cuisine. Open M 8:30am-10pm, Tu-W 8:30am-midnight, Th 8:30am-2:30am, F 8:30am-3am, Sa 10am-3am. MC/V. ❷

BARCELONETA

Barceloneta is mostly home to expensive seafood restaurants advertising paella *menús* (especially along Pg. Joan de Borbó). You have to go farther inside the neighborhood for smaller restaurants and grocery stores. There's a **Spar Express** on P. Juan de Borbó.

- 🔳 **Jai-Ca Bar,** C. Ginebra, 13 (☎932 68 32 65), 2 blocks down Pg. Joan de Borbó and 3 blocks toward the beach, on the corner with C. Baluard. Hugely popular tapas bar serving all kinds of small seafood treats and plenty of beer (€1.70) to wash them down. Most tapas €3-6. Open Tu and Su 9am-10:30pm, W-Sa 9am-11:30pm. MC/V. ❶

- **La Bombeta,** C. Maquinista, 3 (☎933 19 94 45). ⓜBarceloneta. Walk down Pg. Juan de Borbó (toward the beach) and take a left on C. Maquinista. A retro facade marks this tapas bar, which offers deep-fried *bombas* and a variety of seafood tapas. Appetizers €3-10. Entrees €9-12. Open M-Tu and Th-Su 9am-11:45pm. Cash only. ❷

Bar Bitacora, C. Balboa, 1 (☎933 19 11 10). ⓂBarceloneta. Walk down Pg. Juan de Borbó (towards the beach) and take the 1st left after Ronda del Litoral onto C. Balboa. Loud music and tapas (€4-10) draw young, hungry beachgoers. Open Tu-Su 9am-12am. Cash only. ❷

Can Maño, C. Baluard 12 (☎933193082). ⓂBarceloneta. Another busy restaurant serving fresh, simple seafood in a packed dining room. Meat and fish dishes €3-10. Combination plates €6-8. Open M-F 8am-5pm and 8-11pm, Sa 8am-5pm. Cash only. ❷

POBLE NOU

Restaurants in Poble Nou are few and far between. Cheap bar-restaurants are scattered inland, but along the beach food tends to be touristy and expensive. The best bet for a post-beach meal (without being sucked into one of the many pricey and barely distinguishable seafood restaurants lining Port Olímpic) is to walk up Rambla de Poble Nou where a line of more affordable restaurants awaits, catering mostly to locals. Better yet, visit a supermarket or grab a *bocadillo* ahead of time for a beach picnic. If you do find yourself in Poble Nou with a rumbling tummy, however, these are our favorites.

Recasens, Rambla del Poblenou, 102 (☎933 008 123). An array of fine wines, cheeses, and fresh produce line the entrance of this gourmet restaurant. Entrees €10-20. Dinner *menú* €22. Open W 6:30pm-1am, Th-Sa 9-11pm and 11pm-1am. Reservations recommended. MC/V. ❹

Agua, Pg. Marítim de la Barceloneta, 30 (☎932 25 12 72; www.grupotragaluz.com), the last building on the ocean side of Pg. Marítim before Barceloneta. Tourists, trendy *barceloneses,* and GQ business-types enjoy seafood and rice dishes from the beachfront terrace. Vegetarian options. Starters €2.50-12. Entrees €8-20. Wheelchair-accessible. Open M-Th and Su 1-3:45pm and 8-11:30pm, F-Sa 1-4:30pm and 8-12:30am. Reservations highly recommended. AmEx/MC/V. ❸

La Fonda del Port Olímpic, Moll de Gregal, 7-9. ⓂCiutadella-Villa Olímpica. Along the left arm of Port Olímpic as you face the sea. If you need to indulge in some beach-side paella (€10-18), this is the place to do it. The superior seafood draws large crowds. Seafood entrees €17-25. Open daily 12:30pm-1am. AmEx/MC/V. ❹

Can Toni, Rambla del Poblenou, 88 (☎933 00 33 17). ⓂPoblenou. Join locals for seafood tapas on the terrace (€2.50-10 or 3 for €10). Happy hour. Open Tu-Su 8am-midnight. AmEx/MC/V. ❷

Nice Spice, C. Pujades, 20 (☎933 08 95 48; www.restaurantenicespice.com). ⓂPoblenou. This small restaurant specializes in tandoori. Delicious lamb, chicken, seafood, and vegetable dishes. Large television next to bar screens Bollywood-esque variety shows. Entrees €7-10. 10% off takeout over €20. Open M and W-Su noon-4pm and 8pm-midnight. MC/V. ❷

MONTJUÏC AND POBLE SEC

The more time you spend in Poble Sec, an up-and-coming neighborhood nestled between Montjuïc and the Raval, the more you'll love it. Streets that seem empty by day bustle after 9pm; by night, the nearby hillside lends the whole neighborhood an enchanted-forest feel. At dinner time (10pm), head to **Calle Magarit**—the street has several delicious Catalan and Italian restaurants. Dining options are not as plentiful in Montjuïc as elsewhere in the area, but the Fundació Miró, MNAC, Castell de Montjuïc, and Teatre Grec all have pleasant cafes. **Poble Espanyol** has a number of touristy restaurants. *Menús* at these run €10-15.

FOOD

■ **Inopia,** C. Tamarit, 104 (☎934 24 52 31). ⓂPoble Sec. Walk up Av. del Paral·lel 1 block to C. Rocafort; make a right, and Inopia is 1 block up, on your right. You might think that this unassuming tapas bar, which has tile walls adorned with customers' postcards and more stools than tables, is nothing special. You would be wrong. Inopia is run by Alberto Adrià, the kid brother of Ferran Adrià (of El Bulli fame) and also El Bulli's pastry chef; the tapas (€2-10) are innovative takes on more traditional dishes and are always fresh. Try the Bikini with mozzarella and boiled Iberic ham (€4.50) or, for dessert, the strawberries with caramel and chardonnay vinegar (€3.80). Open Tu-F 7-11pm, Sa 1-3:30pm and 7-11pm. Reservations recommended, or expect to wait in a long line. MC/V. ❷

■ **La Tomaquera,** C. Margarit, 58. ⓂPoble Sec or Paral·lel. From ⓂPoble Sec, walk 4 blocks down Av. del Paral·lel to reach C. Margait. From ⓂParal·lel, C. Margait is 5 blocks up. This boisterous, popular Catalan restaurant has no menus and accepts no reservations but serves some of the best *caracoles* and *carnes a la brasa* in town. Try the *butifarra* (€7) or the artichokes (€9.30). Open M-Sa 1:15-3:45pm and 8:30-10:45pm. Cash only. ❷

■ **Quimet i Quimet,** C. Poeta Cabanyes, 25 (☎ 934 42 31 42). ⓂParalel·lel. Walk up Av. del Paral·lel and make a left onto C. Poeta Cabanyes. This tiny and much-loved tapas bar's floor-to-ceiling shelves are stocked with bottles of wine of every caliber. Squish in among the locals who pack the place and eat your fill of innovative *montaditos* (little sandwiches). Open Sept.-July M-F noon-4pm and 7-10:30pm, Sa noon-4pm. MC/V. ❷

Xemei, Passeig de l'Exposició, 85 (☎935 53 51 40). ⓂPoble Sec. Walk 1 block down Av. del Paral·lel and make a right onto C. de la Creu des Molers. Walk 7 blocks up to the end of this street; the restaurant will be directly in front of you. This Venetian restaurant owned by twin brothers serves gourmet Italian fish and pasta in a candlelit restaurant on the Montjuïc hillside. Try the *espresso risotto* with zucchini and crawfish (€18). No lunch menu; only a la carte offerings. Open 1:30-4pm and 6pm-midnight. MC/V. ❸

Bella Napoli, C. Magarit, 12 (☎934 42 50 56; www.bellanapoli.net). ⓂPoble Sec or Paral·lel. From ⓂPable Sec, walk 4 blocks down Av. del Paral·lel to reach C. Margait. From ⓂParal·lel, C. Margait is 5 blocks up. This trattoria is rumored to have the best pizzas (€7-12) in town. Exposed brick walls and white tablecloths make for a classy and cozy setting in which to eat your *provola, bresaola,* tomato, cherry, and rucula pizza (€11) or, on Su, your lasagna (€15). What other restaurant has the confidence to serve only lasagna on Sundays? Open Tu-Su 1:30-4pm and 8:30-midnight. MC/V. ❷

Bar Seco, Pg. de Montjuïc, 74 (☎933 29 90 06). ⓂParel·lel. Walk up C. Nou de la Rambla to Pg. de Montjuïc. This corner bar, nestled at the base of Montjuïc, is the perfect place to sip your *cafe con leche* (with croissant; €2.30) or eat a light lunch. Ingredients are local and organic; try the *bocadillo* "Solo," with apple, walnuts, and gorgonzola. By night, the restaurant is quieter, and white Christmas lights twinkle in the windows. Open M 9am-5pm, Tu-Th 9am-1am, F 9am-2am, Sa 10am-2am, Su 10am-1am. Cash only. ❷

Barramon, C. Blai, 28 (☎934 42 30 80; www.barramon.es). ⓂPoble Sec. Walk up C. Blai. This bar, with an outdoor patio, specializes in the food of the Canary Islands. Try the *almogrote* (€5), a mixture of cured cheese sprinkled with garlic, red pepper, and olive oil, from the island of La Palma, or the lamb marinade (€8.50), which is common on all of the islands. Entrees €5-10. Open M-F 6pm-1am, Sa-Su 1pm-1am. Cash only. ❷

Montalban, C. Magarit, 31 (☎934 42 31 43). ⓂPoble Sec or Paral·lel. From ⓂPable Sec, walk 4 blocks down Av. del Paral·lel to reach C. Margait. From ⓂParal·lel, C. Margait is 5 blocks up. No printed menus—just a chalkboard that lists a lot of delicious, fresh fish dishes—at this neighborhood favorite. The crawfish is a must-try. Open Tu-Sa 2-3pm and 9-10pm and Su 2-3pm; no one is hurried out and meals often take a few hours. Reservations necessary. MC/V. ❹

O Meu Lar, C. Magarit, 24 (☎933 29 70 74; www.omeular.es). ⓂPoble Sec or Paral·lel. From ⓂPable Sec, walk 4 blocks down Av. del Paral·lel to reach C. Margait. From ⓂParal·lel, C. Margait is 5 blocks up. The turf to Montalban's surf, this restaurant serves up wood-grilled meat in a subterranean enclave. Try the rabbit (€7) or the sirloin steak (€24). Open 1:30-4:40pm and 8:30pm-midnight. MC/V. ❹

Taverna Can Magarit, C. Concordia, 21 (☎934 41 67 23). ⓂPoble Sec. Walk up C. Concordia. Fill your glass at one of the large casks of wine at the entrance to this old-fashioned tavern; use it to wash down tasty traditional Catalan fare. Entrees like *buitfarra* with beans and rabbit €9-15. Open M-Sa 9-11:30pm. MC/V. ❸

La Fibula, (☎934 42 48 35). ⓂPoble Sec. Walk up C. Blai. This Moroccan-style tea shop with tiled tables and ornately etched glasses is the perfect place to enjoy conversation or a thick novel. The *teteria* offers over 35 types of tea (€2.30) including caramel, eucalyptus, and kiwi, and nearly as many styles of hot chocolate (€2.80-3.10). Middle Eastern music on the stereo. Sweets (baklava and more) €1.10-2.20. Open daily 9:30am-2pm and 5-10pm. MC/V. ❶

La Soleá, Pl. del Sortidor, 14 (☎934 41 01 24). ⓂPoble Sec. From Av. del Paral·lel, walk up C. de Radas. Make a left onto C. de Magalhaes; Pl. del Sortidor is at the end of the street. This sunny bar has orange and yellow tiles, patio seating, and a menu that includes Mediterranean dishes like hummus (€3.50) as well as more standard fare (nachos; €4.50). Perfect for a quick bite. Open Tu-Sa noon-midnight, Su noon-6pm. MC/V. ❷

Zodiaco, C. Magarit, 17. ⓂPoble Sec or Paral·lel. From ⓂPable Sec, walk 4 blocks down Av. del Paral·lel to reach C. Margait. From ⓂParal·lel, C. Margait is 5 blocks up. This cheerful bar has ladybug-print wallpaper and patio seating on C. Blai. With better options in the neighborhood, this might not be the place to eat a full meal, but it does offer a prime location for people-watching and sipping a coffee or a beer. Open daily in summer 1:30pm-1:30am, in winter 6pm-1:30am. MC/V. ❷

GRÀCIA

Without a doubt, Gràcia is the best place in Barcelona to find authentic cuisine from anywhere around the globe. Traditional markets (see **Shopping,** p. 165) and Catalan menus are popular, but the side streets of Gràcia are *the* place to find reasonably priced ethnic cuisine. Tapas bars dominate **Plaça del Sol** and **Plaça Virreina; Calle Verdi** is your go-to for culturally diverse (Egyptian, Japanese, Lebanese, Mexican, and Pakistani) food.

▧ **Gasterea,** C. Verdi, 39 (☎932 37 23 43). ⓂFontana, L3. Follow C. Astúries for several blocks and make a right on C. Verdi. Yellow walls cast a warm glow in this table-less bar. Grab a seat at one of the counters and dig in to Gasterea's selection of excellent, fresh tapas (€1.10). Beer €2-3. Mixed drinks €5. Open daily 7pm-2am. Cash only. ❶

▧ **Ikastola,** C. Perla, 22 (☎933 68 83 87), off C. Verdi. ⓂFontana, M3. Tired of being a grown-up? Then head to Ikastola (Basque for "nursery school") without letting go of the perks of adulthood (like alcohol). Ikastola has the best *bokatas* in the city, and all the locals know it. Every night, a young, hip crowd of would-be Picassos and Verdaguers overflows onto the small backroom terrace, eager to draw on Ikastola's chalkboards, play the upright piano, and eat sandwiches that would make any lunchbox proud. *Bokatas* €4.50, half portion €3. Salads €7. Beer and wine €2.50-5. Cash only. ❶

L'illa de Gràcia, C. St. Domenec, 19 (☎932 38 02 29; www.illadegracia.com). ⓂFontana or Diagonal. Take C. Gran de Gràcia and turn on C. St. Domenec; the restaurant is 2 blocks down on the left. This spacious and brightly lit vegetarian restaurant has a long menu that will prove a relief to those who tire of persuading tapas-bar owners that ham isn't a vegetable. Salads €4.60-5.70. Crepes (sweet and savory) €4-6. Ice cream

FOOD

ON THE MENU

BEFORE BITING INTO BARCELONA...

Barcelona is as proud of its unique cuisine as it is of its language. Here are a few classic Catalan dishes that you'll probably encounter on your journey. When you're finished salivating over the descriptions, head to Gràcia for the real thing.

Calçots et salbitxada: This messy specialty, often served as tapas, features *calçots*, leek-shaped, double-planted onions native to the region. The outside is barbecued black, which turns the caramel inside sweet. They come with a sauce made with almonds, red peppers, garlic, and olive oil. To eat a calçotada, rip away the outer layer, dip it in sauce, and send it down the hatch. (Don't worry if you think this sounds complicated. If you get it wrong—and you certainly will—the locals will show you how it is done.)

Pa amb tomàquet: Literally translated as "bread and tomato," it's just that. Especially in the summer, when the tomatoes are in season, this simple but delectable treat makes a great tapas or mid-afternoon snack.

Escalivada: Traditionally the delight of shepherds returning from the mountains, this vegetable medley presents the bounty of lush Catalunya with grilled eggplants, red peppers, tomatoes, and onions.

Botifarra amb mongetes: This hearty combination of homemade pork sausages (often spiced

€3-4. Open M-Th 1-4pm and 9pm-midnight, F-Sa and Su 2-4pm and 9pm-midnight. MC/V. ❶

Sol y Lluna, C. Verdi, 50, (☎932 37 10 52). ⓂFontana. Walk up C. d'Asturies, make a right on Torrent de l'Olla, a left onto C. L'Or, and another left onto C. Verdi; Sol y Lluna is on the right. Locals rave about this understated gourmet restaurant, which has a marble bar, wooden tables, and a giant hippopotamus statue. The menu includes large salads such as the *Perigord* (*foie gras*, duck, and caramelized apples; €8.30) and crepes (chocolate and banana, €3.80; Grand Marnier, €4.10). Open M-Th and Su 8-11:30pm, F and Sa 1-3:30pm and 8pm-12:30am. MC/V. ❷

La Gavina, C. Ros de Olano, 17 (☎934 15 74 50). ⓂFontana, L3. Walk down C. Gran de Gràcia and turn left on C. Ros de Olano. Enjoy delicious Italian food in this no-frills pizzeria, complete with a life-size patron saint and confessional candles. Try the *Catalana* (tomato, mozzarella, chorizo sausage, garlic, and artichokes; €16). Gigantic pizzas €8-16. Open Tu 8pm-1am, W-Th and Su 1:30pm-1am, F and Sa 1:20pm-2am. Cash only. ❸

Cantina Machito, C. Torrijos, 47 (☎932 17 34 14). ⓂFontana, L3. Take C. d'Asturies until you hit C. Torrijos and make a right. Mexican food is rare in Spain, but this cantina with colorful walls, straw-covered seats, and a few sombreros serves affordable and surprisingly authentic tacos, mole, guac, and margaritas. Well-known for its Cinco de Mayo celebration. Entrees €7.50-14. Open daily 1-5pm and 7pm-1am. MC/V. ❸

Laila, C. d'Asturies, 17 (☎934 15 52 70). ⓂFontana. Walk down C. d'Asturies. This Lebanese pizzeria's hip, red-and-black graphic decor and long, cushioned benches make you want to sit down and stay awhile. At any time of day, a young crowd lounges, eating gourmet pizzas (€7-11), drinking coffee, and socializing. Open daily 10am-midnight. Cash only. ❸

Niu Toc, Pl. Revolució de Setembre, 3 (☎932 13 74 61). ⓂFontana. This restaurant, popular for business lunches and also with young people, serves a €10 *menù* of Catalan cuisine, day and night. Try the specialty—cod—or steak, or paella. The dinner menu is an especially good deal thanks to this restaurant's location on a plaça that is at the heart of Gràcia's young nightlife scene. Entrees €8-16. Open M-Th 1pm-midnight, F-Sa 1pm-1am. MC/V. ❷

Diamant, C. Asturies, 67 (☎932 17 02 18). ⓂFontana. Walk down C. d'Asturies. This popular cafe and restaurant has cow-print coffee cups and a student-friendly atmosphere. Come in the morning for *café con leche* or at night to chew the cud with your friends. Sandwiches €3-5. Open daily 9am-3am. MC/V. ❶

Sushi Itto, C. Londres, 103 (☎932 41 21 99; www.sushi-itto.es). A classy sushi place fusing Japanese cuisine with Western flavors in eclectic rolls. Nigiri €2.20-4.40. Entrees €7-19. 8-piece rolls €14. Delivery €2. Open M-Su 7:30-11:30pm. MC/V. ❸

Ugarit, C. Verdi, 11 (☎932 17 86 22; www.ugarit.es). ⓂFontana. Walk down C. de Asturies to C. Verdi and make a right; the restaurant is on the right. Tired of *jamón* and *croquetas* and looking for a change of pace? This Syrian restaurant, named after an ancient city, offers *tabbuleh* salads (€8), *couscous* (€13) and more. Dishes €3.90-13. Open daily 1pm-1am. MC/V. ❷

La Llar de Foc, C. Ramon i Caja, 13 (☎932 84 10 25). ⓂFontana. Walk down C. Gran de Gràcia to C. Montseny and make a left. This street turns into Ramón i Caja; the restaurant is on the left. Farm equipment on the walls and red-checkered tablecloths make this just the place to eat down-home, traditional dishes like *escalavida* (grilled vegetabels) and *butifarra* (white sausage). Colorful chalkboard menus outside the restaurant advertise a wide selection of *carnes a la brasa*. Entrees €5.10-14. Open 1-4pm and 8:30pm-midnight. MC/V. ❷

Garda, C. Verdi, 15 (☎934 15 30 57). ⓂFontana. Walk down C. de Asturies to C. Verdi and make a right; the restaurant is on the right. This romantic restaurant channels the decor and dishes of Provence in a uniquely Spanish way. Sip your wine at the bar or recline in a wicker chair and linger over a lamplit plate of camembert with small *chorizos* (€6.90). Entrees €6-15. Open daily 8:30pm-midnight. MC/V. ❸

NUT, C. Verdi, 2 (☎932 10 86 40), at Pl. Revolució de Setembre 1868. ⓂFontana, L3. This stone-walled restaurant could well be in the center of a pyramid: statues of pharaohs and a precariously hanging mummies watch over you as you eat tasty Egyptian fare. Try some hummus (€6), the *ganog* (eggplant with vegetables and lemon; €6), or the *kuchari* (rice with lentils and spices; €7.90). Dinner *menú* €9.90. Open daily 1-4pm and 8am-1am. MC/V. ❷

Cafe Adonis 1940, Bailen 188 (☎934 59 12 92). ⓂDiagonal. Walk down C. de Corsega until you hit C. Bailen; Cafe Adonis 1940 is on the corner. This new restaurant-bar (opened in 2009) has industrial accents, like a rusted chandelier and bottle-lined shelves. Locals appreciate Adonis's tapas (*patates braves;* €2.50) and entrees (hamburgers; €7.50) at dinnertime. Wi-Fi available. Beer $1.90; mixed drinks €5.50. Open M-W 9am-1am, Th 9am-1:30am, F and Sa 9am-2:30am. MC/V. ❷

Origens, C. Ramón y Cajal, 12 (☎932 13 60 31; www.lallavordelsorigens.com). ⓂFontana. Near the Pl. of the Revolució de Setembre 1868. The "Llavor dels Origins" (this location is one of the mini-chain's 4 restaurants)

with cinnamon) and long white beans is consumed in enormous quantities by natives and tourists alike. Let's Go asks that you keep the children's rhyme in mind and consume pork and beans responsibly.

Escudella: This official Catalan dish includes everything you could ever want: pasta, rice, chicken, beans, carrots, and onions. All stew together to make a hearty winter soup, typically served at Christmas dinner.

Esqueixada: *Bacalao* (salted cod) is a staple of Catalan cuisine, used in all sorts of preparations. *Esquiexada* is perhaps the most typical, featuring the preserved fish in a fresh salad with tomatoes, sweet onions, red peppers, and black olives. For a twist that is sure to delight, head to one of Barcelona's four Taller de Tapas.

Panellets: These little balls of almond-y joy are baked to celebrate All Saints Day (Nov. 1). However, the flourless almond confections—sometimes topped with cocoa powder or candied fruit—can be found in bakeries year round.

Crema Catalana: Forget about Crème Brûlée—that French pudding can't hold a blow torch to Crema Catalana. Though the origins of this burnt cream dish are a matter of ongoing dispute, Crema Catalana distinguishes itself from its French cousin with cinnamon and citrus zest.

was, according to its menu, "born in 2000 with the intention of introducing to consumers quality Catalan cuisine and to spread the cultural and gastronomic values of Catalonia." In keeping with this goal, the chic restaurant displays the work of regional photographers and serves up *anxoves* (anchovies; €4.28), *amanida de llenties amb pop* (salad with lentils and octopus; €5.90) and dishes for the less adventurous eater, like *coca de tomaquet* (tomato bruschetta; €5) and *arros amb llet* (rice pudding; €5). Leaving the restaurant, stop in the small front shop and buy the local wines, cheeses, and preserves. Dishes €2-8. Open daily 1:30-5pm and 8pm-1am. MC/V. ❷

al. C. Encarnacio, 56 (☎932 19 82 13; www.alpunt.net). ⓂJoanic, L4. Follow C. Escorial for 2 blocks and turn left on C. Encarnació. Bring your dictionary to this restaurant; all the menus are in Catalan. The venue boasts local art for sale, white paper lanterns, and trendy patrons. Extensive wine list. Lunch entrees €11. Dinner entrees €7.90-€16. Desserts €6.20. Open for lunch Tu-F 1-3:30pm, Sa and Su 1-4pm. Open for dinner Tu-Th 8:30-11:30pm, F and Sa 8:30-midnight. AmEx/MC/V. ❸

Agappe, C. Riera de Sant Miquel, 19 (☎932 37 86 01; www.restauranteagappe.com). ⓂDiagonal. Gray walls, white ceilings, a stainless-steel counter, and enigmatic photographs of an empty burka floating in the desert give this restaurant a sophisticated and ethereal feel. Healthy fusion cuisine includes tuna carpaccio and curried chicken. Lunch entrees €12. Dinner entrees €25. Wheelchair-accessible. Open for lunch M-Su 1:30-4:30pm, for dinner W-Sa 6:30-midnight. AmEx/MC/V. ❸

Punda Maria S.L., between C. Benet Mercade and C. Cristobal Berga. ⓂFontana. Walk downhill down C. Gran de Gràcia and make a right on C. Cigne; Punda Maria S.L. is at the end of Pl. Libertat, on the right. Would-be Rockys (Sylvester Stallone, not the raccoon), this is your mecca: the tiny shop has sold eggs and only eggs for over 100 years. Both chicken eggs and quail eggs are delivered fresh every M. The many teeming baskets of fresh eggs in the shop are eminently photographable. Small eggs €2; medium €2.10; large €2.50 per dozen. ❶

VALL D'HEBRON AND HORTA-GUINARDÓ

In this neighborhood that's mostly residential and proud of it, restaurants are few and far between, but generally worth the trek. For groceries, visit the large **Mercadona** (www.mercadona.es; MC/V) at the intersection of **Calle de Petrarca** and **Calle Duero. Calle de Petrarca** is just down **Passeig de Maragall** from ⓂHorta or just up **Passeig de Fabra i Puig** from ⓂVilapicina.

▨ **El Casinet 1903,** Pl. Santa Eulalia. ⓂVirrei Amat. Walk down Pg. de Fabra i Puig and make a left onto C. d'Amilcar. The plaça will be just off this street, on the right. If you happen to be in the neighborhood, join the locals who pack into El Casinet for its out-of-this-world lunch *menú* (€8.90). Not fancy, but serves immensely satisfying, ample portions of home-cooked dishes like *bacalao* and fried chicken. And you can smoke! Open M-F 1-4pm. Cash only. ❷

A Tavola!, Pl. d'Eivissa. (☎933 57 62 24) ⓂHorta. Walk up C. de Fulton to Pl. d'Eivissa. Cheerful trattoria and pizzeria. If you're still hungry for Italian after dinner (which you shouldn't be), head to the gelateria across the plaça. Caprese €6. Pizzas €8-12. Open daily noon-5pm and 8:30-11:30pm. MC/V. ❷

La Panera, C. d'Horta, 69. ⓂHorta. Walk up C. de Fulton, which turns into C. d'Horta. Pass the branch near to the Metro stop and walk up the street to the less-crowded locale. Part bakery, part cafe, and part restaurant, La Panera is perfect for either a quick snack or a lengthy meal. The back room has cute mismatched tables and chairs. Lunch *menú* €9. Sandwiches €2-4. Open M-Sa 6am-9pm, Su 8am-9pm. MC/V. ❷

Can Cortada, Av. de l'Estatut de Catalunya (☎934 27 23 15; www.gruptravi.com). ⓂMundet, L3. Visible from Pg. de Vall d'Hebron. This impressive 11th-century building,

FOOD

originally a feudal defense tower, was converted into a farmhouse in the 15th century. You can still see the old underground dungeon tunnels and the **L**horse-feeding corner. Feast on hearty Catalan staples like the *filete a la piedra*—meat cooked on a hot stone tableside. The beautiful, flower-filled grounds are a pleasant break from the hot and dusty streets nearby. Be brave and try the frogs' legs (€8.40). Entrees around €10. 3-course meal €18-27. Wheelchair-accessible. Open daily 1-4:45pm and 8pm-1:30am. Reservations recommended. AmEx/MC/V. ❸

Can Travi Nou, C. Jorge Manrique (☎934 28 03 01; www.gruptravi.com). Ⓜ Mundet, L3. Exit Mundet to the left and turn right onto Pg. de Vall d'Hebron. Take a right at C. Jorge Manrique; it's at the end of the street. Nestled in the shade, Can Travi Nou is housed in a 17th-century farmhouse. Outside, several shaded terraces overflow with bougainvillea, and inside, baskets of fresh produce give the large dining rooms a classic feel. Woody Allen set one of the restaurant scenes in *Vicky Cristina Barcelona* here. Try the pig's feet with almonds (€27) or 1 of 4 types of *bacalao* (€22). 3-course meal €24-30. Wheelchair-accessible. Open M-Sa 1:30-4pm and 8:30-11pm, Su 1:30-4pm. Reservations recommended. AmEx/MC/V. ❺

All i Oli, C. Alella, 3 (☎934 08 35 42; www.allioli.com). Ⓜ Fabra i Puig. Walk up C. Fabra i Puig and make a right onto C. de Velia. Make another quick right ono C. Alella. Overlook this restaurant's cheesy decor and focus on its delicious food. Amid faux-stalactites and plastic statues, All i Oli serves up tasty Catalan dishes such as *chuelton de buey* (steak; €23) and *caracoles "llauna"* (snails; €14). All dishes come with *all i oli*—the most delicious of mayonaise-based sauces. Open M and W-Su 1-5pm, 8pm-midnight. AmEx/MC/V. ❹

SARRIÀ

There is one main reason to go to Sarrià to eat: Bar Tomás. The *patatas bravas* mecca of Barcelona and of the world, the venue is well worth the somewhat tiresome trip out. There's no Metro here; you'll have to catch an FCG train or a cab. If you're hungry for something more than *bravas*, or searching for a quick dinner before going out, head to **Calle Santalo** or **Calle Marià Cubí.** These streets have a number of excellent and affordable restaurants.

▨ **Bar Tomás,** C. Major de Sarrià, 47 (☎932 03 10 77). FGC: Sarrià. From the FCG stop, take C. l'Hort de la Vila to C. Major de Sarrià. This unassuming bar serves legendary and possibly life-changing *patatas bravas*. They're spicy, they're salty, and Barceloneses know that you can't eat just one (plateful, that is). Still unconvinced? Ben & Jerry's ran a billboard ad campaign in Barcelona in summer 2009 that read: "Delicious like the 'bravas' of Tomás." *Patatas bravas* €2.40. Take-away €3.90-€5. Open daily noon-4pm and 6-10pm. Cash only. ❶

La Burg, Paseo San Juan Bosco, 55 (☎932 05 63 48; www.laburg.com). FGC: Sarrià. La Burg brings the trendy notion of gourmet hamburger to Barcelona—at decidedly non-gourmet prices. Order 1 of 10 types of hamburger. Veggie burgers available. Burgers come with french fries, *patatas bravas,* or a salad. Burgers €7-9. Open daily 1-4pm and 8-11pm. MC/V. ❷

Can Puyentes, C. Marià Cubí, 189 (☎932 00 91 59). FGC: Gracià. Walk 10min. down C. Marià Cubí; the restaurant is on your left. This popular restaurant has made humility its specialty. Wholly unpretentious, it serves up delicious traditional Catalan dishes in a warmly lit room. Choose from a number of traditional vegetable dishes (like artichokes) and *tostadas,* or try the *botifarra catalana* (Catalan sausage). Entrees €5-12. Open daily 1-4pm and 9pm-midnight. MC/V. ❷

Casa Lizarriturry BCN, C. Castellnou, 37. (☎932 05 30 33; www.lizarriturry.com) FGC: Sarrià. This family-run, open-air corner restaurant is absolutely charming. Sit at 1 of its tables, admire fresh flowers and homemade dessert options, and eat gourmet dishes. Lunch *menú*

FOOD

(€13) includes entrees such as gazpacho, bacalao-and-tomato salad, and lasagna. Entrees €10-20. Open Tu-F 1-4pm and 9pm-midnight, Sa 9pm-midnight. MC/V. ❸

Pizza Via, C. de Francesc Carbonell and C. de Mateu Benet. Ⓜ️Maria Christina. Walk up C. del Capita Arenas to C. de Francesc Carbonell; make a right and walk 1 block down. This casual pizzeria has patio seating, just the place to refuel for cheap. Lunch *menú* €9. Pizzas €6-9. Open M-Sa 1-4pm and 8pm-midnight. Cash only. ❷

Santalo 103, C. Santalo, 103. (☎932 01 97 95) FGC: Mutaner. Hanging lights, flowered wallpaper, and modern chairs make this restaurant-bar both romantic and chic. Serves Mediterranean dishes such as salad with goat cheese, nuts, and honey vinaigrette. Entrees €12-20. Open Tu-Sa 1-3:45pm, M-Sa 8:30-11:30pm. MC/V. ❸

Restaurante Orange, C. Rosari, 52. (☎934 18 10 85) FGC: Tres Torres. Walk down V. de Augusta. This restaurant occupies a beautiful residential house on the fringe of one of Sarrià's mansion-filled neighborhoods. Its dark wooden interior is decidedly formal. The menu is gourmet; serves Italian pasta and Argentinian meat. Try the duck *confit* with bacon and a cabernet reduction (€13). Lunch *menú* €8.90. Entrees €8-18. M-Sa 1-4:30pm and 9pm-midnight. AmEx/MC/V. ❸

Justin Sushi Bar, C. Tuset, 28. (☎934 15 70 32) FGC: Gracià. Cafe by day, sushi bar by evening, and bar by night. Roll with smoked salmon and mango cream cheese €9. Entrees €9-25. Open M-Sa 1-4pm and 9pm-2am. MC/V. ❹

No Me Quite Pa, C. Marià Cubí, 189. (☎934 14 03 76) FGC: Muntaner. Walk down C. Muntaner to C. Marià Cubí and make a right; the restaurant is on your right. Funky green walls and an eclectic mix of dishes. Try the hamburger sampler (€9.20), the chicken with lime and ginger (€6.90), or the grilled monkfish with vegetables (€19). Open M-Sa 1-4:30pm and 8:30pm-midnight, Th-Sa until 1am. MC/V. ❸

Restaurante Japones J8, C. Marià Cubí, 179. (☎934 14 73 26) FGC: Muntaner. Walk down C. Muntaner to C. Marià Cubí and make a left; the restaurant is on your right. A well-lit dining room with light wood tables. Offers both in-house dining and take-away. Lunch *menú* €7.80. Dinner *menús* (€13-20) include miso soup, salad, gyoza, sushi, and more. Fill up on sushi (€4.50-14) or order one of the other specialties, such as a hot-wok of chicken with teriyaki sauce (€5.80). Open daily 1-4pm and 8pm-midnight. MC/V. ❸

PEDRALBES AND LES CORTS

There are several good restaurants in Les Corts. Some are grouped near the metro stop around Pl. de la Concordia; others are further away, but merit the short walk. Although the small bars and cafes near Camp Nou feed hordes of soccer fans on game days, the stadium area is not known for its cuisine, and you're likely to end up paying tourist prices for mediocre food. If you're planning on seeing a game, it might be wise to pack a lunch, or to hold out and head back downtown to eat afterwards.

Fragments Cafe, Pl. de la Concordia, 12 (☎934 19 96 13; www.fragmentscafe.com). Ⓜ️: Les Corts. Walk up C. de Galileu and make a right on C. de Deu i Mata. C. Deu i Mata runs into the plaça. This restaurant has something for everyone--tables in Les Corts' most happening plaça, a trellised terrace out back, a stand-up tapas bar, and a candlelit dining room--all tucked into one, green-shuttered place. Try the white beans with *jamón* and mint (€4.50). Lunch menu €12. Entrees €4-14. Reservations often necessary on weekends. Open Tu-Su 1-4pm and 9pm-midnight. MC/V.❶

El Cargolet Picant, Riera Blanca, 7 (☎933 34 04 54; www.elcargoletpicant.blogspot. com), at the corner of Trav. de Les Corts and C. Aristides Maillol. Ⓜ️Collblanc, L5. Busy even on non-game days, "The Spicy Snail" specializes in, of course, 7 snail dishes (about

€6 each). Less adventurous visitors can choose from a number of delicious tapas on display at the bar (€2-9 per plate). Open daily 7am-1:30am. Cash only. ❷

In Blue, Trav. de les Corts, 300 (☎934 19 11 30). Ⓜ: Les Corts. Walk up Trav. de les Corts. This bar/restaurant has local artists' work on the walls and serves up tasty, home-cooked Catalan dishes like *butifarra* and cod. A convenient place to re-fuel. Lunch menu €9.50. Open M-Sa 1-4pm, 8-11:30pm. MC/V. ❷

L'Arrosseria Xativa, C. Bordeus, 35 (☎933 22 65 31; www.arrosseriaxativa.com). Ⓜ: Les Corts. Walk 10min. up the Trav. de les Corts and make a right on C. Bordeus. This rustic restaurant serves up *paella* and *fideua* the old-fashioned way; you eat out of the pan with a wooden spoon. Simple white walls and fresh flowers on the table make you feel right at home. Try the fava beans with clams (€15.50) or the lobster paella (€24.50). Entrees €13-26. Open M-Th 1-4pm and 8:30pm-midnight, F-Sa 1-4:30pm and 8:30pm-midnight. MC/V.4. ❸

La Tertulia, C. Morales, 15 (☎934 19 58 97; www.arrosseriaxativa.com). Ⓜ: Les Corts. Walk 10min. up the Trav. de les Corts and make a right on C. Morales. This restaurant, which is hidden on a residential street, is a destination in and of itself. The pleasantly rustic venue has exposed brick walls adorned with modern artwork, terra-cotta tile floors, and a dark wood bar. Decidedly fancy, this is not a budget choice, but you will get what you pay for. Try the prawn carpaccio with dill and ginger vinaigrette, or a traditional *fideua* with shrimp and clams. Lunch menu €19.50. Dinner entrees €15-30. M-Sa 1-4pm and 8:30pm-midnight. MC/V. ❸

SANT ANDREU

El Desván Azul, C. Malats, 8 (☎933 12 02 88). ⓂSant Andreu. "The Blue Loft" offers an airy environment and upscale cuisine. Excellent pasta dishes (€8-10) such as tortellini with spinach, Roquefort, and walnuts. Meat and fish entrees €9-17. Weekday lunch *menú* €9.60. Open M 1-4pm, Tu-Th 1-4pm and 9-10:30pm, F 1-4pm and 9-11pm, Sa 9-11pm. MC/V. ❸

Indians, C. de Campo Florida, 52 (☎933 52 72 62). ⓂCongrès. Walk down C. Francesc Tárraga and take a left on C. de Campo Florida. This local favorite serves *pizza de créppes* (€8.30), which substitutes pizza dough with a light egg batter. Patrons often linger after a meal for drinks at the terrace upstairs. Why the name? No one knows. Open M-Sa 8:30pm-12:30am. MC/V. ❸

La Brotxeta, C. August i Milà. (☎933 11 57 13; www.labrotxeta.com). ⓂSant Andreu. Walk up Pg. Torras i Bages, go left on C. de Joan Torras, and continue as it leads onto C. August i Milà. The specialty here is *brotxeta* (€6-12)—grilled meat, poultry, or seafood skewered and hung from a hook, then served with potatoes and aioli. The setting feels cozy and old-fashioned and the service is good. Open M-Th and Su 9am-midnight, F-Sa 10am-2am. Cash only. ❷

El Burro Chilango, C. Cinca, 86 (☎933 45 80 08). ⓂTorres i Bages. The lime green tables make this restaurant feel like a piñata. Mexican standards include fajitas (€11), tacos (€9-10), and burritos (€9.50). Open Tu-Su 1-3:30pm and 8-11:30pm. MC/V. ❷

Tasca i Vins, C. del Cardenal Tedeschini, 32 (☎934 08 27 39). ⓂSagrera or Congrès. From Sagrera, walk up Av. Meridiana and turn left on C. del Cardenal Tedeschini. Other locations at C. Industria, 118 (☎934 35 50 52) and C. Diputació, 304 (☎933 42 53 28). It's big, it's cheap, it's a 4-location chain: embrace it. Paella, sangria, *bocadillos*—this place has anything you could possibly want at unbeatable prices, served around a pretty terrace with a fountain in the center. Breakfast deals (half-sandwich, OJ and coffee; €2.40). 6 *menús* €6.80-14. *Montaditos* €1. Paella €8.50. Sangria pitcher €7. Open M-F 8am-midnight, Sa 1:30pm-midnight, Su 1:30-10:30pm. MC/V. ❷

Rhino's, Pg. Fabra i Puig, 68. (☎933 45 72 67; www.cerveceriarhinos.es). ⓂFabra i Puig. The over-the-top safari theme, complete with life-size model rhinoceros, makes this a fun and kitschy place to enjoy tapas (€3-6) and *bocadillos* (€3-5). Open M-Th and Su 9am-midnight, F-Sa 10am-2am. Cash only. ❶

Barchelona Pg. Fabra i Puig, 32 (☎933 11 26 25). ⓂFabra i Puig. Colorful *cervecería* festooned with paintings of the sea-dwelling creatures being cooked and seasoned for your dining pleasure. Combination plates (€6-12.50) feature Catalan staples like *sepia* and *botifarra. Torrades* €6-13. MC/V. ❷

NOU BARRIS

La Esquinica, Pg. Fabra i Puig, 296. (☎933 58 25 19). ⓂVilapicina or Virrei Amat. Locals flood this traditional tapas restaurant, where their favorite dishes are executed to perfection. The atmosphere can be hectic, but the restaurant maintains a subtle charm with quaint details like the antique keys on the walls. One key opens the safe in the back, in which Eusebi Güell hid his gold before his death. Just kidding. Tapas €1.70-6. Open daily 8:30am-midnight. Cash only. ❷

Conde Dracula, Via Júlia, 68-70 (☎933 50 82 89). ⓂVia Júlia. This vampire-themed *cervecería* is adorned from wall to wall with bats, counts, and spooky paintings (but no mirrors). Tapas (€2.60-5.80) and *torradas* (€4.10-5.50) are the main offerings. Watch your jugular. Open M-Th and Su 9am-1am, F-Sa 9am-2am. Cash only. ❷

Taberna Txapeldun, Pg. Fabra i Puig, 159. (☎933 52 91 01; www.tabernatxapeldun.com). ⓂFabra i Puig or Virrei Amat. Classy tapas restaurant with small culinary concoctions made from fun ingredients, including artichokes, mussels, and tripe. *Montaditos* €1.30-5. Tapas €4-7.90. Grilled fish and meat entrees €8.80-15. Midday *menú* €10. Open M-Th and Su 1-4pm and 7-11pm, F-Sa 1-4pm and 7pm-midnight. Closed Aug. MC/V. ❸

Fragola, C. Lorena, 97 (☎933 59 28 54). ⓂLlucmajor. Quintessential pizzeria, complete with booths, thin crusts, and eccentric matriarch. Small pizzas (€4.20-6.30) with plenty of toppings to choose from. If you're really hungry, try the *pizza da tutto*, piled high with ham, mushrooms, artichoke hearts, tuna and salami. Ice cream €1.30-2.40. Open M and W-Su noon-2am. MC/V. ❷

The New Orleans, Pere d'Artès, 10 (☎933 57 79 57). ⓂVirrei Amat. Just off Pg. Fabra i Puig. One of the best joints around for a coffee (€1-3) to perk up in the morning or a fruity iced tea (€2.40) to cool off in the afternoon. Pastries €1-2. *Bocadillos* €2.30-3.30. Small pizzas €5.20. Open M-Th and Su 7am-midnight, F-Sa 7am-2am. Cash only. ❶

SANTS

Historically an industrial district, Sants boast a surprising number of high-quality restaurants, many of which serve international cuisine. The area around **Plaça Osca**, a block up C. de Riego from C. de Sants, is a good place to explore. Restaurants also line **Passeig de Sant Antoni** and nearby side-streets. For meat, fish, produce, and other groceries try the **Mercat Hostafrancs,** C. Creu Coberta, 93 (☎93 431 86 06; open M-Th 7am-2pm and 5:30-8pm, F 7am-2pm, Sa 7am-3pm).

▧ Blau, C. Tenor Masini, 61 (☎933 30 01 12). ⓂPl. de Sants. Sleek, modern black and white dining area, with delicious food for surprisingly low prices. Treat yourself to the steak medallions with honey and mustard reduction (€9) or pigs' feet stuffed with goat cheese, peppers, and onions (€7). Entrees €6.50-13. Open Tu-Sa 1-4pm and 9pm-midnight, Su 1-4pm. MC/V. ❷

El Setè Cel, C. Riego, 18 (☎934 210 532). Ⓜ Pl. de Sants. Sultry interior with sharp lines and warm colors, nice for a drink or a meal. Antipasto with meats or cheeses €6-17. Entrees €5.50-9.50. Open Tu-W 7pm-1am, Th 7-2am, F-Sa 7-3am. MC/V. ❷

La Paradeta, C. Riego, 27 (☎934 31 90 59; www.laparadeta.com). Ⓜ Pl. de Sants. Other locations at C. Comercial, 7 (☎932 68 19 39) Ⓜ Arc de Triomf; Pg. Simó, 18 (☎934 50 01 91) Ⓜ Sagrada Família; and C. Pacífico, 74 (☎935 34 65 57) Ⓜ Fabra i Puig. Popular self-service restaurant where you order fresh seafood market-style (by weight or unit), which is then prepared simply with oil and garlic. Cooking time is quick, but you may have to wait in line to get your order in; the place is consistently packed and no reservations are accepted. Full meals around €20. Cash only. ❹

Fo Bar, Pl. Osca, 12 (☎691 55 63 29; www.fo-bar.com). Ⓜ Pl. de Sants. Funky blue-green interior doubles as a bar and restaurant for a young crowd. Tasty salads (€4.70-7.10) like escarole with cod, artichoke, anchovies, and olives. Mixed drinks €6. Open Tu-Th and Su 10am-midnight, F-Sa 10am-2am. Kitchen open 10am-11pm. Cash only. ❷

La Parra, C. Joanot Martorall, 3 (☎933 32 51 34), in a steep alley right of C. Sants, 2 blocks from Ⓜ Hostafrancs, L1. Irresistible aromas emanate from the wood terrace, luring passersby to enjoy classic Mediterranean fare in this quaint restaurant. Entrees €9-13. Open Tu-F 8:30pm-midnight, Sa-Su noon-4pm. MC/V. ❷

Tarántula, C. Valladolid, 40 (☎934 11 27 28; www.latarantula.com), Ⓜ Estació Sants. From the station, go down Pg. Sant Antoni, take a right on C. de Santa Catalina, and the 1st left onto C. Valladolid. Warm, friendly restaurant dishes out huge portions of Mexican food. Specialties include the bountiful cactus salad (€9) and a selection of spicy enchiladas. Entrees €9-15. Open M-Th 8pm-1am, F-Sa 8pm-2am. MC/V. ❸

Dhamma, C. Papin, 8 (☎934 911 18 13). Ⓜ Pl. de Sants. Warm, informal dining room with a lunch buffet built around holistic vegetarian cuisine. Shiatsu massage offered upstairs. Call ahead to find out about themed dinners. Buffet M-Sa 1-4pm. MC/V. ❶

Simbad, Pg. Sant Antoni, 15 (☎933 30 23 62). Ⓜ Pl. de Sants, L1/5. Palestinian restaurant with outdoor seating along the *passeig*. Middle-eastern classics like *fattoush* and *kofta*, along with the old stand-bys falafel and shawarma. Combination plates €9-11. Take-away falafel and shwarma €3.50. Open daily noon-midnight. Cash only. ❷

SIGHTS

Barcelona has always been on the cutting edge of the art world. Visitors cross continents not only to see the paintings hanging in fantastic museums, but also to admire imaginative modern architecture and parks designed by world-renowned visionaries. The streets are the galleries for Barcelona's artistic spirit; intricate lampposts and murals light up even the most drab neighborhoods. You'll find the classics—Picasso, Miró, Mir, etc.—but also modern shows at museums like the Tàpies. Concentrated in l'Eixample, the *Modernista* treasures draw architecture aficionados from the far reaches of the world. Parc Güell and Parc Diagonal Mar allow for contemplation surrounded by innovative designs and sculptures. Sprinkled throughout the entire city lie plaças, tree-lined avenues, and corner parks, each with their own character to explore and discover.

RUTA DEL MODERNISME

For those with a few days in the city and an interest in seeing some of the most popular sights, the **Ruta del Modernisme** is the cheapest and most flexible option. The pass provides discounted admission to dozens of *Modernista* buildings in the city, and comes with the purchase of a guidebook (€12); additional adult passes are €5, though an adult accompanying someone under 18 is free. Passes provide a 25-30% discount on the Palau de la Música Catalana, Fundació Antoni Tàpies, the Museu de Zoología, tours of l'Hospital de la Santa Creu i Sant Pau and the facades of La Manzana de la Discordia (Amatller, Lleó i Morera, and Batlló), and map tours of Gaudí, Domènech i Montaner, and Puig i Cadafalch buildings, among other attractions. The pass comes with a map and a pamphlet giving the history of different sights, which is helpful for prioritizing visits. Purchase passes at the Pl. Catalunya tourist office, the Modernisme Centre at **Hospital Santa Creu i Sant Pau,** C. Sant Antoni Maria Claret, 167, or **Pavellons Güell,** Av. de Pedralbes, 7. Centralized info can be found at ☎902 07 66 21, 933 17 76 52, and www.rutadelmodernisme.com. Many sights have tour times and length restrictions; visiting all of them on the same day is virtually impossible.

BARCELONA CARD

Another discount option is the **Barcelona Card.** The card is good for 2-5 days and includes free public transportation (on the Metro, daytime buses, and trains to the airport) and nearly 80 discounts (and sometimes free admission) at museums, cultural venues, theaters, and a few bars and clubs, shops, and restaurants. They are sold at tourist offices, Casa Batlló, El Corte Inglés, the Aquarium, and Poble Espanyol. Prices for 2-5 days range €24-36 for adults and €20-31 for ages 4-12. For students (usually with ISIC card; ISOS accepted less often), it may be cheaper to use student discounts to get into attractions.

BUS TURÍSTIC

Sit back and let the sights come to you. The Bus Turístic stops at 44 points of interest along three different routes (red for the north, blue for the south, and green for the eastern waterfront). Tickets come with an eight-language brochure with information on each sight. A full ride on the red or blue route takes about 2hr., green takes 40min., but the idea is to get off at any place of interest and use the bus (as many times as you want in your allotted days) as a convenient means of transportation. Multilingual guides stationed in every bus help orient travelers and answer questions. You can buy tickets once on board, or ahead of time at **Turisme de Catalunya,** Pl. de Catalunya, 17, in front of El Corte Inglés, and at www.barcelonaturisme.com. Many of the museums and sights covered by the bus offer discounts with the bus ticket; some are closed on Mondays. (Buses run daily every 5-25min. First departure 9-9:30am; no service Dec. 25 and Jan. 1. 1-day pass €20, ages 4-12 €12; 2-day pass €26.)

CIUTAT VELLA

Brimming with cathedrals, palaces, and unabashed tourist traps, Barcelona's oldest neighborhood masks its age with round-the-clock energy. The heart of the Barri Gòtic took shape during Roman times and continued to develop during the medieval period as new ruling powers built over old structures and roads. Today it is the political and historical center of the city, with a split personality that is by turns quaint and overwhelming. Catalan commercialism persists in all its glory with store-lined streets and fine restaurants, but the soul of the neighborhood lies deeper than these attractions, down its tiny, twisting alleyways.

BARRI GÒTIC

The Barri Gòtic is the oldest part of Barcelona; it came into being well before the grid layout in the rest of the city. The Barri Gòtic was settled during Roman times and continued to develop during the Romanesque and Gothic periods. Be sure to set a day aside to wander around the Barri Gòtic and explore the layers of history that have accumulated here.

ESGLÉSIA CATEDRAL DE LA SANTA CREU I SANTA EULÀLIA (THE CATHEDRAL OF THE HOLY CROSS AND SAINT EULALIA). Three separate buildings have existed on this site: an AD fourth-century basilica, an 11th-century Romanesque church, and finally the present Gothic Cathedral, begun in 1298. The much-photographed facade comes from yet another era (1882), when it was added to the main structure by architect Josep Mestres. Mestres worked from a plan drawn up by Frenchman Carles Galtés de Ruán in 1408; this ensured a genuinely Gothic appearance.

In the cathedral's **plaça,** seven stylized letters crafted by Joan Brossa spell out "Barcino," commemorating the original Roman city settled on land that is now Barcelona. The Romans first marched through Spain in the third century BC in an effort to subdue North African powers in Carthage. They subjugated the resident Laietani and settled next to Montjuïc in 210 BC. In 15 BC, in honor of Augustus's rule, the Romans gave the small town the unwieldy name of Colonia Julia Augusta Faventia Paterna Barcino.

As you enter the church, the **cathedral choir** is directly in front of you. The backs of the stalls are painted with 46 coats of arms commemorating the Chapter of the Order of the Golden Fleece, an early United Nations of sorts, held in Barcelona in 1519. Behind the choir you'll find the most important liturgical elements of the Cathedral, including the marble *cathedra* (bishop's throne; thus "cathedral"), the altar with the bronze cross designed by Frederic Marès in 1976, and most notably the sunken **crypt** of Santa Eulalia, one of Barcelona's patron saints. Discovered in the Santa Maria del Mar in AD 877, Santa Eulalia's remains were transported here in 1339. The crypt holds a white marble sarcophagus that depicts scenes from the saint's martyrdom at age 13.

Behind the altar, the **Chapel of Sant Joan Baptista i Sant Josep** features one of the most famous pieces of artwork in the Cathedral, the *Transfiguration of the Lord* altarpiece created by Bernat Martorell in 1450. The elevator to the roof is to the left of the altar, through the Capella de les Animes del Purgatori; it will give you a close-up view of the Cathedral's spires, as well as a bird's-eye view of the entire city.

Just to the right of the tomb is the exit into the peaceful ■**cloister,** home to the Fountain of St. Jordi. Thirteen white geese occupy the cloister, serving as a reminder of St. Eulalia's age at the time of her death. The chapels in the cloister were once dedicated to the various guilds of Barcelona, and a few of them are still maintained today (including the shoe-makers' and electricians'). If you look back toward the interior of the Cathedral, you can see the only remaining piece of the Romanesque structure: the large, arched doorway leading back inside. The earlier fourth-century building was almost entirely destroyed by Muslim invaders in 985; what little is left is visible underground in the Museu d'Història de la Ciutat (see p. 141). Coming from the Cathedral, you'll find the Cathedral museum at the near right corner of the cloister. The museum's most notable holding is Bartolomé Bermejo's renowned oil painting *Pietà*, the image of Christ dying in the arms of the Virgin; it's in the Sala Capitular, to the left upon entrance. The museum also holds the famous monstrance (the receptacle used for holding the Host for communion), made of gold and silver and dripping with precious jewels. Legend has it that the monstrance was given to the cathedral by the last Catalan king, Martí, before he died childless in 1410.

The front of the Cathedral is also the place to catch an impromptu performance of the Sardana, the traditional Catalan dance. Performances generally occur Sunday mornings and afternoons after mass. (Ⓜ*Jaume I, L4. In Pl. Seu, up C. Bisbe from Pl. St. Jaume. Cathedral open daily 8:30am-12:30pm, 1-5pm, and 5:15-7:30pm. Museum open daily 10am-12:30pm, 1-5pm, and 5:15-7pm. Elevator to the roof open M-Sa 10am-12:30pm and 1-6pm. Services Su at noon and 6:30pm. From 1-5pm €5 (includes cathedral, elevator, and museum), otherwise free. Museum €2. Elevator €2.50.)*

PLAÇA DE L'ANGEL. Outside Ⓜ Jaume I is the square where the main Roman gate into Barcelona (Barcino in antiquity) was once located. The *plaça* gets its name from the legend surrounding the transfer of St. Eulalia's remains from Santa Maria del Mar to the cathedral: supposedly the martyred saint's body suddenly became too heavy to carry, and an angel appeared in the *plaça* pointing a finger at one of the church officials, who, it turned out, had secretly broken off and stolen one of Eulalia's toes. The angel statue (facing Via Laietania) commemorates the event, pointing with one arm to her own toe and with her other arm to the culprit. (Ⓜ*Jaume I, L4.)*

ROMAN WALLS. Several sections of the northeastern walls of Roman Barcino are still standing near the cathedral. **Carrer Tapineria,** which runs from Pl. de l'Angel (to the left when you are facing Via Laietana) to Pl. Ramon Berenguer, serves both as parking space for mopeds and a viewing area from which you can see a large stretch of an AD fourth-century barricade under the Palau Reial Major. Continuing along C. Tapineria and making a left onto Av. de la Catedral lands you in **Plaça Seu** (in front of the Cathedral), where you can see the only intact octagonal corner tower left today (part of the Museu Diocesà). To the right of the cathedral are several more Roman towers and a reconstruction of one of the two aqueducts that supplied water to Barcino. (Ⓜ*Jaume I, L4.)*

CARRER DEL BISBE. In Roman times, C. del Bisbe served as the city's main north-south thoroughfare. Today it is lined with various official buildings. As you walk from the Cathedral to C. del Bisbe, on the right is the entrance to the medieval **Casa de l'Ardiaca,** once home to the archdeacon and now the location of Barcelona's newspaper archives. Stop and check out the mail slot designed by Domènech i Montaner in 1902, next to a sculpted tortoise with several swallows—according to one popular theory, an expression of his opinion of the postal service (supposedly as quick as a bird but actually as slow as a turtle).

Directly across from the Casa de l'Ardiaca is the **Capella de Santa Llúcia;** it is not well labeled, but you can enter through one of two small metal doors. The chapel was built in 1268 and is one of only a few remaining Romanesque churches in the entire city. Every December 13, the Day of Santa Llúcia, locals pay their respects to the saint, and the Fair of Sant Llúcia begins around the Cathedral.

Once you exit the chapel, make a left onto C. Bisbe. Walking down the street will take you past the **Palau de la Generalitat** on the right and the Casa de los Canónigos on the left, once home to the religious canons and now the office of the Catalan president. The two are connected by an elaborate neo-Gothic bridge built in 1929 as part of the restoration of the Barri Gòtic. (Ⓜ*Jaume I, L4. Make an immediate left when you exit the main door of the Cathedral, before walking out onto the plaça. Walk to the end of C. de Santa Llúcia; it intersects C. del Bisbe.*)

ROMAN TOMBS. Located in the Upper Barri Gòtic, the Plaça de la Vila de Madrid contains one final Roman site worth visiting: a row of AD second- to fourth-century Roman tombs, lined up just as they originally were along a road leading out of Barcino. (Roman law forbade burial within the city walls.) Look for the tombs underneath the walkways over the pits; the recently restored tombs are significantly lower than the rest of the *plaça*, proof of how much the physical terrain of Barcelona has changed over the past 2000 years. (Ⓜ*Liceu or Catalunya, L3. From Ⓜ Liceu, walk up Las Ramblas (away from the port) and turn right onto C. Portaferrissa. Take the first left onto C. d'En Bot; it will lead directly to the Pl. de la Vila de Madrid. From Ⓜ Catalunya, walk down Las Ramblas and turn left onto C. la Canuda. Make sure not to confuse C. la Canuda with C. Santa Anna; C. la Canuda slopes downward. Walk about 30 yards and Pl. de la Vila de Madrid is on the right.*)

PLAÇA DE SANT JAUME. Pl. de Sant Jaume has served as Barcelona's political center since Roman times. Two of Catalunya's most significant buildings have dominated the square since 1823: the Palau de la Generalitat, headquarters of Catalunya's government, and the Ajuntament, or city hall. (*Generalitat open 2nd and 4th Su of the month 10:30am-1:30pm. Closed Aug. Mandatory tours in Catalan, English, and Spanish every 30min. starting at 10:30am. Free. Ajuntament open 2nd and 4th Su 10am-1:30pm. Free.*)

The **Palau de la Generalitat** is the center of Catalunya's regional government and has served as the seat of power for 128 presidents of Catalunya, from Berenguer de Cruïlles in 1359 to current president José Montilla. The oldest part of the building is the Gothic facade in C. Bisbe, site of the original entrance; the government officials who commissioned it in 1416 were so happy with the St. Jordi medallion designed by Marc Safont that they paid him double what they had originally promised. Most of the center of the palace was added in the 16th and 17th centuries, including the beautiful **Pati dels Tarongers** (Patio of Oranges) and the **Salón Dorado** (Gold Room), a hall with an ornate gold ceiling and tapestries inspired by Petrarch depicting the triumph of honor over death and time over honor. Also notable is the **Salón de Sant Jordi,** whose cupola is visible from the Pl. St. Jaume. Part of the 17th-century additions, this extravagant room features a St. Jordi statue by Frederic Marès and is covered in allegorical paintings depicting the history of Catalunya. *(Pl. St. Jaume. Enter to the right on C. Bisbe. Ⓜ Jaume I, L4. ☎ 902 400 012; www.gencat.cat/palau. Open for tours by appointment only the 2nd and 4th Su of every month 10:30am-1:30pm (application form available online).*

The **Ajuntament** is Barcelona's city hall and office of social-democratic Mayor Jordi Hereu. In the late 14th century, Barcelona's elite Consell de Cent (Council of One Hundred) decided that the site of the original Roman forum would be the perfect place to construct their headquarters. The most impressive room in the building, the **Saló de Cent,** was completed in 1369; King Pere III had his first meeting with the Consell de Cent there in 1373. With red-and-gold brocaded walls, high arches, and a profusion of crystal chandeliers, it oozes with Catalan pride. Smaller but equally stunning is the **Saló de la Reina Regente,** designed in 1860 for plenary meetings and containing a half-dome stained-glass skylight. The **Saló de las Crónicas** wall decorations, created by Josep Marià Sert, depict episodes from Roger de Flor's 14th-century expedition to the Far East. The entrance courtyard, meanwhile, further serves to glorify Catalan culture by displaying sculptures by some of Barcelona's most famous artists, including Josep Llimona, Josep Subirachs, and Joan Miró. *(Pl. St. Jaume. Ⓜ Jaume I, L4. Open Su 10am-1:30pm, last entry 1:15pm. Tours in English at 11am; Spanish at 10:30, noon, and 1pm; Catalan at 10, 11:30am, and 12:30pm, or as needed by large groups. Self-guided tours also allowed; pamphlet guides are available in Catalan, Spanish, English, and French. Free.)*

TEMPLE OF AUGUSTUS. At the end of C. Paradís, a plaque marks **Mont Tàber,** the highest point of Roman Barcino at 16.9m above sea level. Right behind the plaque, inside the protective walls of the Centre Excursionista Catalunya, a local outdoors club, are the four columns from the original Roman Temple of Augustus. These columns used to tower over the center of the ancient roman plaça. *(Ⓜ Jaume I, L4. Inside the Centre Excursionista de Catalunya building. Enter Pl. St. Jaume from C. Bisbe and take a hairpin left turn into tiny C. Paradís. Follow this street around the corner and to the end. Open Oct.-May 10am-2pm and 4-8pm; June-Sept. 10am-8pm.)*

SOUTHERN ROMAN WALLS. In case you haven't had your fill of Roman walls yet, the second concentrated stretch of them is located in what was the southeastern corner of the original city, near present-day **Plaça Regomir** and **Plaça Traginers.** This civic center hosts free art exhibitions in its front room and also showcases a substantial piece of an AD first-century Roman wall. The wall is visible from the street through a glass window but is also accessible from a ramp inside the building.

Soon after passing the civic center, turn left on C. Correu Vell. A tiny alley, C. de Groch, branches off to the left into a space where you can see a stretch of AD fourth-century wall and two square towers. If you then go back and take C. Correu Vell to its end, you will find yourself in the quiet Plaça Traginers, which hosts yet another substantial section of fourth-century walls. Check out the tower on the corner of C. Correu Vell and Baixada de Viladecols, right off Pl. Traginers. It was one of 78 towers that made up the second enclosing wall of Barcino in the AD fourth century, and unlike other Roman sites in the city, it has not yet been tainted by modern construction. *(C. Regomir, 3. Ⓜ Jaume I, L4. From Pl. St. Jaume, take C. Ciutat; just as the street turns into C. Regomir, the Centre Pati Llimona will be on your left. ☎ 932 68 98 96. Centre Pati Llimona open M-F 9am-9:30pm and Sa 10am-2pm and 4-8pm. Free.)*

SANTA MARIA DEL PI. As far as religious buildings go, the Catedral de la Santa Creu tends to usurp tourist attention in the Barri Gòtic. The most popular among locals, though, is the **Església de Santa Maria del Pi**, a small 14th-century church with exquisite Gothic stained glass. The three *plaças* surrounding the church (Pl. del Pi, Placeta del Pi, and Pl. de St. Oriol) are pleasant places for relaxing in the shade. (Ⓜ*Liceu, L3. Take C. Cardenal Casañas from Las Ramblas. Open daily 8:30am-1pm and 4:30-8:30pm. Be sure to observe proper church etiquette. Free.*)

PLAÇA REIAL. The most crowded, happening *plaça* in the entire Barri Gòtic is the Pl. Reial, where tourists and locals congregate to eat and drink at night and to buy and sell at the Sunday morning flea market. **Francesc Daniel Milona** designed the *plaça* in one of Barcelona's first spurts of productive (rather than oppressive) urban planning, replacing the decrepit Barri Gòtic streets with a large, architecturally cohesive *plaça* in the 1850s. Near the fountain in the center of the square there are two street lamps designed by Antoni Gaudí at the very beginning of his architectural career. The *plaça* is a popular place to grab a drink or meal, and some of the Barri Gòtic's most happening and tourist-filled restaurants and bars reside here. Moreover, the regular police patrols make the Pl. Reial one of the safer places to hang out in Barcelona, day or night. (Ⓜ*Liceu or Drassanes, L3.*)

OTHER PLAÇAS IN THE BARRI GÒTIC. Farther toward the water, off C. Ample, the much newer **Plaça Mercé** is a popular spot for weddings as well as for Barcelona's soccer team: the **Església de la Mercé** on one side holds the image of the mother of God to which FCB players dedicate all of their successful games. One last *plaça* worth seeing is the **Plaça de Sant Felip Neri**, a right off C. Bisbe when you are coming from the Cathedral. It is peaceful and pretty today, but it has a rather morbid past: it was once the site of a Jewish cemetery, and in January of 1938 a Civil War bomb ripped through the area, killing 20 children. Shrapnel marks are still slightly visible on the facade of the Església de Sant Felip Neri. (Ⓜ*Liceu, L3 or Jaume I, L4.*)

LAS RAMBLAS

LA RAMBLA

La Rambla is a world-famous cornucopia of street performers, fortune-tellers, pet and flower stands, and artists. A glut of tourists has led to a ton of restaurants and shops that cater to them. Watch your wallet; this is a pickpocketer's paradise. The tree-lined thoroughfare consists of five distinct *ramblas* (promenades). Together, the Ramblas form one boulevard about one kilometer long, starting at Pl. de Catalunya and proceeding down to Rambla del Mar and the Mediterranean.

LA RAMBLA DE LES CANALETES. The portward journey along las Ramblas begins at the Font de les Canaletes, the glorified water pump for which la Rambla de les Canaletes is named; it is recognizable by the four faucets and the Catalan crests (red crosses next to red and yellow stripes) that adorn it. Legend has it that visitors who sample the water will fall in love with the city (if they haven't already) and are bound to return to Barcelona someday. Stationed around here are the first of many living statues that line Las Ramblas during the day. Because of its symbolic position at the top of Las Ramblas on the Pl. de Catalunya, La Rambla de les Canaletes also sees a fair number of political demonstrations and Barça victory celebrations.

LA RAMBLA DELS ESTUDIS. You'll hear the squawking of the caged residents of the next section of Las Ramblas before you see them. The next stretch of Las Ramblas, which extends to C. Carme and C. Portaferrissa, is often referred to as "La Rambla dels Ocells" ("Promenade of the Birds"). A number of stalls here sell birds of nearly every kind: roosters, parrots, ducks, and many, many parakeets. Guinea pigs, iguanas, fish, ferrets, tortoises, and pretty much every other kind of caged creature is also available. The official name of this stretch of rambla comes from the university that used to be located here; *estudis* is Catalan for "studies."

LA RAMBLA DE SANT JOSEP. Here the screeching birds give way to the sunflowers, roses, and tulips on the segment of Las Ramblas commonly known as "La Rambla de les Flors" ("Promenade of the Flowers"). Vendors here have offered a variety of fragrant bouquets since the mid-1800s. In April, the flower stands are joined by book vendors in preparation for the Día de Sant Jordi, a Catalan variation on Valentine's Day. On April 23, couples exchange gifts; women of all ages receive flowers while men receive books.

The hulking stone building at the corner of C. Carme is the Església de Betlem, a Baroque church whose interior never recovered from torching by anarchists during the Spanish Civil War. A bit farther down is the famous traditional Catalan market, **Mercat de la Boqueria** (p. 116), officially named El Mercat de Sant Josep, the oldest of the city's some 40 markets. At Pl. Boqueria, just before the Liceu metro stop, you'll walk across Joan Miró's circular pavement mosaic, created for the city in 1976 and now a popular meeting point.

LA RAMBLA DELS CAPUTXINS. Miró's street mosaic marks the beginning of La Rambla dels Caputxins, the most user-friendly of the five Ramblas and the first of Las Ramblas to be converted into an actual promenade. The pedestrian area widens, and the majestic trees provide a bit more shade. Across from the recently renovated opera house, the Liceu (see this page), a strip of restaurants with outdoor seating vie for tourist euro, offering unremarkable and fairly expensive food.

LA RAMBLA DE SANTA MONICA. Following the tradition of naming the parts of Las Ramblas after the goods sold there, this stretch would most likely be nicknamed La Rambla de las Prostitutas. At night, women of the oldest profession patrol this wide area leading up to the port, beckoning passersby with loud kissing noises and lots of cleavage. During the day, however, this rambla distinguishes itself with skilled practitioners of a different art. These virtuosos can whip up dead-on caricatures in just five minutes. Also along this stretch you are bound to see people playing *trile*, a shell game with three little boxes and a tiny ball. Careful—these guys know how to manipulate that little *bolita* and they often have accomplices in the audience to help rope people in. This part of the rambla will take you all the way down to the Monument A Colom, and beyond that is the short Rambla del Mar leading to Port Vell.

🅰GRAN TEATRE DEL LICEU. After burning down for the second time in 1994, the Liceu was rebuilt and expanded dramatically; a tour of the building includes not just the original 1847 **Sala de Espejos** (Hall of Mirrors), but also the 1999 **Foyer** (a curvaceous bar/lecture hall/small theater). The five-level, 2292-seat **theater** is considered one of Europe's top stages, adorned with palatial ornamentation, gold facades, and sculptures. A brief visit will give you a worthwhile glimpse into the majesty of the theater, but to really experience the place, try to catch a performance. Discount tickets are often available. *(La Rambla, 51-59, by C. Sant Pau. ⓂLiceu, L3. ☎ 934 85 99 00; www.liceubarcelona.com. Box office open M-F 10am-1pm and*

SIGHTS

2-6pm or by ServiCaixa. Short 20min. non-guided visits daily 11:30am-1pm every 30min, €4. 1hr. tours 10am; €8.70, seniors and under 26 €6.70.)

⬛LA BOQUERIA (MERCAT DE SANT JOSEP). La Boqueria is just the place to pick up that hard-to-find animal part you've been looking for, plus any other delicacies you've been craving. A traditional Catalan *mercat*—and the largest outdoor market in Spain—located in a giant, all-steel *Modernista* structure, La Boqueria is a sight to behold. Specialized vendors sell produce, fish, organs, whole pigs, cheese, nuts, wine, and sweets from a seemingly infinite number of independent stands inside. A few excellent cafes have terraces outside and serve dishes incorporating fresh ingredients from the market. *(La Rambla, 89. Ⓜ Liceu. A plate of seafood will generally cost €6-15, mixed seafood platter €20-25, for two €30-37. Open M-Sa 8am-8pm.)*

PALAU DE LA VIRREINA. Once the residence of a Peruvian viceroy, this 18th-century palace houses temporary art exhibits, often featuring contemporary audio-visual installations. Also on display are the latest incarnations of the 10-15 ft. tall dolls which have taken part in the city's Carnival celebrations since 1399. The imposing couple Jaume and Violant, dressed in long, regal robes, are the undisputed king and queen of the Carnival parade. The cultural institute here serves as information headquarters for Barcelona's cultural festivals. *Las Ramblas, 99, at C. Carme. Ⓜ Liceu, L3. ☎ 933 16 10 00. Open Tu-F 11am-2pm and 4-8pm, Sa-Su and holidays 11am-8pm. Free.*

MONUMENT A COLOM. Ruis i Taulet's monument to Columbus towers at the port end of La Rambla. Nineteenth-century *Renaixença* enthusiasts convinced themselves that Columbus was Catalan, not Italian. The statue points proudly in a mysterious direction—not to the Americas, but out over the horizon toward Libya—which some take as error, and others as directions to what would have been Columbus's first refueling point. Take the elevator for an excellent and broad view of the city from a somewhat cramped lookout-point. *(Portal de la Pau. Ⓜ Drassanes. Elevator open daily 9am-8:30pm. €2.50, children and over 65 €1.50.)*

LA RIBERA

⬛PALAU DE LA MÚSICA CATALANA. This is the Graceland of Barcelona. The Orfeó Catalan choir society commissioned *Modernista* master Lluís Domènech i Montaner to design this must-see concert venue, built in 1903. By day, the music hall glows with tall stained-glass windows and a skylight; it comes alive again after dark with electric lights. Sculptures of winged horses and busts of the muses spring from the walls flanking the stage. An inverted glass dome, painted with 40 women dressed as angels, looms in the very center of the ceiling. When the Orféo choir was founded in 1891, it was the first to permit women and men to sing together. The angels on the ceiling were a welcome to those women and an affirmation of their rightful place in the choir. The muses in back, each with a different exotic instrument, are likewise meant to welcome and honor the music of foreign cultures. Back in 1908, foreign and exotic meant Beethoven and Wagner, but even today the Palau hosts a diverse range of musical guests, from high-profile orchestras to bossa nova and pop-rock. The Palau's 3,000-tube organ is finally back in service after a lengthy renovation. *(C. del Palau de la Música, 4-6. ☎ 902 44 28 82; www.palaumusica.org. Ⓜ Jaume I, Urinaona. Mandatory 50min. tours in English every hr. Open daily Sept.-July 10am-3:30pm, Semana Santa and Aug. 10am-6pm. €12, students and seniors €11. Check website for scheduled performances. Concert tickets €8-175. Box office open 9am-9pm. MC/V.)*

⌘PARC DE LA CIUTADELLA. A quick walk from Barceloneta and Barri Gòtic and sandwiched between La Ribera and Poble Nou and, Parc de la Ciutadella is both a refreshing break from the speed of the city and a major cultural and historical site. Take a nap, take a stroll, take a lover—just keep an eye out for jamming musicians. Barcelona's military resistance to the Bourbon monarchy in the early 18th century convinced Felipe V to quarantine the city's influential citizens in a large citadel on the site of what is now Pg. de Picasso. An entire neighborhood was razed and its citizens evicted to make room for the *ciuta-della*, which lorded threateningly over Barcelona. In a popular move, the city demolished the fortress in 1878 and replaced it with the peaceful promenades of Parc de la Ciutadella. Architect Josep Fontseré designed the new park, and brought with him newcomers Domènech i Montaner (of **Palau de la Música Cat-alana** fame, see (see opposite page)) and Antoni Gaudí. Several Modernista buildings went up years later when Ciutadella hosted the Universal Exposition in 1888, including Montaner's stately Castell dels Tres Dragons, now the **Museu de Zoologia.** *(ⓂCiutadella or Marina. Park open daily 8am-11pm).*

⌘HIVERNACLE. Originally built to showcase unusual tropical plants not sturdy enough for the climate of Barcelona, Josep Amergós's iron and glass *hiverna-cle* (greenhouse) now houses white tablecloths and bow-tied waiters alongside a room of exotic fauna, the perfect spot for a tropical afternoon meal or drink. The park's public restrooms also lurk among the greenery. On Wednesday evenings from May through July, the Hivernacle holds jazz concerts (10:30pm, €4); in July, Thursday nights bring free classical music (10:15pm). Farther down the Pg. de Picasso on the other side of the Museu Geologia, the iron-tiered Umbracle, built in 1883 and renovated in 2001, offers a cooler, shadier escape than its brother greenhouse. *(On Pg. de Picasso, behind the Museu de Zoologia. ⓂArc de Triomf, L1. ☎ 93 295 40 17. Currently closed for renovations.)*

ARC DE TRIOMF. Less famous than its French cousin, this monument, just north of the Parc de la Ciutadella, is no less magnificent: the palm-lined walk-way at its feet makes it a charming photo-op. Rather than commemorating a military triumph, the Arc de Triomf was designed as the entrance to the 1888 Exposition. A stylistic nod to the Spanish Moors, the red bricks surround green and yellow ceramic tiles and sculpted bats, angels, and lions. The main facade is a friendly face smiling down at you, dear tourist—it represents the welcom-ing of foreign visitors to Barcelona. *(ⓂArc de Triomf, L1.)*

PARRÒQUIA CASTRENSE. One of the few remaining buildings from the original citadel (and the only one open to the public), this church was built in 1720 for military men who populated what was then a menacing fortress. A quick visit provides a unique glimpse into a past which has literally been demolished in order to build the park. *(Open in winter Sa-Su 11:30am-1:30pm and 4:30-6:30pm, in sum-mer Sa-Su 11:30am-1:30pm and 4:30-8pm. Mass Su 12:30pm.)*

PARC ZOOLÒGIC. Those tired of marveling at brilliant architecture (and with cash to spare) can marvel instead at the brilliant behinds of mandrills and macaques or the aviary of strange and beautiful tropical birds in the Parc Zoològic. Sadly, the zoo's former superstar Floquet de Neu ("Snowflake," the world's only albino gorilla) has passed away, leaving only his humdrum non-albino offspring and a slew of other zoo standards. *(ⓂCiutadella/Vila Olímpica, L4. Follow C. Wellington out of the Metro. The zoo is accessible from a separate entrance on C. Wel-lington. From inside the park, the zoo entrance is next to the Parliament building. ☎ 902 45 75 45; www.zoobarcelona.com. Open daily from Jan. to mid-Mar. and Nov.-Dec., 10am-5:30pm; from mid-Mar. to May and Oct., 10am-7pm; June-Sept. 10am-8pm. Last entry 1hr. before closing. The zoo has* *its own restaurants and snack bars. Wheelchair-accessible. Free dolphin shows with entry every day at 11:30am, 1:30pm, 4:30pm, and 6pm. €16, ages 3-12 €9.60, seniors €8.20. AmEx/D/MC/V.)*

EL FOSSAR DE LES MORERES. Topped with an eternal flame, the Fossar de les Moreres (Mulberry Cemetery) memorial is a significant reminder of the (still ongoing) Catalan struggle for cultural autonomy. The Catalans who resisted Felipe V's troops in 1714 were buried here in a mass grave, commemorated by this monument and a plaque with a verse by the poet Serafí Pitarra: "In the Mulberry Cemetery no traitors are buried. Even though we lose our flags, this will be the urn of honor." Demonstrators and patriots converge here on September 11th, National Day of Catalonia, to commemorate the siege of Barcelona and the subsequent ban on displays of Catalan nationalism. *(Off C. de Santa Maria and next to the church's back entrance.)*

EL RAVAL

PALAU GÜELL. Gaudí completed Palau Güell—a *Modernista* residence built for wealthy patron Eusebi Güell i Bacigalupi (the industrialist, landowner and politician of Parc Güell fame)—in 1890. Güell spared no expense on this house, which, as the only building that Gaudí actually completed that has not undergone any major modifications, is considered to be one of the first true representations of the architect's revolutionary style. Picasso, who famously wanted to "send Gaudí and the Sagrada Família to hell," painted his Blue Period work across the street. Palau Güell was a private residence for the Güell family until 1936. During the Spanish Civil War, the *palau* was turned into a barracks; this left it in such a state of disrepair that its then-owner (Eusebi's daughter) turned it over to the Barcelona city council. Because the building is currently under restoration, visitors can see only the main facade, the ground floor, and the basement—a detailed description of the chimneys that have been renovated, however, is available online. *(C. Nou de La Rambla, 3-5. ⓂLiceu. ☎933 17 39 74; www. palauguell.cat. Partial entrance only. Open Tu-Sa 10am-2:30pm. Free.)*

EGLESIA DE SANT PAU DEL CAMP. Although this small, ancient stone church may not impress at first glance, art and design students will note the decorated columns, vaulted ceilings, and tiny, intricately detailed stained-glass windows that together make this medieval marvel one of the most important examples of Romanesque architecture in the city of Barcelona. Guifré Borrell, the church's founder and the son of Wilfred the Hairy (see **Life & Times,** (p. 41)), was buried here in AD 911. When first founded in AD 912, the church stood in the country, well outside the city walls (thus its name, Sant Pau "of the countryside"). The current church building, constructed in the 12th century, is very much a part of the city. *(ⓂParal·lel L2/3, at the intersection of C. Sant Pau and Carretes, 2 blocks off Av. Paral·lel. Open M-Sa 10am-1:30pm and 4-7:30pm. €2.)*

LA BIBLIOTECA DE CATALUNYA. This library of Catalan studies, housed in the Antic Hospital of Santa Creu of Barcelona (a building that has been slowly restored over the past 15 years), is a cool and calm oasis in the heart of the city. The old Hospital has high, arched stone ceilings that juxtapose nicely with the building's recently completed carrels. The library's collection, founded in 1907 and once housed in the Generalitat, aims to bring together all the most important documents of Catalan history. While the library's main study room is open only to scholars, a part of the room with benches and a short video about Catalan history is reserved for those who come to see the library or to take a break from the tumult of surrounding Raval. *(Carrer de l'Hospital, 56. ⓜLiceu. www. bnc.edu. Open M-F 9am-8pm, Sa-Su 9am-2pm.)*

UNIVERSITAT DE BARCELONA. Overlooking Gran Via, this palatial 19th-century building housed the University of Barcelona until much of its campus moved north to Pedralbes in the 1950s. Today, the philosophy, religion, mathematics, and language departments remain in the regal hallways. The grounds include several beautiful, shady courtyards lined by arches and columns and filled with trees, ponds, and fountains. The library is open to the public for consultation; bring a picture ID. For those looking to sublet a room in a nearby apartment, check the bulletin boards scattered around on the ground floor. *(Pl. Universitat. ⓜUniversitat, L1/2/3. www.ub.edu. Open M-F 8:30am-8:30pm, Sa-Su 10am-8:30pm.)*

EL CALL (JEWISH QUARTER)

Records indicate that Jewish families started moving to Roman Barcino as early as the AD second century. The Jewish quarter sprang to life near the center of town, between present-day Pl. St. Jaume, C. Ferran, C. Banys Nous, and the Església Santa Maria del Pi. Although today there is little indicating its Jewish heritage, for centuries El Call was the most vibrant center of intellectual and financial activity in all of Barcelona; Jews even received a certain amount of governmental support and protection in return for their substantial economic and cultural contributions to the city.

Anti-Semitism spread throughout Europe in the 13th century, however, and Spain was no exception. In 1243, Jaume I ordered the complete isolation of the Jewish quarter from the rest of the city, and he forced all Jews to wear identifying red-and-yellow buttons. Anti-Semitism increased as citizens looked for scapegoats for the plagues and poverty of the 14th century, and in 1348, hundreds of Jews were blamed for the Black Death and tortured mercilessly until they "confessed" their crimes. In 1391, as harassment spread throughout Spain, a riot ended in the murder of nearly 1000 Jews in Barcelona's Call. By 1401, every single synagogue and Jewish cemetery was demolished, making the forced conversion law of 1492 an easy next step (see Catalan Jews). To add insult to injury, Jewish tombstones were pilfered to construct other buildings around that time. If you keep an eye out you may be able to spot some still-discernable Hebrew inscriptions on some of the old, 14th-century walls in Barri Gòtic, for example at Pl. de Sant Iu, above and to left of the gas lamp on the wall opposite the **Museu Frederico Marès.**

One Jewish synagogue was turned into a church, the **Església de Sant Jaume** (C. Ferran, 28) which is still in use today. Some of the only remaining tangible evidence of Jewish inhabitants in El Call is the ancient Hebrew plaque in tiny C. Marlet as well as at the **Associació Call de Barcelona,** which features a collection of relics and ruins from an old synagogue. To get there, take C. Call from Pl. St. Jaume and turn right onto C. Sant Domènech de Call and then left onto C. Marlet. The plaque is at the end of the block and the museum is at the beginning.

One of the best-known alleys in El Call has nothing to do with Jewish history: to the left off the end of C. Sant Domènech de Call (coming from C. Call) is the **Baixada de Santa Eulalia,** which is said to be the place where the city's patron saint was tortured to death, joining the ranks of Christian martyrs (see **Església Catedral de la Santa Creu,** (p. 110). On the wall at the start of the street, a plaque written by Catalan poet Jacint Verdaguer commemorates the legend. *(ⓜLiceu, L3. Associació Call de Barcelona C. Marlet: ☎ 933 17 07 90; www.calldebarcelona.org. Open M-F 10:30am-2:30pm and 4-7pm, Sa-Su 10:30am-3pm. Tour €2.)*

BLUEPRINT BLUES

Many come to Barcelona to learn about Cerdà, the idealistic urban planner famous for designing l'Eixample (see p. 5). Fewer people, however, become acquainted with Antoni Rovira i Trias, the runner up in the selection of plans for the extension.

Trias had drawn out a plan which sought to continue the varied, uneven pattern of streets in the old Barri Gòtic by way of five wedges radiating outward from the city center. Most scholars agree that his vision of l'Eixample was designed to perpetuate the class structure of the neighborhoods, favoring the fancier Pg. de Gràcia at the expense of more working-class barrios.

Perhaps for this reason, Trias' plan was the one selected to be implemented by the upper-class that controlled Barcelona Ajuntament in 1860. It is only because the government in Madrid chose Cerdà, and trumped the Barcelona authorities, that Trias's designs were not carried out.

More attention has been paid to Trias and this crucial moment in the history of the city of Barcelona with the recent book *E.: Antoni Rovira i Trias. Arquitecte de Barcelona* by Eloi Babiano i Sanchez. If you want to get a look at Triaz face to face, there's a statue of him in Grácia at the corner of C. de Providencia and C. de Rebassa.

L'EIXAMPLE

AROUND PASSEIG DE GRÀCIA

When **Ildefons Cerdà** drew up his designs for L'Eixample, he envisioned utopic, green, and well-ventilated city blocks where people from all social classes would live free of the congestion that plagued epidemic-prone old Barcelona. While he succeeded, to an extent—L'Eixample's avenues are indeed tree-lined and sunlit—the neighborhood has never quite realized Cerdà's vision of socio-economic integration (it was, and remains, posh). As Barcelona's bourgeoisie have increasingly moved uptown, the once-residential districts around Pg. de Gràcia have filled with offices and shops. Both in this zone and farther away, Cerdà's interminable blocks and wide-open plaças are broken up by architectural landmarks from every subsequent era. Make sure to look through the avenues' leafy ceilings; glimpses of *Modernista* casas and **Torre Agbar,** Jean Nouvel's spaceship-like, blue- and red-lit glass tower, will be your reward for doing so. Because l'Eixample is so large, the sights and museums in this neighborhood are grouped into three more manageable areas: l'Eixample Dreta, Pg. de Gràcia, and l'Eixample Esquerra.

CASA MILÀ (LA PEDRERA). Although innovative, Gaudí's unusual designs for Casa Milà were unpopular 100 years ago, and the name, La Pedrera (which means stone quarry in Spanish), came about as a result of popular jokes, critiques, and caricatures. The building's namesake, wealthy businessman Pere Milà, hired Gaudí because he liked his work on neighboring Casa Batlló (p. 121). But as the project progressed between 1906 and 1910, Milà's wife, Rosario Segimon, became increasingly unhappy with the appearance and refused to pay the excessive building costs. Gaudí eventually filed a lawsuit against the couple over his fees (he won and promptly gave all of the money to the poor), and the Casa Milà ended up being the only residence he designed where he didn't also craft the furniture. Today, visitors have access to the main floor, the attic, the terrace, and a sample apartment equipped with period furniture. The rest of Casa Milà is inhabited by the lucky (read: wealthy) people who sat on the 20-year waiting list for an apartment as well as several offices of Caixa Catalunya, which acquired the building in 1986 (hence all the pamphlets that read "La Pedrera de Caixa

Catalunya"). The attic, deemed the **Espai Gaudí**, is filled with displays about the construction of this and other Gaudí works, calling attention to the way Gaudí interpreted and expressed natural forms. Casa Milà in particular is built around two central courtyards, with an underground park in the basement and not a single flat wall in the entire space. For a great photo-op, climb to the roof of Casa Milà to get a picture of La Sagrada Família (p. 123) framed by an arch. The summer concert series, *La Nit de Pedrera*, transforms the roof into a jazz cabaret on weekend nights. *(Pg. de Gràcia, 92. ☎ 902 40 09 73; www.lapedreraedu-cacio.org. Open daily Mar.-Oct. 9am-8pm, last admission 7:30pm; Nov.-Feb. 9am-6:30pm. €9.50, students and seniors €5.50. Free audio tour. Concerts last weekend of June-July F-Sa 9pm-midnight. €12, glass of cava included.)*

LA MANZANA DE LA DISCORDIA

According to Greek myth, a piece of fruit was responsible for the Trojan War: the goddess of Discord created a golden apple as a prize for the most beautiful, and divine disharmony ensued. Barcelona has its own competition for the golden apple on the block of Pg. de Gràcia between C. Consell de Cent and C. Aragó, where trademark houses by the three most important architects of Modernism stand side-by-side in proud competition: the Casa Lleó Morera by Domènech i Montaner, the Casa Amatller by Puig i Cadafalch, and the Casa Batlló by Gaudí. Even the most ardent Catalanists haven't wanted to give up the pun in the old name *la manzana*, which in Castilian means both "block" and "apple." The name "Block of Discord" is especially indicative of the contrast (and clash) between the styles and aesthetics of the three houses. All of these creations are renovations of older, pre-existing edifices. To see the architectural contrast most clearly, take a look from across the street.

CASA BATLLÒ. The most fantastical member of the Block of Discord, Gaudí's Casa Batlló sees the most visitors. Gaudí was 52 when he reconstructed this house—one of his first works and completely "Gaudían" in style—after years of developing it. Shimmering and curving in shades of blue and green, the house looks slightly different at every hour of the day. Many see the building as a depiction of the legend of St. Jordi and the **◪dragon.** This interpretation incorporates all the major facets of the facade. The tall pinnacle on the left symbolizes the knight's lance after it has pierced the dragon's scaly back, which is represented by the warped, multi-colored, ceramic roof. The stairway supposedly represents the winding dragon's tail or the curves of his vertebrae, the outside balconies skulls, and the molded columns the bones of his unfortunate victims. Others see the house as having an underwater theme; walls and stained-glass windows are fluid and wavelike, and many of the ceilings spiral as if in a whirlpool. Particularly interesting is the way he tiled the central inner patio, dark blue on the top and lighter on the bottom, in order to distribute the light from above as evenly as possible. Of the many aspects of the building accessible by the tour, highlights include the mushroom-shaped fireplace, the house's dining room with two puzzlingly spaced pillars (only a few inches apart), the back porch decorated with colorful mosaics, and the roof, which allows for a closer look at the facade's scaly tiling as well as a decent view of the city. As you leave be sure to pay your respects to the Gaudí hologram, who salutes as you leave the upper level. *(Pg. de Gràcia, 43. ☎ 932 16 03 06; www.casabatllo. cat. Open daily 9am-8pm. €17, students, BCN card €13. Cash only. Call for group discounts for more than 20 people. Free multilingual audio tour.)*

SIGHTS

CASA LLEÓ I MORERA. In 1902, textile tycoon Albert Lleó Morera hired **Domènech i Montaner** to add some pizzazz to his boring 1864 home on the corner of Pg. de Gràcia and C. Consell de Cent. Montaner responded by creating one of the most lavish examples of decorative architecture in Barcelona, for which he won the Ajuntament's annual prize for Best Building of the Year in 1905. Much of the street-level exterior was destroyed by the Loewe leather shop that now occupies the entry, but if you look up at the second-floor balconies on either side of the corner tribune, you can see two nymphs on each balcony, holding (from left to right) a gramophone, an electric light bulb, a telephone, and a camera, symbols of the new leisure technology available to the bourgeoisie of the early 1900s. There are carved lions on the balcony above the tribune. Mulberry leaves lace around the tops of the tribune's vertical columns. Together these refer to the family name: *lleó* in Catalan means "lion," and *morera* means "mulberry tree."

The mezzanine level of the interior, unfortunately closed to the public, boasts a stunning dining room with glimmering stained-glass windows and detailed ceramic mosaics of the Lleó Morera family picnicking outdoors. The famous furniture that Gaspar Homar originally designed for this room is permanently on display at the Museu d'Art Modern. *(Pg. de Gràcia, 35. Entrance not permitted.)*

CASA AMATLLER. Chocolate mogul Antoni Amatller planted the first seed for La Manzana de la Discordia in 1898, when he commissioned **Puig i Cadafalch** to redo the facade of his prominent home. Cadafalch turned out a mix of Catalan, neo-Gothic, Islamic, and Dutch architecture best known for its stylized, geometric, and multicolored upper facade. The lower exterior of the house also has character; look carefully and you can see the owner's personality inscribed in sculpture. Above the main door, the prominent carving of Catalan hero St. Jordi battling the ◼dragon demonstrates Amatller's Catalan nationalism and the four figures engaged in painting, sculpture, architecture, and music represent Amatller's broad cultural interests. On either side of the main second-floor windows, there are caricatures of Amatller's favorite pastimes. On the left, small monkeys and rabbits busily mold iron (the main Catalan industry of Amatller's time), and a donkey with glasses reads while another plays with a camera; on the right side, frogs and pigs hold glass vases and pottery, a reference to Amatller's passion for vase-collecting. A huge "A" for Amatller adorns the outside of the entrance, intertwined with almond leaves (*amatller* means "almond" in Catalan). The long, single balcony with many doorways is also a traditional element of Catalan architecture.

Inside, the entrance foyer has original iron-and-glass lamps, bright, decorative tiles, and a stained-glass skylight just to the right of the main hallway. The small temporary art exhibit in the back room features various projects relevant to Modernist architecture—for example, miniature architectural models, stained-glass exhibitions, and collections of photographs from that period. Buy some Amatller chocolate to see for yourself whether he deserved his fortune. The apartment where the millionaire lived with his daughter is now home to the Institut Amatller d'Art Hispànic, open to students of the institute.

The Joieria Bagués, which holds a well-known collection of Modernist pieces from the Masriera tradition, occupies the right side of the entrance level. The mseum offers a tour of the store's sparkling dragonflies, nymphs, and flowers. *(Pg. de Gracià, 41. ☎934 877 217. House closed for renovations, expected to reopen 2012. Tours of film and temporary exhibition weekdays at noon, €5. More tours may be offered as renovations continue: call ahead.)*

OTHER SIGHTS ON PASSEIG DE GRÀCIA

If you want to prolong the magical mystery tour of *Modernisme*, a jaunt down the Pg. de Gràcia will acquaint you with equally interesting, though less famous, facades. Start at ⓂCatalunya and make your way up the Pg. de Gràcia. On the right at street level (no. 18), you'll see the **Joieria Roca,** a boxy building with a glass-brick exterior matched with pink. This curving building was way ahead of its time in 1934, so much so that architect Josep Lluís Sert sparked a serious conservative backlash with his unconventional design for the facade. **Casa Olano,** at no. 60, was used as headquarters for the Basque government during the Spanish Civil War; this is commemorated by a plaque above the doorway. The building earned its nickname "Pirate House" from the rendition of sailor and first circumnavigator Juan Sebastian Elcano (he completed the famous voyage after Magellan kicked the bucket in the Phillipines), who glares menacingly down at passersby. Up a little farther, at no. 66, is one of the most attractive corner facades on the Pg. de Gràcia, part of the **Casa Vidua Marfà,** built by Manual Comas Thos in 1905. Today it houses Barcelona's School of Tourism, and though you can't walk through the entire building, you can still walk into the entrance foyer and look up at the multi-colored skylight.

A few blocks up and one block over, at the intersection of Diagonal and Rambla de Catalunya (no. 126), the literally two-faced **Can Serra** is worth a look as well. The original turreted pink-and-peach stone building, constructed in French Gothic style, was completed by Puig i Cadafalch in 1908 and is adorned with a sculpture by Eusebi Arnau of St. Jordi, the ◾dragon, the princess, and some strangely entangled centaurs. The bulk of the house was razed in 1981, and now the old Gothic facade wraps around a smooth, black, glossy structure home to the Diputació of Barcelona.

Still want more? Then go back to Pl. de Catalunya and walk up the Pg. de Gràcia only one block to C. Casp. Turn right and continue for a few blocks to no. 48, **Casa Calvet** (☎93 412 40 12), Gaudí's first apartment building. It was also the only design he ever won an award for during his lifetime: the Ajuntament's first annual prize for Best Building of the Year, given out in 1900. Now the building houses an upscale restaurant with a gorgeous interior colored by stained glass. From Casa Calvet, backtrack half a block to C. Roger de Llúria, turn right, and walk down 2½ blocks. On your right, at no. 56, will be a small passageway leading to the **Torre de les Aigües,** the water tower built by Josep Oriol Mestres in 1879 to supply water to the first houses of l'Eixample. Today it overlooks a small summertime pool for neighborhood children. A half-block farther up, at the intersection of C. Roger de Llúria and C. Consell de Cent, you will see the neatly adorned and painted exteriors of the oldest houses in l'Eixample, built in 1864. Four houses were actually built here at once, one on each corner, for landowner Josep Cerdà (not to be confused with Ildefons Cerdà, the architect who planned l'Eixample), but only this one remains today.

L'EIXAMPLE DRETA

◾**LA SAGRADA FAMÍLIA.** Although Gaudí's unfinished masterpiece is barely a shell of the intended finished product, La Sagrada Família is without a doubt the world's most visited construction site. Despite the completion of only eight of the 18 planned towers (and those the shortest), millions of people make the touristic pilgrimage to witness the work-in-progress. Its construction is entirely funded by popular donations; in the past, the Church told donors their patronage guaranteed them a place in heaven. (Luckily, visitors' entrance fees are considered just such "popular donations.") While it's questionable whether the price of admission will get you through the pearly gates, it will get you into an awe-inspiring world of nature, spirituality, and art. Finished or not, La Sagrada Família has become intertwined with the image of Barcelona.

An extremely pious right-wing organization called the **Spiritual Association for Devotion to St. Joseph (or the Josephines)** commissioned La Sagrada Família. Founded in 1866 in reaction to the liberal ideas spreading throughout Europe, the group was determined to build an Expiatory Temple for Barcelona, where the city could reaffirm its faith to the Holy Family of Jesus, Mary, and Joseph (hence the building's full name, Templo Expiatori de la Sagrada Família). The first architect they chose quit almost immediately when his ideas for the church strayed from those of the project's commissar. Gaudí replaced him in 1884, at the age of 31. For the first 15 or 20 years, private contributions kept the building process going, but as the mood and culture of the city changed with the onset of the modern age, construction slowed drastically, and the Civil War (p. 44) brought it to a complete halt. The war years proved tragic for the temple. First, Gaudí died after being hit by a tram just outside the church's walls in 1926, having overseen the completion of only the Nativity Facade. To make matters worse, in 1936, arsonists on the revolutionary side of the Civil War broke into the crypt, opened Gaudí's tomb, smashed his plaster models, and burned every single document in the workshop in a display of anti-establishment fury.

Today, the building remains under the auspices of the Josephines; architect Jordi Bonet, whose father worked directly with Gaudí, heads up the project with sculptor Josep Marià Subirachs, who finished the **Passion Facade** in 1998. Without Gaudí's exact calculations, the team works from ongoing reconstructions of his original plaster models. The computer models that engineers use to recreate his underlying mathematical logic are so complicated that they have earned an exhibit of their own. As today's workers slowly give shape to what they think Gaudí had in mind, they continue to achieve unprecedented architectural feats. Until now, it was nearly impossible to set a completion date because of the intricacies of the reconstructed models and the unsteady flow of donations. Most recent estimates predict that La Sagrada Família will be finished by 2030. Winged pigs may soar from the towers that same year.

When completed, the front of the temple—the **Glory Facade**—will feature four more bell towers; together the 12 towers will represent the 12 apostles. Above the center of the church will rise a massive 170m **Tower of Jesus,** with a shorter spire just behind it dedicated to Mary. The Jesus tower will in turn be surrounded by four more towers symbolizing the four Evangelists (the authors of the four gospels). As finishing touches, Gaudí envisioned an extravagant spouting fountain in front of the main Glory Facade and a tall purifying flame at the back. Gaudí's dedication to religious themes in his work on La Sagrada Família (see p. 123) has even earned the attention of the Vatican. The continuation of Gaudí's greatest obsession has been fraught with fierce controversy. Some, like Salvador Dalí, have argued that the church should have been left incomplete as a monument to the architect.

Others believe that La Sagrada Família should be finished, but in a more "authentic" manner than has been the case so far. Critics usually attack most vehemently Josep Maria Subirachs i Sitjar's **Passion Facade.** The controversial Passion Facade, which faces the Pl. de la Sagrada Família, portrays Christ's Passion (Catholic lingo for his crucifixion, death, and resurrection). Its abstract, Cubist design contrasts starkly with the more traditional **Nativity Facade,** which depicts Christ's birth and faces the Pl. de Gaudí. Defenders of the facade argue that *Modernisme* has always been about celebrating the vision of individual Catalan artisans—and that this facade does precisely that.

Today's visitors can see detailed paintings of the projected church in the **Museu Gaudí.** Numerous pictures from the early years of the project, sketches by Gaudí, the glass-walled workshop where his models are still being restored, and various sculptures and decorative pieces from the temple are also on display. For a more somber experience, gaze down on Gaudí's crypt, where roses and tea lights line the grave as a statue of Mary watches over the man that lived and died for this church. *(C. Mallorca, 401.* ☎ *932 08 04 14; www.sagradafamilia.org.* ⓂSagrada Família. Open daily Apr.-Sept. 9am-8pm, Oct.-Mar. 9am-6pm. Last elevator to the tower 15min. before close. Guided tours in English (€3) May-Oct. at 11am, 1, 3, 5pm; Nov.-Apr. at 11am and 1pm. €11, students €9, under 10 free. Elevator €2.50. Combined ticket with Casa-Museu Gaudí €13, students €11.)*

ESGLÉSIA DE LES SALESES. This church's anterior bell tower and its intricate brickwork make it distinctive and memorable. **Joan Martorell i Montells** (1833-1906), one of Gaudí's mentors, built the church in 1885. Originally a convent, it was severely damaged during the 1909 **Setmana Trágica** (Tragic Week; see **Life & Times,** p. 41). After its 1945 repair, the church became a school, and then a Catholic parish. Its detailed brick, stone, and glass exterior decorations mark it as a direct precursor to the Modernist movement. *(Pg. de St. Joan, 57.* ☎ *932 65 39 12.* ⓂVerdaguer, L4/5.) Open 6-8pm.)*

OTHER SIGHTS IN L'EIXAMPLE DRETA

STATUES ON AVENIDA DIAGONAL. A good number of Barcelona's more than 400 monuments adorn l'Eixample, where wide streets and open corners lend them plenty of visibility.

MONUMENT TO NARCÍS MONTURIOL I ESTARRIOL. This sculpture of a submarine is a tribute to Estarriol (1819-1885), the inventor of, appropriately, the first submarine driven by combustion engine. *(C. Girona and Av. Diagonal.* ⓂVerdaguer, L4/5.)*

MONUMENT TO ANTON CLAVÉ. Clavé founded many popular choral societies. *(Pg. de St. Joan and Trav. de Gràcia.* ⓂJoanic, L4.)*

MONUMENT TO JACINT VERDAGUER. Verdaguer (1845-1902) was a well-known Catalan poet. Some of his shorter poems are known as songs, namely, "L'Emigrant." *(Pg. St. Joan and Av. Diagonal.* ⓂVerdaguer, L4/5.)*

L'EIXAMPLE ESQUERRA

SCULPTURES IN L'EIXAMPLE ESQUERRA

MEDITATION. Officially entitled Meditation, the bull's thoughtful pose mimics that of Rodin's *The Thinker*. He's easy to miss, but you'll remember his brooding countenance forever. At the opposite end of the avenue, his cousin, **Coquette,** a flirtatious giraffe of questionable virtue, seduces passersby on Av. Diagonal. *(*ⓂCatalunya, L3. From Pl. de Catalunya, walk up La Rambla de Catalunya 1 block to Gran Via; the statue is in the middle of La Rambla, across from Comme-Bio.)*

CASAS IN L'EIXAMPLE ESQUERRA

CASA GOLFERICHS. One of Gaudí's collaborators, **Joan Rubió,** designed this Moorish-influenced, brown brick structure in 1901. Now a civic center, Golferichs hosts courses ranging from "Domestic Economics" to "Ancient Egypt: Art,

Magic, and Myth" as well as conferences, art exhibitions, and summer concerts in the courtyard. *(Gran Via, 491, at the intersection with C. Viladomat. ⓜUrgell, L1. ☎933 23 77 90. M-F 9:30am-10pm, Sa 10am-2pm and 5-9pm. Wheelchair-accessible.)*

CASA DE LACTANCIA. Pere Falques and **Antoni de Flaguerra** designed this *Modernista* residence—now a nursing home. Stone carvings by **Eusebi Arnau** and a mosaic flag of Barcelona can be viewed from outside, but step into the foyer to see the equally impressive wrought-iron interior balcony and delicate stained glass windows. *(Under construction as of summer 2009, but it is still possible to step into the foyer. Gran Via, 475. ⓜUrgell, L1.)*

CASA COMPANY. Puig i Cadalfach constructed this house for a local family in 1911. The creamy white Art Deco facade with painted decorations was converted into Dr. Melcior Colet's gynecology practice in 1940 and later donated to the government of Catalunya. Today, it houses the **Museu de l'Esport** (p. 146). *(C. Buenos Aires, 56-58. ⓜHosptial Clinic, L5. Walk up C. del Comte d'Urgell until you hit C. Buenos Aires. Make a right; the building is 1 block down on the right.)*

CASA DE LES PUNXES (HOUSE OF SPIKES). Also known as **La Casa Terrades,** this is one of the most famous *Modernista* houses in the city. **Puig i Cadafalch** designed the house in 1905 for the Terrades sisters, who wanted to unite three existing buildings on their property. *(Av. Diagonal, 416-420. ⓜJoanic, L4, near the intersection of Av. Diagonal and C. Roger de Llúria.)*

CASA COMALAT. This *casa*, built from 1906-11 and designed by **Salvador Valeri i Pupurull** (1873-1954), has two facades. The one facing Av. Diagonal is symmetrical and well decorated with subtle stone textures. *(Av. Diagonal 442.)*

PALAU DEL BALÓ DE QUADRAS. Puig i Cadafalch designed this house (built 1904-06), which is almost entirely capped in sculptures. It is currently being used as the "Casa Asia," a building intended to encourage cultural communication and exchange with Asia. *(Av. Diagonal, 373.)*

POBLE NOU

OLYMPIC SIGHTS. From 1982 to 1997, the industrious socialist Pasqual Maragall was the mayor of Barcelona. Thanks to his efforts, the city was able to secure the bid to host the 1992 Summer Olympics. Maragall then used the pressure of the international spotlight as an opportunity to completely revamp Barcelona. New athletic arenas and apartment complexes were built, the beaches were cleaned up, the waterfront was remodeled into party central, and the prostitutes were shuffled into less visible neighborhoods.

Further inland, at the intersection with Av. Bogatell and C. Frederic Mompau, is **Plaça Tirant lo Blanc,** the center of Olympic housing in 1992, commemorated by a small statue of a wistful athlete. Returning to the park and heading right toward the Mapfre building brings you to the **Parc del Port Olímpic,** a long, triumphant walkway lined by tall white spires and culminating in Robert Llimos's radiant *Marc* statue. Dedicated to the tragic death of the artist's son, it captures all the youthful optimism and energy of Barcelona in the 1990s. Across the fountain lies the **Parc de Cascades,** home to Antoni Llena's Dalíesque *David and Goliath* as well as Auke de Vries's enigmatic *El Poder de la Paraula* (the Power of Words). To reach Frank Gehry's copper *Peix* (Fish) and the **Port Olímpic,** return to the fountain and turn right toward the water. The fish will be on your right and the port on your left.

CEMENTIRI DE L'EST. Pre-l'Eixample Barcelona desperately needed every inch inside city walls for living space, so in 1773 this cemetery was built outside the walls to bury some of Barcelona's dead elite. Crumbling monuments and miniature churches crowd the back of the plot; toward the front of the cemetery, in the center aisle, there is a statue erected in memory of the thousands of people in Barcelona who died during the Yellow Fever epidemic of 1821. *(At the dead end of Av. Icària. ⓜLlacuna, L4. From the metro, walk down C. Ciutat de Granada toward the waterfront towers; at the T-intersection with C. Taulat, turn right and follow the white walls of the cemetery to the gated opening. Open daily 8am-6pm.)*

OTHER SIGHTS IN POBLE NOU. The neighborhood is best viewed in an easy loop (see Walking Tour). To your left at the intersection of C. de Marina and Avinguda Icària lies the **Parc de Carles I**, with its tall, infamous *Culo de Urculo* statue ("Hercules's ass"). On Av. Icària, huge metal sculptures run down the center of the street and resemble something like a mix of thatched roofs and telephone poles. Named *Pergolas* by architect Enric Miralles, they're an ultra-modern take on the original latticed rooftop gardens with climbing plants common in ancient Egypt. To the right on the second block of Av. Icària is the **Centre de la Vila,** a two-story shopping mall, lacking most of the major store names scattered throughout the rest of Barcelona. It does boast a movie theater, a supermarket, and shops for any basic last-minute beach essentials you might need. *(ⓜCiutadella/Villa Olímpica, L4. Exit the metro with the twin skyscrapers to your right and cross C. Ramon Trias Fargos to get to the intersection of C. de Marina and Avinguda d'Icària.)*

PORT VELL

◼TORRE SAN SEBASTIÀ. One of the easiest and best ways to view the city is on these cable cars, which connect beachy Barceloneta and the Port Vell area with Montjuïc. The full ride takes about 10min. each way, and there's an intermediate stop near Monument a Colom at Jaume I if you want to explore Las Ramblas from the south. Bring your camera to get some postcard-perfect shots of Barcelona. If you're looking to splurge, there's also a fancy restaurant at the top of the San Sebastià tower. *(Walk all the way down Joan de Borbó until you see the beach, then bear right and head to the imposing tower with the cable cars coming out of it. ☎934 41 48 20. Open daily 11am-8pm. To Montjuïc one-way €7, round trip €13, or to the top for the view €4 (free to get up to restaurant). The tower is also accessible from Montjuïc (see the Jardins Verdaguer, p. 130). Jaume I stop currently closed, expected to reopen by November 2009.)*

L'AQUÀRIUM DE BARCELONA. The aquarium features over 20 tanks, focusing mostly on Mediterranean sea creatures. The highlight is the 80m conveyor belt that leads through a glass tunnel surrounded by four million gallons of water and hundreds of fish, sharks, and rays. There is also a cafeteria and a multitude of interactive exhibits for kids. *(Moll d'Espanya. ⓜDrassanes or Barceloneta. Advance tickets ☎932 21 74 74; www.aquariumbcn.com. Open daily July-Aug. 9:30am-11pm; June and Sept. 9:30am-9:30pm; Oct.-May M-F 9:30am-9pm, Sa-Su 9am-9:30pm. €17, 4-12 €12, over 60 €14. Mini-guide available in English. AmEx/MC/V.)*

OTHER SIGHTS. Since hosting the 1992 Olympic games, Barcelona has slowly but surely re-established itself as one of the greatest ports on the Mediterranean. The newest addition to the waterfront is the **World Trade Center,** built in 1999 and designed by the renowned architect I.M. Pei. The low, curved buildings remind many of a cruise ship—fitting, considering the building's proximity to the docks. The ultra-modern complex includes the luxurious **Grand Marina Hotel** (completed in 2002), office space, restaurants and cafes, and a convention center. At the other end of Pg. Colom in front of the post office (a postal

SIGHTS

palace created for the 1929 International Exhibition and a sight in and of itself) is **Cap de Barcelona,** also known as Barcelona Head. This depiction of a woman's face—half surreal and half cartoon—was created by the late American pop artist Roy Lichtenstein for the 1992 Olympics. (Ⓜ*Drassanes, L3, or Barceloneta, L4.*)

MONTJUÏC

CASTELL DE MONTJUÏC. This historic fortress sits high on the hill, and from the external *mirador*, guests can enjoy a multitude of panoramic jaw-droppers and photo-ops. The first section of this massive castle was built in 1640 in just 30 days. Fifty-four years later the main castle was constructed. It continued to expand until 1799, when it grew to accommodate over 3000 people. Nowadays, the Ⓜ**telefèric**—an airborne cable car that runs to and from the castle—is half the fun. Over the long course of its history, the Montjuïc castle has been used for many different purposes: fortress, military prison, and (most recently) museum. In 2009, however, the castle will undergo a complete renovation, and its future incarnation will introduce visitors to a whole new kind of torture. The building will house three civil institutions: the **International Center for Peace** (where opposing groups can meet and resolve their conflicts), the **Space of Memory,** (which will present thematic exhibits on the castle's history) and the **Interpretive Center of Montjuïc** (which will educate its visitors about the geological and biological history of Montjuïc and serve as an urban-planning forum). (*From* Ⓜ*Paral·lel, take the funicular to Parc de Montjuïc and then the cable car to the castle. Parc de Montjuïc bus runs up the mountain, leaving from in front of the telefèric, or you can walk up the steep slope on C. Foc from the same spot.* ☎ *933 28 60 25. Telefèric de Montjuïc open in summer 9am-10pm, in winter 9am-8pm. €6; round-trip €8.30, children €6.30. Castle open daily 8am-8pm. Free.*)

POBLE ESPANYOL. Created for the 1929 International Exhibition, this park features replicas of famous buildings and sights throughout Spain. The courtyards sometimes host performances, and the entire complex is filled with regional craft shops that sell everything from tacky souvenirs to gallery pieces. Tourists new to Spain are likely to find the differences between "regions" minimal and the overall experience rather underwhelming. Those who have been to Cadiz, Granada, Sevilla, Toledo and other Spanish cities will ooh and aah at the realism of each miniature replica. The large open-air courtyard occasionally serves as a performance venue. The **Fran Darell Contemporary Art Foundation** is centrally located and offers a welcome break from the souvenir bazaar around it. For most, Poble Espanyol is a better place to visit at night, when the crowds will give you a taste of what Spain does best: party. (*Av. Marquès de Comillas, 13.* Ⓜ*Espanya or bus #13 or 50.* ☎ *935 08 63 00. Open M 9am-8pm, Tu-Th 9am-2am, F 9am-4am, Sa 9am-5pm, Su 9am-midnight. Last entry 1hr. before closing. €8.50, students and seniors €6.50, ages 4-12 €5.60, after 8pm €5. Prices may vary when there are concerts.*)

FONTS LUMINOSES. The Fonts Luminoses (Illuminated Fountains) run alongside Av. Reina Maria Cristina and are dominated by the huge central **La Font Màgica** (Magic Fountain). The fountains are visible from Pl. d'Espanya, in front of the Palau Nacional. During weekends, colored lights and dramatic music bring the fountains to life in a spectacular display. (*On Av. Reina María Cristina.* Ⓜ*Espanya, L1/L3. Shows May-Sept. Th-Su every 30min. 9-11:30pm; Oct.-Apr. F-Sa every 30min. 7-9pm. Free.*)

CEMENTIRI DEL SUD-OEST. This gigantic Modernist cemetery, dating from 1883, is an amazing complex of stone, brick, sculpture, and stained glass. Because the cemetery is in a seldom-frequented part of Montjuïc, it can be a little deserted. With friends, however, the place's eerie, otherworldly feel is more alluring than alarming. Of special note are the **Amatler family tomb** designed by Puig i Cadafalch (who also designed their house in l'Eixample; see p. 122) and the statuary-topped **Batlló family resting place** (of Casa Batlló fame; see p. 121). In the cemetery's northeast corner, the **Fossar de la Pedrera** commemorates the site where many Republican heroes of the Civil War were rounded up and shot. Stone pillars are engraved with the names of the victims, and an arched statue set in a small pond honors Catalan President **Lluís Companys,** who was assassinated by Franco on this very spot in 1940. *(C. Mare de Deu del Port, 54-58. Bus #38 from Pl. de Catalunya will drop you off across from the main entrance. Or, from inside Montjuïc, follow Av. del Castell to the left with your back to the Castle. The back entrance to the cemetery is a 20min. walk downhill and will be on your left. To get to Fossar de la Pedrera, turn left on Via Santa Eulalia by the cemetery's main entrance and take the 2nd right onto Sant Joseph; follow this paved path and look for Fossor signs. A helpful cemetery map is available from the administration offices at the main entrance, across from the bus stop. ☎ 934 84 17 00. Open daily 8am-6pm. Free.)*

PARC JOAN MIRÓ. Miró's giant **Dona i Ocell** *(Woman and Bird,* 1982) holds court in the center of a park dedicated to the artist. This colorful sculpture rises 22m (72 ft.) into the air, a mosaic of glazed greens, yellows, reds, and blues in homage to Gaudí. Miró changed the name from *Le Coq* after city planners objected. During the summer, particularly in June, Parc Miró is the favorite hangout of firecracker enthusiasts. *(C. Tarragona. Ⓜ Espanya, L1/L3, or Tarragona, L3. A 5min. walk down C. Tarragona from Pl. de Espanya.)*

ANELLA OLÍMPICA. In 1929, Barcelona inaugurated the Estadi Olímpic de Montjuïc (Olympic Stadium) in its unsuccessful bid for the 1932 Olympic games. Over 50 years later, Catalan architects **Federic Correa** and **Alfons Milà,** designers of the Anella Olímpica (Olympic Ring) esplanade, completed the facilities in time for the '92 Games with the help of Italian architect **Vittorio Gregotti.** The Olympic opening ceremonies took place here that year; the stadium is capable of seating 55,000 spectators, or 77,000 with the incorporation of temporary terracing. Nearby, the **Torre de Telefónica,** designed by Valencian Santiago Calatrava, commands the Olympic skyline at 106m (348ft). Today, Montjuïc's Olympic area is still a major tourist attraction. The well-equipped Anella Olímpica lives on, serving the sporting needs of professionals and amateurs alike. Come here to catch a soccer game at the Estadi Olímpic (see **Entertainment,** p. 153) or swim in the Piscines Bernat Picornell. *(The easiest way to get to the Olympic Area is to take the funicular from inside Ⓜ Paral·lel L2/L3 at Av. Parallel and Nou de la Rambla. Turn left out of the funicular station onto Av. Miramar and follow it past the Fundació Miró. The road turns into Av. de l'Estadi; the stadium is on your left. Alternatively, take bus #50 from la Plaça d'Espanya and ask to be let off when you see the stadium on your right. Wheelchair accessible.)*

PAVELLÓ MIES VAN DER ROHE. Renowned as one of the most original works of the famous German architect Mies van der Rohe, this Barcelona landmark is an example of spatial serenity that is far ahead of its time. Van der Rohe built a pavilion for the 1929 International Exhibition, but his contribution—a minimalist marvel of glass, stone, marble, and steel—was demolished in 1930 when no one purchased it. The pavilion standing in its place today is a replica commissioned by the city government; the reconstruction was led by architects Cristtian Circi, Fernando Ramos, and Ignasi de Sola Morales. The open-air courtyards are home to Georg Kolbe's graceful statue, **Morning,** and several copies of van der Rohe's famous **Barcelona Chair,** one of the first tubular steel chairs ever designed. *(From Ⓜ Espanya, L1/L3, follow Av. Reina Maria Cristina until the Font Màgica. Face the Palau Nacional and the Font Màgica; the Pavelló is to the right. ☎ 93 423*

S
I
G
H
T
S

40 16; www.miesbcn.com. Guided tours W and F 5-7pm. Open daily 10am-8pm. €4.50, students €2.30, under 18 free.)

GARDENS OF MONTJUÏC

JARDINS LARIBAL. These trellised, shady 7.8 acres of gardens wind sinuously down the Montjuïc hillside, just beneath the Fundacio Miró. Sit by a lily pond and look out over the city to the Sagrada Família and Torre Agbar; you'll never want to leave. *(Av. Mirimar and Pg. de Santa Madrona; the gardens are accessible from either street. Open daily 10am-sunset. Free.)*

JARDINS JOAN MARAGALL. Joan Maragall i Gorina (1860-1911) was the leader of the *Modernisme* movement in literature. (And the father of 13 kids. Busy guy.) Recline in this park among flowers, fountains, and statues, or wander over to the Albéniz Mansion, which was designed by Juan Moya for the 1929 Exposition. Ideal for a picnic lunch before a visit to the nearby MNAC. *(Av. de l'Estadi 65-69. From the mirador del MNAC, walk to the right, looking at the view, down a flight of stairs, and then up Pg. Sta. Madrona; the entrance to the gardens is just before the T-intersection with Av. de Miramar on the right. Albéniz Mansion ☎ 932 92 42 12. Garden open Sa-Su and holidays 10am-3pm. Free.)*

JARDINS MOSSÉN JACINT VERDAGUER. Named after the Catalan poet Mossén Jacint Verdaguer, these expansive gardens merit a leisurely visit. Walk to the top of the hill where a pond feeds water to geometric pools below—the view from here is spectacular. On C. Montjuïc, the smaller Jardins de Joan Brossa holds the **Carmen Amaya** statue crafted by Josep Cañas i Cañas in 1966, which honors the traditional Catalan Sardana. *(Av. Miramar, between the Fundació Miró and the Castell de Montjuïc. From Ⓜ Paral·lel, L2/L3, take the funicular to Av. Miramar. Turn right out of the funicular and walk along Av. Miramar, then uphill on C. Montjuïc. ☎ 900 30 20 30. Open daily 10am-sunset. Free.)*

JARDÍ BOTANIC. The topography of the Montjuïc mountainside dictates the layout of the beds in Barcelona's botanical garden. The garden focuses on those plants that thrive in a Mediterranean climate (this replaced the earlier strategy, focusing on plants that can't survive a Mediterranean climate). Plants from eight regions are represented: Australia, California, the Canary Islands, Chile, the Eastern Mediterranean, North Africa, South Africa, and the Western Mediterranean. Without a canopy of big trees to protect it, the hillside can be scorching hot in the summer; stroll the garden in the morning or early evening. *(C. Dr. Font i Quer, 2. From the Olympic Stadium, walk up C. Dr. Font i Quer. Buses #50 and #55 also stop in front of the garden. ☎ 934 26 49 35; www.jardibotanic.bcn.es/index_eng.htm. Garden open June-Aug. 10am-8pm. €3.50, under 25 €1.70, under 16 free. Last Su of every month and every Su after 3pm free.)*

GRÀCIA

⊠PARC GÜELL. On a hill at the northern edge of Gràcia lies Barcelona's most enchanting public park, designed entirely by **Gaudí,** and—in typical Gaudí fashion—not completed until after his death. After the pleasing results of his collaboration with Gaudí on Güell's Palau, Eusebi Güell, a Catalan industrialist and patron of the arts, commissioned the renowned architect to fashion a garden city in the tradition of Hampstead Heath and other parks in England, where Güell had spent many years. Güell was fascinated with rank and power (he longed to be granted a title by the king), and he envisioned a utopic community devoid of the lower classes (the turn-of-the-century Beverly Hills). Started in 1900, construction slowed to a halt in 1914 due to financial difficulties, and only three houses were completed. The citizens of Barcelona were put off both by Gaudí's shockingly bold designs and the park's then-great distance from the city. As a result, only two aristocrats signed on and as a housing development it was a complete failure.

As a park, Park Güell is fantastic. In 1918, the Barcelona City Council bought Park Güell, and in 1923 opened the multicolored, dwarfish buildings and mosaic stairways to the public. The park has since been honored as a UNESCO World Heritage Site. The park, with its Catalan themes, religious symbolism, and natural influences (read: beautiful flowers), is a symphony of color and form. The most eye-catching elements of the park—the surreal mosaics and fairy-tale fountains—are clustered around the main entrance on C. Olot. The entrance's Palmetto Gate, a replica of the iron work on Gaudí's *Casa Vicens*, is flanked by two small buildings originally meant to house the community's administrative offices. Visitors today can stop by the LAIE book and gift shop in the house on the left as you face the park entrance. These otherworldly houses were inspired by a Catalan production of Hansel and Gretel; the spire-topped construction belongs to the children, and the other, crowned with a bright red poisonous mushroom, belongs to the witch. Lavishly decorated with fan-shaped mosaics, the roofs resemble edible gingerbread and cream frosting. Behind Hansel and Gretel's house, you'll find the park's restrooms and a popular cafe. (Coffee €1.50; tapas €1-3; bocadillos €3-6. Open during park hours.)

Facing the majestic double staircase, a cavernous stone area to the right, now under construction, was originally meant to house the carriages of park residents. When open, the structure, reminiscent of an elephant, serves as a shaded rest area for visitors. The staircase itself is divided into three sections, each with its own fountain. Tourists jostle to take pictures of their loved ones beside the gaping, multicolored **salamander fountain** as it drools into the basin below. The animal's sleek body is covered with a tightly woven mosaic of green, orange, and blue. Some believe it is a reference to the coat of arms of the French city of Nîmes, the northern boundary of Old Catalunya. At the next level, a curvaceous red mosaic fountain holds a stone interpreted to be either an oracle or the philosopher's stone. The mouth-like bench behind it is entirely protected from the wind and remains in the shade for three seasons (winter is the sunny one).

Stairs lead up to the **Hall of One Hundred Columns (Teatro Griego),** a Modernist masterpiece of 86 Doric columns (but who's counting?). A spectacular open space meant for the community's market, the hall's columns support a ceiling constructed of white-tiled domes. Toward the center, musicians often play classical music, and multicolored medallions are interspersed among the ceiling domes. **Josep Maria Jujol,** Gaudí's right-hand man, created every medallion, using scraps from discarded mirrors, plates, glasses, and even porcelain dolls.

Stairs on either side of the hall lead up to the **Plaça de la Naturalesa,** a barren open area partly supported by the columned hall below and surrounded by the **serpentine bench.** The shape of the bench is not only aesthetically pleasing, but also structurally necessary given the positioning of the columns below. It is also designed to cradle visitors' buttocks and is consequently incredibly comfortable. All of this thanks to the rumored "creative methods" of Jujol. He is said to have made one of the workers sit bare-assed in the wet cement to add that extra, anatomically correct touch. Pieced together from broken ceramic remnants from local pottery workshops, Gaudí and Jujol's multicolored bench is covered with brightly colored flowers, geometric patterns, and religious images. During the park's restoration in 1995, workers discovered that the 21 distinct tones of white are cast-offs from the **Casa Milà** (see p. 120) that had been cemented in the bench. The bench's abstract collage later became a great inspiration for Joan Miró's Surrealist work.

From here, sweeping paths supported by columns (meant to resemble palm trees) swerve through hedges and ascend to the park's summit, which commands tremendous views of the city. A pleasant walk through the grounds begins at the path directly to right when facing the salamander fountain. Follow the wide path past the sunny flower beds and open grassy area and veer right toward the shaded benches. As the path twists uphill, the turreted, pink **Casa-Museu Gaudí** (p. 132) appears on your left. Farther ahead, the **Pont dels Enamorats** offers views of the city all the way to the sea, and Gaudí's stone trees—tall columns topped with agave plants—are interspersed with curved benches. Around the next curve, **Casa Trías** (1905), the park's third house, purchased by the lawyer Trías Domènech and still owned by his family, is surrounded by less scenic walking paths that loop around to the left along Avenue del Coll del Portell. Farther along the wide, main path, past a grassy area with a small playground and plenty of benches, an upward slope spirals to **El Turo de Les Tres Creus**. Originally destined to be the park residents' church, the small tower is topped with a mere three crosses, which appear to form an arrow when you look toward the east. This peak is the park's highest point, offering a dazzling 360° view of the city below. To head back down, follow the twisting path that slopes toward the sea. Check out the views of the Hansel and Gretel houses and other park structures. At the Avenue Sant Josep de la Muntanya entrance, follow a narrow path to the right until it becomes El Viaducte de la Bugadera as it passes Güell's house (now a school) on the right. The irregularly shaped stone columns that support the covered passageway are composed of fascinating shapes. You'll find the statue of **La Bugadera** (the Washerwoman) on one of the last columns in the passageway. Stairs ahead lead back to the Pl. de la Naturalesa. *(Bus #24 from Pl. Catalunya stops at the upper entrance. Info center ☎ 93 284 62 00. Park and info center open daily 9am-dusk. Free.)*

CASA-MUSEU GAUDÍ. Designed by Gaudí's friend and colleague, **Fransesc Berenguer,** the Casa-Museu Gaudí was the celebrated architect's home from 1906 to 1926, when he moved into the Sagrada Família for the months leading up his death. Gaudí's leftover fence work from other projects was used to create the garden of metallic plant sculptures in front of the museum. The three-story house is a great place to examine Gaudí's anatomical furniture designs from the Casa Batlló, paintings of several of his works by notable artists, and his bronze-cast death mask from close-up. The ceilings, different in every room, highlight the otherwise sober spaces with touches of color and eye-catching patterns. Before leaving, peek into the Modernist bathroom where the toilet seat curves in Gaudí's trademark saddle-shape. *(☎ 93 219 38 11. Carretera del Carmel. Inside Park Güell, to the right of the Hall of One Hundred Columns when you are facing away from the sea. Open daily Apr.-Sept. 10am-8pm; Oct.-Mar. 10am-6pm. Last entrance 15min. before closing. €5.50, with ISIC or under 18 €4.50, under 10 free.)*

OTHER HOUSES IN GRÀCIA

When in Gràcia, look up. The neighborhood's narrow, tree-lined streets are home to several of *Modernisme's* lesser-known architectural masterpieces. Casting your eyes skyward can also prove rewarding: warped wrought-iron balconies and brightly patterned walls inform you that yes, you have stumbled upon a masterpiece. Because these buildings are private houses, their interiors are closed to the public. The houses are so distinctive, however, that even a good look at each exterior is well worth the (sometimes lengthy) walk.

CASA VICENS. Gaudí designed Vicens between 1883 and 1888 for a local tile manufacturer; it is fittingly decorated with blocks of cheerful green, white, and yellow ceramic tiles accented with red-painted brick. The famous architect studied Arabic design to come up with the casa's rigid angles. By contrast, the graceful, fluid ironwork of the balconies and the palm-leaf gate foreshadow the architect's style in later projects. In the summer, bougainvillea brims over the right hand corner of the house, adding a pleasing touch of purple. *(C. Carolines, 24-26.)*

CASA RAMOS. Jaume Torres completed Casa Ramos in 1906. Today the house includes three separate buildings that share a façade. The Modernist floral motifs and insect-patterned grilles are eye-catching, despite the fact that its ground floor is now almost entirely occupied by storefronts. *(Pl. de Lesseps, 32, ⓂLesseps.)*

CASA CAMA. Francesc Berenguer designed this building's two stained-glass-enclosed turrets. The building repeats a long-stemmed flower design in the paint job and the window. Notice the beautifully carved wood shutters. *(Gran de Gràcia, 15.)*

CASA FUSTER. Lluís Domenèch i Montaner designed this asymmetrical neo-Gothic building between 1908 and 1911 and made its cylindrical corner tower his focus. Get up close to see the nesting birds, roses, and other intricate designs sculpted at the top of the ground-floor columns. *(Pg. de Gràcia, 132.)*

CASA BONAVENTURA FERRER. Pere Falques completed this house in 1906. It is one of the few Modernist baroque buildings in Barcelona, and is perhaps the least impressive of the houses we list—it looks more like a hunk of rock than anything else. *(Pg. de Gràcia, 113. ⓂDiagonal L3/5 or Fontana L3.)*

PLAÇAS IN GRÀCIA

In the neighborhood's *plaças*, locals gather over long meals at outdoor tables. A quick stroll through the *plaças* is a great way to get acquainted with the area (and, if you're willing to linger, with the locals).

PLAÇA RUIS I TAULET. This plaça is home to the **Torre del Reloj** (clock tower), an emblem of the Revolution of 1868. The tower was designed by architect Antoni Rovira i Trias and built with four faces so that it could be seen from all corners of the neighborhood. The clock itself was the work of Swiss-born Albert Billeter. A plaque on the tower commemorates a human tower that the Castellers (a tradition apparently still practiced in Catalonia) once erected next to the Torre. Facing the plaça is Gràcia's sky-blue town hall, a Modernist work designed by local architect Francesc Berenguer and adorned with Gràcia's coat of arms. *(ⓂFontana. Walk down C. Gran de Gràcia and make a left on C. St. Domenec. The plaça is on your right.)*

PLAÇA LESSEPS. This is where you surface when you come out of the Lesseps metro stop. The public art installed here (which takes the shape of a giant, partially-submerged metal boat) incited great controversy when it was first installed. It is meant to symbolize unity, as this area is the "seam" of Gràcia and the Zona Alta and the intersection of several major roads. *(ⓂLesseps.)*

PLAÇA DEL DIAMANTE. This plaça was made famous by Merce Rodoreda's 1962 novel of the same title, which was translated into English as *The Time of the Doves*. The plaça features a sculpture of La Colometa, the main character in Rodoreda's novel. This is one of the two plaças in Gràcia that nightlife centers (the other is Plaça del Sol). Show up around 8pm and stay as long as you like. *(ⓂFontana. Walk up C. d'Asturies.)*

PLAÇA VIRREINA. This calm *plaça* is bordered by tapas bars, pastel houses, and the Church of St. Joan de Gràcia. On Sunday mornings, the square transforms into a market where locals sell secondhand goods. (Ⓜ*Fontana. Follow the directions to Plaça del Diamante, but continue several blocks farther.*)

PLAÇA DEL SOL. This square is skirted by a fantastic selection of cafes and bars that teem with young locals at night; the neighbors always complain. The *plaça* has a raised concrete center, so join the crowd to talk, drink, and smoke. It also boasts a statue by Joaquim Camps entitled *Astrolabi* that represents a sun dial and the twelve signs of the zodiac. (Ⓜ*Fontana. Walk down C. Gran de Gràcia to Trav. de Gràcia and turn left. Make another left up C. Sol.*)

PLAÇA REVOLUCIÓ DE SEPTIEMBRE 1868. This modest *plaça* is dotted with trees, and celebrates—you guessed it—the Revolution of 1868, also known as **La Septimbrina.** The uprising dethroned Queen Isabel II and ushered in a period now known as the **Sexenio Democrático** (the six democratic years, 1868-1874). The Bourbon dynasty was restored in 1874. Now, the square is bordered by several restaurants. (Ⓜ*Fontana. Walk down C. Gran de Gràcia to Trav. de Gràcia and make a left. Make another left up Torrent de l'Olla; the square is on your right.*)

PLAÇA DE JOHN LENNON. Plaça de John Lennon, created in 1993, honors the rock musician with a record-shaped plaque that reads "Give Peace a Chance" in Catalan. This is a favorite playground for local children *and* their parents. (Ⓜ*Fontana or Diagonal. From Fontana, walk down C. Gran de Gràcia, make a right on Trav. de Gràcia, and then another right on C. Quevedo. The plaça is on the left.*)

PLAÇA RASPALL. This square is a popular gathering spot for Gràcia's gypsy population. A plaque remembers the musician Gato Pérez, who wrote the well-known (in Spain) rumba "Y ahora vengo yo...cantando aunque no sea Moreno" ("And now, here I come—singing although I am not dark-haired"). (Ⓜ*Fontana or Diagonal. From Fontana, walk down C. Gran de Gràcia, make a left on Trav. de Gràcia, a right on Mare de Deu dels Desemperats, and another left on C. Tordera.*)

VALL D'HEBRON AND HORTA-GUINARDÓ

Vall d'Hebron and Horta-Guinardó are not sightseeing meccas. They do, however, have extensive sports facilities and a few nice parks and plaças, almost all of which boast formidable views of the city.

JARDINS DEL LABERINT D'HORTA. Once the private grounds of a wealthy marquis, this Neoclassical 17-acre garden was restored by the architect **Joaquim M. Casamor i d'Espona.** The garden is replete with sculptures of Greek heroes, manicured walkways, a love canal, a cascade, and, of course, the labyrinth. A hot summer afternoon can instantly become a cool, refreshing bit of paradise in this fairy-tale park. (*C. dels Germans Desvalts, 1.* Ⓜ*Mundet, L3. Exit on the right and follow Pg. de Vall d'Hebron, turning left before the Velodróm cycling facility. Jardins are directly behind the Velodróm, up the steep steps.* ☎ *934 28 39 34. Open daily May-Aug. 10am-9pm; Apr. and Sept. 10am-8pm; Mar. and Oct. 10am-7pm; Nov.-Feb. 10am-6pm. €2, under 14 €1.50, under 5 free. Su Free. Tours an additional €2.*)

BIBLIOTECA HORTA-CAN MARINER. This brand new, glass-and-steel library provides a peaceful break from walking the hills of Vall d'Hebron and Horta-Guinardó. The library specializes in books on theater and is filled with 20-somethings (the popular library even has a Facebook page). The library also has free internet and Wi-Fi. (*C. del Vent, 1.* Ⓜ*Horta. From the Metro, walk up C. d'Horta.* ☎ *934 20 82 85. Open M 4pm-11:30pm, Tu 10am-2pm, W 10am-11:30pm, Th 10am-2pm, F 4pm-11:30pm, Sa 10am-2pm. Free.*)

🔲TIBIDABO

To reach Tibidabo by metro, take FCG L7 to Av. Tibidabo, then collect the Tramvia Blau (€4.10 round-trip) to Pl. Doctor Andreu, where the Tibidabo Funicular awaits to take you to the amusement park (runs every 15min. until park closes; €4 roundtrip, refundable with park admission). Or, take the T2 bus which runs from Pl. Catalunya to the Parc d'Attracions every 30min. until the park closes (€2.60 each way).

The name Tibidabo comes from a verse in the Latin Bible where the devil takes Christ to a pinnacle overlooking the many kingdoms of the world and says: *Haec omnia tibi dabo si cadens adoraveris me* (All of this I will give to you if you fall down and worship me). "All of this," in this case, is a gloriously high view of Barcelona spilling into the seemingly endless aquamarine Mediterranean. Besides the view, Tibidabo also offers a popular amusement park dating back to the turn of the century and a church, **El Sagrat Cor** (which ought to prevent any devil worship that might be spontaneously induced by the awesome vista).

Other points of interest on the way up the mountain include the colorful **La Rotonda** in Pl. JFK and the majestic **Casa Roviralta** (Av. Tibidabo, 31), two impressive *Modernista* works by Adolf Ruiz i Casamitjana and Joan Rubió, respectively. Just down the hill from the amusement park is the silver-domed **Observatori Fabra,** built in 1904 and still functioning today. Piercing the skyline next to El Sagrat Cor is the **Torre de Collserola** communications tower, built to satisfy the increased technological demands brought on by the 1992 Olympics.

🔲**PARC D'ATRACCIONS.** The assortment of amusement park rides and attractions offered here are each made infinitely more charming and romantic by its location high above Barcelona and its *fin-de-siècle* origins. The amusement park first opened in 1908, and several of the rides date back to the 1920s, including the iconic **Avión,** a red propeller plane that circles above the park, and the **Atalaya,** a crane-like structure with two rotating arms that reach a height of 550m. The lower levels of the park host the more thrilling rides, including the rollercoaster, log flume, and swinging ship, and are only accessible with a full entrance ticket. Entrance to the **Camí del Cel** (the top level of the park) is free for those who simply care to stroll, enjoy the views, pretend you're in a Woody Allen movie, and munch on cotton candy. Individual tickets (€2) can be purchased only for the *Camí del Cel* rides, which include the Atalaya, Avión, ferris wheel, and Museu d'Automats. *(Pl. Tibidabo, 3-4. ☎ 932 11 79 42; www.tibidabo.es. Park open July-Aug. noon-9pm; Camí del Cel open M-Th 11am-8pm, W-Su 11am-9pm. Off-season hours irregular, but generally park open Sa-Su noon-4pm; Camí del Cel open daily noon-4pm. Check website for more detailed schedules. Most attractions wheelchair-accessible. €25 for full entrance and unlimited rides, 60+ and under 1.1m tall €9, disabled visitors €5; unlimited Camí del Cel rides €11.)*

EL SAGRAT COR. This neo-Gothic Church of the Sacred Heart overlooks the city from the top of Tibidabo. Several additions made after St. John Bosco founded the church in 1886 result in an eclectic pastiche of architectural styles. The church boasts three terraces, each offering a more dizzying view than the last, and a lookout point at its peak (564m) with the greatest view of them all. Stairway to the first terrace is free; to reach the upper levels you have to take the elevator. *(Pl. Tibidabo. ☎ 934 17 56 86; www.templotibdabo.org. Lower stairs and church open 10am-8pm. Elevator to the top open daily 10am-2pm and 3-7pm; €2. Wheelchair-accessible at the lower levels.)*

TORRE DEL COLLSEROLA. Barcelona's sparkling, futuristic communications tower, soaring 560m above sea level, hardly blends in with the area's architecture and remains a point of contention among locals. Built to transmit TV and radio signals for the 1992 Olympics, the tower now has an external glass elevator that takes visitors to the 10th floor, offering spectacular views of the city the whole way up. *(Crta. de Vallvidrera, a short walk from the Parc d'Atraccions. ☎ 934 06 93 54. Open July-Sept. 15 W-Su 11am-2pm and 3:30-8pm. Irregular hours during off-season, but generally open Sa-Su 11am-2pm and 3:30-6pm. Closed Jan.-Feb. Check online for detailed schedule. €5, students €3.50, seniors and ages 4-14 €3.)*

PARC DE COLLSEROLA. Created as part of Barcelona's 1976 General Metropolitan Plan, the Parc de Collserola encompasses acres of greenery easily accessible from the city center. People come here to hike, bike, ride ponies, and drive on designated routes through the forest. Before exploring the park, stop at the extremely useful **Centre d'Informació.** The center has rotating exhibitions about the park and its wildlife, and the helpful staff sells numerous guides and maps in addition to providing free pamphlets. Most are available only in Catalan, and none are offered in English, but for those who plan on exploring the park extensively, it may still be worth it to invest in a more detailed Serra de Collserola map (€10), which shows all the trails spanning the park, and marks points of interest such as picnic areas, vistas, archeological remains, fountains, and historical buildings. It also comes with a guide outlining a range of trails and bike-paths, with descriptions in Catalan of some of the sights along the way. The center also has bathrooms, a snack bar, a public telephone, and a brief informational video about the park, available on request.

Parc de Collserola is full of enough natural and man-made sights to pack a long afternoon escape from the city. Most hiking and biking routes offer good views of the city and surrounding hills, especially the **Passeig Mirador de las Aigues,** an 11km route accessible from the Information Center. There are also more than 50 notable archaeological finds and ruins inside the park. The park has been shaped by civilization since at least the sixth century BC, as the remains of the **Penya del Oro** demonstrate. The area is also dotted with small churches and a chapel; the **Santa Creu d'Olorda** dates back to the 12th century. Walk across the viaduct in Can Ribes, or enjoy a rest in the shady **Font d'en Ribas,** a colorful *Modernista* fountain built around a spring in 1909. The water from the spring was said to have medicinal properties. **Castellciur,** a castle built in the 14th century over 12th-century remains, serves as a particularly good lookout point. Interesting remains from the last two centuries include the turreted **Sanatori Antituberculós.** Nicknamed "El Castell," it was intended as a tuberculosis hospital on Tibidabo but was never completed, and is now in an advanced state of ruin. Also worth noting are the remains of Dr. Salvador Andreu's **Arrabassada Casino.** Opened in 1911 with a proud exterior staircase reminiscent of that of the Paris Opera, the building was closed down by municipal authorities in 1912, and, like El Castell, has thoroughly deteriorated. *(Take the FGC train to Baixador de Vallvidrera and follow the steps above the exit for 10min. Info center at C. Carretera de l'Església, 92. ☎ 932 80 35 52; www.parccollserola.net. Open daily 9:30am-3pm.)*

SARRIÀ

A visit to Sarrià is a pleasant way to see the traditional home of the Catalan bourgeois and a more suburban side of Barcelona. The upper part of Sarrià, closer to the Collserola hills, is the place to stroll and gawk at the lavish gated mansions and private schools, which include Gaudí's **Casa Bellesguard** and **Collegi de les Teresianes.** If you're looking to meander through here, but don't want to sweat profusely, it's probably a good idea to start from above at Ronda de

Dalt and work your way down the steep hill that is Sarrià. The lower, older area of Sarrià is concentrated around the **Plaça Sarrià**, notable for the Neoclassical **Sant Vicenç de Sarrià Church** (1816). The front entrance of the church faces **Calle Major de Sarrià**, the area's main street, which is full of restaurants and cafes. Pl. Sarrià also has an antique market during the summer on Tuesdays (9am-8pm) and a small used-book market on Fridays (9am-8pm). Once a year, on May 11, the small, shady **Plaça Sant Vicenç** off C. Major de Sarrià, hosts **La Fira de Sant Ponç**, a festival honoring the patron saint of herbalists and beekeepers; various medicinal plants, honey products, and cheeses are put out for the occasion.

CASA BELLESGUARD. Now a private home, Casa Bellesguard is closed to the public, but for true Gaudí fanatics, even a peek from the street is worthwhile. Built by Gaudí in 1902, Casa Bellesguard is one of the architect's neo-Gothic designs and resembles something out of a medieval fairy tale. Tall and fairly compact, with one sculpture spire, Casa Bellesguard is adorned with metal grillwork, tiled benches resplendent with blue and red fish, and three Rapunzel-esque balconies. Note the starred, blue-and-white tiles that frame the window above the door. A stone staircase and landing to the left of the entrance gate provide a picturesque view of the building and the surrounding hills. *(C. Belles-guard, 16-20. FCG: Sarrià or Av. Tibidabo. To access the house from above, head to ⓜZona Universitaria. Then catch the #60 bus at Zona Universitària-Escola A E Empresarials (right next to the metro stop) and take it 7 stops to Benedetti-Ronda de Dalt. From Ronda de Dalt, walk down C. de Bellesguard. The walk is short and hassle-free, and the casa will be on your left. To access the house from below, take bus #14, 30, 66, 70, or 72 to Pg. Bonanova, then take C. Escoles Pies up the steep hill to where it dead-ends at C. Immaculada, and make a right. Walk for several long blocks until C. Immaculada dead-ends at C. Bellesguard and make a left up the hill; Casa Bellesguard is on your right.)*

COLLEGI DE LES TERESIANES. The construction of this stately Neo-Gothic building, started by an unknown architect in 1888, was taken over by Gaudí the following year. The building now serves as a Catholic school. Gaudí designed a wing (to the right as you enter the gate), and though constrained by a low budget, he managed to create some innovative features. Legend has it that when Father Osso, the man who hired Gaudí to design the building, pressured the architect to restrain himself, Gaudí replied, "Let's each stick to our own strength; I'll make houses, and you write masses." On the building's facade, a row of repeating letters—JSH for *Jesú Salvate Hombres* (Jesus Saves Men)—adorns the space between two rows of windows. The arcs of the lower windows recall the shape of hands in prayer, and the pineapple shape that tops a tower on the left symbolizes strength. Though Gaudí was content to super-vise most of the wing's construction, he fashioned the iron gate himself, with repeating symbols of Saint Teresa. While these details can be appreciated from outside, it is the school's main internal hallways and two skylights that are admired by architects worldwide for their perfect parabolic arches. *(C. Ganduxer, 85-105. FGC: Bonanova. Bus #14, 16, 72, or 74. ☎ 932 12 33 54. Call in advance to schedule a tour, offered Sept.-June 10:30am-1pm. Free.)*

JARDIN DE LA VILLA AMÈLIA. Sarrià boasts some of the most relaxing and well-manicured public spaces in the city. The 6-acre Jardins de la Villa Amèlia, designed by architect **Joaquim Maria Casamor,** provide families and mid-after-noon loungers with plenty of playgrounds and bench space. Palm trees and eucalyptus-lined paths radiate out from a central fountain, a few feet away from an unobtrusive *chiringuito* (small cafe). As you walk around the pond, note one particularly impressive eucalyptus, estimated to be 115 years old. *(FGC: Sarrià. Walk down C. Cardenal Sentmenat, turn right on C. Dels Vergòs, and cross the Pl. d'Artos onto C. de Santa Amèlia. The parks are 4 blocks down. Open daily 10am-sunset.)*

JARDIN DE LA VILLA CECILIA. Across the street from the Jardin de la Villa Amèlia is the 4-acre Jardin de la Villa Cecilia. Created by architects **Jose Antonio Martinez Lapena** and **Elias Torres,** the garden won a prize for its design. Jardin de la Villa Cecilia is built around a civic center—the Villa Cecilia—and boasts a multilevel canal, shrubbery, a basketball court, ping-pong tables, and a playground. As you walk into the park, note the 1964 sculpture by Francisco Lopez Hernandez; the surreal metal construction, *Ophelia*, appears to float in the canal. *(FGC: Sarrià. Walk down C. Cardenal Sentmenat, turn right on C. Dels Vergòs, and cross the Pl. d'Artos onto C. de Santa Amèlia. The parks are 4 blocks down. Open daily 8am-sunset.)*

PEDRALBES AND LES CORTS

The sights in Pedralbes and Les Corts, though distant from the city center, are worth traveling for.

⊠MONESTIR DE PEDRALBES. Set amid the low-rise apartments of Zona Alta, this monastery makes a surprisingly tranquil, refreshing, and historically interesting break for those with the time to leave the glamour and chaos of downtown Barcelona. Devout Queen Elisenda of Montcada founded the monastery in 1327 to atone for her earthly sins. She chose the name Pedralbes from the Latin *"petras albas"* ("white stones"). The first stone was put in place in March 1326, and by May 1327, the first community of nuns moved in. These were the Poor Clare nuns, the female branch of the Franciscan order. When noble women of the time became widows, they had two choices—remarry or become a nun. Those who chose the latter option often brought with them family riches; because of this, monasteries tended to accumulate wealth and art. Elisenda of Montcada was the fourth and final wife of King James II, and when he died a year after the complex's completion, she chose to leave the court and live near the monastery. When she died in 1364, she left her substantial inheritance to the monastery, and requested to be buried there. Her tomb depicts her in two lights: in the figure that faces the church, she is dressed as a queen, and in the figure that faces the cloister, as a penitent and widow.

Inside the monastery, you can peek into the lives that the nuns led centuries ago; the courtyard, infirmary, kitchen, and dining hall have all been elegantly restored and opened to the public. Though the Poor Clares live on, they have recognized the historical value of the old monastery and bequeathed it to the City of Barcelona; they now reside in adjoining facilities. Inside the old monastery, the cloister (the central courtyard) boasts a garden and a fragrant exhibit. Around the cloister, one can see a series of day cells—the nuns' own personal retreats, diminutive in size but perfect in detail.

Also worth seeing is the **Dormidor.** Once the nuns' sleeping quarters, today, this cavernous hall holds the exhibition "The Treasures of the Monastery." The collections of altarpieces and choir books are intricately crafted, gilded, and in general, dazzling. While the monastery once housed the impressive Thyssen-Bornemisza collection, it no longer does; this collection has been moved to the **MNAC** on Montjuïc (p. 128). The monastery's orange trees, splashing fountains, and shaded walkways create a rare sense of tranquility. *(Baixada del Monestir, 9.*

Ⓜ*Palau Reial, L3. Go north on Av. Pedralbes from Pl. Pius XII (the street is not well labeled, but it is the major roadway) and follow road signs to the monastery. Buses #22, 63, 64, 75 (school days only), 78. ☎ 932 56 34 34; www.museuhistoria.bcn.cat. €6, students €4. 1st Su of every month and every Su 3-8pm free. Open daily 10am-8pm.)*

PALAU REIAL DE PEDRALBES. Located around the corner from the University of Barcelona, the Palau Reial de Pedralbes and its quiet park provide a secluded getaway from the rest of the city. The Palau itself, commissioned by the Güell family for the King of Spain (Alfonso XII) to make their father Eusebi Güell a count, was given to Spain at the International Exposition of 1929. The pale orange mansion is tastefully designed and houses the **Museu de les Arts Decoratives** and the **Museu de Ceràmica** (p. 151). When you walk in, make sure to glance up and examine the impressive ceiling mural. Only real Gaudí enthusiasts will want to check out the much-lauded drinking fountain. The architect constructed it in his early years, and it pales in comparison to his more grandiose works. The fountain is off to the left of the main path to the palace, in a small forest of bamboo shoots. The simple design is a rather small twisting iron ▪dragon that spouts water over a Catalan shield. Above, a bust of Hercules surveys the proceedings. "Rediscovered" in 1983 after decades of neglect, the fountain was restored and now provides water to the numerous students picnicking in the park. *(Av. Diagonal, 686. Ⓜ Palau Reial, L3. At the far end of the park.)*

FINCA GÜELL. The *finca* (farm) was built in 1883, when Gaudí's patron Eusebi Güell extended his estate into Pedralbes. At one point, these pavilions were Güell's summer estate and a working farm. Gaudí recreated the garden of the Hesperides as it is described in *L'Atlantida* by Jacint Verdaguer i Santaló, a great Catalan poet; thus the orange tree atop the pillar at the garden's entrance and the ▪dragon that Gaudí created for this estate's gate. Those disappointed with the relatively unimposing Gaudí iron dragon in the Parc del Palau Reial should head up Av. Pedralbes to see this more menacing monster. Meticulously welded, the animal spreads its wings across the front fence of the farm, flashing fearsome fangs to the curious ones who might be tempted to cross. *(Av. Pedralbes, 7. Ⓜ Palau Reial, L3. A 5min. walk from Av. Diagonal, on the left. ☎ 933 17 76 52. Owned by the University of Barcelona and closed to the public except for guided visits M-F 10:15am and 12:15pm. Call for reservations.)*

MUSEUMS

BARRI GÒTIC AND LAS RAMBLAS

Barri Gòtic is not the place for contemporary art or halls full of the old masters; instead, it is home to a smattering of quirky collections and historical exhibitions.

MUSEU D'HISTÒRIA DE LA CIUTAT. Buried some 20m below a seemingly innocuous old plaça lies one of the two components of the Museu d'Història de la Ciutat: the subterranean excavations of the Roman city of Barcino. This **archaeological exhibit** displays incredibly well-preserved AD first- to sixth-century ruins; through glass sections, you can see huge ceramic wine casks, intricate Roman floor mosaics, and the reused cornerstones that form part of the Roman walls. The fourth-century wall fresco depicting a man on horseback is a particularly beautiful and well-preserved relic. Also accessible through the museum is the **Palau Reial Major,** which was built on top of the fourth-century ruins and served as the residence of the Catalan-Aragonese monarchs. The Gothic **Saló de Tinell** (Throne Room) is supposedly the place where Fernando and Isabel received Columbus after his journey to America, and now hosts exhibitions about contemporary Barcelona. *(Pl. del Rei. ⓂJaume I. ☎ 932 56 21 00; www.museuhistoria.bcn.cat. Wheelchair-accessible. Open Apr.-Sept. Tu-Sa 10am-8pm, Su 10am-3pm; Oct.-Mar. Tu-Sa 10am-2pm and 4-7pm, Su 10am-3pm. Free multilingual audio guides. Pamphlets available in English. Museum €6, students €4. Exhibition €1.80/1.10. Museum and exhibition €6.80/5.10. Under 16 free.)*

CENTRE D'ART DE SANTA MÓNICA. Once a convent, this museum now houses temporary exhibitions and hosts artistic events. The provocative installations housed here are often interactive and tend to be quite elaborate. In April 2009, the museum turned heads by staging an "itinerant musical action" whereby a man played piano while being paraded down Las Ramblas with a man and a woman having passionate simulated sex atop his instrument. There are significant rebuilding phases between shows, so call and make sure the galleries are open before you visit. Just in front of the Museum is the **Punt d'Informació Cultural,** which has all the art-related programs and flyers you could ever want. *(La Rambla, 7. ⓂDrassanes. ☎ 933 16 28 10; www.artsantamonica.cat. Open Tu-Sa noon-10pm. Free. Punt d'Informació Cultural open M-F 9:30am-2pm and 3:30-7:30pm, Sa 10am-2pm.)*

MUSEU DE L'ERÒTICA. This stimulating museum has an odd assortment of pictures, artwork, and artifacts that spans human history and depicts a variety of sexual acrobatics that seem to defy the limits of human flexibility. The 7 ft. wooden phallus is a classic photo-op. Be sure to catch the 1926 porno flick said to have been secretly commissioned by King Alfonso XIII. *(La Rambla, 96. ⓂLiceu, L1/3. ☎ 933 18 98 65; www.erotica-museum.com. Open daily 10am-9pm. €9, students €8.)*

MUSEU DE CERA (WAX MUSEUM). Over 300 wax figures form an endless parade of celebrities, fictional characters, and rather obscure European historical figures. The most recognizable ones have distinctive facial hair, like Fidel Castro and Chewbacca from Star Wars. If the celebrities upstairs are too banal, downstairs you'll find more gruesome depictions of famous martyrs, murderers, and monsters. For those dying to have their picture taken with a wax sculpture of Picasso mid-brush stroke, this is the place to go. *(La Rambla, 4-6 or Pg. de la Banca, 7. ⓂDrassanes. ☎ 933 17 26 49, www.museocerabcn.com. Open July-Sept. daily 10am-10pm; Oct.-June M-F 10am-1:30pm and 4-7:30pm, Sa-Su and holidays 11am-2pm and 4:30-8:30pm. Last entrance 30min. before closing. €10, ages 5-11 and seniors €6, under 5 free. Audioguide €3.50.)*

MUSEU FREDERIC MARÈS. Marès (1893-1991) was one of Spain's better known sculptors, but he also had an insatiable passion for collecting; as he once said, "I make sculptures so that I may buy sculptures." In 1946, in a classic example of the bourgeois patronage of the arts so common in Catalunya, he founded this museum and donated his entire private collection and some of his own sculptures. The building itself was originally part of the Palau Reial Major, home to the monarchs of the Aragonese dynasty from the end of the 10th century through the 15th century.

Inside the museum, the lower floors house a huge collection of Spanish and Hispanic sculpture from pre-Roman times through the 19th century. The majority of these floors are dedicated to an almost endless collection of wooden Christ figures and Mary-with-Jesus carvings, which cannot help but become repetitive to even the most patient (and pious) observer. Also overwhelming but with a bit more variety are the upper floors, containing Marès's "Sentimental Museum," a vast collection of objects daily life during the Romantic era that features cases upon cases of fans, jewelry, combs, timepieces, scissors, pipes, playing cards, dolls, and floral arrangements.

In addition to these collections is a second-floor library dedicated to Marès's own sculpture, accessible by appointment only, and a room on the ground floor dedicated to rotating sculpture exhibits. (*Pl. de Sant Iu, 5-6 or Pg. de la Banca, 7.* Ⓜ*Jaume I.* ☎*932 56 35 00; www.museumares.bcn.cat. Open Tu-Su 10am-7pm, holidays 10am-3pm. €4.20, students and seniors €2.40, under 16 free. Free entry W afternoons and first Su of the month. Free audioguide with deposit of picture ID.*)

MUSEU DIOCESÀ. This small museum tends to be overshadowed by the cathedral next door, but it is a treasure trove for history buffs, as it contains the city's only intact octagonal defense tower from Roman Barcino. The museum's collection of religious artifacts covers two main periods, the Romanesque (12th and 13th centuries), and the Gothic (14th and 15th centuries). Highlights include an almost entirely intact church fresco from 1122 as well as a stunning gold, diamond-adorned **Custodià del Pi,** made in 1587 and originally used in the nearby Santa Maria del Pi church. In Catholicism, the *custodià* is used to store the Host before and after the rite of communion. Still in perfect condition today, it drips with ornate detail and delicate religious symbolism.

The building itself is of interest as well. The round base at the bottom was built by the Romans during the AD first century, the octagonal base on top of that during the fourth century, the next section during medieval times (look for uniform windows), and the fourth during the Gothic period (look for the higher, more delicate row of windows). From the top floor gallery, you can even see blackened stones from fires started by invading Muslim armies in the Middle Ages. The entrance to the museum leads through the original Roman wall and into a Gothic building that was the city's oldest homeless shelter/soup kitchen, the Pia Almoina, before being turned into a prison in the 18th century under the dreaded Felipe V. As you reach the top floors, note the prisoner's etchings still visible near the stairs, and don't miss the excellent view of the cathedral's facade next door. The museum also hosts a series of temporary historical and artistic exhibits. (*Av. de la Catedral, 4.* Ⓜ*Jaume I.* ☎*933 15 22 13. Open M-Sa 10am-2pm and 4-8pm, Su 11-3pm. €6, students and seniors €3, under 7 free.*)

MUSEU DEL CALÇAT (SHOE MUSEUM). This bizarre collection of footwear is a tribute to the ancient guilds of Barcelona, tracing the existence of master shoemakers to an official document signed by the Bishop of Barcelona in 1203. Even today, a few faithful members tend to the guild's chapel in the Cathedral de la Sant Creu. Tucked away in the Pl. Sant Felip Neri, the museum includes reproductions of shoes from as far back as the AD first century. The majority of the collection comes from the past three centuries and includes everything from 18th-century men's sandals to Ronaldinho's winning soccer cleats. When the Via Laietana was built in 1908, the Shoe Museum was dismantled stone by stone and moved to Felip Neri to make room for the new thoroughfare. *(Pl. Sant Felip Neri, 5.* ⓂJaume I. ☎ 933 01 45 33. Open Tu-Su 11am-2pm. €2.50; information pamphlet €1.50.)

LA RIBERA

MUSEU PICASSO. This fascinating museum traces the development of Picasso as an artist with an exhibit of his early works, organized chronologically. The large collection weaves through five connected mansions that were once occupied by Barcelona's nobility. Picasso's friend, Jaume Sabartés, made the museum's founding donation in 1963; the collection was later expanded by Picasso himself, and then by relatives after his death. Though you may not recognize Picasso the Cubist in this collection of his earlier works, the museum gives unsurpassed insight into his formative years as a painter in Barcelona. Visitors will also witness the artist's later experiences in Paris, where he first encountered the impressionists' experiments with light and Cézanne's technique of flatness.

The museum features several noteworthy works from Picasso's Blue and Rose periods, but most impressive of all is the display of the artist's 58 Cubist interpretations of Velázquez's *Las Meninas*. The original painting is a breathtaking, 7ft. portrait of the royal family. Hailed as the finest Spanish painting, *Las Meninas* is often re-interpreted by Spanish painters as a rite of passage of the great. Instead of simply transposing the picture, Picasso reinvents it, transforming the many vantage points of the original into the jarring fragments and lines of vision that would become the trademark of his Cubist technique.

Other exhibits of the museum showcase his early award-winning paintings and his later sculpture. Special temporary exhibitions highlight work by Picasso's contemporaries. As Barcelona's most popular museum, the Museu Picasso often has lines snaking a good way down C. de Montcada; the best times to avoid the museum-going masses are mornings and early evenings. *(C. de Montcada, 15-23. ⓂJaume I, L4. From the metro, head down C. de la Princesa and turn right on C. de Montcada. ☎ 932 56 30 00; www.museupicasso.bcn.es. Open Tu-Su 10am-8pm. Last entry 30min. before closing. Wheelchair-accessible. €9, students and seniors €6, under 16 free. Special exhibits €5.80. Free Su after 3pm. 1st Su of each month free.)*

MUSEU DE LA XOCOLATA. This unique and delectable museum is half educational journey through the history of chocolate, and half-impressive, if largely random, chocolate sculptures. Children will enjoy choco-versions of cartoon characters from Bambi to Homer Simpson. The cafe offers workshops on chocolate sculpting for children under 12, and chocolate tastings paired with wine and liquor for the rest of us. *(Pl. Pons i Clerch, C. del Comerç, 26. ⓂJaume I. ☎ 932 68 78 78; www.museudelaxocolata.com. Open M and W-Sa 10am-7pm, Su 10am-3pm. €4.30, students and seniors €3.70, with Barcelona Card €3, under 7 free. Alcohol and chocolate tasting €7.70; reservations required. Workshops for kids from €5.40; reservations required.)*

MUSEU BARBIER-MUELLER. Relics from the pre-Columbian Americas line darkened rooms in this small museum devoted to the conquistadors' booty. And some fine booty it is: tapestries, carvings, ornaments, vases, sculptures, and jewelry dating from 200 BC fill the halls, taken from Olmec, Maya, Aztec, Cocle, Mochica, and Inca sites in the New World. Be sure to take a look upstairs where some of the most ornate and impressive sculptures lie. *(C. de Montcada, 14. ⓂJaume I, L4. ☎ 93 310 45 16; www.barbier-mueller.ch. Open Tu-F 11am-7pm, Sa 10am-7pm, Su 10am-3pm. Wheelchair-accessible. €3.50, students and seniors €1.70. Free 1st Su of the month.)*

MUSEU DE CIÈNCIES NATURALS. Designed by Lluís Domènech i Montaner, the *Castell dels Tres Dragons* (Castle of the Three Dragons) now serves as a zoological museum. Originally built to hold massive, 600-person banquets for the 1888 Exposition, this building is now lined with stuffed and mounted creatures of all stripes. Just a bit down the park lies the partner geological museum, with a host of gems and fossils on display. Though both museums are undoubtedly educational, their appeal may be limited mostly to those with an insatiable fascination with taxidermy. *(Parc de la Ciutadela. Ⓜ Jaume I or Arc de Triomf. ☎ 933 19 69 12; www.bcn.cat/museuciencies. Open Tu-Sa 10am-6:30pm, Su and holidays 10am-2pm. €4.20, seniors and students €2.70, 16 and under free.)*

GALLERIES

GALERIA MAEGHT. This gallery features an intriguing collection of modern art, mostly by Spanish artists—regulars include Tàpies, Marco del Re, and Pablo Palazudo. Upstairs is a rotating exhibition highlighting specific painters. A wealth of beautiful prints, posters, and art books are for sale on the off chance the originals on the wall are out of your budget. *(C. de Montcada, 25. Ⓜ Jaume I. ☎ 933 10 42 45; www.maeght.com. Open Tu-F 10am-2pm and 4-7pm, Sa 10am-2pm. Free.)*

CIRCULO DEL ARTE. Along with a circulating exhibition, this gallery displays and sells many rare and collectible art books. Signed artworks are also available: you may be able to snag an original Miró print for a mere €80. *(C. de la Princesa, 52, Ⓜ Jaume I. ☎ 932 68 88 20; www.circulodelarte.com. Open M-F 9am-9pm, Sa 10:30am-2:30pm and 3:30-8pm. Free.)*

EL RAVAL

El Raval, home to the MACBA and the University of Barcelona, has "artsy" tattooed on its forehead. The streets below the University (in the direction of Ⓜ Liceu) tend towards a younger crowd; above the University (around Ⓜ Universitat and particularly on C. Consell de Cent) you'll find art galleries galore that host up-and-coming artists hoping to someday make it to MACBA's walls.

MUSEU D'ART CONTEMPORANI (MACBA). The gleaming white MACBA building, designed by American architect Richard Meier in 1995, was the final product of a collaboration between Barcelona's mayor and the Catalan government to restore El Raval by turning the neighborhood into a regional artistic and cultural center (14 years later: mission accomplished). The museum's modernity and scale, as well as sheer brightness, are a startling contrast with the narrow alleys and aging cobblestone streets of the surrounding neighborhood. The building's sparse decor was designed to allow the art to speak for itself, which it has—the MACBA has received worldwide acclaim for its focus on interwar avant-garde art. While the permanent collection provides a general overview of Western contemporary art, it is particularly successful in introducing the public to the works of some acclaimed artists from Barcelona. The main attractions are the highly innovative rotating exhibits and the "Nits de MACBA" (Th and F nights in the summer), when the museum stays open until midnight and the reduced price of admission (€3.50) includes a guided tour. Every year during Sonar (Barcelona's über-popular festival celebrating electronic and experimental music), the museum opens its exhibitions to festival-goers and hosts the Sonarcomplex stage, as well as other Sonar-related activities. To give a feel for what this means, on one Friday of the 2009 festival, there were live concerts at 1, 4:30, 7:30, and 9pm (as well as, of course, several "at night," or after 9pm). During Sonar, entry into the museum is limited exclusively to festival-goers, and the Museum's hours are the same as the Sonar's. *(Pl. Des Àngels, 1. Ⓜ Catalunya.*

☎ 934 12 08 10; www.macba.es. Open M and W-F 11am-8pm, Sa 10am-8pm, Su 10am-3pm. Tours in Catalan and English M and Th 6pm; Catalan and Spanish W and F 6pm, Su noon and 6pm. €7.50, students €6, under 14 free; temporary exhibitions €4. From mid-May to Sept. restaurant and bar service on 1st-fl. terrace. Restaurant and bar phone ☎ 672 20 73 89.)

CENTRE DE CULTURA CONTEMPORANIA DE BARCELONA (CCCB). The center's striking architecture incorporates an early 20th-century theater with its 1994 addition, a sleek wing of black glass. CCCB hosts expositions, symposia, and courses having to do with its major themes (simple matters like the human condition, cosmopolitanism, public space, and creativity). It now has a cafe, gallery space, screening room, and bookstore. Along with MACBA, it is also a main daytime venue for the Sonar music festival. Check the center's exhaustive website or the *Guía del Ocio* for scheduled events. *(Casa de Caritat. C. Montalegre, 5.* Ⓜ*Catalunya or Universitat.* ☎ *933 06 41 00; www.cccb.org. Open Tu-W and F-Su 11am-8pm, Th 11am-10pm. Exposicions €4.70, students €3.60, under 16 free. 2 exposicions for €6. 1st W of the month, Th 8-10pm and Su 3-8pm free.)*

GALLERIES

Though you'll find galleries throughout The Raval and L'Eixample, many are similar and not all will interest you. Rather than take our word for it, browse along the streets near **Consell de Cent** (Ⓜ Pg. de Gràcia), or ask the tourist office for a list of galleries.

GALERIA SENDA. This multi-level gallery has a long history of modern art and multimedia exhibitions. *(Consell de Cent, 337.* Ⓜ*Pg. de Gràcia.* ☎ *934 87 67 59; www. galeriasenda.com. Open M-Sa 10am-2pm and 4:30-8:30pm. AmEx/MC/V.)*

GALERIA LLUCIA HOMS. This long, thin gallery works with young contemporary artists of varying nationalities and media. Exhibitions in 2009 spanned modern sculpture, photography, graphic design, and more. *(Consell de Cent 315.* Ⓜ*Pg. de Gràcia.* ☎ *934 67 71 62; www.galeriallluciahoms.es. Open M-F 10am-2pm and 4:30-8:30pm, Sa 11am-2pm and 5:30-8:30pm. AmEx/MC/V.)*

L'EIXAMPLE

AROUND PASSEIG DE GRÁCIA

🎨**FUNDACIÓ FRANCISCO GODIA.** This museum was created in 1998 by Godia's daughter in order to open his private art collection for public viewing. **Francisco Godia** (1921-1990) was a bizarre combination of astute businessman, accomplished Formula One race car driver, and passionate supporter of the arts. His collection boasts a huge variety of works and artists over the span of nearly a millennium. From an impressive collection of 12th-century religious sculptures and paintings to modern works by such names as Picasso and Tapiés. Highlights include Saragossa's stunning *Virgen de la Leche* (1374), Solana's bold, dark-lined *Bullfight at Ronda* (1927), Francesc Gimeno's life-like *Mother and Daughter* (1898), and the popular *At the Racecourse* (1905) by Ramon Casas. The Fundació also organizes exhibitions featuring private collections from throughout Spain. Be sure to check out the front room filled with Godia's racing trophies, proof that fast cars, engine grease, and art *can* go hand-in-hand. *(C. Diputació 250.* Ⓜ*Pg. de Gràcia, L2/3/4.* ☎ *932 72 31 80; www.fundacionfgodia.org. Open M, W-Sa, and Su 10am-8pm. Free guided tours Sa-Su noon in Spanish and Catalan; otherwise call ahead for a guided tour, €6. Wall descriptions and printed guides are in English, Catalan, and Spanish. Wheelchair-accessible. €6. MC/V.)*

MUSEU DEL PERFUM. Located in the back of a perfectly ordinary-looking perfume store, the Museu del Perfum is easy to miss. The collection inside, however, should not be overlooked. It showcases nearly 1000 perfume containers, from second-century BC Roman vials to gold and silver plated perfume flasks from the 18th and 19th centuries to Chanel no. 5. Take a gander at the highly original designs, including a mouse, a lightbulb, the Eiffel Tower, and a suicidal bottle with a knife-shaped throat applicator. Even Salvador Dalí took a crack at this little-known art form, with a huge bottle he called "The Sun King." *(Pg. de Gràcia 39. ⓂPg. de Gràcia. ☎932 16 01 21; www.museodelperfume.com. M-F 10:30am-2pm and 4:30-8pm, Sa 11am-3pm. Wheelchair-accessible. €5; students and seniors €3.)*

MUSEU EGIPCI. In 1993, the wealthy Jordi Clos decided to turn a private passion into Spain's only museum dedicated entirely to Pharaonic Egypt. More than 500 Egyptian artifacts and several displays focused on tombs, mummies, and the beliefs surrounding death in ancient Egypt pack two whole floors. Be sure to take a look at the small collection of mummified animals, including a falcon and a crocodile. Catch Egypt-related dramatic performances every night at 9pm, complete with a tour and a glass of cava. *(C. Valencia, 284, just to the left of Pg. de Gràcia when you're facing Pl. de Catalunya. ⓂPg. de Gràcia, L2/3/4. ☎93 488 01 88; www.museuegipci.com. Open M-Sa 10am-8pm, Su 10am-2pm. Closed Dec. 25-26 and Jan. 1. Descriptions in Spanish and Catalan. Free tours in Spanish and Catalan Sa 11am and 5pm; call ahead to hire an English guide. Wheelchair-accessible. €11; students and over 65 €8. Performances €25. MC/V.)*

L'EIXAMPLE ESQUERRA

FUNDACIÓ ANTONI TÀPIES. Antoni Tàpies's massive and bizarre wire sculpture, *Cloud with Chair*, atop Domènech i Montaner's red brick building announces this collection of contemporary abstract art. The top floor of the foundation is dedicated to famous Catalans, particularly Tàpies, while the other two floors feature temporary exhibits of other modern artists' work. Tàpies is one of Catalunya's best-known artists; his works often defy definition, springing from Surrealism and Magicism, and drawing inspiration from Picasso and Miró. Most of his pieces mix painting and sculpture, and are generally referred to as collage, although he also creates abstract sculptures. Most of his paintings include a "T" in some form, a symbol that has been variously interpreted (or misinterpreted) as a religious cross, sexual penetration, and the artist's own signature. In truth, no one knows the real meaning, if there is one. Tàpies's use of unorthodox materials—including objects found in the trash—and his dark, dirty colors are often construed as a protest against the dictatorship and the subsequent urban alienation pervading Spain's cities. Everyday materials, like sand, glue, wood, marble powder, dirt, and wire show the eloquence inherent in simplicity. The other highlights are the rotating exhibitions on the two lower floors—some of the best modern photography and video art in the city, as well as film screenings and lectures. In summer, check out DJ nights on the terrace, with free drinks and after-hours gallery access. *(C. Aragó, 255. ☎934 87 03 15. ⓂPg. de Gràcia. Closed for renovation as of summer 2009. Call for more information.)*

MUSEU DE L'ESPORT. Puig i Cadafalch's Casa Company once housed the **Museu de l'Esport** collection; most of the collection (including its 40-some Olympic torches) was recently moved to the **Olympic Museum** on Montjuïc, but a few genuinely interesting relics, like photographs and medals from the one-time Olympics of Catalonia, remain. Now, the house is less a destination in itself than another stop on your tour of Barcelona's *casas*. That said, if you do happen to be in the neighborhood, the museum is quaint and charming, and definitely worth the 15min. it takes to see its entire holdings. *(C. Buenos Aires, 56-8.* Ⓜ*Hospital Clínic, L5. Walk north on C. Villarroel and turn left onto C. Buenos Aires.* ☎ *934 19 22 32. Open M-F 10am-2pm and 3-5pm. Free.)*

PORT VELL

MUSEU MARÍTIM. The **Drassanes Reiales de Barcelona** (Royal Shipyards of Barcelona) consists of a series of huge indoor bays in which entire ships could be constructed and stored over the winter. The Maritime Museum traces the evolution of shipbuilding and life on the high seas. The centerpiece is a life-size replica of a 16th-century galley, displaying holographic oarsmen rowing with all their might. Recommended mainly for the nautically inclined. *(Av. Drassanes, off the rotary around the Monument a Colom.* Ⓜ*Drassanes.* ☎ *933 42 99 20; www.diba. es/mmaritim. Open daily 10am-7:30pm. Free audio guide and entrance to museum. €6.50; ages 11-16, students, and seniors €5.20; ages 6-10 €3.25. Museum and Golondrinas port tour €9.60/7.40/5.30. Free Su after 3pm.)*

BARCELONETA

🖾**MUSEU D'HISTÒRIA DE CATALUNYA.** The last gasp of the old city before you hit the packed beaches of Barceloneta, the Museu provides a patriotic introduction to Catalan history, politics, and culture. The detailed displays, diagrams, and artifacts (all with English captions) all help thread together the centuries of background behind all the historical sights you've been marveling at in Barcelona. The city's entire history is here: Neolithic tools; artifacts of the Roman and Islamic rules of the AD first millennium; exhibits on the repression of Catalunya by Felipe V; the *Renaixença* and development of *Modernisme;* the Civil War; the rule of Franco, and the resurgence of culture and industry since Franco's death. (Whew.) Recreations of a 1930s Spanish bar, an AD eighth-century Islamic prayer tent, and other dioramas make the museum a full sensory experience. *(Pl. Pau Vila, 3. Near entrance to the Moll d'Espanya; left walk out toward Barceloneta.* ☎ *932 25 47 00; www.mhcat.com. Open Tu and Th-Sa 10am-7pm, W 10am-8pm, Su 10am-2:30pm. €4; under 18 and students €3; university students, under 7, and over 65 free. Free 1st Su of the month.)*

POBLE NOU AND PORT OLIMPIC

MUSEU DE CARROSSES FÚNEBRES. This small collection of 22 plush 19th- and early 20th-century horse-drawn hearses is pretty morbid. But, the museum *is* full of intriguing facts on Spanish funerals. Who knew only virgins could ride to their graves in white carriages? *(C. Sancho de Ávila, 2.* Ⓜ*Marina, L1. From the metro, follow Av. Meridiana away from C. Marina until its intersection with C. Sancho de Ávila. Enter the gray office building right on the corner labeled Serveis Funeraris de Barcelona, S.A., and ask at the info desk inside for the Museu de Carrosses.* ☎ *902 07 69 02; www.sfbsa.es. Open M-F 10am-1pm and 4-6pm, Sa-Su 10am-1pm. Wheelchair-accessible. Free.)*

MONTJUÏC AND POBLE SEC

🖾**MUSEU NACIONAL D'ART DE CATALUNYA** (PALAU NACIONAL). Designed by Enric Catá and Pedro Cendoya for the 1929 International Exposition (see **Life and Times,** p. 41), the Palau Nacional has housed the Museu Nacional d'Art de

Catalunya (MNAC) since 1934. The museum's main hall is a public event space that resembles a wedding cake in its white, cream, and pink detailed splendor, while the ground-floor wings are home to the world's finest collection of Catalan Romanesque art (to your left as you walk in) and a wide variety of Gothic pieces (to your right). The Romanesque frescoes, now integrated as murals into dummy chapels, were salvaged in the 1920s from their original, less protected locations in northern Catalunya's churches. Their restoration creates a surprisingly spiritual tour through the medieval masterpieces. The museum's Gothic art corridor displays paintings on wood, the medium of choice during that period. The chronological tour of the galleries underlines the growing influence of Italy over Catalunya's artistic development, and ends with a breathtaking series of paintings by Gothic master **Bernat Martorell.**

Upstairs, you'll find MNAC's collections of Modern art (to the left), of Numismatics (coinage; slightly to the right), and of drawings, prints, and posters (farther to the right). The Modern Art collection comprises Catalan works of art that date from 1800 to the 1940s. Not surprisingly, the collection reflects the avant-garde movements that held sway in Catalunya at the time: *Modernisme* and *Noucentisme.* Its highlights include works by Fortuny, Casas, Rusinol, Gaudí, Jujol, Picasso, Gargallo, and Julio Gonzalez. Gaudí's 1907 "Confidant from the Batlló House" chair is one highlight. The Numismatics collection is a heist movie waiting to happen. It includes more than 134,000 pieces of money (Spanish coins, medals, and valuable papers) and walks the visitor through the history of Catalonia's coinage from Antiquity to today. The drawings, prints, and posters collection includes pieces that date from the 16th century to the beginning of the avant-garde. The museum's Fortuny collection is particularly acclaimed. *(From Ⓜ Espanya, walk up Av. Reina María Cristina, away from the twin brick towers, and take the escalators to the top. ☎ 936 22 03 76; www.mnac.es. Open Tu-Sa 10am-7pm, Su and holidays 10am-2:30pm. Wheelchair-accessible. €8.50, students and seniors €6, under 14 free. First Su of the month free. Audio tour included.)*

◼**FUNDACIÓ MIRÓ.** Miró's pieces are a personal and poignant tour through 20th-century Spanish history; the fundamental optimism of his later works and the generosity he demonstrated throughout his life have made him one of Spain's—not just Catalunya's—most beloved artists. More than a museum, the Fundació Miró is a foundation to support contemporary art and young Catalan artists as well as a rotating collection of 11,000 of Miró's works and pieces by other artists inspired by Miró's unique style. Designed by Miró's friend Josep Luís Sert, the Fundació links interior and exterior spaces with massive windows and outdoor patios. Skylights illuminate an extensive collection of statues, paintings, and *sobreteixims* (paintings on tapestry) from Miró's career. The Fundació also sponsors music recitals in the summer months, and occasionally hosts film festivals (check the website for listings).

The first room of the permanent collection features the *Tapestry of the Foundation,* a colorful and wall-sized depiction of a woman. Outside, between rooms 11 and 12, The *Mercury Fountain* created by Miró's good friend Alexander Calder, commemorates the war-torn town of Almaden. Room 16 displays Miró's **Dream Paintings** (1925-1927), an eerie depiction of a world where "the pull of gravity" no longer exists. **The Constellation Series,** the more poetic of Miró's works, is on display in room 17. Pick up a headphone set from the ticket desk to guide you to some of the most famous pieces in the foundation. *(Take the funicular from Ⓜ Paral·lel or catch the Park Montjuïc bus from Pl. Espanya. ☎ 934 43 94 70; www.fundaciomiro-bcn.org. Library open M and Sa 10am-2pm, Tu-F 10am-2pm and 3-6pm. Fundació open July-Sept. Tu-W and F-Sa 10am-8pm, Th 10am-9:30pm, Su and holidays 10am-2:30pm; Oct.-June Tu-W and F-Sa 10am-7pm, Th 10am-9:30pm, Su and holidays 10am-2:30pm. Last entry*

15min. before closing. €8, students and seniors €6, under 13 €4. Temporary exhibitions €4/3/4.
Headphones €4. Concert tickets €10.)

MUSEU OLIMPIC DE L'ESPORT. Prepare for some serious sensory overload. As visitors walk down a spiraling ramp, videos, photographs, and display cases of historical artifacts bombard with information on the history and ethic of sports. For sports enthusiasts and couch potatoes alike, the museum is worth a visit: its exhibits cover genuinely interesting subjects like major upsets and the history of sports for the disabled. Downstairs, the displays are interactive, and visitors can measure their high jump or long jump against gold medal heights and lengths—a fun, if humbling, experience. *(Av. de l'Estadi, 60. From the funicular, walk up Av. de Miramar, which it becomes Av. de l'Estadi; the museum is on your left. ☎ 932 92 53 79; www.museuolimpicbcn.com. Open Apr.-Sept. Tu-Sa 10am-8pm; Oct.-Mar. Tu-Sa 10am-6pm, Su and holidays 10am-2:30pm. €4, students €2.50, under 14 free.)*

MUSEU ETNOLÒGIC. This museum, which will be of great interest to anthropology enthusiasts but perhaps of little interest to the uninitiated, has an extensive permanent collection that includes more than 10,000 items from around the world. The museum's exhibits draw attention to the overarching lifestyles of those in the cultures that produced the artifacts; the Catalan section, for example, shows the role of each object in a stockbreeding society, while the Australian Aboriginal section shows weapons and paintings as they are used and understood in a hunter-gatherer society. Visitors leave the museum not just having seen thousands of unrelated objects, but with a sense, if only a shallow one, of each culture represented. *(Pg. Santa Madrona, downhill from the funicular or uphill from Museu Arqueològic. ☎ 934 24 68 07; www.museuetnologic.bcn.es. Open June-Sept. Tu-Sa 10am-6pm, Su 10am-2pm and 3-8pm. Oct.-May Tu, Th and Sa 10-7pm; W and F 10am-2pm; Su 10am-2pm and 3-8pm. €3, students and seniors €1.50. 1st Su of every month and every Su 3-8pm free.)*

MUSEU ARQUEOLÒGIC DE CATALUNYA. Founded in 1932, the Museu Arqueològic is located in the beautiful Palau de Artes Graficas, constructed in 1929 for the Exposición Universal. A tour of the galleries' jewelry, earthenware, sculptures, mosaics, and countless other artifacts will take you from prehistoric times to the Medieval Ages in Catalunya and the Balearic Islands. Unfortunately, much is left to the imagination, as the historical context and explanations are somewhat sparse. Several rooms feature a collection of Carthaginian art from Ibiza, fascinating models of huge megalithic funeral monuments, and excavated relics from the Greco-Roman city of Empúries in surrounding Catalunya. *(Pg. Santa Madrona, 39-41. From Ⓜ Espanya, L1/L3, take bus #55 up the hill to the Palau Nacional. When you are facing the Palau Nacional, the museum is to the left. From the Museu Etnologic, walk down Pg. de Santa Madrona and the museum will be on your left. ☎ 934 24 65 77; www.mac.es. Open Tu-Sa 9:30am-7pm, Su and holidays 10am-2:30pm. €3; ages 16-18, disabled, students and children of single-parent households €2.10, under 16 and 1st Su of every month free.)*

VALL D'HEBRON AND HORTA-GUINARDÓ

MUSEU DE CARRUATGES. This museum has 46 exhibits that include work carriages, luxury carriages, and 600 or so coachmen's accessories. The Piera family, whose company was in charge of street cleaning and refuse collection in the early 1900s, oversaw this museum's creation. This is not a destination in and of itself unless you are a wild-hearted carriage enthusiast, but worth seeing if you're in the area. *(Pl. de Josep Pallach, 8. Ⓜ Mundet or buses #10, 27, 60, 73, 76, 85, and 173 all stop nearby. From the Metro, walk down Av. Can Marcet and make a right onto Pl. de Joan*

Comudella. Pl. de Josep Pallach is off Pl. de Joan Comudella. ☎ 934 27 58 13. Open Su 10am-1pm. Groups can organize tours during the week 10am-1pm by calling in advance. Free.)

TIBIDABO

MUSEU D'AUTÒMATS. An amusing collection of 19th- and 20th-century automated displays, from models of ski slopes and the park itself to full-fledged jazz bands, dancers in ballrooms, and a winking gypsy. Just press the green buttons and watch 'em go. Be sure to catch the morbid (and of course automated) re-creation of a decapitation and a hanging, all in miniature. (Open July-Aug. M-Th 11am-8pm, W-Su 11am-9pm; Sept.-June open daily noon-4pm. €2, free with admission to Parc d'Atraccions.)

MUSEU-CASA VERDAGUER. Jacint Verdaguer, the most celebrated poet of the Catalan literary *Renaixença*, lived in this 18th-century house before his death in 1902. Verdaguer is known for winning a Catalan poetry contest with his epic poem *L'Atlantida*. The rooms have been preserved as they were before his death, and detailed explanations of the artist's life and works fill the house; unfortunately for many visitors, all the explanations are in Catalan. The path up to the museum is covered in his poetry, also of course in Catalan. (C. Carretera de l'Església, 104. FGC: Baixador de Vallvidrera. Follow signs from the train station. ☎ 932 04 78 05. Open Sa-Su 10am-2pm. Free.)

MUSEU DE LA CIENCIA. Located at the halfway stop on the bus or tram from Pl. JFK to Pl. Dr. Andreu, the recently renovated science museum covers every topic imaginable, from robotics and physics to biology and archeology. It features hundreds of displays and interactive exhibits as well as temporary exhibitions and a planetarium. Especially impressive is the *Bosc Inundat*, a giant recreation of a swampy Amazonian forest filled with large and menacing fish and garish tropical birds. (C. Teodor Roviralta, 55. FGC: Tibidabo. Buses #17, 22, 58, 75 stop at Pl. JFK and buses #60 and 196 stop in front of the museum. ☎ 932 12 60 50. Open Tu-Su 10am-8pm. €3, students and children €2, seniors free. Planetarium €2, students and seniors €1.50.)

PEDRALBES AND LES CORTS

Museums in Pedralbes and Les Corts cater to the obsessed. Whether your passion is soccer, *Modernisme*, or fashion, there's a museum here that will impress you with its original, well-curated exhibits. On a hot day or a rainy day, leave the city center, head here, and educate yourself. There aren't many dining options around, so it might be wise to pack a picnic.

■MUSEU DEL FÚTBOL CLUB BARCELONA. Busloads of tour groups from all over the world pour into this museum, making it one of Barcelona's most visited—it sees more than 1,200,000 visitors per year. The museum merits all the attention it gets, as it pays fitting homage to one of soccer's greatest clubs. Any sports fan will appreciate the history of the team that began in 1899 when a Swiss soccer star, Hans Gamper, moved to Barcelona and gathered a group of eager players. Some of the team's recent greats include Maradona, Ronaldo, Luis Figo, Rivaldo, Ronaldinho, Messi, and Henry. Room after room displays countless cups the team has won, including the coveted European Cup, which it won in 1992, 2006, and 2009, and the Copa del Rey, which it has won 25 times, more than any other club. The museum includes soccer-related art and past team photos. Check out some of the funky uniform variations on the familiar blue and burgundy team colors. The high point, especially if you can't get to an actual match, is the chance to enter the **Camp Nou** stadium itself—with a capacity of 98,787, it is the biggest stadium in Europe. In addition, the tour shows you the dressing rooms, a tunnel to the playing field, players' benches, the press rooms, the chapel, and the presidential box. In the same complex, a gift shop sells all varieties of official FCB merchandise. *(Next to the stadium. ⓂCollblanc. Enter through access gate 7 or 9. ☎ 934 96 36 08. Open M-Sa 10am-6:15pm, Su and holidays 10am-2pm. Museum and Camp Nou tour €17. Free parking.)*

MUSEU DE LES ARTS DECORATIVES. The quirky Museum of Decorative Arts presents European home furnishings and household objects from as far back as the Middle Ages. The displays are ordered chronologically; walking through, you can see the influence of each age on the objects that we live among today. The Romanesque-Gothic display emphasizes knights' nomadic lifestyles and the need for their possessions to be portable. The Renaissance display includes several large, ornate, inlaid chests of drawers and coffers that beg to be opened (a sign forbids visitors to do so). The 19th-century collection of furniture hints at how the Catalan bourgeoisie once lived; particularly striking is an 1815 Catalan sleigh bed and its side table. Check out the pieces of metal sculpture, cast iron, and mosaic tiles and observe Modernism's influence in the realm of interior design. The museum's eclectic collection also contains 20th-century industrial objects, such as Juma's 1977 *Sabata de Talo*, an ash tray shaped like a woman's high-heeled shoe, and a collection of motorcycles. If that isn't enough, a broad range of temporary exhibitions are held throughout the year. *(Av. Diagonal, 686. Bus #7, 33, 63, 67, 68, 74, 75, 78, L51, or L61 or ⓂPalau Reial, L3. On the 2nd floor of the Palau Reial, opposite the Museu de Ceràmica. ☎ 932 56 34 65; www.dhub-bcn.cat/ca/museus. Admission will also get you into the Museu de Ceràmica (p. 151) and the Museu Téxtil (p. 151). Open Tu-Sa 10am-6pm, Su and holidays 10am-3pm. €4.20, students under 25 €2.40, under 16 free.)*

MUSEU DE CERÀMICA. The display in the Museu de Ceràmica traces the evolution of Spanish ceramic sculpture from the 11th century to the present. The exhibits showcase skillfully crafted plates, tiles, jars, and bowls gathered from all regions of Spain. Artists and art historians will want to read the plaques discussing each era's symbolism and firing technique. The five rooms of 20th-century ceramics display abstract works by Picasso and Miró as well as other artists; imagine drinking sangria out of a pitcher designed by the master of Cubism himself. *(Av. Diagonal, 686. Bus #7, 33, 63, 67, 68, 74, 75, 78, L51, or L61 or ⓂPalau Reial, L3. On the 2nd floor of the Palau Reial, opposite the Museu de les Arts Decoratives (p. 151). ☎ 932 56 34 65; www.museuceramica.bcn.cat. Ticket will also get you into the Museu de les Arts Decoratives and the Museu Téxtil (p. 151). Open Tu-Sa 10am-6pm, Su and holidays 10am-3pm. €4.20, students under 25 €2.40, under 16 free.)*

MUSEU TÉXTIL I D'INDUMENTÀRIA. This museum offers a quick tour of the history of European fashion, from bustles and sadistic corsets to V-necks and miniskirts. The main exhibit—"Dressing the Body"—juxtaposes old with new, highlighting historical influence on modern design and the ways that clothing distorts the body. In the first display, for example, a 2008 dress by Emilio de la Morena with a flared hot pink tulle skirt is shown side-by-side with 16th-century dresses worn by noblewomen; an adjacent screen discusses why designers want to make the waist appear narrow and the hips wide. Fashionistas will ooh and ah at the museum's collection of contemporary jewelry. *(Av. Diagonal, 686. Bus #7, 33, 63, 67, 68, 74, 75, 78, L51, or L61 or ⓂPalau Reial, L3. On the 3rd floor of the Palau Reial. Take the stairs to the left of the main staircase, as you ascend. ☎ 932 56 34 65; www.dhub-bcn.cat/ca/museus. Ticket will also get you into the Museu de les Arts Decoratives (p. 151) and the Museu Ceràmica (p. 151). Open Tu-Sa 10am-6pm, Su and holidays 10am-3pm. €4.20, students under 25 €2.40, under 16 free.)*

ENTERTAINMENT

BEACHES

Barceloneses love their coast. The entire strip between Torre San Sebastiá and Parc de Diagonal-Mar is lined with public beaches. Due partially to strong riptides, few bathers swim more than a few meters from shore; the number one beach activity is tanning. Topless tanning is common on all the city beaches, and people begin to lose their suit bottoms toward the nether regions of **San Sebastià** although the only official nude beach is **Platja Mar Bella**. Barcelona's beaches are crowded at almost any time of day, but crowds tend to thin out on the eastern stretches. The beaches are cleaned every night by large sifting tractors. There are restaurants near practically all the beaches, although they become less frequent toward **Nova Mar Bella**. *(Beach info ☎ 932 21 03 48; www.bcn.cat/platges. Dogs, camping tents, motorcycles, soap, music, and trash are not allowed on the beaches. Shower stations, police, first aid, and info available on all beaches, June-Sept. 10am-7pm. All beaches have lifeguards June-Sept. daily 10am-7pm, Mar.-June Sa-Su 10am-7pm. Lockers at police stations. Nova Icaria, San Sebastiá, and Nova Mar Bella are fully wheelchair-accessible and provide bathing assistance services in July and Aug.)*

BARCELONETA. Barceloneta's two main beaches, **Platja San Sebastià** and **Platja Barceloneta** (adjacent to one another), are the neighborhood's biggest draws. These are the closest to Barceloneta and ⓂCiutadella as well as to Port Vell and Las Ramblas. Expect Platja Barceloneta to be the most crowded stretch of sand in Barcelona. The farthest tip of Platja San Sebastiá, near Torre San Sebastiá, offers more privacy, but with a summer-long public fiesta going on at the popular beaches next door, who needs it?

POBLE NOU. The beaches to the north of Port Olímpic (left, facing the water) include Platja Nova Icària, Platja del Bogatell, Platja Mar Bella, and Platja Nova Mar Bella. (From the port to Nova Mar Bella is about a 20min. walk.) Closest to the port Olímpic is the short **Platja Nova Icaria**. This beach is busy; it often fills up with families and volleyball players. Next is **Platja del Bogatell,** one of the most coveted tanning areas. Base Nàutica Mar Bella marks the end of Bogatell and the beginning of **Platja Mar Bella,** a section of which is designated nudist, secluded behind dunes. **Mar Bella** is the gay beach; a rainbow flag marks the spot. **Nova Mar Bella** and **Platja Llevant,** which lie just past Platja Mar Bella (the end of which is marked by the restaurant La Oca Mar) host mostly teenagers and 20-somethings. As they require the longest walk to reach, fewer tourists find their way out to these beaches and there tends to be some space available even on weekends.

COSTA MARESME

For those who tire of the crowded beaches of Barcelona, there's plenty more coastline just a short train ride away. Some of the beaches below are worth a visit, though there's no need for too much planning in advance. Since the C-1 RENFE line travels right along coastline with sand and surf in plain view, play it by eye and hop off at first stop that piques your interest.

BADALONA. This is the quickest way to escape the crowded Barcelona beaches (and many locals know it). The sand stretches for three kilometers,

NO WORK, ALL PLAY

HOGUERAS DE SANT JOAN

Things really heat up when Barcelona's residents celebrate the arrival of summer and La Noche de San Juan, the anniversary of the death of St. John the Baptist, whose Spanish name is San Juan.

This fiesta has its origins in ancient celebrations of June 21, the summer solstice and the longest day of the year.

On the night of June 23, locals light "purifying" firecrackers and bonfires (hogueras), and party even harder than usual. Downtown and the waterfront are notoriously wild, but residents hold private parties in all parts of the city.

In other parts of Catalunya, early spring brings a similar celebration known as las fallas (the figures). During this rite, locals walk down a mountain carrying large, burning figures, which they then throw into a bonfire in the city plaça.

Another Sant Joan tradition is to eat a coca (a traditional Catalan pastry) served with cream and pine nuts.

Definitely the most enduring tradition for the night of Sant Joan, however, is spending the whole night eating and drinking with friends.

so you ought to be able to find a place of your own. Crowds begin to thin out as you walk north. *(RENFE stop: Badalona, C1. 20min. from Pl. Catalunya.)*

PLATJA D'OCATA. Right next to the train stop, this wide beach attracts a lot of daytrippers from Barcelona, but is large enough to provide plenty of space for volleyball nets and, of course, hours of tanning. *(RENFE stop: Ocata, C1. 30min. from Pl. Catalunya. Lifeguard on duty from June 24 to Sept 11 11:30am-7:30pm.)*

PLATJA DE MATARÓ. Technically made up of three smaller beaches (**Platja de Sant Simó, Platja del Callao** and **Platja del Varador**), Mataró is a spacious and sporty stretch of sand with kayak and wind-surfing rentals as well as goals set up for beach soccer. *(RENFE stop: Mataró, C1. 40min. from Pl. Catalunya. Facing the sea, Varador is just to the left of the train stop. Sant Simó and Callao are farther along in the same direction. Lifeguard on duty from mid-May to Aug. 10am-6pm.)*

PLATJA MUSCLERA. Musclera is a bit farther out of the way and more difficult to reach, but the pleasant and fairly secluded nude section on the left half of the beach (facing the sea) makes it worth it. *(RENFE stop: Caldes d'Estrac, C1. 50min. from Pl. Catalunya. Station is right across from Platja Pg. del Mar. Walk left (facing the sea) to reach Platja Musclera, which is the next beach over. Lifeguard on duty July-Aug. 10am-6pm.)*

BOWLING

Bowling Pedralbes, Av. Dr. Marañón, 11 (☎93 333 03 52; www.bowlingpedralbes.com). ⓂCollblanc or Zona Universitaria. 14 lanes and a bar just a block from the Camp Nou stadium make for a welcome late-night change of pace. 1 game M-F afternoons (before 5pm) €1.50, M-Th evenings €2.50, F-Su evenings €4.80, Sa-Su afternoon, €3.80. Shoe rental €1. Pool tables (€1.50 per game) and foosball also available. Fixed lunch *menú* €9.50. Open M-Th 10am-2am, F-Sa 10am-3am, Su 10am-12am. MC/V.

FESTIVALS

While Barcelona works hard to distinguish itself from the rest of Spain, the city shares at least one thing in common with the rest of the country: it knows how to have fun. For information on all festivals, call the tourist office (☎933 01 77 75; open M-F 10am-2pm and 4-8pm) or check the "Agenda" or "Diary" on www.bcn.es. Double-check sight and museum hours during festival times, as well as during the Christmas season and *Semana Santa*.

The streets fill with book vendors and rose sellers on the **Festa de Sant Jordi** (St. George; Apr. 23), the Catalan take on Valentine's Day; the day officially celebrates Catalunya's patron saint with a feast. Men give women roses, and women give men books. In the last two weeks of August, city folk jam at Gràcia's **Festa Mayor;** lights blaze in *plaças* and music plays all night as two dozen streets compete to be the best decorated. On September 11, the **Festa Nacional de Catalunya** brings out traditional costumes, dancing, and Catalan flags hanging from balconies. Barcelona's main festival, the **Festa de Sant Joan,** takes place the night of June 23. You might as well surrender to the all-night beachside partying (and erratic nightclub hours); ceaseless fireworks and bonfires in the street will keep your eyes wide open anyway. The largest Barcelona celebration, however, is the **Festa de Mercè,** the weeks before and after September 24. To honor the patron saint of the city, *barceloneses* revel with fireworks, Sardana dancing, and concerts.**Santa Eulàlia,** the city's female patron saint, is celebrated February 12-13.

FILM

INDEPENDENT AND ARTHOUSE CINEMA

Though the giant, Hollywood-oriented **Cinesa** theaters are the most prominent options for movies, Barcelona also fosters an array of small theaters that prefer to show independent and foreign films, usually at independent prices. Check the *Guía del Ocio* or other cultural guides for film festivals and screenings that are sometimes held at cultural centers like CCCB or even clubs like Sala Apolo. The Cine section in the *Guía del Ocio* denotes subtitled films with **V.O.** (original version) *subtitulada*; other foreign films are dubbed *(doblado)*, usually in Spanish. Most theaters have a discount day (usually Monday or Wednesday).

Filmoteca Aquitània, Av. Sarrià, 33, (☎934 10 75 90). Ⓜ Hospital Clínic. Shows classic and cult films that span the medium's history, often as part of an extended series dedicated to particular directors, actors, and themes (100 American Films, all of Elia Kazan, and so on). All films screened in V.O. with subtitles in Castilian or Catalan. Tickets €2.70, students and seniors €2. 10 tickets €18. MC/V.

Méliès Cinemas, C. de Villarroel, 102 (☎93 215 11 88; www.cinesmelies.net). Ⓜ Urgell. Shows mostly independent films on its 2 screens, usually a year or two after their release, always in V.O. with subtitles in Castellano. M €4.50, Tu-Su €6.

Casablanca-Kaplan, Pg. de Gràcia 115 (☎932 18 43 45). Shows independent foreign films in V.O. along with nearby **Casablanca-Gracias** (Girona, 175; ☎934 59 03 26; currently undergoing renovations but expected to reopen by the end of 2009). Tickets €6.50, M €4.80. Cash only.

Arenas Cine-Gay, C. Disputació, 5 (☎934 23 11 69). Ⓜ Espanya. Off C. Tarragona just below Princep Jorgi. Shows a selection of action, comedy, and drama from the last decade. Main screen not exclusively gay. Check *Guia del Ocio* for movie times. Tickets €7.50.

Renoir Floridablanca, (☎93 426 33 37), Port Vell, in Moll d'Espanya next to the Aquàrium. Ⓜ Universitat.7 screens that show foreign and independent films, catering to nearby university students. Films always shown in V.O. Tickets M €5, Tu-Th and Su €6.50, F-Sa €7. MC/V.

Maldà, C. del Pi, 5 (☎934 81 37 04; www.cinemalda.es). Ⓜ Liceu. Inside Galerías Maldá. Only 1 screening room, but an ambitious selection of contemporary foreign independent films, screened in VO with Castilian subtitles. Keep an eye out for double features and small film festivals hosted here. Tickets M €5, T-Th €6.50, F-Sa €7.

VOID, Ferlandina, 51. (☎934 43 42 03; www.void-bcn.com). Ⓜ️Universitat. George Clooney watches 2 movies a day in his personal screening room, and now you can, too. This video club rents out a 30-person capacity screening room where you can watch whatever you want, either from the club's extensive collection or BYO (2hr. €40). Also rents movies from said collection (€3 per 3 days). Open Tu-Su 4:30-10:30pm. Cash only.

A MOVIE UNDER THE STARS. Head up the hill to Sala Montjuïc, an annual 5-week film series in the moat of Castell de Montjuïc. Bring a picnic, settle down on the lawn, and listen to live music before the show. Summer (from late June to early Aug) M, W, F at 8:30pm; buy tickets at the castle the day of (€5, deckchair rental €3) or online at www.servicaixa.com.

ENGLISH LANGUAGE AND HOLLYWOOD CINEMA

Icaria-Yelmo, C. Salvador Espriu, 61 (☎932 21 75 85; www.yelmocineplex.es), in the Olympic Village. With 15 screens, major releases are sure to pass through here and are always shown in V.O. The place for your *Harry Potter* and *Pirates of the Caribbean* fix. Tickets €7.40, M €5.70, matinees €5.90.

Cinesa Maremagnum (☎902 33 32 31), Port Vell, in Moll d'Espanya next to the Aquàrium. Ⓜ️Drassanes. 8 screens show mainstream film releases, usually dubbed in Castellano. Tickets available by phone or ServiCaixa. Tickets €7.40, W €5.60. MC/V.

IMAX Port Vell, Moll d'Espanya s/n. (☎932 25 11 11; www.imaxportvell.com). Ⓜ️Barceloneta. Along Port Vell, next to Maremagnum. Boasts an IMAX screen, an Omnimax 30m in diameter, and 3D projection. Get tickets at the door, through ServiCaixa, or by phone. Open noon-11:20pm. Tickets €13, matinees €8.10. MC/V.

GYMS AND RECREATIONAL SPORTS

The tourist offices or the online directory (www.barcelonaturisme.com) can provide info about swimming, cycling, tennis, squash, sailing, hiking, scuba diving, whitewater rafting, kayaking, and most other sports.

DiR Fitness Club, 12 branches throughout Barcelona, including one at C. Gran de Gràcia, 37 (branch ☎934 15 55 50; central ☎902 10 19 79; www.dir.es). A popular Barcelona gym chain with every amenity imaginable, from steam bath, solarium, and personalized fitness programs to fingerprint-scan entrance; 13 locations. Prices depend on time of day, age, and number of days per week, but generally €4.25 per day (plus €2 membership card, purchased once); monthly passes range €40-200 depending on location and services. Open M-F 7am-10:15pm, Sa-Su and holidays 9am-7:15pm. MC/V.

Piscines Bernat Picornell, Av. Estadi, 30-40 (☎934 23 40 41; www.picornell.com), to the right when facing the stadium. Test your backstroke in the Olympic pools with stadium seating overlooking the city. €4.80 for outdoor pool (long-term passes available); €9.20 for workout facilities including sauna, massage parlor, and gym. Sa 9pm-11pm and winter M 4:15pm-6pm are nude days. Outdoor pool open June-Sept. M-Sa 9am-9pm, Su 9am-8pm; Sept.-May daily 7:30am-4pm. Workout facilities open M-F 8:45am-11:30pm, Sa 7am-8:45pm, Su 7:30am-3pm. MC/V.

Club Natació Atlètic-Barceloneta, on Plaça del Mar, Pg. Joan de Borbó, across the street from the Torre San Sebastià cable car tower.(☎93 221 00 10; www.cnab.org), offers outdoor and indoor pools in addition to beach access, a sauna, a hot tub, and a full weight room. Memberships start at €27 a month. Joining fee €56. Non-members €7 per day. Open M-F 6:30am-11pm, Sa 7am-11pm, Su and holidays 8am-5pm. AmEx/MC/V.

Nova-Icària Sports Club, Av. Icària, 167 (☎93 221 25 80; atenciousuari@novaicaria. com), on the corner of C. Arquitecte Sert. ⓂCiutadella/Port Olímpic, L4. A full-service sports club, with weight lifting, aerobics, a pool, tennis courts, basketball courts, and more. Membership €33 per month, €67.50 start-up fee. Non-members €6.65 per visit. Open Su 8am-4pm, M-F 7am-11pm, Sa 8am-11pm. Closed holidays.

Centre Muncipal de Tennis, Pg. Vall d'Hebron, 178 (☎93 427 55 00) and Centre Muncipal d'Esports, Pg. Vall d'Hebron, 166 (☎93 428 39 52). ⓂMontbau, L3. Exit metro opposite Jardins de Pedro Muñoz Seca. Turn right down Pg. de Vall D'Hebron; the tennis center will be directly in front of you. The centers offer tennis and racquetball courts, a pool, yoga, and more. Monthly pool membership €52. Non-members pay per visit. Single visit €6 before 4pm, €3.35 after 4pm; under 12 €3.75 before 4pm, €2.10 after 4pm. Open M-Th 10am-8pm, F-Su and holidays 8am-9pm. Wheelchair accessible. MC/V accepted for membership payments only.

MUSIC, THEATER, AND DANCE

Barcelona offers many options for theater aficionados, though most performances are in Catalan (*Guía del Ocio* lists the language of the performance). Reserve tickets through **TelEntrada** (24hr. ☎902 10 12 12; www.telentrada.com), **ServiCaixa** at any branch of the Caixa Catalunya bank (24hr. ☎902 33 22 11, for groups 88 80 90; www.servicaixa.com; open M-F 8am-2:30pm), or www. ticktackticket.com—the Spanish Ticketmaster. The **Grec** summer festival turns Barcelona into an international theater, music, and dance extravaganza. For information about the festival, ask at the tourist office, check out www.barcelonafestival.com, or, during the festival, stop by the booth at the bottom of Pl. de Catalunya, on Portal de Angel.

In the past decade, Barcelona has managed to establish itself as a major stop for touring bands—especially during summer music festivals. **Sónar,** the grandaddy of them all, comes to town in mid-June, attracting renowned DJs and electronica enthusiasts from all over the world for three days (and very long nights) of concerts and partying. Besides Sónar, major music festivals include **Summercase** (indie and pop), **Primavera Sound** (more indie and pop), and **Jazzaldia.** Check www.mondosonoro.com or pick up the *Mondo Sonoro* festival guide at hostels and bars. For info on cultural activities in the city, swing by the **Institut de Cultura de Barcelona (ICUB),** Palau de la Virreina, La Rambla, 99. (☎933 16 10 00; www.bcn.cat/cultura. Info office open daily 10am-8pm. Most performances around €18-30.) Check www.barcelonaturisme.com for occasional 10% discounts. **Palau de la Música Catalana,** C. Sant Francese de Paula, 2 (☎932 95 72 00; www.palaumusica.org; ⓂUrquinaona), to the right off Via Laietana near the level of Pl. Urquinaona, also sells concert tickets. (Concert tickets €8-175. Box office open M-Sa 9am-9pm, Su from 1hr. prior to the concert. No concerts in Aug.; check the *Guía del Ocio* for listings. MC/V.)

Palau de la Música Catalana, C. Sant Francese de Paula, 2 (☎902 44 28 82; www. palaumusica.org) ⓂJaume I, L4, in La Ribera, off Via Laietana near Pl. Urquinaona. Head up Via Laietana to the intersection of C. Ionqueres. Performances most often feature choirs and orchestras, but the venue also hosts pop and rock artists from time to time. Box office open M-Sa 10am-9pm, Su from 2hr. before show time. No concerts in Aug.; check website or the Guía del Ocio for listings. Concert tickets €8-175. MC/V.

Centre Artesà Tradicionàrius, Tr. de Sant Antoni, 6-8 (☎932 18 44 85; www.tradicionarius.com), in Gràcia. ⓂFontana. Catalan folk music concerts Sept.-June. Tickets €6-12; frequent free concerts. Also dance, music workshops, and summer festivals; inquire for details. Open Sept.-July. M-F 11am-2pm and 5-9pm. Cash only.

Gran Teatre del Liceu, La Rambla, 51-59 (☎934 85 99 13; www.liceubarcelona.com). ⓂLiceu. Founded in 1847, destroyed by fire in 1994, and recently reopened, Liceu has regained its status as the city's premier venue for opera, ballet, and classical music. Reserve tickets in advance. Box office open M-F 1:30-8pm, Sa-Su and holidays 1hr. before showtime. 24hr. ticket sales at ServiCaixa. AmEx/MC/V.

L'Auditori, C. Lepanto, 150 (☎932 47 93 00; www.auditori.com), in L'Eixample between ⓂMarina and Glòries. Home to the city orchestra (the BOC) and host to visiting chamber, choral, and jazz groups. Concerts from late Sept. to mid-July. Tickets €6-50; special performances up to €120. Available by phone, through ServiCaixa or TelEntrada, or at ticket windows (open M-Sa noon-9pm, Su 1hr. before show starts). MC/V.

HIGH CULTURE, LOW BUDGET. The Gran Teatre del Liceu sells nosebleed seats at low prices. Beware of the cheapest tickets (€7-9) unless you want to sit behind an obstruction. Students with ID can arrive at the theater 2hr. before showtime (1hr. on weekends) and pick up remainder seats at a 30% discount. This is best attempted on weekdays, when seats more frequently go unsold.

Teatre Lliure, C. Montseny, C. Montseny, 47 (☎932 18 92 51; www.teatrelliure.com), in Gràcia. ⓂFontana. Showcases contemporary theater productions from summer festivals to Shakespeare. Call or check website for information. Tickets may be purchased at the theater or by calling Tel Entrada. Wheelchair-accessible. Shows May-Oct. Tu-Sa 9pm, Su 7pm; Nov.-Apr. Tu-Sa 9pm, Su 6pm. Tickets M-W balcony €12, orchestra €16; Th-Su €15/19. 20% discount for students.

Teatre Grec, 38 (Tel-Entrada ☎902 10 12 12; www.grec.bcn.es), across from the Museu d'Arqueològia. From ⓂEspanya, L1/L3 take bus #55 to Montjuïc. Located in the picturesque Jardins Amargós, the Teatre Grec was carved out of an old stone quarry in 1929 under the direction of Ramon Reventós. The open-air Grecian-style amphitheater is the namesake and occasional host of the Grec Barcelona Summer Theater Festival (p. 154). Most theater performances are in Spanish or Catalan, but there are plenty of music and dance shows. Outdoor cafe open July daily 8pm-3am.

Mercat de Les Flors, C. Lleida, 59 (☎93 426 18 75; www.bcn.es/icub/mflorsteatre). From ⓂEspanya, L1/L3, take bus #55 to Montjuïc. A converted flower market, now one of the city's major theater venues and a stage for the Grec festival. The Mercat de Les Flors and Teatre Grec will soon be incorporated into the Ciutat del Teatre (City of Theater)—a home for theater performance and training in Barcelona. For tickets, call Tel Entrada or stop by the Palau de la Virreina at Las Ramblas, 99.

Teatre Nacional de Catalunya, Pl. de les Arts, 1 (☎93 306 57 00; tickets 93 306 07 06; www.tnc.es), near the intersection of Av. Diagonal and Av. Meridiana. ⓂGlòries, L1, in l'Eixample. This national theater hosts classical theater and ballet in its main room (usually 1-2 shows per month) and various contemporary music, dance, circus, and textual performances in accompanying spaces. Tickets for the main room €20-24, students and seniors 20% discount. Available over the phone, through ServiCaixa (www.servicaixa.com), or at ticket windows (open M noon-3pm and 4-9pm, Tu-Sa noon-9pm, Su noon-6pm; shorter hours in winter).

Palau d'Esports Sant Jordi, on Montjuïc. (☎93 426 20 89). This huge venue hosts big-name musicians. For concert info, check www.agendabcn.com or the Guía del Ocio.

Palau de la Generalitat, at Pl. Sant Jaume (☎93 402 46 16; www.gencat.es). ⓂJaume I, L4, in the Barri Gòtic. The Palau hosts a free bell concert on the 1st Su of every month at noon.

JAZZ, POP, AND ROCK 'N' ROLL

Apolo, Nou de la Rambla, 113 (☎934 41 40 01; www.sala-apolo.com), ⓂParal·lel. The first place to look for major indie acts to come through Barcelona (think people like Nouvelle Vague and Camera Obscura). Hosts its fair share of electronica and hip-hop artists as well, along with Flamenco shows the first W of every month (www.myspace.com/flamencoobsessions). Beer €4. Mixed drinks €8. Tickets €12-22, usually available online at www.sala-apolo.com. MC/V.

Jamboree, Plaça Reial, 17 (☎933 19 17 89; www.masimas.com), ⓂLiceu. Boasts a jazz series that's been active since the 60s and still brings relevant musicians (Elvin Jones and Art Farmer have appeared here). Also ventures into funk and hip hop with WTF Jam Sessions (M 9pm-1:30am, €4). Upstairs, **Tarantos** holds flamenco shows (daily 8:30, 9:30, 10:30pm; €7) Jazz performances Tu-Su 9 and 11pm. Tickets (€10-12) available through www.telentrada.com. AmEx/MC/V.

Sidecar, Plaça Reial, 7 (☎933 17 76 66; www.sidecarfactoryclub.com). ⓂLiceu. Hosts pop and rock shows. Tends to showcase more local acts and fewer internationally imported bands compared to other Barcelona concert venues. Check website for listings. Tickets (€6-14) often available through www.atrapalo.com. Cash only.

Razzmatazz, C. Pamplona, 88, and Almogàvers, 122 (☎932 72 09 10; www.salarazzmatazz.com). ⓂMarina. This massive converted warehouse now hosts a wide range of big name musical acts from reggae to metal to electro-pop (big name means big name: Gossip, Offspring, and so on). This is where Barack Obama goes when he's in Barcelona. Just kidding. Check website for upcoming concerts. Most tickets (€12-30) available online through Telentrada or Ticketmaster. AmEx/MC/V.

BeCool, Pl. Joan Llongueras, 5. (☎933 62 04 13; www.salabecool.com). ⓂHospital Clínic. Walk up C. Comte d'Urgell, left on Diagonal, and right onto C. Beethoven; Pl. Joan Llongueras will be on your left. Opened in 2006, this venue has quickly become a common stop for indie bands touring Europe. When the show ends, weekend DJ sessions begin and last until dawn. Check website for upcoming shows and online ticket sales (€5-22). Beer €4. Mixed drinks €7-8. Cover €12, 1 drink included. Open Th-Sa 1-6am. MC/V.

Salamandra, Av. Carrilet, 235, and Av. Carrilet, 301. (☎933 37 06 02; www.salamandra.cat). ⓂAv. Carrilet. 2 rooms host an eclectic spread of performers, from black metal to baltic folk ensembles (a little more of the former than the latter). Check website for upcoming shows and online ticket sales.

FLAMENCO

Although Catalunya does not have a tradition of flamenco, a dance which originated with the gypsies in southern Spain's Andalucía, the tourist industry has fed the demand for flamenco venues. Though shows are geared toward tourists, in no way does that reflect poorly on their quality; some of the best flamenco musicians and dancers in Spain pass through these establishments.

El Patio Andaluz, C. Aribau, 242 (☎93 209 33 78), in Gràcia. ⓂDiagonal. From the Metro, take a left on Diagonal and turn right on C. Aribau. Lively Andalusian-themed restaurant showcases traditional Spanish flamenco. Show and 1 drink €30; show and *menú* from €54. Daily shows at 9:30pm and midnight. Call 9am-7pm for reservations. El Patio's red-paneled bar, **Las Sevillanas del Patio,** stays open until 3am for drinks and dancing.

Guasch Teatre, C. Aragó, 140 (☎93 323 39 50 or 93 451 34 62). ⓂUrgell, L1, in l'Eixample. Presents both children's theater, like Cinderella and Gulliver's Travel's, and adult theater. Often showcases flamenco; call for schedules. Tickets €6-18. Children's theater generally shown Th 6pm, F-Sa 12:30pm, Su 5:30pm; adult theater Th 9pm,

TOUR DE... HUH?

In 2009, stages six and seven of the Tour de France took place around Barcelona.

We were confused, too, but don't worry: we checked, and Barcelona is, in fact, in Spain. The famous bicycle race, which alternates every other year between clockwise and counterclockwise circuits of France, also occasionally makes forays into neighboring states. In 2007, the race passed through Belgium, London, and Spain. In 2008, there was an Italian stage. In 2134, stage four will take place on Io, one of Jupiter's moons.

The race in 2009 visited a handful of countries: Andorra, Italy, Monaco, Spain, and Switzerland. Barcelonese took to the streets on July 9th and 10th to watch the competitors vie for the yellow jersey. Stage six, which ran from Girona to Barcelona, was a flat stage and Thor Husovd, from Norway, won it. Stage seven, from Barcelona to Andorra-Arcalis, was mountainous; Brice Feillu, from France, finished first.

If you happen to be in town during June or July, do your research at www.letour.fr. And if you forget, but happen to see a pack of bikers rush by, who knows? Maybe you just saw Lance.

F-Sa 10pm, Su 7:30pm. Ticket office opens 1hr. prior to performance.

OLYMPIC FACILITIES AT MONTJUÏC

SOCCER
Estadi Olímpic de Montjuïc, Pg. Olímpic, 17-19 (☎93 426 20 89, 24hr. 90 210 12 12). The stadium hosts free soccer games for Barcelona's second beloved team, R.C. Deportivo Espanyol, a.k.a. los periquitos (parakeets). Open daily 10am-8pm. Obtain R.C. Deportivo Espanyol tickets from Banco Catalana.

SWIMMING
Piscines Bernat Picornell, Av. Estadi, 30-40 (☎93 423 40 41; www.picornell.com), to the right when you're facing the stadium. Test your swimming skills in the Olympic pools, two gorgeous facilities surrounded by stadium seating. A favorite for families and sunbathers. There is also a small cafe inside the complex. €4.40 for outdoor pool, €8 for pool and workout facilities including sauna, massage parlor, and gym. Outdoor pool open Su 9am-8pm, M-Sa 9am-9pm. Workout facilities open Su 7:30am-8pm, M-F 7am-midnight, Sa 7am-9pm.

THE OUTDOORS

Those looking for a little greenery make their way to the lovely Collserolas, which offer plenty of opportunities for hiking, biking, picnicking, and horseback riding. For other outdoor activities, such as hiking Montserrat, see **Daytrips,** p. 195.

PARC DE COLLSEROLA
The **Centro d'Informació,** Carretera de l'Església, 92, has all the information you'll need on activities in the park. Pamphlets and basic maps are available for free and the staff can advise you on various facilities and options in and around the park. (See **Tibidabo,** p. 135; ☎932 80 35 52. www.parccollserola.net. FGC: Baixador de Vallvidrera, then follow signs to center. Open daily 9:30am-3pm.)

HIKING
The information center provides numerous useful guides to trails in the park. For those who want to stay close to the entrance, there are six hikes, marked with a variety of colors, that start and end near the center itself. The red path to the **Font**

de la Budellera (Budellera Spring), is an easy hike to the Torre de Collserola, Tibidabo, or the town of Vallvidrera. The leaflet "Walks Around," available for free at the center, gives a detailed description of each color-coded itinerary, which range from 15min. (green path) to 2¼hr. (purple path). More detailed maps and guides (€6-18) are offered, which though they can help you navigate more extensive routes through the massive park, are almost exclusively in Catalan. Separate English guided tours can be arranged in advance (€97 per group of 25) and last about four hours. (Call ☎932 80 35 52 for more info.)

BIKING
Biking in the park is limited to paths which are at least 3m wide, but there are plenty of them. The maps for sale list some bike routes (in Catalan) and most roads are marked with signs indicating whether they are bicycle-friendly. Unfortunately, there's no bike rental shop near the park. You'll have to rent one downtown and bring it up on an FGC train (see **Bike Rentals,** p. 31). Most FGC stations are equipped with escalators and ramps along the stairwells. One of the most popular paths, not far into the park, is the **Passeig Mirador de las Aigues,** which offers bikers and hikers a view of Barcelona along an 11km trail. To get there, take the FGC from Pl. de Catalunya to the Peu del Funicular stop, catch the funicular, and press the request button to get out halfway up, at C. de Aigües.

HORSEBACK RIDING
There are six stables in the park, but most of them are far from public transportation. One exception is the Hípica Sant Cugat, Av. Corts Catalanes, s/n. Guides here lead excursions into Parc de Collserolla (€21 per hr.) and offer horseback-riding classes (€200 for 10hr.). Call ahead to reserve a space. (From ⓂFabra i Puig catch the A4 bus to Sant Cugat; get off at the gas station and walk 3min. to the stable. ☎936 74 83 85; www.hipicasantcugat.es. Open daily 10am-2pm and 4-6pm.)

SKATING

Skating Pista de Gel, C. Roger de Flor, 168 (☎93 245 28 00), between C. Aragó and C. Consell de Cent, in l'Eixample. ⓂPg. de Gràcia, L2/3/4. One of only two ice-skating rinks in the city, and the only one open year-round and at night. Open M-F and Su 10:30am-1:30pm and 5-8:30pm, Sa 10:30am-1:30pm and 5-9pm. €9, with skates €12. Cash only.

SPECTATOR SPORTS

FÚTBOL CLUB BARCELONA
For the record, the lunatics covered from head to toe in red and blue stripes didn't just escape from an asylum—they are **F.C. Barcelona (Barça)** fans. A visit to Camp Nou, home of FCB, can be compared to a religious experience for many fans. The team, commonly referred to as El Barça, has the motto of "més que un club" (more than a club), and it's easy to see why. El Barça is a symbol of Catalunya and its proud people, and the team carries the political agendas of the entire region (see More than a Rivalry, p. 166). The club has a devoted worldwide following, and boasts more than 100,000 members. Even the Pope, while visiting Barcelona in 1982, signed the membership book and became an honorary member. The FCB also has teams in several other sports—including

basketball, rugby, and roller hockey—that play in other buildings in the Camp Nou complex, which includes basketball courts, a mini-stadium and the Palau Blaugrana (Blue-Burgundy Palace).

Camp Nou, on C. Aristides Maillol. ⓂCollblanc. Head down C. Francese Layret and take the 2nd right onto Trav. de les Corts. A block later, turn left onto C. Aristides Maillol, which leads to the ticket office and museum entrance (see Sights & Museums, p. 114). ☎93 496 36 00; www.fcbarcelona.com. Tickets available for all club sport events. Ticket office open Sept.-June M-F (and the day before matches) 9:30am-1:30pm and 3:30-6pm; July-Aug. 8am-2:30pm.

GETTING TICKETS

Inaugurated in 1957, Camp Nou stadium was expanded in 1982 to hold 120,000 for the World Cup, and is today Europe's largest fútbol ground. However, getting tickets to a Barça match is not always easy; hardcore FCB fans already have tickets, leaving slim pickings for visitors. Matches usually take place on Sunday evenings at 9pm, and the bigger the match, the harder it is to get in. Entradas (tickets) are available at the ticket office and usually go on sale to the public the Thursday before the match. A number of scalpers also try to unload tickets for copious amounts of cash in the days before the match. At the ticket office, expect to pay €30-60, and bring your binoculars, as most available seats are on the third level. The seats may be in the nosebleed section, but even at that height, any Barça match is an incredible experience. The cheap seats offer a bird's eye view of the action and gorgeous views of the mountains of Tibidabo and Montjuïc. Even if you can't tell which player scored the goal, you'll have just as much fun celebrating it with 70,000 newfound friends.

BULLFIGHTING

Catalunya is not the stronghold of bullfighting in Spain; bullfights will typically not sell out and will be dominated by tourists.

Plaça de Toros Monumental, Gran Via de les Corts Catalans, 743 (☎93 245 58 02; www.torosbarcelona.com). ⓂMonumental. Built in 1915 by Ignasi i Morell, the bullring is one of the few prominent buildings in the city that draws overtly from Arabic architectural influences; it is a rare touch of Andalucía in Catalunya. The corrida (bullfighting) season runs Apr.-Sept., with fights every Su at 7pm. Tickets (€18-95) may be purchased at the bullring; ticket window open M-Sa 11am-2pm and 4-8pm; Su 11am-1pm. Tourist visits to the bull ring are also permitted during those hours; adults €4, children €3. Tickets may also be purchased at C. Muntaner, 24 (☎93 453 38 21; fax 93 451 69 98). Cash only.

WATERFRONT ACTIVITIES

For those who are done bronzing and want to do something active, there are several options around Port Vell and Vila Olímpica, both on water and land. Boating and beach sports abound, and there's a coastal bike path (4km).

BOAT TOURS

Las Golondrinas (☎934 42 31 06; www.lasgolondrinas.com), on Portal de la Pau. ⓂDrassanes, L3. At the foot of the Monument a Colom, in Port Vell. double-decker ferries chug around the entire Port Vell, as far as Montjuïc and back. (35min., €6, ages 4-10 €2.60). A longer excursion includes a tour of Port Olímpic. (1½hr.; €13, seniors and students €10, ages 4-10 €5). Ticket office open daily July-Sept. 10am-9pm, Oct.-Mar. 11am-6pm, Apr.-June 10am-7pm. Closed from Dec. 15 to Jan. 3. MC/V.

Catamarán Orsom (☎934 41 05 37, fax 934 41 21 14; www.barcelona-orsom.com), right next to Las Golondrinas on Portal de la Pau in Port Vell. ⓜDrassanes, L3. This 75 ft. catamaran will take you on a more upscale, relaxing sail around the Barcelona with full bar service. The afternoon rides feature live Jazz. 1½hr. cruises at noon (€13, ages 11-18 and seniors €9.50, ages 4-10 €6.50, under 4 free). Jazz cruises at 3:30 and 6pm (€15, ages 11-18 and seniors €13, ages 4-10 €6.50, under 4 free). Cash only.

WATERSPORT RENTALS

Base Náutica de Mar Bella (☎932 21 04 32; www.basenautica.org), on Platja de la Mar Bella. The Mar Bella nautical base offers classes in windsurfing (€185 per 10hr.), catamaran sailing (€216 per 12hr.), kayaking (€124 per 10hr.), and diving and navigation. The base also rents kayaks (€14 per hr.), windsurfing boards (€23 per hr.), and leads group trips. Summer camps offered for children (5-day €105, 10-day €212). Membership (€183 per year) brings a 10-30% discount off all courses and rentals. Open daily May-Aug. 10am-8pm, Sept.-Oct. and Apr. 10am-7pm, Nov.-Mar. 10am-5:30pm.

Centre Municipal de Vela (☎932 25 79 40; www.vela-barcelona.com), at Moll de Gregal Port Olímpic, in the left corner of the port as you walk toward the water, lower level. Like the nautical base, the municipal sailing center offers lessons in windsurfing, sailing, and navigation as well as member services including saunas and massages. This posh workout palace is a more expensive, elite option than the nautical base, with a plethora of offerings; check the website or pick up an informational newsletter at the front desk. Membership is €201 annually, ages 15-20 €160, under 15 €125. Family rates available. Open daily May-Aug. 9am-9pm, Mar.-Apr. and Sept.-Oct. 9am-8pm, Nov.-Feb. 9am-6pm.

IN RECENT NEWS

(NOT) TAKING THE BULL BY THE HORNS

In May 2009, Prou—the anti-bullfighting platform—announced the collection of over 180,000 signatures backing a ban bullfighting in Catalunya. Residents of the 65 towns represented in the petition are demanding the outlaw of bullfights and other traditional spectacles that result in the death of an animal. With nearly four times the number of signatures required to stage a debate, the motion will now be presented to the Catalan Parliament. While many Catalan political parties remain undecided on the ban, anti-bullfighting advocate Eric Gallego is confident that Catalunya could outlaw the sport by November of 2009.

Bullfighting has long been recognized as symbol of Spanish culture, immortalized by Ernest Hemingway as an "art...in which the degree of brilliance in the performance is left to the fighter's honor." It remains a multimillion-dollar industry in Spain, maintained largely by tourism. But a growing awareness of animal rights—especially among young people—fuels anti-bullfighting activism in Catalunya.

While only less than 30 percent of the Spanish population professes an interest in the sport, fans are purportedly diehard. Gallego claims that even a strategic compromise of Portuguese-style "light" bullfights—in which the bull is not publicly killed—will not suffice. "Spaniards would not go to such *corridas,*" he said. "Here, the public wants to see the animal get killed."

SHOPPING

A shopaholic's paradise, cosmopolitan Barcelona is littered with stores for all audiences and price ranges. The fashionista meccas are **Plaça Catalunya** and **Passeig de Gràcia** in l'Eixample. Those on the prowl for typical European women's clothing—and if you're lucky, big discounts—should check out **Calle Portaferrissa, Calle Pelai** in front of Pl. Catalunya, and **Avinguda Portal de l'Àngel**. A stroll down **Calle d'Avinyó** and its smaller side streets will prove beneficial for anyone into underground fashion, as will a trip to La Ribera or Gràcia's hip boutiques. Less expensive jewelry, accessories, and other knick-knacks can be found on **Calle Boqueria**. For more legitimate jewelry, meander into one of the treasure chests on **Calle Call**. One good destination for bargain-hunting is **Carrer Girona**, between C. Casp and Gran Via, in l'Eixample. There, you'll find a small string of discount shops offering clothing, shoes, bags, and accessories. (Ⓜ Tetuán. Walk 2 blocks down Gran Via and take a left on C. Girona.) **Carrer Bruc,** one street over, offers more retail delights for bargain hunters. Be aware that stores marked "Venta al Mejor" are wholesalers who don't take kindly to browsing. Another area to try for discounts is the **Mercat Alternatiu** (Alternative Market) on C. Riera Baixa in El Raval. (Ⓜ Liceu. Take C. de l'Hospital—a right off La Rambla facing the ocean—and follow it to C. Riera Baixa, the 7th right, shortly after the stone hospital.) This short street is crammed with secondhand and thrift stores. For a department store, **El Corte Inglés** by Pl. Catalunya holds anything and everything between its massive walls (including a supermarket in the basement).

ART AND FILM

Cinemascope, C. de la Perla, 29 (☎ 932 37 27 20). Ⓜ Fontana. Walk down C. Gran de Gràcia and make a left onto C. de Montseny. This street turns into C. de la Perla. Film buffs will drool over this small shop, which sells rare DVDS, movie posters, T-shirts, and more. Open M and W 5-9pm, Th-Sa 11am-2pm and 5-9pm, Su 5-9pm. Cash only.

Mostra d'Art, Pl. Sant Josep Oriol. Ⓜ Liceu. This weekly art display makes the plaça it's set in all the more charming. For 3 decades, local artists have set up their easels and displayed their canvases for perusal (and purchase) by the tourists sipping coffee and eating tapas on the square. Open Sa 11am-8:30pm, Su 10am-2:30pm.

BOOKS

La Central del Raval, C. Elisabets, 6 (☎ 902 88 49 90; www.lacentral.com and www.centralcafe.com), off La Rambla in El Raval. Ⓜ Catalunya. Literature and nonfiction in 7 languages in a spacious bookstore and cafe (a rare combination here in Barcelona), born in 1693 as the Gothic-style Església de la Misericòrdia. Pocket Catalan/English and Catalan/Spanish dictionaries €12. Open M-F 10am-9:30pm, Sa 10am-9pm. AmEx/MC/V.

Come in Librería Anglesa, C. Balmes, 129 (☎ 934 53 12 04; www.libreriainglesa.com). English books and a selection of classic novels. Bulletin boards feature ads for travel partners or language instructors. Open M-Sa 9:45am-2pm and 4:30-8:15pm. MC/V.

Documenta, C. Cardenal Casañas, 4 (☎ 933 17 25 27; www.documenta-bcn.com), just steps off La Rambla, located in the old Cu-Cut! publishing house, which was forcibly shut down by the army in the 1930s. Decent selection of English novels and travel guides. Open M-Sa 9:30am-8:30pm, Su and holidays 11am-2:30pm and 5-8:30pm. AmEx/MC/V.

FNAC (www.fnac.es) has 3 locations: Triangle mall in Pl. Catalunya (☎933 44 18 00; open M-Sa 10am-10pm), ⓂCatalunya; Av. Diagonal, 3-35 (☎935 02 99 00; open M-Sa 10am-10pm), ⓂBesòs Mar; L'Illa Centre Comercial, Av. Diagonal, 557 (☎934 44 59 00; open M-Sa 10am-9:30pm), ⓂMaría Cristina. AmEx/MC/V.

Happy Books, C. Pelai, 20, (☎933 17 07 68; www.happybooks.com). ⓂUniversitat. A good selection of Barcelona guidebooks in both English and Spanish (€10), English/Catalan and English/Spanish dictonaries, and English-language novels downstairs. Open M-Sa 10:30am-8:30pm. MC/V.

Hibernian Secondhand English Bookshop, C. Montseny, 17 (☎932 17 47 96; www.hibernian-books.com). ⓂFontana. Walk down C. Gran de Gracía and make a left on C. Montseny. Book lovers will experience glee upon discovery of this small shop selling secondhand English books. Divided by genre (art, philosophy, thriller). Shelf of €1 books (mostly romance novels) at back of store. Open M 4-8:30pm, Tu-Sa 10:30am-8:30pm.

The Watergate Bookshop, Pl. Vicenç Martorell, 2 (☎933 43 58 38). ⓂCatalunya. Walk down Las Ramblas, make a left on C. Elisabets, and then the 1st right onto C. de les Ramelleres. The plaça is on the right, and the restaurant is in the far right corner. Alternatively, ⓂCatalunya. Walk down C. de Pelai and make a left onto C. de les Ramelleres; the plaça is about 3min. down, on the left. "Strange and rare books for insane minds," read advertisements for the Watergate Bookshop. After several weeks of backpacking through Europe with your college roommates, you should have a good sense of which one to send here. He or she can leaf through "The Anarchist Cookbook," or buy the President Obama paper dolls that they've been searching for. Open M 4:30-9pm, Tu-Sa 11am-2:30pm and 4:30-9pm. MC/V.

CLOTHING

Clink, C. Verdi, 14, (☎933 02 88 68). ⓂFontana. Walk down C. d'Asturies to C. Verdi. C. Verdi is home to many a cute boutique; this one stands out with its collection of brightly colored dresses (€20-30) with distinct prints and fabrics. Has an excellent selection of (modern) women's hats and some accessories too. Open M-Sa 10am-10pm. Closed Su. MC/V.

Instinto, C. Asturies, 15 (☎932 17 82 99). ⓂFontana. Walk down C. Asturies. This women's clothing store has clothes in exceptionally bright colors, made of exceptionally soft fabrics. A great place to pick up a present to take home to your mom—and who knows? You might luck out and find something that you like too. Shirts and skirts €20-40. Open M-F 10am-2pm and 4:30-8:30pm, Sa 10:30am-2:30pm and 5-8:30pm. MC/V.

Mercat Raval, Rambla de Raval. (☎648 09 19 54, www.mercatraval.com) ⓂLiceu. Clothing market with booths of colorful, funky dresses, designer sleeveless T-shirts, and trendy accessories. Open from Sept. to mid-July Sa and Su 9am-11pm.

El Piano Tina Garcia, C. Verdi, 20 (☎934 15 51 76). ⓂFontana. Walk down C. d'Asturies to C. Verdi. This boutique has a selection of distinctive garments (€20-30) for women; down the street at C. Verdi, 15, you'll find **El Piano Man,** a sister store for men. Open M-Sa 10am-10pm. Closed Su. MC/V.

Sombreria Mil, C. Fontanella, 20 (☎933 01 84 91). ⓂUrquinaoa. Looking to avoid sunburn the stylish way? This hat shop has everything from feathered ladies' hats to trucker caps. They're fun to try on, even if you're not looking to buy. Open M-Sa 9:30am-8:45pm. MC/V.

MAJOR CHAINS

Blanco, C. Pelai, 1 (☎933 18 23 40; www.blancoint.com). Affordable clothing usually true to the year's (or season's) styles. Much like the United States brand Old Navy, right down to the pop music playing in the dressing rooms. MC/V.

Camper, Rambla Catalunya, 122 (☎932 17 23 84; www.camper.com) or Passeig de Gràcia, 100 (☎934 67 41 48). "Mediterranean" designer sneakers for both men and women. MC/V.

Desigual, Las Ramblas, 136 or Pg. de Gràcia, 47 (☎933 04 31 64; www.desigual.com). "Atypical fashion." This popular Spanish designer brand emphasizes bright colors and wild patterns; in United States terms, think J.Crew meets Pacsun. MC/V.

El Corte Ingles, Plaça de Catalunya, 14 (☎933 06 38 00; www.elcorteingles.es) or Av. Diagonal, 617 (☎933 667 100). A large, upscale department store selling everything from dishware to diamonds. Extremely convenient, but pricey. AmEx/MC/V.

Mango, Paseo de Gràcia 8-10 (☎934 12 15 99; www.mango.com) or Paseo de Gràcia, 65 (☎932 157 530). A competitor of stores like H&M and Topshop. In 2007 this chain released a 25-piece collection designed by Penelope Cruz. MC/V.

Zara, C. Pelai, 30 (☎933 01 09 78; www.zara.com) or Pg. de Gràcia, 16 (☎933 18 76 75). A women's clothing chain that manufactures designer knock-offs. Usually falls in the center on a spectrum of classic to trend-of-the-week. MC/V.

MARKETS

CIUTAT VELLA

Mercat de Sant Josep/La Boqueria, La Rambla de Sant Josep. ⓂLiceu. Come to buy *jamón serrano* or mussels for dinner, or to ogle the tongues, hearts, and feet of recently slaughtetred critters. The front area of this popular, somewhat touristy market sells delicious and cheap snacks like fresh smoothies. Open M-Sa 8am-10:30pm. Some vendors MC/V, some cash only.

Fira del Collectiu d'Artesans d'Alimentació, Pl. del Pi. ⓂLiceu. Artisanal food merchants sell organic, locally produced food. Honey, herbed cheeses, and homemade pastries and breads. Open 1st and 3rd F, Sa, and Su of each month 10am-9pm.

GRÀCIA

Mercat de la Llibertat, Pl. de la Llibertat (☎93 415 90 93). ⓂDiagonal or one block off Via Augusta from FGC: Gràcia. Originally designed as an open-air market by Berenguer in 1875, this market was covered years later. The wrought iron gates and floral details are particularly impressive, as is the drinking fountain at the front of the market, which bears Gràcia's shield. Vendors offer everything from fresh eggs to dried fruit. Open M 5-8pm, Tu-Th 8am-2pm and 5-8pm, F 8am-8pm, Sa 7am-3pm. Though some vendors may accept MC/V, it's a good idea to bring cash.

Mercat de L'Abaceria Central, at the intersection of Trav. de Gràcia and C. Torrijos (ⓂFontana or Joanic). This market is conveniently located in the heart of Gràcia . The produce stalls are inside, while outside vendors sell flowers, clothing, and trinkets. Open M-Th 7am-2:30pm and 5:30-8:30pm, F-Sa 6am-3pm and 5-8:30pm. Some vendors MC/V, some cash only.

POBLE SEC

Mercat Sant Antoni, Ronda Sant Pau/Carrer Comte d'Urgell. Ⓜ️Sant Antoni. Larger than downtown's La Boqueria and less touristed, this open-air market selling fresh fruits, vegetables, eggs, bread, and more makes for an unusually delightful grocery shopping experience. Su from 8am-3pm there is a book market outside of the food market. M-Th and Sa 7am-2:30pm and 5:30-8:30pm, F 7-10:30pm, Closed Su. Some vendors MC/V, some cash only.

LES CORTS

El Mercat de les Corts,Trav. de les Corts. Ⓜ️Les Corts. A large, indoor market selling fresh fruits, vegetables, eggs, meat, and more. Open M-W and F-Sa 10am-9pm. Some vendors MC/V, some cash only.

ODDITIES

Enrique Tomas, C. Rogent, 94 (☎934 33 56 69; www.enriquetomas.com). Ⓜ️Clot. Walk quite a ways (several blocks) up C. Rogent. If you have a passion for *jamon iberico,* then this is the place for you. From the moment you walk into this corner shop, you'll smell (and smell like) the most delicious of pigs. Sandwiches €3.60. Legs of ham €30-300. MC/V.

G. I. Joe's, C. Hospital, 82 (☎93 329 96 52; www.gijoebcn.com) Ⓜ️Liceu. Other location at C. Tallers, 82 (☎93 302 12 91). Ⓜ️Universitat. If you forgot to pack a gas mask or steel-toed army boots, G. I. Joe's is here to serve you. You'll also find backpacks, army jackets, T-shirts, pants, and lots of camo. Open M-Sa 10:30am-2pm, 5-8:30pm. MC/V.

El Ingenio, Rauric, 6 (☎93 317 71 38; www.el-ingenio.com). Ⓜ️Liceu. Walking down C. Ferrán from Las Ramblas, take a left onto C. Rauric. Guarded by a stern *gigante* (giant), this toy store has all kinds of bizarre and amusing items for sale. Inside you'll find more giant heads along with practical joke kits, juggling supplies, wooden figurines, wigs, costumes, and hundreds of other entertaining trinkets. Open M-F 10am-1:30pm and 4:15-8pm, Sa 11am-2pm and 5-8:30pm. AmEx/MC/V.

LTW, C. Tallers, 29. (☎933 18 36 62; www.ltwtattoo.com). Ⓜ️Universitat. Highly esteemed tattoo and piercing shop and home of renowned tattoo artist Jondix, who specializes in Thai-style Buddhist designs. Plan ahead: there's a 2-month wait for an appointment. Piercings from €21. Tattoos from €82. Open M-Sa 10:30am-8:30pm. Cash only.

Mercat de Numismática i Filatèlia, Pl. Reial. Ⓜ️Liceu. In case you were wondering, some Spaniards do enjoy collecting things besides legs of *jamon ibérico,* and this market is proof. As the name of the market suggests, the emphasis here is on numismatics (coin collecting) and philately (the study of stamps), so go get your dork on. Open Su 9am-2:30pm.

Olokuti, C. Asturies, 36 (☎932 17 00 70; www.olokuti.com). Ⓜ️Fontana. Walk down C. Asturies. If you like to think of yourself as a conscientious consumer, head to this eco-friendly shop selling "world" books, music, scarves, underwear, and more. Some baby items like bibs and rattles. Handmade purses €9-40. Open daily 11am-9:30pm. MC/V.

Te Quiero, C. Torrijos, 9 (☎932 84 60 00). Ⓜ️Fontana. Walk down C. Gran de Gràcia, make a left onto Tr. de Gràcia, and then another left onto C. Torrijos. This incense, tea, and book shop is the perfect antidote to the chaos of Gràcia's nearby street market. A small back room has low tables, floor cushions, natural light, and lovely plants. Get a new book, read it over a cup of tea, and get your daily dose of zen. Books €8-12. Tea €1.20-3. Open M-Sa 10am-2pm and 4-8:30pm. MC/V.

Verkerke, C. del Cardenal Casañas, 10-12 (☎933 02 01 86). ⓜLiceu. Filled wall-to-wall with posters of all different kinds for your browsing pleasure. Artistic masterpieces, bands, movies, kittens, you name it, all in large scale (€8-15). Open M-F 10:30am-2pm and 4:30-8:30pm, Sa 11am-2:30pm and 5-9pm. AmEx/MC/V.

ON THE FRONT LINES OF THE THRIVING MUSIC BUSINESS

C D Drome, C. Valldonzella, 3 (☎933 17 46 46; www.cddrome.com). ⓜUniversitat. Hip record store specializing in electronica and house. DJ your own personal dance party at the vinyl listening stations. Open M-Sa 10:30am-8:30pm. MC/V.

Guitar Shop Barcelona, Tallers, 27 (☎934 12 19 19). ⓜUniversitat or Catalunya. Walk down C. Tallers. A large, professional shop selling guitars and guitar accessories. Flyers advertise concerts and lessons. Open M 5-8:30pm, Tu-Sa 10am-2pm, 4:30-8:30pm. MC/V.

Revolver Records, Tallers, 11 and 13 (☎934 12 73 58 or 02 16 85; www.discos-revolver.com). ⓜPl. Catalunya. 2 record stores on the same block. On the right, you'll find a good selection of indie and alternative CDs, with an emphasis on metal. The store to the right has more classic rock as well as some jazz and oldies. Open M-Sa 9am-11pm. MC/V.

Wah Wah Records, C. Riera Baixa 14 (☎934 42 37 03; www.wah-wahsupersonic.com). ⓜLiceu. Eclectic mix of vinyl and CDs with a specialty in 60s garage and psychedelia. Also runs its own record label, which re-releases unfairly forgotten gems across a variety of genres. Open M-Sa 11am-2pm and 5-8:30pm. MC/V.

WE HAVE A GREAT IDEA FOR A FIRST DATE

Condoneria, Pl. Sant Josep Oriol, 7 (☎933 02 77 21; www.condoneria-bcn.com). ⓜLiceu. Good-humored sex shop with a wide selection of vibrators, toys, lubes, condoms, and countless other items that might tickle your fancy (among other things). Open M-Sa 10am-3pm and 4-8:30pm. MC/V.

SHOPPING

NIGHTLIFE

Barcelona truly lives by night (and all the way until early morning). Its wild and varied nightlife treads the precarious line between slick and kitschy. In many ways, the city is a tourist's clubbing heaven: things don't get going until late (don't bother showing up at a club before 1am) and keep going for as long as you can handle it—frequently 6am. Yet for every full-blown dance club, there are a hundred more relaxed bars, from Irish pubs to gay clubs to absinthe dens. Check the *Guía del Ocio*, available at newsstands, for even more up-to-date listings of nighttime fun, as the hot spots change often. *Barcelona Week*, the English arts weekly, also has listings.

BARRI GÒTIC AND LAS RAMBLAS

When night falls, the distinction between upper and lower Barri Gòtic becomes much clearer. The area above C. Ferran, dominated by shops, restaurants, and hostels, virtually shuts down by midnight, while **Carrer Ferran** and below becomes a human river of tourists and locals weaving their way from bar to bar. There are a few clubs and several hybrid bar-clubs in and around **Plaça Reial,** but overall the Barri Gòtic is more of a place for drinking and hanging out than for wild and crazy dance parties like the ones in Maremagnum or Montjuïc (p. 185).

While Barri Gòtic has some nightlife, it is a favorite tourist spot and as such attracts drug dealers, pickpockets, and prostitutes. Prostitutes tend to stick to Las Ramblas or other major streets (C. Ferran, C. Avinyó) and it's best not to let them get a hold of your arm or clothing as they may soon try reaching for your pockets. Drug dealers tend to stick to sidestreets and alleys which come just off the main streets and plaças (i.e. Pl. Reial, Pl. Trippy, C. Avinyó) but generally leave passersby alone once they make it clear they're not interested. With its ancient, randomly arranged streets, Barri Gòtic is an easy place to get lost in. Get an idea of where you're going before you head down a street; you don't want to end up alone in the middle of one of the many narrow, empty sidestreets. When in doubt, you can always go back to Las Ramblas and work your way up and down the neighborhood from there. At night, the main drag is certainly host to its fair share of unsavory characters trying to sell beer, sex, and drugs, but it does offer light and the protection of crowds. Overall, the area is well-policed and whispers of "hashish" are probably the only indications of lawlessness that you'll encounter.

Just a short ways into the maze of Barri Gòtic is the infamous Plaça "Trippy." Located at the end of C. Escudellers from Las Ramblas, this square, officially named Plaça George Orwell, has long garnered a reputation for attracting an alternative crowd and the trade of illicit substances. It is rumored that the government removed all of the benches here to discourage loitering and drug dealing; how successful they were is debatable. More recently, a 24hr. closed-circuit surveillance camera has been installed in the square, in a superbly ironic gesture (given the plaça's original name) meant to further curtail drug sales. Nowadays the trippiness of yore is gone, but you're sure to find a ready supply of smiley, rattily-clothed guitar players as well as some less smiley drug-dealers around the corner.

171

! IT TAKES TWO. Of course traveling in groups at night is always a good idea, but it can be especially helpful in Barri Gotìc. Even a single companion, especially of the opposite sex, can work wonders in decreasing the amount of attention you receive from unsavory characters. Women accompanied by men are sure to receive fewer catcalls by drunken tourists and locals, and men with a female companion will be spared a great deal of harassment by prostitutes.

BARS

El Bosq de les Fades, Pg. de la Banca, 16 (☎933 17 26 49), near the Wax Museum. ⓂDrassanes. This spooky cafe-bar used to be the horror section of the Wax Museum and retains a fairytale look, with gnarled trees, gourd-lanterns, and a wishing well. Fills up early, so it's a good place to start the night. Beer €3. *Cava* €3. Tequila Sunrise €7.20. Open M-Th and Su 10am-1am, F-Sa 10am-2am. MC/V.

Barcelona Pipa Club, Pl. Reial, 3 (☎933 02 47 32; www.bpipaclub.com). ⓂLiceu, L3. Unmarked—look for the small plaque on the door to the left of Glaciar Bar, on your left as you enter the square from Las Ramblas, and ring the doorbell. Don't let the pseudo-secrecy deter you. A welcoming place for late-night drinks. The decor is 100% Sherlock Holmes, the music mostly jazz and fusion, and the people are a mix of local bartenders, artists, and tourists in the know. An impressive collection of pipes from around the world is housed in a side-room along with a small pool table (€1.50 a game). Live music (often jazz) F 11pm. Mixed drinks €7, beer €4. Open daily 11pm-4:30am. Cash only.

Shangó, C. d'En Groch, 2 (☎662 10 51 65). ⓂJaume I. Walk down Via Laietana and take a right on C. d'Àngel Baixeras. Continue as it turns into C. Gignàs and take a right on the small C. d'en Groch. This colorful bar blasts Latin beats and attracts young locals with its delicious mojitos (€6). Free salsa classes Tu and W at 11pm. Beer from €2.20. Happy hour 9-11pm. Open daily 9pm-3am. Cash only.

Smoll Bar, C. Comtesa de Sobradiel, 9. ⓂLiceu, L3. Between Pl. Reial and Via Laietana. As promised, this chic, neon-lit bar is quite small, and fills up quickly and reliably. Be prepared to get cozy with a young, mostly gay crowd. Beer €3.50. Mixed drinks €6-7. Open M-Th 9:30pm-2:30am, F-Sa 9:30pm-3am. Cash only.

Sincopa, C. Avinyò, 35. ⓂLiceu, L3. Coming from Las Ramblas, take a right off C. Ferran. Bright, instrument-laden walls enclose a lively young crowd. Always blasting music, mostly Latin. When the upside-down musicians on the ceiling orient themselves you know you've had too much to drink. Wine €3. Mixed drinks €7. Open daily 6pm-3am. Cash only.

13 Bar, C. Lleona, 13. ⓂLiceu, L3. Coming from Las Ramblas, take a right off C. Ferran onto Avinyó and a left onto C. Lleona. At the end of this inconspicuous sidestreet lies a bar with a dark sense of humor and a crowd of locals. Presents a perfect mix of devilish music and fruity drinks. Beer €2.50. Wine €2.50. Mixed drinks €5. Happy hour 10:30-11pm. 2 for 1 drinks Su. Open M-Th and Su 8pm-2am, F-Sa 8pm-3am. Cash only.

La Ria, C. Milans, 4 (☎933 10 00 92). ⓂLiceu, L3. Coming from Las Ramblas, take a right off C. Ferran onto C. Avinyó and follow it until you see C. Milans on your left. Crowds pack into this tapas bar for the small array of cheap and tasty *montaditos* (€1.20) and beer (€2). Wine €3. Open M-Th noon-4pm and 6pm-1:30am, F-Sa noon-4pm and 6pm-3am. Cash only.

Andú, C. Correu Vell, 13 (☎646 55 39 30). ⓂSant Jaume I, L3. Coming from Pl. Sant Jaume, take a left off C. de la Ciutat. Stay on Avinyó. This cozy wine bar sports a well-executed antique look and attracts a young, sophisticated crowd. Good for an early glass of wine (€2.50-5) or a late bite to eat. Bottles €9-15. Sangria €5-15. Tapas

NIGHTLIFE

€2.50-5. Meat and cheese platters €15. Open daily 8pm-3am. Kitchen closes at midnight. MC/V.

Oviso, C. Arai, 5 (☎www.barnawood.com). Ⓜ️Liceu, L3. A youthful and colorful crowd to match the bright wall murals, befitting a bar right in the middle of Plaça Trippy. Serves food and fresh fruit juices during the day. Beer €2. Mixed drinks €6-7. Open M-Th and Su 10am-2:30am, F-Sa and holidays 10am-3am. Cash only.

Margarita Blue, C. J. A. Clavé, 6 (☎934 12 54 89). Ⓜ️Drassanes, L3. Walk past the wax museum and take a left. It's off Las Ramblas, about 1 block from the port. This Mexican-themed bar draws a 20- and 30-something crowd with small blue margaritas, tropically painted walls, and a strangely arranged wall of mirrors behind the bar. Small Mexican dishes (€3.50-8) accompany the tequila. A wider array of mixed drinks (€7) than most. Open M-Th and Su 7pm-2:30am, F-Sa 7pm-3am. Kitchen closes at 1am.

Schilling, C. Ferran, 23 (☎933 17 67 87; www.cafeschilling.com). Ⓜ️Liceu, L3. One of the more laid-back and spacious wine bars in the area, with dim lighting, velvet seat cushions, and bottles climbing the walls. Crowd gets younger as the night goes on. Excellent sangria (pitcher €18). Wine €3. Mixed drinks €8. Serves breakfast and sandwiches (€4-6) during the day. Open daily M-W 10am-2:30am. MC/V over €10.

Las Cuevas del Sorte, C. Gignàs, 2 (☎932 95 40 1). Ⓜ️Liceu, L3. Coming from Las Ramblas, take a right off C. Ferran, turn left on C. Avinyó, and left again on Gignàs. Soft lighting and walls that resemble rock formations upstairs, an actual cave with mosaic pillars illuminated by a disco-ball downstairs. DJ from 11pm on likes to start off the night with 60s ballads and old-school soul. Beer €3. Sex on the Beach €4.50. Mixed drinks €6-8. Happy hour 7-10pm. Open M, W-Th, and Su 7pm-2:30am, F-Sa 7pm-3am. Cash only.

Santamónica, Pl. Reial, 11-12 (☎933 01 13 64). Ⓜ️Liceu, L3. Dim, red-tinted light and zebra-patterned cushions make this one of the snazzier places around to lounge in and enjoy a drink. Beer €4. Mixed drinks €6-7. Open daily 5pm-3am. MC/V.

Blondie, C. D'en Roca, 14 (www.blondie-bcn.com). Ⓜ️Liceu, L3. Go up C. Casañas and make a left on C. d'en Roca. Punk-themed bar devoted primarily to its namesake. Try one of the punk-rock drinks, the specialty being, of course, the Blondie (vodka, campari, peach juice, and cava; €8). Beer €2.50. Open M-Th and Su 8pm-2am, Fr-Sa 10pm-3am. MC/V.

Glaciar Bar, Pl. Reial, 3 (☎933 02 11 63; www.glaciarbarcelona.com). Ⓜ️Liceu, L3. In the near left corner coming from Las Ramblas. Glaciar has a rather small but nicely decorated interior; most people sit outside in the Pl. Reial. A chill place to hang our with a beer and look out upon an otherwise hectic square. Start your night off with tapas (€2-6) or *bocadillos* (€3-6). Beer €2.50. ½L of sangria €7. Open M-Th and Su 11am-2:30am, F-Sa 11am-2:30am. Cash only.

Casa El Agüelo, C. Avinyó, 37 (☎933 10 23 25). Ⓜ️Liceu, L3. Take a right off C. Ferran, coming from Las Ramblas. A cozy tavern whose decor is somewhere between medieval Catalunya and the American West. Brick walls, fireplaces, long wooden tables, and a cavernous, dungeon-like basement. A good place for cheap beer with a big group of friends. Beer €2.80. Mixed drinks €7. Open M-W and Su 7pm-1:30am, Th 7pm-2:30am, F-Sa 7pm-3am. Cash only.

CLUBS

Karma, Pl. Reial, 10 (☎933 02 56 80; www.karmadisco.com). Ⓜ️Liceu. The club downstairs may look like a colorfully lit wind tunnel, but it hosts a lively and fun atmosphere. DJ will not hesitate to play classic pop-rock throwbacks for all to sing along to. Beer €4. Mixed drinks €6-8. Club cover €10 includes 1 drink. Bar open Tu-Su 6pm-2:30am. Club open Tu-Su midnight-5am.

Harlem Jazz Club, C. Comtesa de Sobradiel, 8 (☎933 10 07 55). ⓂLiceu, L3. Between Pl. Reial and Via Laietana. Live music varies: blues, jazz, reggae, flamenco, and acoustic rock attract international musicians from as far away as Senegal, Kenya, Brazil, and Cuba. After the live music is over, plenty will stay and more will trickle in to dance late into the night. 2 sessions per night: Tu-Th and Su 10:30pm and midnight, F-Sa 11:30pm and 1am. The 2nd session is always much more crowded, especially on weekends. Beer €3.50. Admission €4-8, usually includes 1 drink. Cover F-Sa €7.50. Open Tu-Th 9pm-3am, F-Sa 9pm-5am, Su 9pm-5am during the summer. Get a schedule for the month at the front door. Cash only.

Jamboree, Pl. Reial, 17 (☎933 19 17 89; www.masimas.com). ⓂLiceu. A disorienting maze of stone arches and swirling lights thumps with hip hop; 2nd floor plays 80s and 90s pop. Dance floors fill up between 2-3am. Earlier in the night this popular venue hosts live jazz. Beer €5. Mixed drinks €9-10. Jazz 9 and 11pm €4-12. Cover €10; look for flyers with discounts. Difficult to get in on nights with lists. Open daily 9pm-1am; nightclub open M-Th and Su 12:30am-5am, F-Sa 12:30am-6am. Upstairs, Tarantos hosts flamenco shows (€6). Open daily 8-11pm.

New York, C. Escudellers, 5 (☎933 18 87 30). ⓂDrassanes, L3. Right off Las Ramblas. Once a strip joint, New York is now the biggest club in the Barri Gòtic; drink tables overlook the red and black, strobe-lit dance floor for your voyeuristic pleasure. Crowds don't arrive until after 3am; music includes reggae and Brit-pop. Cover 11:30pm-2am €6 includes 1 beer; 2-5am €13 includes 1 drink. Open Th-Sa midnight-5am. Cash only.

Soul Club, C. Nou de Sant Francesc, 7 (☎933 02 70 26; www.soulclub.es). ⓂDrassanes, L3. Take the 2nd right off C. Escudellers; it's on your left about 100 ft. down. The softly curved walls house a room of young jazz, funk, and soul aficionados. Dance floor is relatively small, but the expertly chosen tunes are sure to get people on their feet. Beer €3.50. Mixed drinks €7.50. Cover F-Sa €5 includes 1 cheap drink. Open M-Th and Su 11pm-2:30am, F-Sa 11pm-3am. Cash only.

Boulevard Culture Club, Las Ramblas, 27 (☎933 016289). ⓂLiceu, L3. Large, hi-tech club with bright pixellated lights raining upon the dance floor. Pumps electronica for a young, mostly tourist, crowd. Guys free until 1:30am, girls until 2:30am. Cover €13, with flyer €10. Beer €6. Mixed drinks €9-10. Open M-Th midnight-5am, F-Sa midnight-6am.

LA RIBERA

La Ribera's nightlife scene is more local and more varied than the scene on La Rambla. When the gas lantern goes on in front of Església de Santa Maria each night, people begin to migrate from small backstreet bars to second-floor sheesha lounges.

El Copetín, Pg. del Born, 19 (☎607 20 21 76). ⓂJaume I. Cuban rhythms invade this casual, dimly lit nightspot. Copetín fills up before some places open, making it a good place to start the night. When the bartenders break out the maracas and cowbell, be ready to get down. Mojitos €7. Open M-Th and Su 6pm-2:30am, F-Sa 6pm-3am. Cash only.

Ribborn, C. Antic de Sant Joan, 3 (☎933 10 71 48; www.ribborn.com). ⓂBarceloneta. Deep crimson light and an eclectic music selection, from jazz to funk to soul. Beer €2.50. Mixed drinks €7. Jazz piano W 9pm. Happy hour Tu-Sa 7-10pm. Open Tu-Su 7pm-3am. MC/V.

El Born, Pg. del Born, 26 (☎933 19 53 33). ⓂJaume I. Sit at the marble counter over the basins where they used to sell fish, or follow the tiny spiral staircase for more casual seating. Free Wi-Fi. Beer €2. Open Tu-Su 10am-2:30am. MC/V over €10.

Pitin Bar, Pg. del Born, 34 (☎93 319 59 87; www.pitinbar.com). Ⓜ Jaume I. A shiny interior on the 1st floor and a cozy attic upstairs fill up nightly with the young and the young-at-heart. Start off with a beer (€2.50) and if that doesn't do enough for you, contemplate a shot of absinthe (€3.50). Or just skip right to the absinthe. Open Sept.-May Tu-Su 10am-2am, June-Aug. daily 10am-2am. Cash only.

Alma, C. de Sant Antoni dels Sombrerers, 7 (☎933 19 76 07). Ⓜ Jaume I. The tattoos and body piercings on display in this bar rival its dramatic red decor. Come during happy hour (8:30-9:30pm) to snag €4 mixed drinks and €8 pitchers of sangria. Open M-Th and Su 8:30pm-2:30am, F-Sa 8:30pm-3am. Cash only.

No Se, Pg. del Born, 29 (☎671 48 59 14). Ⓜ Jaume I. Walk down C. Princesa, make a right onto C. Montcada, and follow it until Pg. del Born. Perhaps in keeping with its laid-back name, this bar doesn't try as hard as some of its competitors on the busy Pg. del Born. The intimate space has a few canvases thrown up on the walls and a relaxing ambience. Mixed drinks €8-10. Open daily 8pm-2:30am. MC/V.

Kama, C. del Rec, 69 (☎932 68 10 29; www.kamabar.com). Ⓜ Barceloneta. Walk up Pl. del Palau, make a right on Av. del Marqués de l'Argentera, and a left on C. del Rec; the bar is on the right. Kama means "desire" in Sanskrit. At this fuschia-lit restaurant, you'll find what you desire—assuming that it's Indian dishes like *kheema mutter* and *palak paneer*, mixed drinks, and a sharp, cosmopolitan ambience. Lunch *menù* €10. Entrees €15-26. Mixed drinks €8-10. Open M 8:30pm-midnight, Tu-Sa 1-4pm and 8:30pm-midnight, Su 8:30pm-midnight. MC/V.

Cactus Bar, Pg. del Born, 30 (☎933 10 63 54; www.cactusbar.cat). Ⓜ Jaume I. Walk down C. Princesa, make a right onto C. Montcada, and continue until Pg. del Born. Walk toward the beach; the bar is a ways down, on the left. This corner bar has simple metal decor, windows ideal for people watching, and a prime location on a popular street. Come during the day to try the walnut-raisin bread with Roquefort cheese (€3.80), or show up at night for a caipirinha (mixed drinks €8.50). Open M-Sa noon-2am, Su noon-midnight. MC/V.

Berimbau, Pg. del Born, 17 (☎933 19 53 78). Ⓜ Jaume I. Walk down C. Princesa and make a right onto C. Montcada. Turn on Pg. del Born; the bar is down the street, on the left. This Brazilian bar's low wicker chairs give it a beachy, laid-back feel. Brazilian music plays in the background. Mixed drinks €8-10. Open daily 6pm-2:30am. MC/V.

Princesa 23, C. Princesa, 23 (☎932 68 86 18; www.princesa23.es). Ⓜ Jaume I. Walk down C. Princesa. Shamelessly touristy and fun enough to get away with it. Princesa 23 serves mojitos and caipirinha cheap (€3.50) to an international crowd until 11pm and then keeps serving them for full price late into the night. Tasty food ranging from tapas and paella to wraps and hamburgers (€3.50-10). Large TVs, a quote by Kahlil Gibran scrawled across the walls, and late-night DJs spinning pop, R&B, and electronica mean that this restaurant has something for everyone. You may hate yourself for loving it here, but you're probably come back. Open M-Th 11am-2:30am, F-Sa 11am-3am, Su 11am-2:30am. MC/V.

Creps al Born, Pg. del Born, 12 (☎932 69 03 25). Ⓜ Jaume I. Walk down C. Princesa and make a right onto C. Montcada. It will hit Pg. del Born. This bar offers crepes and mixed drinks. Sit in the red and black space and wash down your Gran Marnier crepe (€5.90) with...some more Gran Marnier. Crepes and salads €3.90-5.90. Open M-Th 1:30pm-2am, F-Sa 1:30pm-3am, Su 1:30pm-2am. Cash only.

Palau Dalmases, C. Montcada, 20 (☎933 10 06 73). Ⓜ Jaume I. Walk down C. Princesa and make a right on C. Montcada. Enter the central courtyard of this one-time Baroque palace through its nondescript door and you'll immediately feel like a courtier. The gilded decor is glitzy to the point of gaudy, but a fun, if

NIGHTLIFE

expensive jaunt back in time. Drinks from €7. Opera music Th 11pm. Cover €20; includes 1 drink. Open Tu-Sa 8pm-2am, Su 6-10pm. MC/V.

Mudanzas, C. Vidrieria, 15 (☎933 19 11 37). ⓜJuame I. Walk down C. Princesa and make a right on C. de Montcada. Cross the Pg. del Born; C. Montcada turns into C. Vidrieria. Black and white checkered floors, marble tabletops, and taupe walls give this bar a retro feel that attracts a local and tourist crowd at all ages. Smoke a cigarette while sipping a martini at the bar, or take 1 of the venue's free magazines to the mezzanine. Mixed drinks €8-10. Open M-Th 5pm-2:30am, F-Sa 5:30pm-3am, Su 5pm-2:30am. MC/V.

Local Bar, Fossar de les Moreres, 7 (☎93 319 13 57; www.localbar.es). ⓜJaume I. The hip flock here for live jazz and an electro-funk DJ (Th-Su 11:30pm). The walls are plastered with local art and fliers for live music. Beer €3. Mixed drinks €7. Open M-Th and Su 9pm-2am, F-Sa 9pm-3am. MC/V.

Mirame Linda, Pg. del Born, 15 (☎933 10 37 27). ⓜJaume I. Exotic mixed drinks draw a friendly, diverse crowd. Sit at the bar practice your Catalan—the mojitos (€6) should help. Open M-Th and Su 5pm-2:30am, F-Sa 5pm-2:30am. Cash only.

EL RAVAL

If you stick to the Northern part of El Raval, you'll find yourself in hip, creatively decorated, colorful (literally) bars with a young, laid-back crowd—true to the artsy nature of the area. Be sure to check out **Calle Joaquim Costa,** near the MACBA, which packs in numerous distinctive and happening venues in just a few short blocks. As you move away from the University and MACBA, bars become more functional than artsy and cater more to tourists than to locals. Be aware that around Las Ramblas there are many wily pickpockets, around Las Ramblas del Raval prostitutes linger on the street corners, and in the depths of El Raval the streets can be eerily deserted late at night.

BARS

▩ **Marsella Bar,** C. de Sant Pau, 65. ⓜLiceu. Don't be deterred by the tarnished mirrors and blackened bottles—they add to the cowboy charm of this oldest of Barcelona's bars (built in 1820). Religious figurines grace the walls of the bar, famous among locals for its *absenta* (absinthe; €5). Beer €3.20. Mixed drinks €5-6. Open M-Th 11pm-2am, F and Sa 11pm-3am. Cash only.

▩ **Betty Ford,** Joaquin Costa, 56 (☎933 04 13 68). This local favorite is the place to see and be seen—amid chic and simple decor and raucous conversation. Happy hour 6-9pm offers fancy mixed drinks for €4; try a Manhattan or sugar-sweet mojito. Beer €2.50-4. Open M and Su 6pm-1:30am, Tu-Th 2pm-1:30am, F-Sa 2pm-2am.

Bar Almirall, C. Joaquín Costa, 33 (☎933 18 99 17, casalmirall@telefonica.net). ⓜUniversitat. Marble floors and countertops, black chairs, dim lamps, and laid-back clientele. It's house policy to stop you after your 3rd absinthe (€5-7), but the staff is fond of saying that you won't make it there anyway. Beer €2-4. Mixed drinks €6-7. Free Wi-Fi. Open M-Th 5pm-2:30am, Sa until 3am, Su 7pm. Cash only.

Bar Ra, Pl. de la Garduña (☎933 01 41 63, reservations 61 595 98 72; www.ratown.com). ⓜLiceu, L3, just behind Las Ramblas's *Boqueria* market. Everything about Ra exudes cool, from its erotic Hindu mural to the individually painted tablecloths to the waiters themselves. Artfully prepared international food offerings use fresh ingredients from the nearby *Boqueria* market. Try the excellent vegetarian lasagna (€7.50) and duck magret with mango sauce (€9.50), or come for Sunday brunch in the sun. Entrees €6.50-13.

Beer €2.50. Mixed drinks €6.50. Open M-Th 9am-midnight, F-Sa 9am-2:30am, Su noon-midnight. AmEx/MC/V.

L'Ovella Negra, C. Sitges, 5 (☎933 17 10 87; www.ovellanegra.com). ⓂCatalunya, L1/3. From Pl. de Catalunya, go down Las Ramblas and take the 1st right onto C. Tallers; C. Sitges is the 1st left. Young English-speaking tourists and some university students saddle up at a tavern that feels like a medieval stable. Cheap beer and sangria (huge pitcher of either €7.30) and Foosball tables. Lunch menu €6.10. Open M-Th 9am-2:30am, F 9am-3am, Sa 5pm-3am, Su 5pm-2:30am. Cash Only.

Sant Pau 68, C. de Sant Pau, 68 (☎934 41 31 15). ⓂLiceu. Floral wallpaper contrasts with painted black silhouettes and hanging bottle lights, perfectly mixing smooth and gritty. Beer €2. Mixed drinks €6. Open M-Th and Su 8pm-2:30am, F-Sa 8pm-3:30am. MC/V.

London Bar, C. Nou de la Rambla, 34 (☎933 01 25 40; www.londonbarbcn.com), off Las Ramblas. ⓂLiceu, L3. Locals and unruly expats rub shoulders at this smoky and always crowded *Modernista* tavern, which celebrated its 100th birthday on Día de Sant Joan (June 23) 2009. Beer €3. Wine €3. Mixed drinks €6.50-9. Absinthe €5. Open Tu-Th and Su 7:30pm-4:30am, F-Sa 7:30pm-5am. AmEx/MC/V.

Rita Blue, Placa Sant Agusti, 6 (☎933 42 40 86; www.ritablue.com), on C. Hospital off Las Ramblas. ⓂLiceu, L3. Sister to Rita Rouge. Live house music plays downstairs W-Su 11pm. DJs, poetry slams, other performances. Beer €2.20; mixed drinks €5.40-8. Call for dinner reservations. Open M-Th and Su 6pm-2am, F-Sa 6pm-3am.

Rambla Raval 10, Rambla del Raval, 10. ⓂLiceu or Paral.lel. Walk down C. Sant Pau until you reach the Rambla del Raval. When you walk into this bar, which is likely to be dark, packed with youth, and playing loud music, look up at the chandelier; it's made entirely of mini bottles of alcohol. Order a *piel de iguana* (iguana skin; 2 for €9) and lose yourself in the upbeat atmosphere. Mixed drinks €4.50-8. Open M-Th 8pm-2am, F-Sa 8pm-3am. Cash only.

La Masia, C. Elisabets, 16 (☎933 02 24 30). ⓂLiceu. Walk up Las Ramblas and make a left onto C. Elisabets. This bar, which maintains a charming traditional Spanish simplicity, has booze, cheap tapas (almonds €1.50; other dishes €1.50-8), and a great location right on the seam of the MACBA and El Raval districts. Happily chatting students fill the tables on weekend nights. Beer €2-3. Mixed drinks €5-6. Open M-Th 10am-2am, F-Sa 10pm-3am, Su 10pm-2am. MC/V.

Xhiwat Buen Cafe, C. Ramalleres, 26 (☎933 01 04 63). ⓂCatalunya. Walk down C. Pelai and make a left on C. de Jovellanos. This unpretentious and intimate shawarma, tea, and hookah restaurant has low tables, floor mats, and a friendly owner who will make you feel right at home. *Menù* includes bread, hummus, falafel salad, and shawarma (€8). Beer €2. Open M-Sa 1pm-2am. Cash only.

Manchester, C. Valldonzella, 40 (☎663 07 17 48; www.manchesterbar.com). ⓂUniversitat. Walk down the Ronda de Sant Antoni and make a left onto C. Joaquin Costa. Then make another left onto C. Valldonzella. This red-lit bar has old cassette tapes on the walls, ugly-chic artwork, and live music some nights. Check their Myspace for performance calendar. Mixed drinks €5-7. Open M-Th 7pm-2:30am, F-Sa 7pm-3am, Su 7pm-2:30am. Cash only.

Oddland, C. Joaquim Costa, 52 (☎934 12 00 49; oddland_bcn@hotmail.com). ⓂUniversitat. Walk down Ronda de Sant Antoni and make a right on C. Joaquim Costa. Tall green tables, funky walls with plaster and amoeba-shaped splotches, and a projected black-and-white movie on the back wall make this bar decidedly odd—but in a happy sort of way. Happy hour 6-10pm; mixed drinks €4. Serves snacks. Open M-Th 7pm-2am, F-Sa 7pm-3am. Cash only.

Café de les Delicies, Rambla del Raval, 47. ⓂLiceu or Paral.lel. Walk down C. Sant Pau until you reach the Rambla del Raval; the bar is on the right. Turquoise walls, wood tables, and fresh flowers make this bar feel like a trendy household kitchen—a great place to kick back for a quiet conversation with friends. At one end of the bar, you'll find leather sofas and books to read. Mixed drinks €6. Open M-Th 10am-2am, F-Sa 10am-3am. Cash only.

Tra.lers, C. Trallers, 39-41 (☎934 12 78 43). ⓂCatalunya. Walk down C. Pelai and make a left on C. de Jovellanos, then another left on C. Trallers. Restaurant by day and bar by night. No-frills black walls and L-shaped floorplan give it a grunge-chic feel. Convenient location near to the Pl. de Catalunya means that the venue gets rowdy at night. Lunch menù €10. Mixed drinks €5-7. Open M-Th 11am-2am, F-Sa 11am-3am, Su 11am-2am. MC/V.

Bar Centric, C. Ramelleres, 27 (☎933 01 81 35). ⓂCatalunya. Walk down C. Pelai and make a left on C. de Jovellanos. This historic-looking tapas bar has etched-glass windows, warm lighting, wooden booths, and a great location. Residents at the affiliated Hosteleria Grau and students come in the early evening. Beer €2-4. Open 8:30am-9pm. MC/V.

The Quiet Man, Marqués de Barbera, 11 (☎934 12 12 19). ⓂLiceu, L3. Take C. Unió off Las Ramblas; after 2 blocks it becomes Marqués Barbera. As authentic an Irish pub as you'll find in Barcelona, with homey decor, a good collection of Beleek (fine Irish china), and a friendly Irish staff. Late-night fish and chips (large, €7; small, €3.50), live music (pop or rock F-Sa midnight, Su 8:30pm), pool and foosball tables, and a private room available with reservation. Wi-Fi. Pints of imported drafts €4.40. Mixed drinks €7. Open M-W and Su6pm-2:30am, Th-Sa 6pm-3am. Cash only.

Ambar, C. St. Pau, 77 (☎628 08 74 01). ⓂParal·lel. Walk up C. de Sant Pau. On Ambar's big, warehouse-like walls you'll find ornate wallpaper and empty frames. Low velvet chairs make for comfy lounging right off Las Ramblas del Raval. Olives €1.50. Beer and wine €2. Mixed drinks €6. Open M-Th and Su 8pm-2am, F-Sa 8pm-3am. MC/V.

Muy Buenas, C. Carme, 63 (☎934 42 50 53). ⓂCatalunya, L1/3/4. The bar's modernista decor suggests a time warp back to the early days of the last century. Serves Middle Eastern and Cuban food (entrees €7-14). Come after 1am for mojitos, caipirinhas, and late-night freshly cooked pizzas. Beer €1.50-3. Mixed drinks €6-8. Poetry readings Su and W 9pm. Open M-Th 8:30am-2am, F-Sa 8:30am-3am, Su 7pm-2am. Kitchen open daily 1-5pm and 8pm-12:30am. MC/V.

Pepino, C. Nou de la Rambla, 44 (☎934 43 86 36). ⓂDrassanes. Walk up Las Ramblas and make a right on C. Nou de la Rambla; it's a ways down on your right. "Pepino" means cucumber; come to this red-lit bar and order a "Pepino goes to Moscow" (with cucumber, ginger, lime, ginger ale, ice and vodka). You can't help but notice the mannequin over the bar, but also check out the black-and-white movie playing on the wall over the entrance. Entrees €6-10. Open M-Th 6:30pm-2:30am, F-Sa 7pm-3am. Kitchen open until midnight. AmEx/MC/V.

Pastis, Santa Mónica, 4 (☎933 18 79 80). ⓂDrassanes, L3. Walk 1 block up Las Ramblas and turn left on Santa Mónica. An older crowd of absinthe and pastis drinkers come to enjoy live music in this small, old tavern. Every square inch is covered with something of interest: portraits, pictures, paper cranes, mannequins suspended from the ceiling, etc. Absinthe and pastis €5. Beer €3. Mixed drinks €6.50. Live tango Tu 10:30pm; other live music W, Th, Su. Open Tu-Th and Su 7pm-2am, F-Sa 7pm-3am. MC/V.

Bar Pepe, Valdonzella, 36. ⓂUniversitat. Walk down C. Valdonzella toward C. Joaquin Costa; it's on your right. This dive bar has graffitied walls, but it's right near the university and drinks are as cheap as they get. Beer €2. Mixed drinks €3.50 until 9pm, then €5. Open daily 1-5pm and 8pm-12:30am. Cash only.

Hostel-Bar, C. Nou de la Rambla and C. Guardia. Ⓜ Drassanes. Walk one block up Las Ramblas and turn left on Santa Monica; it's at the end of the block on your left. What this bar lacks in decoration it makes up for in colorful clientele. Folks from all walks of life stumble into this corner haunt, where beer is €2, shots are €1, and the "jarra hostel bar" (a house specialty) is €12. The bar is affiliated with a hostel and guests get discounted drinks. Wi-Fi. Open M-Th 8am-2am, F-Sa 8am-3am, Su 10am-midnight. Cash only.

CLUBS

Moog, C. Arc del Teatre, 3 (☎933 01 72 82; www.masimas.com/moog). Ⓜ Liceu or Drassanes. Industrial metal walls and swirling green lights betray this as the techno headquarters of Barcelona, though the upstairs dance floor blasts music from the 80s and 90s. Look for discount flyers on Las Ramblas. Cover €10. Open daily midnight-5am, weekends until 6am. W especially popular. MC/V at bar.

Valhalla Rock Club, C. Tallers, 68 (www.myspace.com/valhallaclubderock). Ⓜ Universitat. Walk down C. Tallers. A must-visit for rockers, goths, and death-metal enthusiasts. The club's 2009 summer lineup included artists such as Los Mercenarios and Riot of Violence. Check their MySpace page for upcoming shows and covers. Happy hour daily; kegs until 10pm. Open M-Th 6pm-2:30am, F-Sa 6pm-3am, Su 6pm-2:30am. Cash only.

L'EIXAMPLE

L'Eixample has upscale bars and some of the best—though not exclusively— gay nightlife in Europe. (Thus the area's nickname "Gaixample.") Some clubs can be difficult to get to, into, or back from; you may want to check out transportation ahead of time. Be sure to look up the NitBus schedule or the cost of a taxi home.

BARS

🏛 **Z:eltas,** C. Casanova, 75 (☎934 50 84 69; www.zeltas.net). Complete with shimmering cloth hangings, feather boas, and low white couches, this exotic bar welcomes a classy clientele—usually gay—to sip a drink and enjoy the ambience. Wine €3. Beer €4.50. Mixed drinks €7. Open daily 10:30pm-3am. MC/V.

Les Gents que J'aime, C. València, 286, downstairs (☎932 15 68 79). Ⓜ Pg. de Gràcia. You'll feel like Serge Gainsbourg at his hippest lounging in this dark, subterranean bar's velvet furniture. Background soul, funk, and jazz soothe patrons enjoying drinks like Les Gents (kiwi, lime, and pineapple juice; €7). Shotgun the chairs tucked beneath the staircase. Beer €4. Mixed drinks €6-7. Open daily 7pm-2:30am. AmEx/MC/V.

Espit Chupitos (Aribau), C. Aribau, 77 (www.espitchupitos.com). Ⓜ Universitat. From Pl. de la Universitat, walk up C. Aribau. Colloquially known as "The Chupito Bar" (the bar has grown so popular that there are actually now three locations in Barcelona), this bar serves shots with flair. Servers perform when delivering so-called spectacle shots (€2): the Harry Potter shot involves lighting the bar on fire and the Monica Lewinsky shot…well, let's just say it's best ordered for an unsuspecting friend. Other locations at Carrer de la Unió 35 and Passeig de Colom 8. Open M-Th and Su 8pm-2:30am, F and Sa 8pm-3am. MC/V.

Dietrich Gay Teatro Cafe, C. Consell de Cent, 255 (☎934 51 77 07). Ⓜ Universitat or Pg. de Gràcia. An unflattering caricature of a semi-nude Marlene Dietrich greets patrons at this inclusive gay bar. Beer €3.50. Mixed drinks €6. Drag shows, acrobatics, and dancing; check with the restaurant ahead of time. Open M-Th and Su 6pm-2am, F-Sa midnight-3am. MC/V.

FROM THE ROAD

PRIDEBARCELONA '09

From June 20-28, 2009, Barcelona threw its first Gay Pride week. Spain is—politically, at least—a gay-friendly country (same-sex marriages have been legal nationwide since 2005), and Barcelona has been dubbed the San Francisco of Spain. In short, expectations were high.

A parade began at 5:30pm in the Plaça Universitat (on the edge of the so-called Gaixample) and ended in a float village and street party that included live music performances.

The party continued throughout the week as numerous bars and clubs threw Pride-specific free-entry nights, or two-for-one specials. (Check Barcelona Pride's website for a listing of specific deals.)

The rest of the week saw live music, movie showings, family picnics, sporting events, and even church services specifically celebrating GLBT pride. Debates were held in Catalan on topics such as "GLBT Politics in European Cities" and "GLBT Spirituality." Barcelona's GLBT community and its supporters were out en masse, working to open lines of communication between gays and straights, raise awareness, and make the most of what was arguably the party of the year—and in Barcelona, that's saying something.

Watch out, San Francisco: the gauntlet has been thrown.

- Justine Lescroart

La Chapelle, C. Mutaner, 67 (☎934 53 30 76). ⓂUniversitat. Walk up C. Mutaner. La Chapelle's decor juxtaposes antique devotional carvings with ultra-modern bubble lights. Gay-friendly. Beer €2.50. Mixed drinks €5. Open daily 4pm-2am. MC/V.

Atame, Consell de Cent, 257 (☎934 54 92 73). ⓂPg. de Gràcia or Universitat, L2/3/4. The door of this gay bar is draped in a rainbow flag, but otherwise the decor is sleek and minimalist. A mostly male, friendly, and energetic crowd shows up 7 nights a week for drag shows and more. Beer €2-3. Mixed drinks €6-7. Open M-Th and Su 6pm-2:30am, F-Sa 6pm-3am. MC/V.

Dow Jones, C. Bruc, 97 (☎932 07 63 75). ⓂPasseig de Gràcia. Walk down C. Arago until you hit C. Bruc; make a left. At this stock-market themed bar, drinks (€2.50-7.50) are priced according to how frequently they're ordered, with the constantly-changing prices displayed on a TV screen. The best of i-banking (nice drinks) with the best of NASDAQ (large, lively crowds). The walls are papered in the *Financial Times*. Open M-F 7:30am-3am, Sa-Su noon-3am. MC/V.

Plata Bar, C. Consell de Cent, 233 (☎934 52 46 36). Stainless steel patio tables and a mostly male clientele spill from this corner bar onto the sidewalk. Colored lighting makes for a fun ambience. Open M-Th 6pm-2:30am, F-Sa 6pm-3am. MC/V.

Underground by Axel, C. Aribau, 33 (☎933 23 93 93). ⓂUniversitat. Walk up C. Aribau. Located in the "heterofriendly" (read: gay) Axel Hotel, this bar is all about steel, glass, and urbane animal magnetism. Happy hour M-F 8:30-11:30pm; 2-for-1 mixed drinks. Open daily 10:30am-2am. MC/V.

El Gato Negro, Consell de Cent, 268 (☎699 77 36 74). ⓂUniversitat. Walk up C. Aribau and make a right onto Consell de Cent. Part of the Espit Chupitos franchise (see p. 179). Both are usually bustling, so head to one if the other is full. Open Tu-Su 8pm-2:30am. MC/V.

Momo's Bar y Copas, Consell de Cent, 319 (☎934 87 33 14). ⓂUniversitat. Walk up C. Aribau and make a right onto Consell de Cent. Salsa, Merengue, and Bachata classes; call ahead for the season's schedule. Shots €2. Open daily 8pm-3am. MC/V.

Bar Snooker, C. Roger de Llúria, 42 (☎933 17 97 60; www.snookerbarcelona.com), between C. Gran Via and C. Diputació. ⓂTetuán, L2, or Pg. de Gràcia, L2/3/4. This large lounge bar has red velvet chairs, neon-green and blue lit pool tables, and an impressive list of scotches. Singles night W 8pm. Mixed drinks €8. Open daily 6pm-3am. AmEx/MC/V.

Topxi, C. València, 358 (☎932 07 01 20), just off Pg. St. Joan. Ⓜ️Verdaguer, L4/5. A small, unpretentious bar-club that just happens to put on some of the most flamboyant drag and strip shows in the city—in intimate quarters. The orientation of the crowd varies by night and by show; call ahead to find out which way the evening swings. Cover €8-10; includes 1 drink. Open M-Th and Su 12:10am-5am, Sa 12:10am-6am. Cash only.

Berlin, C. Muntaner, 240 (☎932 00 65 42). Ⓜ️Diagonal, L3/5. A slice of streamlined German style in Barcelona. Corner bar with marble accents and huge, naked light bulbs attracts area hipsters and l'Eixample yuppies. Beer €2 during the day, €4 at night, Mixed drinks €9. Open M-F 10am-2am, Sa 11am-3am. MC/V.

Caligula, C. Consell de Cent, 257 (☎934 51 48 92). Ⓜ️Pg. de Gràcia, L2/3/4. Bar designed in a pan-Asian style invokes a romantic atmosphere with draped fabrics, tea lights, music, Buddha statues, and massive floral arrangements. A crowd gathers around the bar and sidewalk tables. Transvestite spectacles after 10pm. Beer €4.20. Mixed drinks €6-9. Wheelchair-accessible. Open daily 8pm-3am. Cash only.

Aloha, C. Provença, 159 (☎934 51 79 62). Ⓜ️Hospital Clìnic, L5. Barcelona's Hawaiian paradise—complete with exotic caged birds, leis, and plenty of bamboo. 2 pool tables and a wide liquor selection. All sorts of people find their haven in Hawaii here. Cross the bridge by the waterfall to find the dark, intimate tiki huts perfect for private parties of 2 to 20; call ahead to reserve a table. Try the *coco loco* (coconut milk and rum; €6). Open M-Th and Su 6pm-2:30am and F-Sa 6pm-3am. Cash only.

Moon Cafe, C. Provença, 213 (☎934 88 17 21). Ⓜ️Diagonal. Red lights line the windows of this welcoming corner bar and restaurant where a young crowd enjoys drinks and cross-cultural tapas (€3-7) late into the night. Open M-Th 7am-2am, F-Sa 7am-3am. AmEx/MC/V.

CLUBS

🔲 **Mojito Club,** C. Rosselló, 217 (☎654 20 10 06; www.mojitobcn.com). Ⓜ️Diagonal. Buenavista salsa dance studio (☎932 37 65 28) by day and Mojito Club by night, this venue lures a fun-loving crowd with early-evening lessons and late-night Latin beats. Brazilian party W with free samba lessons at 11:30pm and R&B all night. Cover €10; includes 1 drink. For those taking regular lessons, cover may be waived. Open daily 11pm-5am. MC/V.

🔲 **La Fira,** C. Provença, 171 (☎650 85 53 84). Ⓜ️Hospital Clínic or FGC: Provença. A crowd swarms the circus-tent dance floor surrounded by carousel swings, carnival mirrors, and a fortune teller. The watchful sphinx perched atop the bar will make sure you don't go overboard with the wide selection of shots. Variety of shows and parties, often with entrance fee or 1 drink minimum. Open Th-Sa 11:30pm-3am. Cash only.

Luz de Gas, C. Muntaner, 246 (☎932 09 77 11; www.luzdegas.com). Ⓜ️Diagonal, L3/5. Chandeliers, gilded mirrors, and deep red walls set the mood in this swanky uptown music venue. Concerts include the occasional big-name jazz, blues, or soul performer like Branford Marsalis, Bonnie Raitt, or Monica Green; thousands of performances have taken place here. After 1am, the chairs are folded up and the luxurious club becomes a high-class disco playing pop music. If you're looking to finish a conversation or talk about the show, head upstairs to the quieter glassed-in balcony. Beer €6. Mixed drinks €10. Cover €18; check the Guía del Ocio for specific show listings and times. Wheelchair-accessible. Open daily 11:30pm-5am. MC/V.

La Madame, Ronda de St. Pere, 23, between C. Bruc and Pl. Urquinaona. Ⓜ️Urquinaona. A mixed gay-straight crowd fills the 2 huge dance floors of this popular club. Pounding house music by the Maintee Group's locally esteemed DJs. Beer €5. Mixed drinks €8. Wheelchair-accessible. Cover €15-20; includes 1 drink. Open F-Su midnight-6am. MC/V.

Zac Club, Av. Diagonal, 477 (☎933 21 09 22; www.zac-club.com). Ⓜ️Hospital Clìnic, L5. Big names, such as Lenny Kravitz and the Cindy Blackman Group, sometimes come to perform in this intimate disco setting. Live jazz, funk, and blues nightly midnight-2am. A smaller dance floor and plenty of bar room makes this a great place for people that shun the gyrating masses of larger venues. Drinks €4.20-7.20. Cover €10-15; includes 1 drink. Open Th-Sa 12:30am-dawn.

Aire, C. València, 236. (☎934 54 63 94; www.arenadisco.com) ⓂPg. de Gràcia, L2/3/4. One of Barcelona's biggest and most popular lesbian clubs. Throngs of women crowd the multicolored dance floor, grooving to pop, house, and 80s classics. Women-only strip show from 6-10pm 1st Su of every month. Cover €5-10; includes 1 drink. Open Th-Su 11:30pm-3am. Check out the Arena family's other gay discos, some of the most popular in the area: **Arena Classic** at C. Diputació, 233 plays 80s tunes; **Arena Dandy** at Gran Via, 593 pumps techno beats. The popular **Arena Madre** at C. Balmes, 32 is mostly for men, as is the more relaxed **Punto BCN** bar at C. Muntaner, 63. MC/V.

Roxy Blue, Consell de Cent, 294 (www.roxyblue.es). ⓂUniversitat. Walk up C. Aribau and make a right on Consell de Cent. Ubiquitous blue sparkling lights and 3 dance rooms make the new Roxy Blue Society Club a safe bet for a night of glamour. Music varies by night (check the web page) and includes R&B, soul, hip hop, minimal, electronica, and techno. Cover €12-18. Open W-Th midnight-5am, F-Sa midnight-6am. MC/V.

Antilla, C. Aragó, 141 (☎934 51 45 64; www.antillasalsa.com). ⓂUrgell. Walk up C. Comte de Urgell and make a left on C. Aragó. Wild neon lighting and a large, open dance floor make this salsa school and dance club a local favorite. Cover €10; includes 1 drink. Lessons for dancers of all levels Tu-Sa 5-11pm. Club open Tu-W 11pm-4am, Th 11pm-5am, F-Sa 11pm-6am. MC/V.

La Suite, C. Villarroel, 216 (☎658 31 45 03). Elegant and exclusive (Playboy has been known to throw its official parties here), La Suite plays R&B, hip hop, and rap in black-and-gold rooms. Cover €18. You may be able to get in for free before 2:30am if you visit their Facebook page (search "Suite Club Barcelona") and sign up. Open Th-Sa midnight-6am. MC/V.

Salvation, Ronda de St. Pere, 19-21, between C. Bruc and Pl. Urquinaona. ⓂUrquinaona. The place to come if you've sinned...and want to keep on sinning. A popular gay club with 2 huge dance floors and pounding house music. Beer €5. Mixed drinks €8. Wheelchair-accessible. Cover €11; includes 1 drink. Open F-Su midnight-6am.

Illusion, C. Lepanto, 408 (☎932 47 36 00), right below ⓂAlfons X, L4. A favorite destination for students and local kids in their 20s, this club is more happening in winter than in summer. 2 dance rooms: house music in the main and salsa in the smaller. Go-go shows tease the audience every 15min. or so, starting around 3am. Beer €4. Mixed drinks €6. Hosts a gay session ("T Dance") Su 7pm-midnight. 18+. Cover Su €8, F €7, Sa €9. Open F midnight-5am, Sa 6-10pm (16+) and 12:30-5:30am. Closed Aug. Cash only.

Arena Madre, C. Balmes, 32 (☎934 87 83 42; www.arenadisco.com). ⓂPg. de Gràcia, L2/3/4. One of Barcelona's most popular gay clubs. Young men populate the bulk of the dance floor (as well as several cages) moving to pop and house music under intense strobe lights. Striptease M. Cover Su-F €6, Sa €12; includes 1 drink. Open daily 12:30pm-5:30am. Check out one of the other equally popular Arena-affiliated clubs: **Arena (Sala Classic)** at C. Diputació, 233 plays handbag music; **Arena (Sala Dandy)** at Gran Via, 593 plays pop hits from decades past. Go to **Aire** at C. Valencia, 236 for a mostly lesbian crowd. Cash only.

Sol, C. Villarroel, 216 (☎932 37 86 58). ⓂHospital Clínic, L5, or Diagonal, L3/5. Barcelona's beautiful, uptown crowd hits the wooden, elegantly lit dance floor or mingles upstairs on the couches. Downstairs disco plays pop and house; upstairs is smaller, more laid-back, and plays less intense disco. Mixed drinks €5-7.50. Cover €10; includes 1 drink. Open Th-Sa midnight-5:30am.

Divine, Balmes, 24 (☎933 17 22 48; www.dDivine.com). ⓂUniversitat. Divine entertains dinner guests with a night-long drag show including song, dance, and hilarious

NIGHTLIFE

attempts to translate her jokes for English-speaking audience members. Between acts be sure to compliment Divine on her make-up. Entrees €16-24. Restaurant open M-F 12-4pm, W-Sa 10pm-2am. Drag show W-Sa 9:30pm. MC/V.

Hyde Club, Pg. Domingo, 3 (☎654 20 10 06; www.hydebcn.com). ⓜPg. de Gràcia. Go west on C. de València and right on the narrow Pg. de Domingo. Mingle with the elite, well-dressed crowd in the midst of a swanky gold interior at this upscale club. See if you can work up the nerve to go out onto the dance floor without spending too much money on €10 drinks. Wheelchair-accessible. No jeans or sneakers. Lounge open M-Th and Su midnight-3am. Club open Th-Sa midnight-6am. MC/V.

BARCELONETA AND PORT VELL

Maremagnum, the one-time mecca of Barcelona nightlife, has shifted its focus toward being purely a daytime shopping mall, shutting down all but one of its clubs after a series of violent altercations took place on its premises at night. Today, beach nightlife has shifted toward Port Olímpic and Pg. Marítim, although a handful a worthwhile bars can be found in Barceloneta.

Absenta, C. Sant Carles, 36. ⓜBarceloneta. Walking down Pg. Joan de Borbó and take a left on C. Sant Carles. A green interior with vintage posters suits the star beverage at this absinthe bar, although most choose to sit out on the terrace during summer. Beer €2.50. Wine €2.80. Absinthe €4-7. Open M, W-Th, and Su 11am-2am, Tu 6pm-2am, F-Sa 11am-3am. Cash only.

Ke?, C. del Beluart, 54. (☎932 24 15 88) ⓜBarceloneta. Walking down Pg. Joan de Borbó, take a left on C. Sant Carles and another left at the plaça onto C. del Beluart. Decor meanders between tropical surf, the American west, and Popeye the Sailor. Hosts an equally eclectic crowd, from rowdy beachgoers to locals using the Wi-Fi on the back sofa over a beer (€2). Open daily 11:30am-2:30am. Cash only.

PASSEIG MARÍTIM DE PORT OLIMPÍC

If what you need is a crowded dance floor and loud music, this is the place to find it. The strip along the lower level of Port Olímpic hosts a string of side-by-side clubs (with a few shisha bars and late-night fast-food joints sprinkled in between for good measure), each trying to drown out the music of the club next door. None of the clubs has a dress code, nor do they charge cover, so hop around until you find one you like. Though these clubs might not be quite as sleek as some of the more exclusive ones nearby, they attract plenty of young partiers looking for a good dance floor.

Opium Mar, Pg. Marítim de la Barceloneta, 34 (☎902 26 74 86; www.opiummar.com). The indoor-outdoor restaurant serves seafood until 1am, at which point the DJ starts blasting house music and the place turns into a glitzy, colorful club. When they aren't platform-dancing, bikini-clad waitresses serve drinks as chic patrons bust a move. Beer €8. Mixed drinks €10-15. Wheelchair-accessible. Cover €20 includes one drink. Restaurant open daily 1pm-1am. Club open M-Th and Su midnight-5am, F-Sa 1am-6am. AmEx/MC/V.

El Gran Casino, C. Marina, 19 (☎932 25 78 78; www.casino-barcelona.com), under the fish. Blackjack, American roulette, French roulette, slots, and *punto banco* are the action here. Attracts mostly an older crowd. Must be 18 to play. No sneakers or beach clothes; collared shirt recommended for men. Passport required. Wheelchair-accessible. Entrance fee €4.50. Open daily 1pm-5am. MC/V.

Shoko, Pg. Marítim de la Barceloneta, 34 (☎932 25 92 00; www.shoko.biz). Like its neighbor, Opium Mar, this is a terraced restaurant by day and exclusive club by night. It may appear mellow during dinner, but by 2am it's packed with a crowd dancing to techno and house. Beer €6. Mixed drinks €10. Wheelchair-accessible. No cover, but look sharp: no sneakers, beach clothes, or lame shirts. Restaurant opens daily at noon. Club open daily noon-3am. AmEx/MC/V.

Catwalk, C. Ramón Trias Fargas, 2/4 (☎692 64 14 29; www.clubcatwalk.net). ⓂPort Olímpic. Sleek interior blasting house downstairs and hip hop and R&B upstairs. Attracts elite partiers from all over the world (even some from Barcelona itself), and during peak club hours you can expect to see a line running halfway down the block. Beer €7. Mixed drinks €12. Cover €20. Open Th and Su midnight-5am, F-Sa midnight-6am. MC/V.

Ice Barcelona, C. Ramón Trias Fargas, 2 (☎932 24 16 25; www.icebarcelona.com). Of all the gimmicks designed to separate tourists from their money, this has got to be one of the most elaborate. Behind the outdoor terrace and bar lies a room made entirely of ice. This small "icebar" is equipped with a small dance floor, TV screens, and various ice-sculptures, including an obligatory representation of la Sagrada Família. If curiosity gets the best of you, €15 will grant you access to the icebar along with a drink, fur jacket, and gloves, which will be much appreciated, especially by those in shorts and flip-flops. Beer €3.50. Mixed drinks €7-9. Open daily 2pm-3am. MC/V.

POBLE NOU

If you want to party in Poble Nou, trade in your skimpy clubbing outfit for something a little more grunge, brush up your foosball skills, and be prepared to jam to heavy metal with Spanish teens or classic rock with the 30-somethings. This neighborhood is the place to be for hard rock and alternative music. Locals have put abandoned warehouses to good use in the blocks around ⓂBogetell, L4. The drinks here are remarkably cheap, and as the patrons are (young) locals, not tourists, the crowd flow is the reverse of the rest of the city: packed during the school year and slower in summer.

Razzmatazz, C. Pamplona, 88, and Almogàvers, 122 (☎932 72 09 10; www.salarazzmatazz.com). ⓂMarina. A warehouse complex with 5 rooms: Pop Bar, The Loft, Razz Club, Lo*Li*Ta, and Rex Room, each with its own live music specialty. Everything from pop to electro to rock. Beer €3.50. Mixed drinks €7.50. Cover €15, includes access to all 5 clubs and 1 drink. Concert prices vary; call ahead or check the website. Open F-Sa and holidays 12:30am-6am. AmEx/MC/V.

L'Ovella Negra (Megataverna del Poble Nou), C. Zamora, 78, (☎933 09 59 38; www.ovellanegra.com). ⓂBogatell or Marina. On the corner of C. Pallars. This warehouse-turned-tavern has a strange medieval-industrial vibe. Foosball and pool tables line the back room, where the stone walls and iron rafters may have you confused about the century you're drinking in. Beer €1.80; pitchers €2.30. Open M-W 7am-5pm, Th 7am-5pm and 10pm-2:30am, F 7-3am, Sa 5pm-3am. Kitchen open all night, serving *panzzas* (pizza) and *creptilles* (crepes) among other snacks. Cash only.

Sala Rock Sound, C. dels Almogàvers, 116 (☎www.salarocksound.com). ⓂBogatell. Walk up C. Zamora 2 blocks and take a right on C. dels Almogàvers. Dark, smoky bar with concrete floors and just the right amount of grime. If you brought your Ramones or AC/DC T-shirt, now's the time to break it out. Beer €3. Shots €2.50. Blues jam sessions every Su at 8pm. Live rock, often with a cover (€4-12). Open F-Sa 10pm-3am. Cash only.

Lokotron, C. Almogavares, 86 (☎934 14 11 38). ⓂMarina. Walk down C. Almogavares. Come to Lokotron for techno and house music as late or early as you want. Open Th-Su 11pm-5:30am, though some travelers report the disco being open until 9 or 10am. MC/V.

MONTJUÏC AND POBLE SEC

Club Apolo is the main nightlife draw in this neighborhood, but within its sidestreets, Poble Sec offers some of the best off-the-beaten-path late-night hangouts in the city. Lower Montjuïc is home to **Poble Espanyol** ("Spanish Village"), a recreation of famous buildings and sights from all over Spain, and a nightlife hotspot during the summer.

THE AFTERMATH

Sometimes partying until 6am just isn't enough. Catering to the insatiable hunger of Barcelona's most hardcore hedonists are *los afters*, a set of late-night establishments that get started just when the clubs close (5 or 6am) and keep the alcohol flowing and the music playing well into the next day. The *afters* tend to be more popular in the winter, when it's still dark enough at 6am to stay in the party mindset, and the weather isn't good enough to induce guilt for sleeping through the entire next day.

These after-hours clubs exist in a legal gray area. Some have managed to escape scrutiny by locating themselves just outside the city; buses wait outside some of the major clubs in Barcelona at closing time to cart people over. Others exploit a legal loophole whereby private clubs can set whatever hours they'd like, and so would-be partygoers, in order to partake, are required to buy "memberships" (usually around the same price as a typical cover).

In July 2009, legislature was passed that finally seeks to legally define and regulate after-hours clubs, and while it might lead to some closures, it could also finally allow a niche of professionally operated, licensed *afters* to serve early morning revelers on the up and up.

Tinta Roja, C. Creus dels Molers, 17 (☎934 43 32 43; www.tintaroja.net). Located just off Av. Paral·lel in a newly pedestrian section of Poble Sec. Red tinted lights, red velvet chairs. The dance floor gets serious, especially during tango classes W 9-10:30pm, (call for details). Specialties include tropical mixed drinks (€7) and Argentine *yerba-mate* (€4.80) Open Th 9:30pm--2:30am, F-Sa 9:30pm-3am. Cash only.

La Terrazza, Avda. Marquès de Comillas, s/n (☎932 72 49 80). On weekend summer nights, Poble Espanyol succumbs to the irrepressible revelry of La Terrazza, an outdoor dance club to one side of the village where you can sway along to techno with the masses. Get here after 2am and you may find yourself in a line of up to 100. Beer €6. Mixed drinks €9-10, although bars scattered in Poble Espanyol stay open late and serve cheaper alcohol. Cover €18, gets you into the village and club, plus 1 drink. Open June-Oct. Th midnight-5am, F-Sa midnight-6am. MC/V.

Mau Mau, C. d'En Fontrodona, 33 (☎60 686 06 17). ⓂParal·lel, L2/L3. Follow C. d'En Fontrodona as it bends right, past C. Blai. Look for a gray door on the left as you walk up the street and ring the bell. Young locals sprawl out on sofas for drinks in this massive, inimitably cool hideout. Films screened Th-Sa at 10pm. Residents from Barcelona buy year-long memberships (€12), but out-of-towners need only sign in at the door. Beer €3. Mixed drinks €6. Open Th-Sa 10:30pm-3am. Cash Only.

Torres de Ávila (☎93 424 93 09), next to the main entrance of Poble Espanyol. ⓂEspanya, L1/3. A million-peseta construction that was at the height of club chic when it was built in the 80s. Torres is still going strong as one of the city's hottest night spots, complete with glass elevators, 7 bars, and a summertime rooftop terrace with gorgeous views of the city. DJs spin house and techno. Drinks €5-10. Dress to impress. Cover €18, includes 1 drink. Open Th-Sa midnight-6:30am.

Instinto, C. Mexic 7-9, (www.salainstinto.com) parallel to Av. Reina María Cristina and close to Poble Espanyol. ⓂEspanya, L1/3. Small warehouse converted into a nearly tourist-free dance club. Themed nights of music alternating between hip hop, drum 'n' bass, and latin rhythms. Strong mixed drinks €8-10. Cover €12, includes 1 drink. Open W-Th and Su midnight-5am, F-Sa midnight-6am. Cash only.

242, Carrer d'Entença, 37. ⓜEspanya. One of the longest running afters still operating within the city of Barcelona itself. Serious partiers trickle into this industrial setting once the clubs close for even more alcohol and electronica. Mixed drinks €10. Beer €5. €15 cover includes 1 drink. Open M and F-Su 6-11am. MC/V.

Rouge, C. Poeta Cabanyes, 21 (☎93 442 49 85). ⓜParal·lel, L2/L3. From Av. Paral·lel, turn onto C. Peeta Cabanyes. Look for the door on your left and ring the bell. Distinguished, vintage decor bathed in warm red light make this a hip bar and lounge with a clientele and a cocktail menu to match. Try the BCN Rouge with vodka, berry liqueur and lime (€6.50). Beer €2.50. Open W-Th and Su 8pm-1am. F-Sa 8pm-3am. Cash only.

XiX, Rocafort, 19 (☎ 93 423 43 14; www.xixbar.com). ⓜPoble Sec. The chairs leaning off the wall defy gravity, and after enough mojitos (€6.80) and blue gimlets (€6.50) you might be drunk enough to defy gravity, too. Good place for an early drink with a local crowd. Open M-Th 6:30pm-2:30am, F-Sa 6:30pm-3am. MC/V for orders €15 or higher.

Bodega del Onze, C. Blai, 8 (☎93442 71 16). ⓜParal·lel. Swimming in lights, with a mismatched set of red leather and leopard print furniture, this relaxed bar is good for a pre-club drink, especially during happy hour (11pm-1am; 2 mojitos or *caipirinhas* €6.) Beer €2.50. Mixed drinks €5. Open M-Th and Su 7pm-2am, F-Sa 7pm-3am. Cash only.

Club Apolo/Nitsaclub, C. Nou de la Rambla, 113 (☎93 301 00 90; www.sala-apolo. com). ⓜParal·lel, L2/L3. Cheekily-themed club nights (i.e., Nasty Monday, Crappy Tuesday) bring droves even on weekday nights. F-Sa nights "Nitsaclub," a hip-hop/pop/soul extravaganza, features a slew of international guest DJs. Come early on M for "Anti-Karaoke" and watch locals stumble and soar through American rock and pop, usually with a thick Spanish accent (M 10-12:30am; €7, includes 1 beer). Beer €4. Mixed drinks €8. Cover €8-12, includes 1 drink. Open daily 12:30-6am, although club schedule varies according to live performance schedule; check online. MC/V.

ZONA ALTA

The area around C. Marià Cubí has great nightlife, but you'll have to take a taxi (or the NitBus). For more accessible fun in Gràcia, head to Pl. del Sol to find the **Eldorado,**Pl. del Sol, 4 (☎932 10 59 00; www.eldoradobcn.com; open daily 10pm-2:30am; terrace from 7pm), or the more relaxed **Café del Sol,**Pl. del Sol, 16 (☎934 15 56 63; open M-Th and Su 12:30pm-2:30am, F-Sa 12:30pm-3am).

GRÀCIA

Gràcia is all about busy-but-intimate bars—the kind of venues where you run into friends and have to raise your voice to talk with them. Some of them have modern, relaxing decor, and colored lighting—Vinil is orange, Nictalia purple—while others, like Cafe del Sol and Blues Cafe, leave it to their clients and the drinks to make the ambience. If you feel a bit more adventurous, head to **Plaça de la Revolució de Septiembre 1868** or **Plaça del Sol** and take it from there; in this young, vibrant neighborhood, you really can't go wrong.

BARS

▨ **Vinil(),** C. Matilde, 2 (☎669 17 79 45; www.vinilus.blogspot.com). This bar's dim orange lighting, mismatched pillows, mellow background music, and screened daily movies make you never want to leave. Beer and wine €2.70. Mojitos and *caipirinhas* (the only mixed drinks served) €6. Open in summer M-Th 8pm-2am, F-Sa 8pm-3am; in winter M-Th and Su 8pm-2am, F-Sa 8pm-3am.

Cafe del Sol, Pl. del Sol, 16 (☎932 37 14 48). ⓜFontana. Walk down C. Gran de Gràcia, make a left on C. Ros de Olano and then a right on C. Cano/C.Leopoldo Alas. Locals pack the 8 tapas bars around Pl. del Sol every night and spill out into the plaça. This mainstay offers perfect tostadas (€3-5) and tapas (€1.70-5) as well as beer (€2-3), wine, and mixed drinks (€5-6). Come for lunch and take your tapas out into the plaça. Open M-Th and Su noon-2:30am, F and Sa noon-3am.

Nictalia, C. St. Domenec, 15 (☎932 37 23 23). ⓜFontana. Walk down C. Gran de Gràcia to C. St. Domenec and make a left; Nictalia is 2 blocks down on the left. Step into this intimate bar and feel the magic—it's got blue fairy lights, purple walls, and colorful chalkboards (not to mention a buzzing crowd of locals and cheap shots). Beer €2-3. Mixed drinks €5. Shots €1.80. Open M-Th 6:30pm-2am, F and Sa 6pm-3am. Cash only.

Sol Soler, Pl. del Sol, 21-22 (☎932 17 44 40; www.myspace.com/solsolertapas). ⓜFontana. Walk down C. Gran de Gràcia and make a left onto C. de Ros de Olano. Follow the noise and make a right onto Pl. del Sol. This beloved corner bar is on Pl. del Sol, the center of Gràcia's nightlife. Also open during the day, Sol Soler is a longtime local favorite and unquestionably the real deal. Crowd in with students around tables, shout to be heard, and feel like a local. Open M-W noon-1:30am, Th-Su noon-2:30am.

Bar Canigo, C. Verdi, 2 (☎932 13 30 49). ⓜFontana. Walk down C. Gran de Gràcia and make a left on C. Ros de Olano. Keep walking (about 6 blocks) until you hit C. Verdi. A classic student haunt. Bar Canigo has cracked mirrors, pool tables, and a young, fun-loving clientele; noisy tables of friends jumble happily around long faux-marble tables to guzzle beers (€2-4). Mixed drinks €5-6. Open M-Th 8pm-2am, F-Sa 8pm-3am, Su 8pm-2am. MC/V.

Café del Teatre, C. Torrijos, 41 (☎934 16 06 51). ⓜFontana. Walk down C. Gran de Gràcia and make a left onto C. Montseny. Walk 8 blocks; it's on the right. This corner bar has *Modernista* stained-glass accents, green lighting, alluring if slightly eerie statues of black cats behind the bar, and a prime location. The mojitos are especially good. Open M-Th 10pm-2am, F-Sa 10pm-3am. Cash only.

La Cervesera Artesana: Pub-Brewery, C. Sant Augusti, 14 (☎932 37 95 94). ⓜDiagonal. Walk down C. Corsega and then make a left onto C. Sant Agusti. It's up ahead, on the left. The only bar in Barcelona to brew its own beer, the Cervesera has long been making locals proud. Try the peppermint home brew (a pint €4.90); you might like it so much that you will take a case home with you. *Pica-pica* also served. Open M-Th 6pm-2am, F-Sa 6pm-3am, Su 6pm-2am. MC/V.

L'Astrolabi, C. Martinez de la Rosa, 14. ⓜDiagonal. Walk down C. Corsega and then make a left onto C. Sant Agusti. This street turns into C. Martinez de la Rosa. L'Astrolabi is shortly up, on the right. A crowd of intimate regulars gathers at this nautically-themed bar to listen to and play live music 7 nights a week. The scene is more campfire than rager. Beer €2-4. Mixed drinks €5-6. Live music from 10pm. Open 8pm-2am. Cash only.

El Otro Bar, Travessera de Gràcia, 167 (☎933 23 67 59). ⓜFontana. Walk down C. Gran de Gràcia until you reach Trav. de Gràcia. Make a left. Even on weeknights, this Irish pub bustles. Colored chalk boards in the street advertise drink specials. Open M-Th 9pm-2am, F-Sa 9pm-3am, Su 9pm-2am. Cash only.

DeDues Cocktail & Bar, C. Torrent de l'Olla, 89 (☎934 16 14 96; www.dedues.es). ⓜFontana. From the Metro, walk down C. Asturies until you hit C. Torrent de l'Olla. Walk 5½ blocks down C. Torrent de l'Olla. This posh *cocteleria* (the walls are bedecked with orange floral swirls) specializes in mojitos and caipirinha (€4). Open M-Th 8:30pm-2:30am, F 8:30pm-3am, Sa 6:30pm-3am. MC/V.

Mond Bar, Pl. del Sol, 21 (www.mondclub.com). ⓂFontana. Walk down C. Gran de Gràcia and make a left onto C. Ros de Olano. Follow the crowds or the noise to Pl. del Sol. The sign above this bar's door reads "Pop Will Save Us." True to this, Mond Bar is your pop oasis in this happening but electronica-dominated plaça. iPod battles Th. Open M-Th 7pm-2:30am, F-Sa 7pm-3am, Su 7pm-2:30am. Beer €2-4. Mixed drinks €5-6. Cash only.

Mi Bar, C. de les Guilleries, 6. ⓂFontana. Walk down C. Gran de Gràcia and make a left on C. Montseny. Continue for 6 blocks, then make a right on C. de les Guilleries. This hideaway bar is glam-meets-graffiti; the walls are scrawled with red and black paint, but chandeliers and mirrors add a touch of class. Pool table in the back room. Drinks €3-8. Open M-Th, F-Sa until 3am, and Su 11pm-2:30am. Cash only.

Velcro Bar, C. Vallfogona, 10 (☎610 75 47 42). ⓂFontana. Follow C. de Asturies to C. Torrent de l'Olla and make a right. After 3 blocks on this street, make a left onto C. Vallfongona. White tables, lilac twinkle lights, and a location away from the madness of Gràcia's plaças makes this a favorite with young locals. Movies are played nightly on the back wall. Mixed drinks €5-8. Open nightly 7pm-2:30am. MC/V.

Stinger, C. Corcega, 338 (☎932 17 71 87). ⓂDiagonal. This bar, which is located between the student zone of Gràcia and the 5-star hotels on Pg. de Gràcia, straddles the line between cozy and classy. Convenient to the Metro, it's a good place to drink your first round. Mixed drinks €6.20-6.90. Open M-Th 6:30pm-2:30am, F-Sa 6:30pm-3am. Closed Aug. MC/V.

Enigma, C. Martinez de la Rosa, 27 (☎695 27 91 82). ⓂDiagonal. Walk down C. Corsega and make a left onto C. Sant Agusti. This street turns into C. Martinez de la Rosa; Enigma is on the left. Not much mystery here—this bar has a pool table, cheap drinks, and a clientele of would-be punks. Games of pool during the week free, weekends €2. Shots €2. Open in summer daily 8pm-2:30am; in winter daily 6pm-2:30am. Cash only.

Flann O'Brien's, C. Casanova, 264 (☎932 01 16 06; www.flannobrienbcn.com). ⓂDiagonal, L3/5. Authentic, boisterous Irish pub with barrels for tables and rugby shirts hanging from the ceiling. Popular with locals and Barcelona's English-speaking expats for almost 2 decades. Top off your evening with a Guinness or a mixed drink (€6). Live music Th-Sa 11:30pm. Open M-Th and Su 6pm-2:30am, F and Sa 6pm-3am.

La Baignoire, C. Verdi, 6, (☎606 33 04 60). ⓂFontana. From the Metro, walk down C. d'Asturies past Pl. del Diamante until you hit C. Verdi. Locals gather around busy La Baignoire's elegant, high tables to chat, drink cava, and sip mixed drinks (€6) before heading to more raucous venues. Open M-Th 6pm-1:30am, F and Sa 6pm-2am, Su 6pm-1am. MC/V.

Blues Café, C. La Perla, 37 (☎93 416 09 65). ⓂFontana, L3. Follow C. Astúries to C. Verdi, turn right, walk 2 blocks to C. Perla, and turn left. Plastered with photos of blues legends. Plenty of cheap beer (€2) to go around. Mixed drinks €4.50. Open Su-Th 6:30pm-2:30am, F-Sa 6:30pm-3am. Cash only.

St. Germain, C. Torrent de l'Olla, 113 (☎934 15 22 07). ⓂFontana, L3. Turn left on C. d'Asturies and right on C. Torrent de l'Olla; walk 3 blocks; St. Germain is 3 block down on the right. On this bar's cheerful red walls you'll find framed, old-fashioned travel posters, a mini-mural of Picasso's *Guernica,* and projected black-and-white movies. The bar is downright cozy. Beer €1.80. Mixed drinks €5.50. Tapas, crepes (€4-6), and quiche (€4). Open M, W, Th, and Su 6pm-2:30am; F and Sa 6pm-3am. Cash only.

Pippermint, C. Bori i Fontestà, 20 (☎932 08 00 00, www.pippermintbcn.com). Pippermint serves the largest drinks you'll ever see—and they all come with straws. *Cuba libre* (rum and coke; 6L) €40. Beer (13L) €71. Sangria (13L) €98. Also has normal-sized drinks (1L; €12-14) for tamer (or smaller) groups. University Bar every Th. Open daily 4pm-3am. MC/V.

Amberes, C. Perla, 34. ⓂFontana. Walk down C. Gran de Gràcia and make a left on C. del Montseny. The street turns into C. Perla. This bar feels like the trendiest living room you'll ever step into with its blue walls, blue furniture, and a large mural of a Rubens nude. Beer €3.50. Mixed drinks €6. Happy hour M-F 7-10pm (2 mixed drinks for €10). Open M-Th and Su 7pm-2am, F and Sa 7pm-3am. Cash only.

Bamboleo, C. Topazi, 24 (☎93 217 32 60). ⓂFontana, L3. A few blocks up C. Topazi from Pl. del Diamante. A good place to end the night. Cuban bar hosts salsa, techno, and rock DJs. Friendly, informal pool games and turns on the foosball table. *Calimochos* (red wine and coke), mojitos, and piña coladas €6 each. An unbelievably long list of *chupitos* (shots; €3). 2-for-1 drinks until 12:30am. Open daily 9pm-3am. Cash only.

Berlin, C. Muntaner, 240 (☎932 00 65 42). ⓂDiagonal. Take Av. Diagonal to C. Muntaner; Berlin is on the right. Dim lighting, cheerful orange and red walls, young clientele, outdoor seating. Also serves food throughout the day. Croquetas €6.50. Bruschetta €7. Beer €2-4. Mixed drinks €7. Open M-W 10am-2am, Th-Sa 10am-3am.

Chatelet, C. Torrijos, 54 (☎932 84 95 90). ⓂFontana, L3. From Fontana, walk down C. d'Asturies. Make a right onto Torrent de l'Olla, then a left onto C. l'Or. Chatelet is on the next corner, on the right. This bar boasts dazzling chandeliers and a Mondrian-inspired wall. Delicious panini—come early in the evening for a quick bite and try the Provenzal (ham, goat cheese, tomato, and herbs; €4.50). Happy hour until 10pm (2 mixed drinks; €8). Shots €3. Open M-Th and Su 6pm-2:30am, F and Sa 6pm-3am. Cash only.

CLUBS

▨ Otto Zutz, C. Lincoln, 15 (☎932 38 07 22; www.ottozutz.com). FGC: Gràcia or ⓂFontana. Japanimation lighting and 3 dance floors make this one of Barcelona's most popular clubs. Named in honor of the legendary 70s club Autozut. Upstairs you'll find local DJs playing electronica; downstairs, you'll hear hip-hop and R&B. VIP access and private parties possible with reservation. Beer €6. Mixed drinks €6-12. Cover €10-15, includes 1 drink. Look for flyers at bars and hotels to get in free before 2am. Open W-Su midnight-6am. MC/V.

KGB, C. Alegre de Dalt, 55 (☎932 10 59 06; www.salakgb.net). ⓂJoanic, L4. Walk along C. Pi i Maragall and take the 1st left; to get a cab home, come back to Pi i Maragall. Techno and loud rock play to a mixed crowd of students and Soviet secret agents. Occasional live concerts 9pm. Beer €4-6. Mixed drinks €6-8. Cover €10, includes 1 drink. Open Th 1-5am, F-Sa and nights before public holidays 1-6am. Cash only.

Nick Havanna, C. Rosello, 208 (☎607 49 79 81; www.nickhavanna.com). FGC: Provenca. Spaniards and tourists looking *muy pijos* (very fly) dance beneath a metal, domed ceiling and rainbow lighting and grind to pop hits. Check out the rotating slide projections. Dress to impress (no sneakers). Drinks €6-8. Cover €10. Open Th-Sa, midnight-5am. MC/V.

Duvet, C. Córcega, 327 (☎93 237 43 22; www.duvet.es). ⓂDiagonal. It's right on C. Córcega, across the street from the Metro. This live music venue and club has nightly events that range from dance lessons to live music to DJs. Dance lessons Tu. Ladies' night W. The best of the 80s and 90s (with some modern hits) F and Sa. Ballroom Su. Open nightly. Cover and exact times vary by event, so check ahead online. MC/V.

NIGHTLIFE

VALL D'HEBRON AND HORTA-GUINARDÓ

This small *barrio*, far removed from, well, everything, takes great pride in its small-town feel. There aren't many nightlife options out here, but the few that you do find, probably in **Plaça d'Eivissa,** will be jam-packed with groups of close friends who are more welcoming to strangers than folks in other more touristed parts of town. Figure out your transportation beforehand, because getting home can prove tricky. Subways run until midnight on weeknights, until 2am on Fridays, and continuously on Saturdays. A cab ride to Pl. Catalunya will cost around €18.

BarCafe Louise Se Va, Pl. d'Eivissa, 11 (www.louiseseva.com/barcafe). ⓂHorta. Young locals pack into BarCafe, where the *flautes* (flutes of drinks) are named after musical icons ranging from Elvis to U2. Fill up before heading to the venue's eponymous sister club. *Flautes* €2-4. Try the *Red Hot Chili Peppers* (sausage; €3). Open daily 5pm-2:30am. Cash only.

Quimet d'Horta, Pl. d'Eivissa, 10 (☎933 58 19 16). ⓂHorta. From the Metro, walk up C. de Fulton. A local favorite for over 100 years. Though the restaurant's much-loved mascot parrot has died, the venue continues to thrive. Salads and sandwiches €2-8. Open M-Tu and Th-Su 9am-midnight. MC/V.

El Frankfurt 1978, Pl. d'Eivissa, 4. ⓂHorta. Walk up C. de Fulton until you reach Pl. Eivissa. This local tapas bar has a stained-glass window and extensive patio seating. Bustles with young locals late into the night. Tapas €2-8. Entrees €5-10. Sangria €2.50. Open daily 1pm-2am. Cash only.

Samba Brazil, Pl. Stes. Creus (☎934 20 66 53). ⓂHorta. From the Metro, walk down C. del Tajo. It's set a bit off the street, so if you get lost, ask a local to point you in the right direction. Paintings of the jungle and topless Brazilian women decorate the brick walls of this spacious and popular bar. It feels like being inside a 1933 issue of *National Geographic.* The leafy outdoor terrace is a great place to meet young locals. Su live music. Mixed drinks €6-7. Open M-W and Su 7:30pm-3am, Th-Sa 7:30pm-3:30am. Cash only.

Club Louise Se Va, C. Santa Amália, 26-30 (☎934 29 98 56; www.louiseseva.com/sala). ⓂHorta. Walk down Pg. de Maragall and make a left onto C. Santa Amália. Tired of rubbing shoulders with tourists? On weekend nights, an intimate crowd of locals packs this red-walled dance club—the only one in the area. Th blues, funk, and soul. Cover less than €10. Open Th 11pm-4am, F-Sa 11:45pm-6am. Cash only.

TIBIDABO

Although pricey and hard to access, the few bars in Tibidabo offer fabulous, shimmering night views of Barcelona from on high. Unless you have really good shoes and willpower, getting here by taxi is the way to go. Ask the driver for the number of the taxi company to call on the way back.

🆇 **Mirablau,** Pl. Dr. Andreu (☎934 18 58 79). Next to Mirabé (see p. 191). 2 terraces and the full window inside the bar afford spectacular views. On weekends, the crowd drifts downstairs to the nightclub. Open all day for those who care for an early drink and a view of Barcelona before nightfall. Mixed drinks €6-11. Wine and beer €4.70-6 (cheaper before 11pm). Sa-Su 1-drink min. Open M-Th 11am-4:30am, F and Sa 11am-5:45am. AmEx/MC/V.

Merbeyé (☎934 17 35 49), in Pl. Dr. Andreu. Set slightly back from the cliff, with a sultry interior that greets loungers for tapas and drinks. The outdoor canopy attracts easygoing crowds, with 80s pop tunes ablare. Creative drinks include the Merbeyé (Cointreau with cava and cherry brandy; €8.50). Open W 7pm-1am, Th and Su noon-2am, F-Sa noon-4am. MC/V.

Mirabé, Manuel Arnus, 2 (☎934 34 00 35; www.mirabe.es), in Pl. Dr. Andreu. A supremely elegant bar overlooking the Mediterranean shore. Potted palms and a small pond only heighten the luxury of the large terrace frequented by well-dressed professionals. Beers €4.50. Mixed drinks €9.50. Open Tu-Su 7pm-3am. MC/V.

CLUBS WHOSE NAMES ALLUDE TO THE 1941 ORSON WELLES FILM *CITIZEN KANE*

Rosebud, Carrer d'Adrià Margarit, 27 (☎934 18 88 85; www.rosebud.es). Across from Museu de la Ciencia. Only the most elite, well-dressed revelers make it past the iron gate and up the red-carpeted stairs to the Xanadu-esque decadence that lies beyond. A list posted at the door bans (among other things) T-shirts, hair that is inappropriately long or unkempt (for men), and white socks. Cover €10 includes 1 drink. Open Th-Su midnight-6am. MC/V.

SARRIÀ

Sick of expats and backpackers guzzling Guinness? The eclectic mix of late-night cafes, bars, and clubs around **Plaça Molina** is packed with established hot spots and savvy Barcelonese who know better than to join the tourists on Las Ramblas at night. Nearby, **Calle Marià Cubí** hops on weekend nights; its tightly-packed drinking and dance venues helpfully obviates the need to make subway transfers under the influence.

Bar Marcel, C. Santaló, 42 (☎932 09 89 48), at C. de Marià Cubí. FCG: Muntaner. Walk about 7min. down C. Muntaner and turn right on C. Marià Cubí. Before midnight, this enormously popular bar masquerades as a quiet, unassuming cafe. But when the clock strikes 12, locals pack the place in search of cheap booze. Certainly not the fanciest bar in the neighborhood, but possibly the most beloved. Coffee €1.20. Beer €2-4. Mixed drinks €6. Open daily 7:30am-2am. MC/V.

Solidarik, C. Amigo, 37 (www.solidarik.com). FCG: Muntaner. Walk 2 blocks up V. Augusta and turn left on C. Amigo. All profits at this sleek bar go toward alleviating problems in 3rd-world countries. See the website for annual projects. Mixed drinks €6-7. Open Th-Sa 10pm-3am. MC/V.

Alkimia, C. Amigo, 35 (☎627 54 56 07). FCG: Muntaner. Walk 2 blocks up V. Augusta and turn left on C. Amigo. The centerpiece of this bar is a corrugated-metal, spiral staircase that leads to a 2nd fl. Upstairs is dark and noisy (in a good way) on the weekends. Th happy hour; 2 drinks €8. Open Th-Sa 11pm-3am. Cash only.

Manhattan, C. Amigo, 23 (☎634 06 68 31). Walk 2 blocks up V. Augusta and turn left on C. Amigo. This bar's black leather chairs and black tables channel New York chic and pictures of the big apple adorn the walls. The mojito(€6) is a specialty. Open Tu-Sa 6pm-3am. MC/V.

Eternity Cafe, C. Amigo 22-24 (☎93 534 12 25). FGC: Muntaner. Walk 2 blocks up V. Augusta and turn left on C. Amigo; continue down. This bar has white armchairs, white walls, and a white wrought-iron railing separating the small upstairs from the downstairs. Mixed drinks €5-8. Open M-W 10pm-2am, Th-Sa 10pm-3am. MC/V.

Punto, C. de l'Avenir, 66 (☎627 91 85 13). FGC: Muntaner. Walk 2 blocks up V. Augusta and turn left on C. Amigo. Walk down this street until you hit C. de l'Avenir; make a right. A straightforward bar decorated in black and orange. Mixed drinks €5-8. Open Th-Sa 11pm-3am. Cash only.

Uno, C. Tuset, 1 (☎932 00 17 48). ⓜ: Diagonal. Walk up Av. Diagonal and make a right onto C. Tuset. Serves breakfast in the morning and morphs into a bar at night. Red and green lighting, a large downstairs lounge, and an older clientele. Lunch menu €8-9. Open M-W 8am-10pm, Th-Sa 8am-3am. MC/V.

DANCE BARS

Bubblic Bar, C. Marià Cubí, 183 (☎93 414 54 01). FCG: Muntaner. Walk about 7min. down C. Muntaner and turn right on C. Marià Cubí. Etched glass windows and a mini-malist interior. DJs spin English and Spanish pop and house. Beer €3. Mixed drinks €5. Open Th-Sa 11:30pm-3:30am. MC/V.

Silk, C. Marià Cubí, 172 (☎696 29 13 70). FCG: Muntaner. Walk about 6min. down C. Muntaner and turn right on C. Marià Cubí. This long, thin bar plays funk, hip hop, rap, and soul. The dance room in the back gets packed on weekend nights. Mixed drinks €4-4.50. Happy hour before midnight; 2 drinks €7. Open Th-Sa 11pm-3am. MC/V.

Minimal, C. Marià Cubí, 173 (☎933 62 02 00). FGC: Muntaner. Walk about 7min. down C. Muntaner and turn right on C. Marià Cubí. Minimal decor keeps the focus on the essential—drinks and music. Long and thin, like Silk (they're in the same building), but here it's okay to dress down. Mixed drinks €6-8. Open Th-Sa 11:30pm-3am. Cash only.

CLUBS

Sutton, C. Tuset, 13 (☎934 14 42 17; www.thesuttonclub.com). ⓜDiagonal. Walk up Av. Diagonal and make a right onto C. Tuset. At this swanky club, you'll find gogo dancers, several VIP lounges, and—if you're there on the right night—free-flowing champagne. Dress to impress—no jeans, and dress shoes are required. Cover €15-20. Open Th-Sa midnight-morning. MC/V.

Universal Lounge Club, C. Marià Cubí, 182 (☎932 01 35 96; www.universalbcn.com). FCG: Muntaner. Walk about 7min. down C. Muntaner and turn right on C. Marià Cubí. This 2-story club has billowy white curtains, spacious dance floors lit in red (downstairs) and blue (upstairs), and is conveniently located near the many bars on C. Marià Cubí. 16+. Weeknights no cover, F-Sa after 2am €18; includes 1 drink. Open M-W and Su 11:30pm-3:30am, Th 11:30pm-4:30am, F and Sa 11:30pm-6am. MC/V.

PEDRALBES AND LES CORTS

Nightlife in Pedralbes and Les Corts is limited. If none of the places below strikes your fancy, consider walking to nearby Sarrià, where options abound, or take the metro downtown.

🅰 **Infussion,** C. Deu i Mata, 10 (www.infussionbar.com). ⓜLes Corts. Walk up Trav. de les Corts and make a left on C. de Galileu. Then make a right on C. Deu i Mata; the restaurant is ½ block down, on your right. Order your mojito (€5.50) at this sultry bar and head past the Arabian Nights-style bar to the back room, where a cast-iron tree decorated with white lights throws faux moonlight over a a lounge area of floor mats and bean bag chairs. Hookah pipes available. Open M-W 8:30pm-2am, F-Sa 8:30pm-3am. MC/V.

Taia, Pl. de la Concordia, 2 (☎934 19 79 09). ⓜLes Corts. Walk up C. de Galileu and make a right on C. de Deu i Mata that runs into the plaça. This bar-cafe has zebra-print walls, yellow leather booths, and a young, cheerful staff. Lunch menú (€10) includes staples like hamburgers. By night, locals spill out onto the patio drinking beer and moji-tos (€6). Free Wi-Fi. Open daily 11am-2am, F-Sa 11am-3am. MC/V.

Bikini, Av. Diagonal, 547 (☎933 22 08 00; www.bikinibcn.com). ⓜMaria Christina. Walk down Av. Diagonal. There are professional dancers on the bar in swimsuits to inspire your own moves. Local DJs. Concerts some nights at 9pm; check the web site for specifics. Cover €10-20. Open Tu-Sa midnight-dawn, Su 10:30-dawn. MC/V.

SANT ANDREU

Trenta Nits, C. Gran de Sant Andreu, 123 (☎93 274 41 69). ⓜFabra i Puig. Walk east on Pg. de Fabra i Puig and make a left on C. Gran de Sant Andreu. When you think of night, what do you think of? Stars? Moons? The color blue? The Beastie Boys? That's what this bar thinks of too—blue walls, stars, and moons decorate the entrance. Popular with 20-something locals, who nod along to pop-punk classics favored by the resident DJ. Beer €2. Mixed drinks €6.50. Cafe by day and restaurant by night. Weekday *menù* €9. Open M 9am-5pm, Tu-Th 9am-2am, F 9am-2:30am, Sa-Su 7pm-2:30am. AmEx/MC/V.

2d2dspuma, C. Manigua, 8 (☎661 23 02 09; www.2d2dspuma.com). ⓜMaragall or Congrès. The name (pronounced *Dos Dedos de Espuma*) refers to the preferred beer head size of the bartender (2 fingers' worth) and is just one manifestation of the expertise on tap here. The menu lists over 150 varieties of beer from all over the world; if the selection is too overwhelming the bartender will be happy to guide you. During the day you can purchase your favorite draft from the store behind the bar. Check the website for beer tasting sessions (€25). Beer €1.90. Open M-Th 9am-3pm and 6-11:30pm, F-Sa 6pm-2am Cash Only.

Torre Rosa, C. de Francesc Tàrrega, 22 (☎93 340 88 54; www.torrerosa.com). ⓜCongrès. This white-walled, turn-of-the-century house is now adorned with pink neon lights and serves an impressive array of mixed drinks, which locals sip on the tree-lined terrace on warm summer nights. Beer €3.50. Mixed drinks €8. Open daily 7am-2:30am. MC/V.

La Torreta, Pg. Fabra i Puig, 98 (www.latorreta.eu). ⓜFabra i Puig. Inside this tower lies a smoky neighborhood bar filled with locals and enough room to bust a move should the music strike you just the right way. Beer €2.20. Mixed drink of the day €4.50. Open daily 7pm-3am.

NIGHTLIFE

DAYTRIPS

MONTSERRAT ☎938

A 1235m peak of limestone, quartz, and slate protruding from the Río Llobregat Valley, Montserrat (Sawed Mountain) is an inspiration to its 2.5 million annual visitors. A millennium ago, one wandering mountaineer claimed to have spotted the Virgin Mary; as the story spread, pilgrims flocked to the mountain. The Monastery of the Virgin, founded in 1025 by the opportunistic Bishop Oliba, is tended today by 80 Benedictine monks. The site attracts those who come to see the Black Virgin of Montserrat, her ornate basilica, the complex's art museum, and panoramic views of Catalunya from the mountain's stunning rocks.

▐▌ TRANSPORTATION AND PRACTICAL INFORMATION

FGC (☎932 05 15 15) line R5 runs to Montserrat from Ⓜ Espanya (1hr.; every hr. 8:36am-5:36pm; return from Montserrat 10:33am-10:33pm; round-trip including cable car €13.70); get off at Montserrat-Aeri. From there, catch the █Aeri cable car right by the station, the coolest way to ascend to the monastery. (Runs daily Mar.-Oct. every 15min. 9:40am-2pm and 2:35-7pm. Price included in bus combo fare or €8 round-trip by itself, one way €5, ages 4-13 €4.50. Additional times in summer; call ☎938 77 77 01.) Another option is to take the FGC's train, the **Cremallera de Montserrat.** (☎902 31 20 20; www.cremallerademontserrat.com.) From Barcelona, this requires a combined R5 train plus the Cremallera (Rack Railway) instead of the cable car (Cremallera €6.50-7.30, children €3.60-4, retired €5.85-6.55; combined, including train from Pl. Espanya, €13.70-14.4 0/10.80-11.20/13.05-13.75). Get off the FGC one station later, at Monistrol de Montserrat, and take the railway up (every 20-30min.). **Autocars Julià buses** run to the monastery, from near Estació Sants. (Leave Barcelona daily 9:15am and return June-Sept. at 6pm, Oct.-May at 5pm. Call ☎934 90 40 00 for reservations. €10. MC/V.) If you plan to use the funiculars, consider buying the **Tot Montserrat** (€28.60, children €17, retired €25) at tourist offices or in Ⓜ Espanya; it includes tickets for the FGC, cable car, funiculars, Museu de Montserrat, and a meal. Also available is the **Trans Montserrat** (€13.85/7.95/12.55), same as the Tot but without the Museu and the meal. Beyond the first 30 min., there is car parking fee. Call ☎938 35 03 84 for a **taxi** (from Barcelona €85).

Visitor services are in Pl. Creu, the area straight ahead from the top of the Aeri cable car steps and the Cremallera station. The **info booth** in Pl. Creu provides free maps, schedules of religious services, and advice on mountain navigation. An audioguide with a booklet on Montserrat is €5, and an audio guide with headphones for two is €6.50. (☎938 77 77 77. Opens daily 9am, closes 5:45-8pm depending on season). For more information, buy the *Official Guide to Montserrat* (€7.50) or the museum guide (€4). Services include: **ATMs** and **bank** at La Caixa, next to the **info booth** (open M-F 9:15am-2pm; Oct.-May M-F 9:15am-2pm, Sa 9:15am-1:30pm); **public bathrooms** to the right up the stairs if you're facing the tourist office; **ambulance** (inquire at info booth); the **Patronat del Parc Natural** (☎938 35 05 91); and the **post office** (open M-F 10am-1:30pm, Sa 10am-noon).

ACCOMMODATIONS AND FOOD

Cel·les Abat Marcet ❶ has beautiful apartments with bath, kitchen, and heating. (☎938 77 77 01; ask for Cel·les. Reception daily 9am-1pm and 2-6pm. From €15-29.50 for one person, €27.50-44 for two. Min. 2 nights; discounts for longer stays.) **Camping Montserrat ❶** is a 5min. walk past the funiculars on the road that goes uphill. Its library has out-of-print climbing books for Montserrat, and the mountain-savvy staff can put you in touch with climbing guides. (☎938 77 77 77; ask for camping. No parking on the site but available near Pl. Creu, €5 for 3 days. Open Apr. 1-Oct. 31. €3 per person, €2 for kids under 12, €2.50 per tent. Reception open 8am-2pm and 5pm-9pm Cash only.)

Food options in Montserrat are limited and aimed entirely at tourists trapped on a mountainside with no other alternatives. Pack food for your hike before coming or else descend into buffet hell. You can pick up some snacks at the small **Queviures supermarket** in Pl. Creu (open daily 9am-6:30pm). For a quick meal, **Bar de la Plaça ❶** is an option. (*Bocadillos* and hamburgers €3-4.50. Open M-F 9:30am-5pm, Sa-Su 9:30am-6:40pm. Cash only.) A new **cafetería ❶**, in Pl. Creu, has limited self-service food options. (Sandwiches €3.50-4.20. Salads €3.45-4.50. Steak and fries €5.80. Open M-F 8:45am-7pm, Sa-Su 8am-8pm. MC/V.) There's a very popular **self-service cafetería ❷** up the hill to the right from the cable car steps (in the building with the red "Mirador" sign), with wider selection and included in the price of the Lucky Tot Montserrat card. (With card, 2 dishes, chosen from *paella*, pasta, and meat, plus dessert and bread, drinks not included; otherwise, *paella* €6.60, meat and fish €4-7, salads €4-5. Open daily noon-4pm.) A fancier alternative, **Restaurant de Montserrat ❹**, is located in the same building. (*Menú* €23; children's dishes available. Open Mar. 15-Nov. 15 daily noon-4pm. AmEx/MC/V.)

SIGHTS

Above Pl. Creu (facing the info booth, take the stairs up and to the right), the beautiful **basílica** looks onto Pl. Santa Noría. Inside the courtyard, next to the main chapel entrance, a marble hallway through side chapels leads to an elevated shrine with the 12th-century Romanesque **La Moreneta** (the Black Virgin), an icon of Mary. (Hallway open daily 8-10:30am and noon-6:30pm; in summer also Sa-Su 7:30-8:15pm. Expect a line in summer.) For many years it was revered as a Black Virgin, until it was discovered that the statue was merely very dirty; the custom stuck, however, and it was subsequently painted black. The **Escalonia boys' choir** performs in the basilica (Aug. 21-June 29 M-F 1pm; Su noon and 7:30pm; schedules may change; check www.escalonia.net). Also in Pl. Santa María, closer to the stairs up from Pl. Creu, the small **Museo de Montserrat** has art ranging from a mummy to Picasso's *Old Fisherman* and Dalí's *El Mariner*, as well as works by Degas, Renoir, and Monet. (Open daily June 26-Sept. 15 10am-7pm; Sept. 16-June 25 10am-5:45pm. €6.50, students and over 65 €5.50, ages 6-12 €3.50, under 8 free, temporary exhibits €3.)

HIKES

Some of the most beautiful areas of the mountain are accessible only by foot. The steep **Santa Cova funicular** descends from Pl. Creu to the **Rosario Monumental,** which winds along the face of the mountain past 15 religious sculptures by notable Catalan artists, culminating at the ancient hermitage **Santa Cova** where the Virgin Mary sighting took place. (Funicular daily every 20min. 10am-1pm and 2-5:45pm. Round-trip €2.70, students and over 65 €2.45, ages 3-14 €1.50. Santa Cova chapel open Apr.-Oct. daily 10:30am-5:15pm; Nov.-Mar.

M-F 11:30am-4:15pm, Sa-Su 10:30am-4:30pm.) Take the **Sant Joan funicular** up the hill for inspirational views of Montserrat, the monastery, and surrounding towns. (Daily every 20min. in summer 10am-6pm. Check the signs for the last return. Round-trip €6.60, students and over 65 €5.95, ages 10-14 €3.60; joint round-trip ticket with the Santa Cova funicular €7.45/6.70/4.10.) Upstairs in the upper station you'll find an exhibit on the funiculars and the **Nature Hall,** containing a model of Montserrat and some of the mountain's history. The **Sant Joan monastery** and **shrine** are only a 20min. tromp from here, and **Sant Jerónim** (the area's highest peak at 1236m), with its views of Montserrat's jagged, mystical rocks, is worth the 1hr. trek from Pl. Creu (1hr. from the terminus of the Sant Joan funicular). The paths are long and winding but not difficult—after all, they were made for guys wearing very long robes.

SITGES ☎938

Forty kilometers south of Barcelona, the beach town of Sitges (pop. 27,000) deserves its self-proclaimed title, "jewel of the Mediterranean." Sitges gained prominence in the late 19th century as one of the principal centers of the *Modernista* art movement; today, the town's sweeping bays, crystalline water, beautiful tanning grounds (there are 300 sunny days per year), and friendly residents give the town an irresistible *je ne sais quoi*. Young and fun-loving tourists flock to Sitges for its vibrant party scene; the town's bars and clubs, though predominantly gay, are enthusiastically hetero-friendly. Although the town makes an ideal daytrip along the coast, consider staying for a few nights—you won't regret it.

TRANSPORTATION

Trains: Cercanías trains (a.k.a. Rodalies; RENFE ☎902 24 02 02, www.renfe.es/cercanias) run from **Estació Barcelona-Sants** to **Sitges** (Line 2 dir: St. Vicenç de Calders or Vilanova, 30min., every 15-30min. 5am-midnight, €2.80).

Buses: Mon Bus (☎938 93 70 60; www.monbus.cat) connects the Barcelona **airport** to Pg. de Villafranca in **Sitges** (M-F every hr. from airport 7:40am-11:40pm, from Sitges 5:55am-11:55pm, Sa-Su every 2hr. from airport 9:40am9:40pm, from Sitges 7:25am-8:55pm; €2.90). Late-night buses operate from Pg. de Villafranca to Rambla de Catalunya in Barcelona and back (12:11-4am, €2.90).

Taxis: ☎938 94 13 29. Run between **Barcelona** and **Sitges** (€60-65). Use only in case of severe nightlife emergency.

Car Rental: ☎938 11 19 96. To reach the beaches and the *cales* (caves), rent a car in Barcelona or Sitges at **Europcar,** on the 1st fl. of the Mercat, to the right from the train station. AmEx/MC/V.

ORIENTATION AND PRACTICAL INFORMATION

Most people arrive at the train station on **Carrer Carbonell** in the northern part of town. From there, the town center is five minutes away by foot, and the beach 10 minutes. To reach either, take a right as you leave the station and the third left onto **Carrer Sant Francesc.** This leads to the old town and intersects **Carrer de les Parellades,** the main strip of stores and restaurants running parallel to the ocean. Any street off Parellades will lead to the waterfront. **Passeig de la Ribera** runs along the central and most crowded beaches.

Tourist Office: C. Sinia Morera, 1 (☎902 10 34 28; www.sitgestur.com). From the station, turn right on C. Carbonell and take the next right at the roundabout onto Pg. de

Vilafranca. The office is 1 block up on the left. Free maps and monthly bulletin of events in ▓**Sitges Agenda.** Open from mid-June to mid-Sept. M-Sa 9am-8pm; from late-Sept. to early June M-F 9am-2pm and 4-6:30pm. Branches at the train station, at Pl. Eduard Maristany, and near the beach, below the church, at Pg. de la Ribera. **Agis,** C. Lope de Vega 9 (☎619 79 31 99; www.sitges.com/agis). Offers **guided tours** of the city (€10-17). **Jafra Natura** (☎627 97 85 66; www.jafranatura.com) takes visitors through the bordering Garraf Natural Park.

Police: Pl. Ajuntament (☎938 11 00 16 or 938 10 97 97).

Red Cross: Pl. de l'Hospital (☎938 94 02 26).

Hospital: Hospital Sant Camil, Carretera de Puigmoltó, Km. 0.8 (☎938 96 00 25). **Center for Adult Primary Care (CAP),** Av. dels Camis dels Capellans.

Internet Access: Sitges PC, C. Angel Vidal, 2 (☎938 11 10 46; www.sitgespc.com). €1 per 20min. Fax, printing, photocopying. Open M-F 9:30am-2pm and 5-8:30pm, Sa 10:30am-1:30pm and 5-9pm. **Il Piacere,** C. Sant Gaudenci, 6 (☎938 10 23 37; www.ilpiaceres.com) has free **Wi-Fi** in a spacious, chic bar. Th live music. Open M-Sa 8am-12:30am, F and Su 9am-2pm and 6pm-midnight. AmEx/MC/V.

Post Office: Pl. d'Espanya (☎938 94 12 47). Open M-F 8:30am-2:30pm, Sa 9:30am-1pm. No package pickup Sa. **Postal Code:** 08870.

▛ ACCOMMODATIONS

Accommodations are difficult to find on summer weekends and are expensive, particularly for solo travelers. Be sure to call well in advance for a room (although the nightlife is crazy enough that you may not need a bed of your own).

Hostal R. Parelladas, C. de les Parellades, 11 (☎938 94 08 01; hostalparellades@hotmail.com), 1 block from the beach. The common area has a large terrace and a piano. The 8 cozy, well-kept rooms all have fans; some have balconies. Wi-Fi. Singles €30; doubles with bath €60; triples with bath €75. AmEx/MC/V (but cash preferred). ❷

Hostal Bonaire, C. Bonaire, 31 (☎938 94 53 26; www.bonairehostalsitges.com). 10 rooms 1 block from the beach. Ask for one of the rooms with a terrace overlooking party-prone C. Bonaire. All rooms have TVs; some have A/C. Reception 24hr. Singles in summer €45, in winter €36; doubles €55-65/45-50. MC/V. ❹

Hotel Central Normandie, C. Sant Bartomeu, 20-22 (☎938 94 99 14; www.central-normandie.com). 47 pristine and centrally located rooms. Classy lounge bar with pool table. Bath, A/C, and safe. Breakfast and daily newspaper included. Free internet and Wi-Fi. Singles €50-70; doubles €60-80. MC/V. ❺

Hotel Playa de Oro, C. San Bartomeu 11 (☎938 94 92 57; www.hotelplayadeorositges.com). Don't be scared off by the fish tank and Inquisition-style furniture in the lobby; this hotel's rooms are modern and immaculately kept, with fans and baths with slate tiling. Singles €45-60, with breakfast €50-65; doubles €60-80/70-90. MC/V. ❺

Hotel Liberty and Apartments, C. Illa de Cuba, 45 (☎938 11 08 72; www.hotel-liberty-sitges.com). The friendly, English-speaking owners of this hotel keep their guests feeling pampered. Spotless rooms have baths, A/C, flatscreen TVs, mini-fridges, and kettles with tea and coffee. Large breakfast-brunch included and served in an orchid-filled conservatory. The owners can organize airport pick-up and drop off, wine tastings, and bike tours. Rooms €68-135; penthouse with lounge, kitchen, terrace, and fireplace €90-160. MC/V. ❺

El Xalet, C. Illa de Cuba, 35 (☎938 11 00 70; www.elxalet.com). 24 ornate, flowery, and somewhat aging rooms. All have A/C and baths. Each bath comes with a tub, hairdryer, soaps, and slippers. Breakfast included. Wi-Fi. Singles €40-65; doubles €60-100. MC/V. ❺

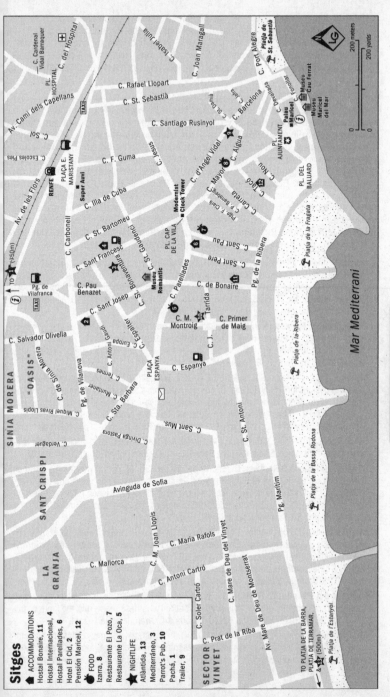

DAYTRIPS

Sitges

ACCOMMODATIONS
Hostal Bonaire, 11
Hostal Internacional, 4
Hostal Parellades, 6
Hotel El Cid, 2
Pensión Maricel, 12

FOOD
Izarra, 8
Restaurante El Pozo, 7
Restaurante La Oca, 5

NIGHTLIFE
Atlàntida, 13
Mediterráneo, 3
Parrot's Pub, 10
Pachá, 1
Trailer, 9

Mar Mediterrani

Hotel El Cid, C. Sant Joesp, 39 (☎938 94 18 42; www.hotelsitges.com). From the train station, take a right, pass the rotunda, and take the 4th left off C. Carbonell. All 77 rooms come with baths, safes, and fans. Small pool, garden, and bar. Breakfast included. Reserve at least a month ahead. Open Apr.-Oct. Singles €48-82; doubles €71-107; triples €103-156. Discounts for stays of 6 nights or longer. MC/V. ❺

◘ FOOD

Many of the restaurants in Sitges are tourist traps, especially on the beachfront. Nevertheless, the food here is world-class. Venture far down C. de les Parellades or on the pleasant side streets to escape the generic scene. If you crave waterfront dining, head to C. Port Alegre, where you'll find fewer crowds and a greater variety of restaurants. Sitges isn't cheap, and you'll generally pay at least €20 for dinner, but expect to get your money's worth. Groceries are available at **Suma,** C. Carbonell, 24, across from the train station. (☎938 94 12 00. Open M-Sa 9am-9pm, Su 10am-2pm. MC/V.) Alternatively, swing by the **Mercat de Sitges,** C. Carbonell, 26, next door to the train station, which has fruit and vegetables, meat, fish, and cheese vendors as well as several cafes and bakeries and even a clothing store. (Open M 8:30am-2pm, Tu 8:30am-2pm and 5:30-8:30pm, W 8:30am-2pm, Th-Sa 8:30am-2pm and 5:30-8:30pm.)

Izarra, C. Major, 24 (☎938 94 73 70), behind the museum area. Basque tapas bar good for a quick fix or a leisurely meal. Ask for a *plato* and grab whatever looks tasty, from Basque seafood concoctions to more traditional Spanish *croquetas*. Tapas €1.40. Entrees €6.50-15. Delicious *sidra* (cider) €1.50. *Menù* available 1:30-4pm and 8:30-11pm. Bar open daily 9am-midnight. MC/V. ❸

El Superpollo: Pollastres a L'Ast, C. San Jose, 8 (☎938 94 57 54). Crackling chickens roast on a spit in the doorway of this no-frills, mouthwatering venue. Quarter chicken €2.20, half €4, whole €8. Also serves french fries and chicken *croquetas*. Open daily 11am-midnight. Delivery 8-11pm. MC/V. ❶

Alfresco Cafè, C. Mayor, 33 (☎938 11 33 07, www.alfrescorestaurante.com). Healthful, gourmet choices found on chalkboard menus that change regularly, with relaxing music and modern, white decor. Check out the mouthwatering desserts in the glass case at the bar. Lunch *menù* €16. Mixed green salmon salad with sesame seeds, caramelized onions, and garnish €14. Free Wi-Fi. Open M and W-F noon-11pm, Sa-Su 10am-11pm. MC/V. ❸

Sol de Roc, C. 1 de Maig, 1. This crepe shop just off the beach will provide a quick fix to your midday or late-night hunger. Sweet €2-3.30. Savory €3-4.50. Open 4pm-midnight. Cash only. ❶

Usaka Sushi Bar & Take-Away, C. Port Alegre, 15 (☎938 94 70 11; www.osakasushibar. com). A sushi bar just off of Platja de Sant Sebastia means ocean views and fresh fish. Rice-paper roll with brie, lettuce, fruit, and a meat of your choosing (chicken, duck, or soft-shell crab) €7.50-11. Rolls €5.75-15. Entrees €10-20. Open Tu-F noon-4pm and 8pm-midnight, Sa-Su noon-midnight. MC/V. ❹

Buenos Aires, C. Port Alegre, 21 (☎938 11 23 44; www.buenosairesgrill.es). Serves Argentina's specialty—meat. Choose your cut, a side, and a sauce, and go home happy. Prime beef *entrecote* €13. Filet €23. Sides (baked potato or vegetables) €3-4. Some seafood options available. Waterfront seating. Open in summer daily noon-12:30am, in winter daily noon-4pm and 8pm-midnight. ❸

La Pizza del Pecado, C. Parellades, 76 (☎938 94 62 65). Cheap slices of deep-dish pizza and delightfully greasy *empanadas* (stuffed pastries) make this the perfect pitstop. Slices €2.30. *Empanadas* €2.30. Salads €4. Open daily 8am-3am. ❶

Ma Maison, C. Bonaire, 28 (☎938 94 60 54). This vast, gay-friendly restaurant has outdoor seating and intricately detailed walls. Mediterranean entrees from a different menu every 2 months. Dinner *menù* €22. Su is *paella* day in winter. Open daily 8:30pm-midnight. MC/V. ❹

👁 SIGHTS

Tourists flock to shop, eat, and drink on the pedestrian walkway **Carrer de les Parellades,** but wise locals stick to the side streets and the peaceful beaches that are located farther up the coast.

PALAU MARICEL. Across the street from the waterfront museums, fragments of Spanish artistic culture unite with *Modernista* ceramics, on C. Fonollar, built in 1910 for the American millionaire Charles Deering. Prepare to be wowed by its sumptuous halls and rooftop terraces. Guided tours are available on some summer nights (July-Sept.) and include a glass of *cava* (sparkling wine) and a castanet concert in the rooftop *claustro* (cloister). (☎ 938 94 03 64. Days and times vary; call ahead for reservations. €10.)

MORELL'S MODERNISTA CLOCK TOWER. As soon as you come into the Plaça at the intersection of C. de les Parellades and C. Sant Francesc, stop and look high up above the Òptica store for this whimsical clock tower. It's easy to miss. (Pl. Cap de la Vila, 2.)

MUSEUMS. Sitges has neatly united its museums under one consortium; they have the same hours and prices, and combo tickets are available. Seven blocks from the clock on C. Fonollar, the **Museu Cau Ferrat** hangs high over the water's edge. Once the home of a driving force of *Modernista* architecture, Santiago Rusiñol (1861-1931), and a meeting place for the young Pablo Picasso and Ramón Casas, the building is a shrine to *Modernista* iron and glass work, sculpture, ceramics, and painting, featuring pieces by El Greco and Picasso. Farther into town, the **Museu Romàntic,** C. Sant Gaudenci, 1, off C. de les Parellades, is an immaculately preserved 19th-century house filled with period pieces like music boxes and two surprising collections: over 400 antique dolls from all over the world and over 25 intricate dioramas of 19th-century life in Sitges. (General info ☎ 938 94 03 64; www.diba.es/museus/sitges.asp. All museums open July-Sept. Tu-Sa 9:30am-2pm and 4-7pm, Su 10am3pm; Oct.-June Tu-Sa 9:30am-2pm and 4-7pm, Su 10am-3pm. Guided tours hourly in summer in Museu Romàntic €3.50, students and seniors €2; combo ticket for several museums €6.50/4.)

🏖 BEACHES

Sitges's sky-blue waters and proximity to Barcelona make it a viable alternative to the crowded sands of Barceloneta and Port Olímpic. At **Platja de la Fragata,** the main beach farthest to the left as you face the sea, sand sculptors create new masterpieces every summer day. By midday, the beaches close to downtown can become almost unbearably crowded; the best beaches, with calmer waters and more open space, like **Platja de la Barra** and **Platja de Terramar,** are a 1-2km walk away (or catch the L2 bus from the train station to the stop next to Hotel Terramar and walk a bit back toward town). If you decide to walk, you will pass several small beaches, including **Platja de la Bassa Rodona,** popular with gay sunbathers. Rocks partly shield these beaches from waves, creating a shallow ocean swimming pool that extends far into the water and is ideal for children. Farther down, the water is bluer and there's more open sand to claim. Sitges is also well known for its peaceful nude beaches. **Platja de l'Home Mort** can be reached by walking past Terramar until you hit a golf course at the end of the sidewalk. Walk on the beach past the golf course, and **l'Home Mort** is in a small cove behind the hills where the train tracks run by the coast. Alternately, flaunt your birthday suit at **Cala Morisca,** on the opposite side of the city, past **Platja d'Aiguadolç.** To reach **Platja del Balmins,** with clear water ideal for snorkeling, walk past the church and **Platja de Sant Sebastià,** go around the first

DAYTRIPS

restaurant you come to, and then take the dirt walkway between the coast and the high white walls of the cemetery. The path will go up and down a slope; the beach is a quiet cove before the port.

NIGHTLIFE

Sitges makes an easy daytrip and an arguably better night-trip. The wild clubs are the perfect escape from the confines of civilization. The places to be at sundown are ◼**Carrer Primer de Maig** (which runs directly from the beach and Pg. de la Ribera) and its continuation, **Carrer Marquès Montroig,** off C. de les Parellades. Bars and clubs line both sides of the small streets, overflowing onto the roads and blasting pop and house music from 10pm to 3am. The clubs here are wide open and accepting, with a vibrant crowd of people, gay and straight. Other popular spots can be found on **Carrer Bonaire** and **Carrer Sant Pau,** but most open only on weekends. The tourist office has copies of **Gay Life** (www.gaylifesitges.com), a map of Sitges including a guide to gay-friendly hotels, restaurants, bars, clubs, and sex shops.

Parrot Terrace, Pl. Industria, 2 or C. Primer de Maig, 2 (www.parrotsclub.com). Sit beneath one of Parrot's fringed, rainbow-colored umbrellas smack in the middle of C. Primer de Maig and ogle the hunks in trunks who walk by. Open daily 10am-3pm and 5pm-3am. MC/V.

Bar Perfil, C. Espalter, 7 (☎656 37 67 91). Located ½ block from C. Sant Francesc, this music bar attracts mainly gay locals and is well-known as an "after" on W. Open in summer daily 10:30pm-3:30am. MC/V.

Atlàntida, Platja les Coves (☎934 53 05 82; www.clubatlantida.com). It's about 3km from the city, and buses run from the Calipolis Hotel. On busier nights they may stop a 10min. walk from the club. For a crowded, sweaty, and shirtless "disco-beach" scene, check out this club. Tu gay night (www.gaybeachparty.com). Cover €10-20. Open Tu-Su midnight-6am. MC/V.

Trailer, C. Àngel Vidal, 36 (☎693 55 94 40; www.trailerdisco.com). Gay-friendly cafe-club. W and Su foam parties. Th dark room and strippers. Cover €10-20 with drink. Invitation flyer grants free admission. Open in summer daily 1-6am; in winter only F, Sa, and holidays. MC/V.

Organic, C. Bonaire, 15 (www.theorganicdanceclub.com). Men and boys come here to dance *au naturel* (well, almost). W latest hits. Th singles night. F 50/50: pants or top, you choose. Cover €10-15. Look for flyers to get in for free; sign up for the VIP guest list online and always get in free before 3:30am. Open in summer daily 2:30am-6am, in winter Sa 2:30am-6am. MC/V.

FESTIVALS

When celebrating holidays, Sitges pushes the boundaries of style and spares no extravagance.

Carnaval, in late Febr. or March. A preparation for fasting during the first week of Lent. Spaniards crash the town for a frenzy of parades, dancing, costumes, and vats of alcohol. Sa and Tu nights are the wildest.

Rallye de Coches de Época, in late March. An antique-car race from Barcelona to Sitges.

Festa de Corpus Cristi, in late May or early June. Townspeople collaborate to create intricate carpets of fresh flowers in the **Concurs de Catifes de Flors.**

Orgullo, in late June. The parties get even wilder than usual during this gay pride week.

Festival Sitges Jazz Internacional, in July or Aug. Part of the larger Sitges Music Festival.

Festa Major, Aug. 21-27. In honor of the town's patron saint, Bartolomé. Watch *papier-mâché* dragons, devils, and giants dance in the streets. Fireworks on Aug. 23.

Festa de la Verema, in Sept. Competitors tread on fresh grapes on the beach for the annual or grape harvest.

Festivitat de Santa Tecla, Sept. 22-23. Rock music, jazz, theater, movies, parties, and sports.

Festival Internacional de Cinema de Catalunya, in Oct. This film festival is perhaps Sitges's biggest event.

COSTA BRAVA   ☎975

Skirting the Mediterranean Sea from Barcelona to the French border, the Costa Brava's cliffs and beaches draw throngs of European visitors—especially French—in July and August. Early June and late September can be remarkably peaceful; the water is warm and the beaches are much less crowded. In winter, the "Wild Coast" lives up to its name, as fierce winds batter quiet, practically empty beach towns. These rocky shores have long attracted romantics and artists like Marc Chagall and Salvador Dalí, a Costa Brava native. No wonder, then, that the Costa Brava is so distinctively Catalan—this is a region that prides itself on its history and on the architectural and artistic treasures it holds. Among these are Dalí's house in Port Lligat and his museum in Figueres. Certain towns have survived the summer-tourist onslaught better than others (Cadaqués has fared well), but there are still clear waters and pine-covered cliffs almost everywhere you turn.

TOSSA DE MAR   ☎972

With 12th-century medieval ruins abutting long stretches of beach, Tossa de Mar (pop. 5893) has been a magnet for artists and romantics since French artist Marc Chagall fell in love with it in 1934. Shortly thereafter, in 1951, actress Ava Gardner fell for Spanish bullfighter Mario Cabrera during the filming of *The Flying Dutchman* here, much to the chagrin of her then-husband, Frank Sinatra. Like many coastal towns, Tossa suffers from the blemishes of tourism, but the beaches, Vila Vella (old quarter), and good Catalan food leave no doubt as to why Chagall called Tossa "blue paradise."

DAYTRIP

▐ TRANSPORTATION

Buses: In Tossa de Mar, the bus station is on Av. Pelegrí at Pl. de les Nacions Sense Estat. Ticket booth open daily 7:15am-12:15pm and 2:30-7:45pm. **Sarfa buses** (☎972 34 09 03; www.sarfa.com). To: **Barcelona** (80min., 18 per day 7:30am-11:30pm, €11); **Girona** (1hr., 10:30am and 7pm, €4.901); **Aeroport Girona** (1hr., June 25-Aug. 31 11:25am and 3:40pm, €8). MC/V. **Pujol** (☎972 34 03 36) takes the scenic route to **Lloret del Mar** (20min.; June-Aug. every 30min. 8am-9:10pm; Sept.-May every hr. 7:40am-8:40pm; €1.40).

Boats: Slow service to towns and otherwise inaccessible *cales* (coves) along the coast, including Lloret and Sant Feliu. **Viajes Marítimos** (☎972 36 90 95; www.viajesmaritimos.com) and **DofiJet Boats** (☎937 61 00 58 or 972 37 19 39; www.dofijetboats.com) depart daily every hr. 9:40am-5:40pm (€15-28). 30min. to Lloret; 1hr. to Blanes. Buy tickets and board on Pg. de Mar, on the beach in front of the first-aid stand. **Fondo Cristal** (☎972 34 22 29; www.fondocristal.com) and **Magic Vision** (☎972 34 16 24; www.magicvision.com) provide glass-bottom boat tours from the right-hand side of the beach.

Car Rental: Viajes Tramontana, Av. Costa Brava, 23 (☎972 34 28 29). Rentals provided by **Olimpia** and **SACAR.** 23+. Credit card, driver's license, and passport required. From €44 per day. Open daily June-Aug. 9am-2pm and 4-9pm; in spring and fall 10am-1pm and 4-7pm. **Viajes Internacional,** C. Peixaterias, 1 (☎972 34 02 41). AmEx/MC/V.

Taxis: (☎972 34 05 49), outside the bus station, in front of Edifici La Nau.

⚔🛈 ORIENTATION AND PRACTICAL INFORMATION

Buses arrive at **Plaça de les Nacions Sense Estat,** where Avinguda del Pelegrí and Avinguda Ferran Agulló meet; the town slopes down to the waterfront. From the station, make a right onto Av. del Pelegrí, then a left onto C. La Guardia. The street narrows, curving around to become C. Socors and then **Carrer Portal;** any street downhill to the left will lead to the beach, while staying on C. Portal will take you to the old quarter, known as the **Vila Vella** (5min.). Running along Tossa's main beach, the **Platja Gran,** is the hyper-touristy **Passeig del Mar.**

Tourist Office: Av. del Pelegrí, 25 (☎972 34 01 08; www.infotossa.com), by the bus terminal at Av. Ferran Agulló and Av. del Pelegrí. Hiking info and a posted schedule of upcoming events. Weekend guided hikes and walks (usually Sa-Su 9am). English spoken. Open June-Sept. M-Sa 9am-9pm, Su and holidays 10am-2pm and 5-8pm; Oct. and Apr.-May M-Sa 10am-2pm and 4-8pm; Nov.-Mar. M-Sa 10am-2pm and 5-8pm. **Branch,** Av. Palma, right on Platja Gran. Open June-Sept. daily 10am-2pm and 4-8pm; Oct. and Apr.-May Tu-Su 10:30am-1:30pm and 4-7pm.

Bank: Banco Santander Central Hispano, Av. Ferran Agulló, 2 (☎902 24 24 24). **ATM** on the street. Open June-Sept. M-F 8:30am-2pm; Oct.-May M-F 8:30am2pm and Sa 8:30am-1pm.

Police: Municipal Police, Av. del Pelegrí, 14 (☎972 34 01 35). English spoken.

Pharmacy: Farmàcia Castelló, Av. Ferran Agulló, 12 (☎972 34 13 03). Open July-Sept. daily 9:30am-1:30pm and 4:30-9pm; Oct.-June daily 9:30am-1:30pm and 4:30-8pm.

Medical Services: Casa del Mar, Av. de Catalunya (☎972 34 18 28). Primary care and immediate attention. The nearest hospital is in **Blanes,** 30min. south.

Internet Access: Ciberlocutori Karabila, C. Maria Auxiliadora, 13 (☎972 34 31 97). €0.50 per 15min. Fax and printing. Open daily 10:30am-midnight. **Cyberstar,** C. Nou, 1 (☎660 12 60 29). €0.30 per 20min., with a €1 minimum. Fax, pre-paid minutes for your mobile and printing. Open daily 10:30am-2:30pm and 3:30pm-midnight. **Tossa Bar Playa,** C. Socors, 6. €0.50 per 10min. Open daily July-Aug. 9:30am-10pm; Sept. and May-June 9:30am-7pm.

Post Office: C. María Auxiliadora, 4 (☎972 34 04 57), down Av. del Pelegrí from the tourist office. Open M-F 8:30am-2:30pm, Sa 9:30am-1pm. **Postal Code:** 17320.

🏠🏕 ACCOMMODATIONS AND CAMPING

Tossa de Mar is a seasonal town; many accommodations, restaurants, and bars are open only from May to October.

🛏 **Fonda Lluna,** C. Roquetes, 20 (☎972 34 03 65; www.fondalluna.com). From Pg. del Mar, turn right onto C. Peixeteries, veer left onto C. Estolt, walk uphill, and make a left on C. Roquetes. Tidy rooms sport summery prints and come with baths, roof access, and sweeping views. Breakfast included. Free internet and Wi-Fi. Book ahead in summer. Regular rooms June-July €22, Aug. €26, Sept.-May €20. With lunch and dinner €40/40/36. MC/V. ❶

L'Hostalet de Tossa, Pl. de l'Església, 3 (☎972 34 18 53; www.hostalettossa. com), in front of the Església de Sant Vicenç. 32 hotel-quality doubles with baths; some with balconies, TVs, and fans. Foosball and pool tables (games €1). Breakfast included. High-season singles €40-51; doubles €77-82. Low-season singles €36-38; doubles €61-65. MC/V. ❹

Camping Can Martí (☎972 34 08 51; www.campingcanmarti.net), at the end of Rambla Pau Casals, off Av. Ferran Agulló. A popular campground near a wildlife reserve.

Hot showers, telephones, pool, restaurant, and a small store. High season tents €9 per person; €5 per car; €6 per child. Low season tents €6;4;4. MC/V. ❶

FOOD

Most restaurants in Tossa specialize in seafood and have reasonably priced *menús*, but the best food and ambience is found in the old quarter. For groceries, head to **Can Palou,** C. La Guardia, 25.

La Lluna, C. Abat Oliva, 10 (☎972 34 25 23). Follow the stairs down from Far Rocafar, or go through the castle's stone gate, make a right, and keep climbing. Flavorful Catalan specialties served in the coziest of dining rooms or on the flower-filled terraces. Whet your appetite with one of the fruit *pâtés,* from the mountain region of Catalunya (€4.30), and follow with a large farmer's bread toast covered in caramelized onion, artichoke, mushroom, asparagus, and melted brie (€6.70). Finish with the *crema catalana* (€3.70). Tapas €1.40-9.40. Open in summer daily 11am-4pm and 6-11:30pm; late Sept.-June M and W-Su 11am-4pm and 6-11:30pm. MC/V. ❶

6'9, C. Nou, 6 (☎972 34 14 34). Locals rave about this fusion restaurant, where the chef mixes traditional Catalan and modern culinary styles. Set back from the bustle, 6'9 is clean and lit by lamps. The restaurant's name is a pun—"nou" means nine in Catalan, and the restaurant is located at #6. *Menú* €13, with over 30 dishes to choose from. Open daily 1-3:15pm and 7:30-10:15pm. MC/V. ❸

Restaurant Bar Marina, C. Tarull, 6 (☎972 34 07 57). Follow the signs to Plaça Esglesia; it's to the right of the church. Tossa is chock-full of overpriced restaurants that cater to tourists; this is one of the cheapest. Green-and-white checkered tablecloths and decent food. Lunch *menù* €10. Mixed *paella* €9.50. MC/V. ❷

SIGHTS AND BEACHES

CENTRE D'INTERPRETACIÓ DELS FARS DE LA MEDITERRÀNIA. Inside the walled fortress of the Vila Vella, an escalating spiral of medieval alleys and steep stairways lead all the way to a picture-perfect view of the city and the surrounding *cales* (small coves), as well as this recently opened museum, where an audio-visual exhibit captures the glory and the drama of lighthouse construction and maintenance. (☎972 34 33 59. Open June-Aug. 10am-8pm; Sept.-May 10am-6pm. €3, students €2, under 12 free.)

MUSEU MUNICIPAL. This museum is located at the tiny Pl. Pintor J. Roig y Soler and housed in the 14th-century Villa dels Ametllers. The museum has a collection of astonishingly well-preserved Roman mosaics dating from the AD fourth to fifth centuries, as well as 1920s and 30s Modern art. The room dedicated to Marc Chagall holds *El violinista celest,* one of his only remaining works in Spain, as well as letters he wrote to the mayor of Tossa. (☎972 34 07 09. Open June-Aug. M and Su 10am-2pm and 4-8pm, Tu-Sa 10am-8pm; Sept.-May Tu-Sa 10am-2pm and 4-6pm, Su 10am-2pm. €3, students €2.)

VILA VELLA RAMPARTS. Tossa del Mar's Vila Vella is the sole remaining fortified medieval town on the Catalan coast. The old town's distinctive stone buildings are, for the most part, 14th- to 18th-century restorations of what were originally 12th-century buildings. The perimeter walls and battlements, however, are by and large unchanged. Of the four original 12th-century towers, three—the **Joanas Tower** (overlooking the bay), the **Clock Tower** (at the entrance to the parade ground), and the **Codolar Tower** (overlooking Codolar Beach)—remain intact. The fourth tower was replaced by the present-day lighthouse. (*Plaça de l'Esglesia. Free.*)

PARISH CHURCH OF SANT VICENC. This church was built between 1755 and 1776, at a time when the congregation had outgrown the 15th-century church in Vila Vella. Built in a Neo-Classical style, the church was originally decorated with Baroque altars and images; unfortunately, most of these disappeared during the Spanish Civil War. Since then, the paint work has been restored and the church continues to serve parishioners. *(Placa de l'Esglesia. Free.)*

BEACHES. Tossa's main beach, surrounded by cliffs and the Vila Vella, draws the majority of beachgoers. To escape the crowds, visit some of the neighboring coves, accessible by foot. The tiny ▓**Es Codolar** rests under the tower of Vila Vella, hugged by wooded cliffs.

▓ NIGHTLIFE

Bars line the narrow streets near the old quarter, packed closely together, so you can stroll down C. Portal and Pg. del Mar and take your pick.

Mar i Cel, C. Estolt, 4 (☎655 83 43 50). If you're in the mood for some *Modernista*-inspired decor and want to schmooze with a younger, local crowd, this place—complete with brightly colored mosaic tiles and billiard tables—is just for you. Pool €1.50 per game. Beer €2.50. Open *Semana Santa* to Nov. daily 9:30pm-3:30am; Dec. to *Semana Santa* F-Sa 9:30pm-3:30am. Cash only.

Bar La Pirata, C. Portal, 32 (☎972 34 14 43). Don an eye patch to blend in at this small establishment and its companion bar **Piratín,** C. Portal, 30, with ship-worthy skull and crossbones decor inside and a tranquil view from tables overlooking the sea below at ▓**Es Codolar.** House sangria €4. Open May-Sept. daily 11am-3am. Cash only.

Bar del Far del Mar. If you don't mind a bit of an uphill walk, then check out this new place, nestled romantically at the foot of the functioning lighthouse on the peak of the Vila Vella. Tart mojitos and a sweet, sweeping view. Mixed drinks €6. Appetizers €2.10-19. Open June-Sept. daily 10am-1am; Oct.-May Tu-Su 10am-6pm. Cash only.

Far Rocamar Bar i Disco, C. Es Cars, 5 (☎972 34 35 56; www.farrocamar.com). This new bar, right next to La Pirata, has a malachite countertop, green lighting, and a monopoly on the Vila Vella disco scene. Mixed drinks €6-7. Open in summer daily noon-2:30am. Disco open 10pm-6am, in winter F-Sa 10pm-6am. AmEx/MC/V.

CALELLA DE PALAFRUGELL

Calella de Palafrugell's beautiful stretches of small beaches and rocky coves draw vacationers to bask in the Mediterranean sunlight and admire the boat-filled bay. Though locals refer to it simply as "Calella," it is not to be confused with the town of Calella on the Costa del Maresme, nor with the nearby Palafrugell, a 15-minute bus ride from Calella de Palafrugell.

▓▓ TRANSPORTATION AND PRACTICAL INFORMATION. Sarfa buses run from Barcelona to Palafrugell (2½hr; Sept.-June 7-8 per day, July-Aug. 14 per day; €16) and from Palafrugell to Calella de Palafrugell and Llafranc (15-20min.; July-Aug. 24 per day, Sept. and June 12-16 per day, Oct.-May 4-5 per day 7:40am-4pm; €1.40). For **taxi** service, call **Rádio Taxi** (☎972 61 00 00) or **Taxis Europa** (☎639 13 26 33); both operate 24hr. A taxi from Palafrugell to Calella de Palafrugell should cost around €12. The Calella de Palafrugell **tourist office** is located at C. de las Voltes, 4. (☎972 61 44 75. Open daily June 10am-1pm and 5-8pm; July-Aug. 10am-8pm.) The **hospital, CAP Alsina i Bofill,** is in Palafrugell on C. d'Angel Guimerá, 6 (☎972 61 06 07). **Internet** access is available at **Pizzeria La Chispita** and **Vent del Mar** (see **Food,** p. 207). Both charge €1 per 15min. The **post**

office is on Pl. de las Escoles. (Open M-F 9am-11:30am, Sa 9:30-11am.) **Postal Code** (Palafrugell): 17200.

▐▐ ACCOMMODATIONS AND FOOD. Hotel prices in Calella de Palafrugell range from expensive to outrageous—many budget travelers choose to stay in neighboring Llafranc or inland at Palafrugell proper, which both offer beds at more reasonable rates. **The Hotel Mediterrani ❺,** C. Francesc Estrabau, 40, is (believe it or not) one of the most reasonable in Calella de Palafrugell. More affordable rooms are simply furnished, and a comfortable lounge area and dining room feature beautiful views of the bay (as do the most expensive rooms). (May-Oct. ☎972 61 45 00, Nov.-Apr. 932 09 91 13; www.hotelmediterrani.com. All rooms have private baths and TVs. Breakfast included. Singles €55-70; doubles €70-138, with view €104-150. MC/V.) **Hotel Port Bo ❺,** C. August Pi y Sanyer, 6, compensates for a more obstructed view of the sea by offering spotless rooms with TVs, A/C, and balconies, as well as a pool. (☎972 61 49 62 or 972 61 50 86; www.hotelportbo.com. Free Wi-Fi and internet. Singles €58-72 low season, in high season €81-88; doubles €76-94/€110-120. MC/V.) Ishmael and Queequeg pitch their tents at **Moby Dick ❶,** C. Costa Verda, 16-28. Look for the white whale made of ship's line to find this convenient campground close to the water. (☎972 61 43 07; www.campingmobydick.com. Reception 9am-9pm. Open Apr.-Sept. €3.40-5.70 per adult, tent, and car; €1.80-3.30 per child. Bungalows €50-99. Cash only.)

At **Restaurant Sol Ixent ❸,** C. dels Canyers, 24, on the right end of the bay facing the water, a modest outdoor patio boasts a magnificent view away from the touristy section of the boardwalk. Fresh salads, seafood, pasta, and rice dishes (including various vegetarian options) run €6.50-18. Try the arugula salad with mixed greens, pears, and shredded Manchego cheese for €8. (☎972 61 50 51. Open daily June-Sept. and Oct.-May Sa-Su 1-11pm. MC/V.) **La Clova ❷,** C. de Codina, 6, offers a reasonably priced mid-day *menú* (€9.90) and even cheaper combination plates (€6.50-10) along with friendly service and a warmly decorated dining room. (☎972 61 56 85. Open daily 1-4pm and 7-10pm. MC/V.) For a quick *bocadillo* (€3.50-4.50) before heading to the shore try **Vent del Mar ❶,** C. Pi Roig, 2, a sunny, laid-back cafe offering combination plates (€10-14). (☎972 61 47 66. Open daily 9-12am. MC/V.) If you've had it with Spanish food and just want a slice of the familiar, **Pizzeria Chispita ❷,** C. del Pintor Joan Serra at C. de Chopitea, will satisfy. (☎972 614 881. Pizzas €7-9. Salads €7. Open from Mar. to mid-Sept. 10:30am-11:30pm. Cash only.)

▐▐ NIGHTLIFE AND FESTIVALS. Nightlife in Calella de Palafrugell consists mostly of pubs that close relatively early. There are some festivals, such as **Festival Jardins de Cap Roig,** a series of concerts in July and August headlined by big-name international artists like James Taylor and Leonard Cohen. (For more information, contact Fundació Caixa de Girona, ☎902 44 77 55 or visit www.caixagirona.com. General admission tickets €25-65.) The **Costa Brava Jazz Festival** also brings music to Calella de Palafrugell in July and August. The **Festa Mayor de Sant Pere** takes place in Calella de Palafrugell at the end of June, honoring the town's patron saint. On the first Saturday of July the **Cantada de Havaneres** is celebrated in Calella de Palafrugell, where hundreds of people gather to hear the *havaneres,* 19th century sea-shanties named after the Cuban city from which they originated. Llafranc holds its **Festa Major de Santa Rosa** with dances and activities around August 30. If you are here the first Saturday of September, check out the **Mercat Boig** ("crazy market") in Pl. del Promontori, where practically anything and everything is sold (but mostly crafts and antiques).

DAYTRIPS

⚠ OUTDOOR ACTIVITIES. For most, a trip to Calella de Palafrugell means a tranquil and picturesque day of tanning, swimming, and eating. For the less lethargic, however, the Camino de Ronda trail extends in both directions following the coastline of Calella up to Llafranc in the north and leading toward the Jardí Botànic de Cap Roig in the south. It's about a 40min. hike from the center of Calella. (☎972 61 45 82. Open June-Sept. 10am-8pm, Oct.-May 10am-8pm; €6.) A free map of the trail and all of Calella de Palafrugell is available at the tourist office. **Poseidon Nemrod Diving,** based on Platja Port Pelegri, offers introductory scuba-diving lessons including a half-hour dive (€50; with 2 dives €80). Other more extensive courses (€180-360) are available, and experienced divers can rent equipment and hire guides to explore the underwater creatures amongst the nearby reefs. (☎972 615 345; www.divecalella.com. Open Apr.-Oct.)

GIRONA (GERONA)   ☎972

Modern Girona (pop. 92,000) is Catalan through and through, but it's been almost everything else over the course of history. A Roman *municipium* and then an important medieval center, the "city of four rivers" was an exemplar of the Spanish settlements where Christians, Jews, and a small number of Arabs coexisted in peace. Girona was the home of the renowned *cabalistas de Girona,* a group of 12th-century rabbis credited with early developments in the school of mystic thought called Kabbala. Although Jews were banned from the city in 1492, you can still walk the streets (or, more accurately, the staircases) of El Call, the old Jewish quarter. In more recent years, the *Ajuntament* of Gerona returned to the city's roots by changing its name back to the original Catalan—Girona—in 1980. Now, this many-splendored metropolis enjoys international recognition as a cyclist's paradise—former Tour de France hero Lance Armstrong called the city home during training season.

▐ TRANSPORTATION

Flights: Aeropuerto de Girona-Costa Brava, Termino Municipal de Vilobi d'Onyar (☎972 18 67 08; www.aena.es, choose Girona from the dropdown menu), 12km from the city, is small and services a few regular flights on **Iberia** (☎902 40 05 00; www.iberia.com) and **Ryanair** (☎ 807 38 38 11; www.ryanair.com). **Barcelona Bus** (☎902 36 15 50; www.barcelonabus.com) runs shuttles from Girona, Barcelona, and the Costa Brava to the airport (from the Girona bus station every hr. 4am-midnight, return every hr. 4:30am-12:30am, €2; from Barcelona 23 per day 3:45am-7:30pm, return 28 per day 8:30am-12:15am, €12). A taxi to the airport from Girona's old city costs about €20-25, at night €30.

Trains: RENFE (☎902 24 02 02; www.renfe.es), in Pl. d'Espanya to the southwest of the city center. Open M-Sa 5:45am-11pm, Su 6:30am-11pm, info 6:30am-10pm. Trains to: **Barcelona** (1¼-1½hr.; M-F 23 per day 6:11am-9:28pm, Sa-Su 18 per day; €6.20-€7.10), change at Maçanet for coastal train; **Figueres** (30-40min.; M-F 22 per day 7:16am-9:39pm, Sa 13 per day 8:20am-9:39pm, Su 16 per day 8:20am-10:13pm; €2.80-€3.10) via **Flaçà** (15min., €1.50-€1.70); **Milan, ITA** (11hr.; Tu, Th, Su 10:15pm; €168, under 26, over 60, and students with ISIC €118); **Paris, FRA** (10½hr.; 10:17pm; €175, under 26, over 60, and students with ISIC €123); **Zurich, CHE** (13hr.; Tu, Th, Sun 9:25pm; €170, under 26, over 60 and students with ISIC €119).

Buses: Next to train station, 5min. from city center. **Sarfa** (☎972 20 17 96). Info open M-F 7:30am-8:30pm, Sa-Su 8:45am-noon and 4:30-8:30pm. Buses to: **Cadaqués** (2hr.; Sept.-June, M-F 6:30pm, July-Sept. daily 9am, 6:30pm; €9.30); **Palafrugell** (1hr.; M-F 16 per day 7am-8:45pm, Sa-Su 11 per day; €5.30) for connections to **Calella** and **Llafranc; Tossa de Mar** (40min.; Sept.-June M-F 6:30pm, July-Aug. 10:30am, 7pm; €5.20). **Teisa** (☎972 20 02 75; www.teisa-bus.com) info open July-Aug. M-F 7:45am-8:30pm, Sa 8:45-11am, Su 8:45am-12:15pm and 4:45-5:30pm; Sept.-June M-F 7:45am-8:30pm, Sa 8:45am-11am, Su 4:45-5:30pm. Buses to: **Lérida** (2½hr.; M-F 3 per day 7:30am-7:15pm, Sa-Su 8:30am, 5:30pm; €22); **Ripoll** (2hr.; M-F 7 per day 7:15am-8:15pm, Sa-Su 2 per day; €11). **Barcelona Bus** (☎972 20 24 32; www.barcelonabus.com). Express buses to **Barcelona** (1¼hr.; M-F 5 per day 7am-7:15pm, Sa-Su 3 per day; €11) and **Figueres** (50min.; M-F 5 per day 8:05am-8:20pm, Sa 2 per day, Su 3 per day; €4.70)

◾⬛ ORIENTATION AND PRACTICAL INFORMATION

The Riu Onyar divides the city into old and new sections. Eleven bridges, mostly pedestrian, connect the two banks. The **Pont de Pedra** leads into the **Barri Vell** (old quarter) by way of C. dels Ciutadans, one block off the bridge, which turns into C. Bonaventura Carreras i Peralta and then C. Força, leading to the cathedral and **El Call,** the historic Jewish neighborhood. The **train** and **bus terminals** are situated off **Calle Barcelona** in the new town. To get to the old city from a bus, walk through the terminal, across the parking lot and Pl. Espanya, turn left onto C. Barcelona, and go straight (a bit more than 3 blocks) until you reach a plaça. Bear right on the plaça and right again onto the small C. Nou; it will take you across Pont de Pedra to the historic area. The iron bridge to the right was built by the Eiffel Company, a modest Parisian firm.

Tourist Offices: Rambla de la Llibertat, 1 (☎972 22 65 75; www.ajuntament.gi/turisme), by Pont de Pedra in the old town. English spoken. Pick up the biweekly *La Guia,* which is in Catalan, but has event listings. Also has listings of hotels, hostels, pharmacies, art galleries, theaters, libraries, and classes with addresses and phone numbers. Open M-F 8am-8pm, Sa 8am-2pm and 4-8pm, Su and holidays 9am-2pm. The **Punt de Benvinguda** office, C. Berenguer Carnicer, 3 (☎972 21 16 78) is 7 blocks up on the other side of the river. Open M-Tu 9am-5pm, W-Sa 9am-8pm, Su 9am-2pm.

Police: Policia Municipal, C. Bacià, 4 (☎972 41 90 92). To report theft, contact the **Mossos d'Esquadra,** C. Vista Alegre (☎972 18 16 00).

Hospital: Hospital de Girona "Josep Trueta," Av. França, s/n (☎972 94 02 00).

Internet Access: Alberg de Joventut Cerverí de Girona (HI), C. dels Ciutadans, 9 (☎972 21 80 03; www.xanascat.net; alberg_girona@tujuca.com). This youth hostel offers internet access to non-guests. €1 per hr. Open to public 9am-10pm. The cafe **El Sol,** Pl. del Vi, 9 (☎972 22 08 92) also has several computers. €0.50 per 10min. Open daily 7am-11pm.

Post Office: Av. Ramón Folch, 2 (☎902 19 71 97), in the brick building with the golden dome. Open M-F 8:30am-8:30pm, Sa 9:30am-2pm. **Postal Code:** 17001.

▌ ACCOMMODATIONS

There are enough hostels in Girona to find a room without much trouble, but some are no less expensive than the hotels in the new city. The best locations are within a couple of blocks of the river on either bank. If you have your heart set on particular digs, call ahead in the summer.

▨ **Pensión Residència Bellmirall,** C. Bellmirall, 3 (☎972 20 40 09; bellmirall1@telefonica.net). To your right when facing the Museu d'Art. Pricey but well worth it. 7 delightful rooms, most with private bath, in a 14th-century house by the main cathedral—complete immersion in the history and charm of Girona. Common area has TV. Breakfast served on the sunny and flower-filled garden patio. Free Wi-Fi. Open Mar.-Sept. Singles €40; doubles €75-85; triples €95. Reserve well in advance. Cash only. ❹

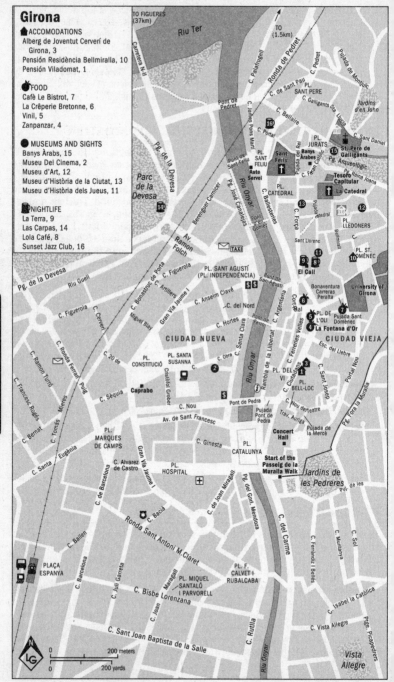

Girona

ACCOMODATIONS
Alberg de Joventut Cerverí de
  Girona, 3
Pensión Residència Bellmiralla, 10
Pensión Viladomat, 1

FOOD
Cafè Le Bistrot, 7
La Crêperie Bretonne, 6
Vinil, 5
Zanpanzar, 4

MUSEUMS AND SIGHTS
Banys Àrabs, 15
Museu Del Cinema, 2
Museu d'Art, 12
Museu d'Història de la Ciutat, 13
Museu d'Història dels Jueus, 11

NIGHTLIFE
La Terra, 9
Las Carpas, 14
Lola Café, 8
Sunset Jazz Club, 16

Pensión Viladomat, C. Ciutadans, 5 (☎972 20 31 76). The rooms are well-decorated, the bathrooms are spotless, and the price is right. At the center of midday action but quiet at night. All rooms have heaters and TVs; many have balconies and large windows. Singles with shared bath €23; doubles €42, with bath €62; triples with bath €85. Cash only. ❶

Alberg de Joventut Cerverí de Girona (HI), C. dels Ciutadans, 9 (☎972 21 80 03; www.xanascat.net). Plain walls and metal bunks, soldier, but good location and prices. Common sitting rooms have TVs, board games, and videos. Breakfast included; dinner €6.20-7.40; full board €11-14. Lockers included; bring your own lock or buy one (€5). Linens included. Towels €5. Laundry: wash €2.50, dry €1.50. Internet €1 per hr. Bike rental €6 per 3hr., €15 per day. Check-in after 3:30pm, but free luggage storage. Dorms July-Sept. €19-22, Oct.-June €15-18. Non-HI members €2 more. Higher rates for 26+. AmEx/MC/V. ❶

🍴 FOOD

Girona boasts exciting local cuisine, both savory and sweet. Local specialties are *botifarra dolça* (sweet sausage made with pork, lemon, cinnamon, and sugar) and *xuixo* (sugar-sprinkled pastries filled with cream). A good place to eat on the cheap is **Calle Cort-Reial** at the top of C. Argenteria. **Pl. de la Independència,** Girona's restaurant hub, offers both high-end and cheaper options, most of which have tables on the square. Join locals at the covered **mercat municipal** located in Pl. Salvador Espriu. (From the tourist office facing Pont de Pedra, walk left past Pl. Cataluña and cross the river at Pont de l'Areny. ☎972 20 19 00. Open M-Sa 6am-2pm. Cash only.) Get your **groceries** at **Caprabo,** C. Sèquia, 9, a block off the Gran Viade Jaume I. (☎972 21 45 16. Open July-Aug. M-Sa 9am-9pm, Sept.-June 9am-2pm and 5-9pm. MC/V.)

Cafè Le Bistrot, Pjda. Sant Domènec, 4 (☎972 21 88 03). Eat on the stone steps of the Convent de Sant Domènec with a view of the old city below, or inside amid Art Nouveau posters. Specialty creations are the *pizzas de pagès* (farmer's bread pizzas; €6-8) made on typical Catalan round bread. Lunch *menú* M-F €14, Sa-Su €17-20. Open daily 1-4pm and 8pm-1am. MC/V. ❸

La Crêperie Bretonne, C. Cort-Reial, 14 (☎972 21 81 20; www.creperiebretonne.com). Girona is 1000km from Paris, but don't tell the diners at this popular crepe joint, which brings a youthful atmosphere and tasty eats to the historic district. The food is cooked in a small bus bound for the town of Cerbère, but you can eat it on the cozy alley terrace or in the train-themed interior while it's fresh (never reheated). Offers both sweet and savory crepes with unique fillings like goat cheese, walnut and raisins or onion, potato and codfish (€2.80-8.60). Equally unusual salads €9-10. Open M-F 1-4pm and 8-midnight, Sa-Su 1pm-midnight. MC/V. ❷

Vinil, C. Cort Reial, 17 (☎972 21 64 40). If you took Vinil's mantra, *"som el que mengem,"* (you are what you eat) to heart, then you'd be a caramelized goat cheese salad with apple, dried fruit, and onion, or a pumpkin and cabbage risotto. Green chairs and walls make for a funky decor to match the eclectic ingredients. Salads and pastas €8-11. Fish and meat entrees €9-20. Open M and W-Su noon-5pm and 7pm-1am, Tu 7pm-1am. MC/V. ❸

Zanpanzar, C. Cort Reial, 10-12 (☎972 21 28 43). The simply decorated interior houses a selection of extraordinary tapas. The array of *montaditos* (€1.50) boast toppings like quail egg, blueberry relish, and *morcilla,* a Spanish version of blood sausage stuffed with rice and spices. Look on the menu for I-dare-you tapas like beef cheeks with *foie gras* (€6.50) and peppers stuffed with oxtail (€3.80). Beer €1.80, *sidra* €1.40. Open M-W 7pm-midnight, Th-F 7pm-1am, Sa 12:30-4pm and 7pm-1am, Su 12:30-4pm and 7pm-midnight. MC/V. ❷

ⓒ SIGHTS

Start your self-guided historical tour of the city at the **Pont de Pedra** and turn left down the tree-lined **Rambla de la Llibertat.** Continue on C. Argenteria, bearing right across C. Cort-Reial. C. Força begins on the left up a flight of stairs.

▧EL CALL. The part of the old town around C. Força and C. Sant Llorenç was once the center of Girona's thriving medieval Jewish community ("call" comes from *kahal,* Hebrew for "community"). Under Rabbi Moshe Ben Nahman, the 13th century Call in Girona was pivotal in the development and spread of the Jewish mystical discipline of the Kabbalah. In the 14th century, hostilities began to mount against the Jewish community in Spain, and in 1492, all Jews who had not been converted or killed were forced into exile. In present day Girona, however, Jewish history and culture are duly commemorated. The site of the last synagogue in Girona now serves as the Centre Bonastruc Ça Porta. The center includes the prominent **Museu d'Història dels Jueus,** which details Jewish life, culture, and belief in the Call, and traces their persecution and flight after the Inquisition. Be sure to lose yourself (quite literally) in the narrow, winding stone staircases that surround the museum. *(C. Força, 8, halfway up the hill. ☎ 972 21 67 61; ajgirona.org/call. Center and museum open June-Oct. M-Sa 10am-8pm, Su 10am-3pm; Nov.-May M-Sa 10am-6pm, Su 10am-3pm. Wheelchair-accessible. Museum €2, students and over 65 €1.50, under 16 free. Audioguides €4. 2hr. guided walking tours of the Barri Vell, including El Call, are available through Ajuntament de Girona i Patronat Call de Girona (☎ 972 21 16 78; puntb@girona-net.com); tours leave from C. Berenguer Carnicer, 3. Tours March 18-Nov. 18 Tu-Su at 10:30am; €10, under 14 free. Tour price includes museum entrance. Offered in English and Spanish.)*

CATHEDRAL COMPLEX. The breathtaking Gothic **Catedral de Girona** rises 90 steps from the *plaça.* Its tower, along with that of **Sant Feliu,** defines the Girona skyline. The **Torre de Charlemany** and **cloister** are the only structures left from the 11th and 12th centuries; the rest of the building dates from the 14th-17th centuries. Look at the keystone of the world's widest Gothic **nave** (23m); the builders eschewed solid stone in favor of a hollow rock with a wood "cork" for fear of weighing the structure down and collapsing it. A door on the left leads to the trapezoidal cloister and the **Tresor Capitular** museum, which holds some of Girona's most precious paintings, sculptures, and decorated Bibles. Its most famous piece is the **Tapis de la Creació,** an 11th-century tapestry depicting the events of Genesis. *(Museum ☎ 972 21 44 26; www.catedraldegirona.com. Open Apr.-Oct. M-F 4:30-8pm, Sa 10am-4:30pm, Su 2-8pm; Nov.-Mar. M-F 10am-7pm, Sa 4:30-7pm, Su 10am-2pm. Wheelchair-accessible with advance notice. Cathedral, tresor, and cloister €5, students and over 65 €3, ages 7-16 €1.20, under 7 free. Su free.)*

SCENIC WALKS. Girona's renowned **▧Passeig de la Muralla,** a 2km trail along the fortified walls of the old city, can be accessed at several points: at the **Jardins de la Francesa** (behind the cathedral), the **Jardins d'Alemanys** (behind the Museu d'Art), and the main entrance at the bottom of the Rambla in Pl. de la Marvà. *(Open daily 8am-10pm.)* Behind the St. Pere de Galligants church (by the Museu d'Arqueologia), you can go up on a *mirador* for great views of the city. Behind the cathedral, the walk coincides with the equally beautiful **Passeig Arqueològic.** This path skirts the northeastern medieval wall and also overlooks the city. For the less athletic, a small green train offers a guided tour (30min.) of the main sights of the old town, including the town hall, cathedral, Església de Sant Feliu, El Call, and the walls. *(Tour leaves in summer daily from the Pont de Pedra every 45min. 10am-1pm and 3-6pm. Less frequently in the winter; check at the tourist office. Available* *in English. €4, children under 10 €3.50.)* Alternatively, relax in the flower-filled Jardins del la Francesa or the shady and tranquil Jardins d'Alemanys.

MUSEU DEL CINEMA. This unusual collection of artifacts, clips, and heavy machinery might be better described as a museum of light-trickery, as over half the museum deals with pre-film forms of illusion and entertainment. The exhibit begins with a five-minute introductory video, which dramatically summarizes the development of optical amusement chronicled by the museum, beginning with Asian shadow puppets and continuing on to the invention of the camera obscura (ninth-12th centuries), the "magic lantern," kinetoscopes, and eventually daguerreotypes, 35mm, Edison, and TV as well as the viewing culture that developed with each advance. Plenty of interactive examples along the way, along with an extensive collection of early camera and film machinery, spice up the exhibits. *(C. Sèquia, 1. ☎ 972 41 27 77; www.museudelcinema.cat. Open May-Sept. Tu-Su 10am-8pm; Oct.-Apr. Tu-F 10am-6pm, Sa 10am-8pm, Su 11am-3pm. Wheelchair-accessible. €4, students and over 65 €2, under 16 free. AmEx/MC/V.)*

🎸 NIGHTLIFE

Nightlife in Girona ranges from finger-snapping coffeehouses to rock bars and crowded *discotecas*. In the summer, the main attraction is **Las Carpas** (the tents), a congregation of outdoor dance floors, bars, and swirling lights in the middle of the **Parc de la Devesa**. The *discotecas* here engage in a symbiotic relationship appropriate to their forest environment, each feeding off of each other's energy and clientele even as they try to blast their music the loudest and sell the most drinks. (Beer €3, mixed drinks €7. Open May-Sept. 15 M-Th and Su 11pm-3:30am, F-Sa 11pm-4:30am.) A trek up C. Pedret will lead to some more options for late-night drinking and dancing, while back in the old quarter you can find a handful of more mellow bars to start the night out.

Lola Café, C. Forca, 7 (☎ 972 22 88 24; www.lola-cafe.com). Super-modern chandeliers counterbalance old, stone walls to create a sophisticated ambience for the snappy, well-dressed crowd. Mixed drinks €7.50. Open daily 11pm-3am. MC/V.

La Platea, C. Fontclara, 4 (☎ 972 41 19 92; www.localplatea.com), next to the Pont d'en Gomez. Flashing neon green stairs, white leather stools, mock-Gothic chandeliers, and pop music to boot. Mixed drinks €8-10. Open Th-Sa midnight-6am.

Siddharta, C. Pedret, 116 (☎ 972 22 04 20). Siddharta specializes in pitchers of Tisane and fruity concoctions with cognac and other liquors. The bar is littered with stone arches, though part of the floor and walls consist solely of gravel and uncarved rocks, which will appeal to your conflicted inner ascetic as you sip fancy drinks. Mixed drinks €7-8; 1½L pitchers €16. Nirvana free. Open daily 8pm-3am. Cash only.

🎊 FESTIVALS

Starting on the second Saturday in May, government-sponsored **Temps de Flors** (www.gironatempsdeflors.net) exhibitions spring up all over the city; local monuments and pedestrian streets swim in blossoms for two whole weeks and the courtyards of Girona's finest old buildings are open to the public (ask for the *"mapa de flors"* from the tourist office). Summer evenings often inspire spontaneous Sardana dancing in the *plaça*. Girona, along with the rest of Catalunya, lights up for the **Focs de Sant Joan** on the night of June 23, featuring fireworks and bonfires. For *Viernes Santo*, the Friday of **Semana Santa**, *Cofrarías*, or church groups, dress up in Old World costumes. Keep an eye out for the men from San Luc decked out in full Roman soldier regalia, including cavalry and weapons. At the end of June, the **Festival de Músiques Religioses del Món** (☎ 972 20 76 34; www.ajuntament.gi/musiquesreligioses) draws choirs and artists from all over the world to perform in the cathedral and on its grand steps, including everything from Tanzanian dance troupes to classical piano recitals. The patron saint, **Sant Narcís,** is celebrated for five days at the end of October, with parades, street-fairs and of course, plenty of fireworks.

FIGUERAS (FIGUERES) ☎972

Sprawling Figueras (pop. 42,000) is functional, not beautiful. Other than the major sights, much of the city has fallen into disrepair. Nevertheless, it is the capital of Alt Empordà county and a major gateway city to France and the rest of Europe. In 1974, the mayor of Figueras asked native Salvador Dalí to donate a painting to an art museum the town was planning. Dalí saw his chance and ran with it, donating an entire museum. The construction of the Teatre-Museu Dalí catapulted the artist to even greater international renown. To this day, Dalí's mind-bending, erotic works lure and entrance a multilingual parade of Surrealism's devotees.

▐▞ TRANSPORTATION AND PRACTICAL INFORMATION

Trains: Pl. de l'Estació (☎902 24 02 02). To **Barcelona** (2hr.; M-F 21 per day, Sa-Su 15 per day; €9-11), **Girona** (30-40min.; M-F 21 per day, Sa-Su 15 per day; €3.10), and **Portbou** (30-40min.; 11 per day; €3.10).

Buses: Buses leave from the **Estació d'Autobusos** (☎972 67 33 54), on the left side of Pl. de l'Estació if your back is to the train station. **Sarfa** (☎972 67 42 98; www.sarfa. com) open 6am-9pm. If closed, buy tickets on the bus. To **Cadaqués** (1hr.; July-Aug. 7 per day 8am-8:30pm, Sept.-June 4 per day; €4.80) and **Palafrugell** (1hr.; Sept.- June M-F 2 per day, July-Aug. 12:15 and 8pm; €6.70). **Barcelona Bus** (www.barcelonabus.com) runs to **Barcelona** (2¼hr.; M-F 4 per day 7:45am-8:15pm, Sa 2 per day 11am-4:15pm, Su 3 per day 7:45am-6:15pm; €16) via **Girona** (1hr., €4.80). Buy tickets on bus, platform 4.

Taxis: Taxis line La Rambla (☎972 50 00 08) and the train station (☎972 50 50 43).

Car Rental: Hertz, Pl. de l'Estació, 9 (☎972 67 02 39). 25+; must have had driver's license for 1 year. All-inclusive rental €46-67 per day. Open M-F 9am-1pm and 4-7pm, Sa 9am-1pm. AmEx/MC/V. **Avis,** Pl. de l'Estació (☎972 51 31 82), in the train station. 23+; credit card only. Rental from €67 per day. Open M-Sa 9am-1:30pm and 4-7pm. AmEx/MC/V.

✦▞ ORIENTATION AND PRACTICAL INFORMATION

From the tip of **Plaça de l'Estació** with your back to the train station, bear left on C. Sant Llàtzer, walk six blocks to C. Nou (the 3rd main road), and take a right to get to Figueras's tree-lined **Rambla.** To reach the **tourist office,** walk all the way up La Rambla and continue on C. Lasauca straight out from the left corner. The blue, all-knowing "i" beckons across the rather treacherous intersection with Avinguda Salvador Dalí.

Tourist Offices: Main Office, Pl. Sol s/n (☎972 50 31 55; www.figueresciutat.com). English spoken. Open July-Aug. M-Sa 9am-9pm, Su 9am-3pm; Sept. M-Sa 9am-9pm; Oct. and Apr.-June M-F 8:30am-3pm and 4:30-8pm, Sa 9:30am-1:30pm and 3:30-6:30pm; Nov.-Mar. M-F 8:30am-3:30pm. 2 additional summer **branches,** in the train station (open July-Sept. 15 M-Sa 9:30am-1:30pm and 4:30-7pm) and in front of the Teatre-Museu Dalí (open July-Sept. 15 M-Sa 10am-2:30pm and 4:30-7pm).

Currency Exchange: Banco Santander Central Hispano, La Rambla, 21. Open M-F 8:30am-2pm, Sa 8:30am-1pm; April-Sept. 8:30am-2pm. **ATMs** on La Rambla.

Police: Av. Salvador Dalí, 107 (☎972 51 01 11). To report a crime, contact the **Mossos d'Esquadra,** C. Ter s/n (☎972 54 18 00).

Hospital: Hospital Comarcal de Figueres, Ronda Rector Arolas s/n (☎972 50 14 00), behind and to the left of the Dalí museum.

Internet Access: Ciber Empordá, C. Empordá, 14, (☎972 67 84 63). €0.30 per 15min., €1.10 per hr. Open daily 10am-10pm. **Café de Nit** offers free **Wi-Fi** to customers (see **Nightlife,** p. 207).

Post Office: C. Santa Llogaia, 60-62 (☎972 50 54 31). Open M-W and F 10am-1:30pm and 4-8pm, Th 10am-8pm, Sa 10am-1:30pm. **Postal Code:** 17600.

ACCOMMODATIONS

Many visitors to Figueras make the journey a daytrip from Barcelona; in spite of this (or perhaps because of it), quality, affordable accommodations are easy to find. Many hostels are on upper floors above bars or restaurants. Others are closer to La Rambla and Carrer Pep Ventura. Inquire at the tourist office about hostels and pensions.

Hostal La Barretina, C. Lasauca, 13 (☎972 67 64 12; www.hostalbarretina.com). Walk up La Rambla to its end and take a left on C. Lasauca; the hostel is a block up on the left. Hotel-like luxury—each room has TV, A/C, heat, and bath. Reception in the restaurant downstairs. Breakfast €3, other meals €10. Internet €2 per hr. Wheelchair-accessible. Reservations recommended. Singles €30; doubles €48. MC/V. ❷

FOOD

The restaurants surrounding **La Rambla** on the small side streets tend to be of higher quality than those near the Teatre-Museu Dalí that serve *paella* to the masses. The extensive outdoor **market** at Pl. del Gra has an amazing fruit and vegetable selection. (Open Tu, Th, Sa 5am-2pm.) At the same square is the supermarket **Caprabo,** Pl. del Gra, s/n, in case you miss the outdoor market. (☎972 50 98 66. Open M-Sa 9am-9pm.)

Cafè Hotel París, La Rambla, 10 (☎972 50 07 13). Everything is natural and home-made, down to the coffee ice cubes for iced coffee. By day, the outdoor patio's wicker chairs attract those seeking the breeze and a chat, while red leather chairs lend the establishment a low-key but sophisticated feel by night. Tasty entrees like macaroni with spinach, bacon, and mushrooms (€6.90) and rabbit with snails and thyme (€6.90). Tapas €2-3.50. Entrees €7-12. *Menú* €13. Open M-F 8:30-11pm, Sa 8:30-11:30pm, Su 9-11pm. MC/V. ❷

Restaurant Hotel Duran, C. Lasauca, 5 (☎972 50 12 50; www.hotelduran.com). Walk up La Rambla to the end and look for C. Lasauca on the left. One of Dalí's haunts. You can eat in the dining room, complete with arches and green chandeliers, where he once held court. Be sure to check out the photos of and menus designed by the famed Surrealist in the hotel lobby. Delicious *canelones* (cannelloni) €10. Appetizers €13-25. Entrees €13-26. *Menú* €18. Open daily 12:45-4pm and 8:30-11pm. AmEx/MC/V. ❹

SIGHTS

TEATRE-MUSEU DALÍ. Welcome to the world of the Surrealist master. This site, the self-proclaimed "largest surrealistic object in the world," held the Figueras's municipal theater before it was destroyed at the end of the Spanish Civil War. Dalí's personal mausoleum/museum/monument is ego worship at its finest. Naughty cartoons, trippy sculptures, a dramatic, traditional tomb, and a pantheon of paintings of Gala, his wife and muse, immerse the audience in his world. Stay alert to the many optical illusions and tricks that pervade the museum, including stereoscopic paintings, holograms, and the portrait of Gala naked at a window which doubles as a depiction of Abraham Lincoln. The collection includes *Soft Self-Portrait with a Slice of Bacon*, *Poetry of America*, *Galarina*, and *Galatea of the Spheres*. A small number of hand-selected works by other artists, including El Greco, Marcel Duchamp, and Modest Urgell, round out the collection. Don't miss the Mae West Room, furnished to create a giant, eerie representation of Dalí's "Photograph of Mae West-cum-Apartment." The museum is large and takes at least an hour to see, regardless of your chosen route. *(Pl. Gala i Salvador Dalí, 5. From La Rambla, take C. Sant Pere 3 blocks up, or just follow the crowds and signs at every street corner. ☎ 972 67 75 00; www.salvador-dali. org. Open July-Sept. daily 9am-7:45pm; Oct. and Mar.-May Tu-Su 9:30am-5:45pm; Nov.-Feb. 10:30am-7:45pm; June daily 9:30am-5:45pm. Last entry 45min. before close. €11, students and seniors €8, groups over 25 €7 per person, under 8 free.)*

MUSEU EMPORDÀ. This collection traces art from the town and region, from Romantic landscapes to works of *Noucentisme* from the turn of the century to contemporary Catalan art. Look for canvases by Modest Cuixart and Ramon Pujol Boira, as well as a few by Tapiés and Dalí. Temporary exhibitions vary widely. "Un Art que Perviu" (2008) showcased sculptures of the female body by Catalan artists, while the 2007 exhibit "Recto-Verso" displayed the backs of famous canvases. *(La Rambla, 2. ☎ 972 50 23 05; www.museuemporda.org. Open Tu-Sa 11am-7pm, Su and holidays 11am-2pm. €2, students €1. Free with entrance to Dalí Museum, temporary exhibitions always free.)*

CASTELL DE SANT FERRAN. A 10-minute walk from the Museu Dalí, this massive 18th-century castle-fortress, built to defend against the French during border disputes, commands a spectacular view of the surrounding countryside and at 320,000 sq. m, it is the largest fortress of its kind in Europe. A tour of the underground passages, tunnels, and waterways is offered by reservation only. *(Av. Castell de Sant Ferran. Follow Pujeda del Castell from Museu Dalí. ☎ 972 50 60 94; www.lesfortalesescatalanes.info. Open daily from July to mid-Sept. 10am-8pm, from mid-Sept. to June 10:30am-3pm. Free. Guided tours of the central fortress, €3, student, €2. Tour of underground passages €15.)*

MUSEU DEL JOGUET DE CATALUNYA. Winner of Spain's 1999 National Prize of Popular Culture, this museum showcases over 5000 antique toys. Skates, board games, dominoes, dolls, rocking horses, playing cards, and countless other sources of pre-television childhood amusement litter the display cases, including the toys of famous Catalans like Joan Miró and Salvador Dalí, which they donated themselves. Don't miss the impressive selection of Christmastime *caganers* ("shitters"...really), a Catalan favorite. *(Sant Pere, 1, off La Rambla. ☎ 972 50 45 85; www.mjc.cat. Open June-Sept. M-Sa 10am-7pm, Su 11am-6pm; Oct.-May Tu-Sa 10am-6pm, Su 11am-2pm. €5, students, seniors, and under 12 €4. Audioguide €3.)*

◙ NIGHTLIFE

A bit removed from touristy Rambla, **Plaça del Sol**, behind the tourist office, contains nearly all of the town's nightlife. **Cafè de Nit**, Pl. del Sol, s/n, offers pool in the back (€2 per game) and mixed drinks for €5-7. Crowd onto the terrace out front or enjoy your *caipirinha* under the artistic lights inside. *(☎972 50 12 25. Free Wi-Fi. Beer €2.30, before 9pm €1.50. Open daily 5pm-2:30am. Cash only.)* Before you go out for a late night of drinks and dancing in Pl. del Sol, however, you may want to stop by **Lizard Café**, C. San Domènec, 7, where you can chill out in the book-lined lounge in back, play cards, or checkmate a hottie while nodding along to psychedelic rock. (☎666 13 07 81. Beer €1.30. Open M-Sa 6pm-2:30am. Cash only.)

CADAQUÉS AND PORT LLIGAT ☎972

Forty years ago, Cadaqués (pop. 2900) was a well-kept Catalan secret. Only a trickle of French tourists visited every summer, and the town had closer diplomatic relations with Cuba than with the rest of Catalunya. The distinctive variety of Catalan spoken here is a testament to the enduring individuality of this drop-dead gorgeous beach town. The whitewashed houses, terra-cotta roofs, and azure bay have attracted artists, writers, and musicians ever since Dalí built his summer home on the neighboring beach, Port Lligat, in the 1930s. From September to May, the town is best experienced as a daytrip, as many food and entertainment establishments close in the low season; however, keep in mind the limited transportation options for a same-day return.

▐ TRANSPORTATION

Buses: Sarfa (☎972 25 87 13). Ticket office open daily July-Aug. 7-8:30pm; Sept.-June opens 15min. before every departure. To **Barcelona** (2¾hr.; July-Aug. 4-5 per day 7:45am-7:45pm; Sept.-June M-F 6:45am, 3:15pm, Sa-Su 6:45am, 5pm; €21), **Figueres** (1hr.; July-Aug. 6-7 per day 7am-7:45pm, Sept.-June 4 per day M-F 7am-6:15am, Sa-Su 8:30am-7pm; €4.80), and **Girona** (2hr.; July-Aug. 8:40am and 5:10pm, Sept.-June M-F 7am; €9.30). The **bus stop** is in the parking lot across from the ticket office. On your way there, stop at the indexed map on the wall to your right to orient yourself. Then head left past the ticket office and turn right onto Av. Caritat Serinyana; the waterfront Plaça Frederic Rahola (known to locals as Ses Herbes) is 4 blocks from this roundabout.

Taxis: Taxi Josep Giró (☎696 61 17 84) and **Olé Taxi** (☎626 52 68 32).

Bike Rental: Rent@Bit, Av. Caritat Serinyana, 9 (☎972 25 82 26; www.rentabit.net). Rents scooters and bikes for exploring the remote areas around Cadaqués. Open daily 9:30am-8pm. Bikes €20 per day, €75 per week. Scooters €40 per day, €245 per week; hourly rates available. Internet €0.50 per 5min., €4 per hr. MC/V.

Cadaquésrent, Av. Caritat Seinyana, 6. (☎678 431 722) rents motorbikes. €15 per 2hr., €40-55 per day. 4-person boat €120 in low season; in high season €140 per ½-day, per day €180/€210; 7-person boat €210/220 in low season, in high season €280/300. Open 9:30am-7:30pm. MC/V.

▐ PRACTICAL INFORMATION

Tourist Office: C. Cotxe, 2 (☎972 25 83 15). Off Pl. Frederic Rahola, on a small street running alongside the beach. Offers an excellent *plànol turístic* (map) as well as a listing of hotels and hostels. Open from July to mid-Sept. M-Sa 9am-9pm, Su 10am-1pm 5-8pm; from mid-Sept. to June M-Th 10am-1pm and 3-7pm, F-Sa 10am-1pm and 3-8pm, Su 10am-1pm.

Bank: Banco Santander, Av. Caritat Serinyana, 4 (☎972 25 83 62). Open Oct.-Mar. M-F 8:30am-2pm, Sa 8:30-1pm; Apr.-Sept. M-F 8:30am-2pm. **ATMs** line the last few blocks of Av. Caritat Serinyana and the Passeig.

Police: C. Carles Rahola, 9 (☎972 15 93 43).

Medical Services: C. Nou, 6 (☎972 25 88 07).

Internet Access: Telecomunicaciones Cadaqués, Riera de Sant Vicenç, 4 (☎972 25 92 48), a block off Pl. Frederic Rahola. €0.50 per 15min., €2 per hr. Open daily 9:30am-

1pm and 3:30-10pm. **Casino** (see **Nightlife**) and **Rent@Bit** (see **Bike Rental**) also offer slightly more expensive internet.

Post Office: Av. Rierassa, 1 off Av. Caritat Serinyana (☎972 25 87 98), 2 blocks from the bus station. Open M-F 8:30am-12:30pm, Sa 9am-11am. **Postal Code:** 17488.

ACCOMMODATIONS AND CAMPING

As Cadaqués is a beach town, many accommodations only open during the summer, and often require reservations.

Hostal Cristina, Riera de Sant Vicenç, s/n, (☎972 25 81 38). By the water, to the right of Av. Caritat Serinyana on the plaça. Cheerfully painted rooms with beautifully tiled baths, A/C, and TVs. Reception 8am-10pm. Breakfast included in summer. Free internet for guests. Dogs allowed. June-Sept. singles €45; doubles €66-76. Oct.-May. singles €35; doubles €56-66. AmEx/MC/V. ❹

Hostal Vehí, C. de l'Església, 6 (☎972 25 84 70). A short walk from the water, across from the tall white church. Follow signs from bus stop or Pl. dr. Trémols. Spiffy bedrooms with immaculate shared baths, A/C, hairdryers, and TVs, some with balconies, nestled amid narrow cobblestone streets and hanging ivy. Breakfast €6. Reserve ahead. Singles €35; doubles €45, with bath €75. Prices vary with season. MC/V. ❸

La Fonda, C. Tórtora, 64. (☎972 25 80 19). Go up C. Miguel Rosset, bear right as it turns into C. Maltret and take a sharp right onto C. Tórtora. A bit of an uphill walk from the center of town, but offers cheerful, pastel-colored rooms with TVs and fans. Many feature a view of the picturesque countryside. Breakfast €6. Wi-Fi in restaurant downstairs. Singles €45; doubles €50-55. MC/V. ❹

Camping Cadaqués, Ctra. Port Lligat, 17 (☎972 25 81 26). 100m from the beach on the way to Dalí's house; follow the signs for Hotel Port Lligat. The campground can get crowded, but it's clean and close to the beach and the center of town. Showers with hot water, pool, restaurant, supermarket. Internet €1 per 15min. Reception 8am-10pm. Quiet hours midnight-8am. Campground open Apr.-Sept. €7.50 per person; €9.50 per tent; €7.70 per car. MC/V. ❶

FOOD

Tourists in Cadaqués (many of them French) expect only the best. Even the seaside restaurants in the town serve respectable food, but you may find more interesting choices in the back streets. The exquisite fresh food ought to justify the relatively high prices. **Valvi,** on Riera de Sant Vicenç a block from Pl. Frederic Rahola, sells groceries for portside picnics. (☎972 25 86 33. Open June-Sept. M-Sa 8:30am-9pm, Su 9am-2pm; Oct.-May M-Sa 8:30am-3pm and 4-8:15pm, Su 8:30am-3pm. MC/V.)

Can Shelabi, C. Riera, 9 (☎972 25 89 00). Like its name, this restaurant is a fusion of Catalunya and Morocco—"can" is "house" in Catalan, "Shelabi" is the owner's Moroccan nickname. *Tajine* (couscous stew with beef or chicken cooked in a ceramic dish; €14-16) is the house specialty. Stop by in the afternoons to enjoy the sweet mint tea amid the turquoise, burnt orange, and yellow walls. *Menú* (€12) offered weekdays includes appetizer, entree, drink, and dessert or coffee. Entrees €11-17. Open daily 1-4pm and 7-11pm. MC/V. ❸

Al Gianni, C. Riera, s/n (☎972 25 83 71). The owner has been preparing the town's freshest food by hand for 15 years, served on a terrace with climbing vines. Pastas with shellfish, colorful risottos, and fresh fish fill the menu. Entrees €7-11. Meat and fish €12-20. Kitchen open M-F 7pm-midnight, Sa-Su 1-3pm and 7pm-midnight. MC/V. ❸

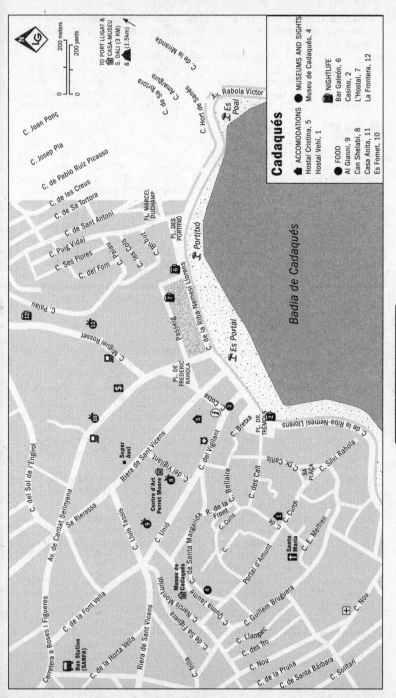

TO PORT LLIGAT &
CASA-MUSEU
S. DALI (3 KM)
& (1.5km)

C. de la Miranda

C. Joan Ponç

C. de Sa Tortora

C. Amargura

C. Hort de Sants

Av. Rabola Víctor

Es Poal

C. Josep Pla

C. de Pablo Ruiz Picasso

C. de les Creus

C. de Sa Tortora

C. de Sant Antoni

PL. MARCEL DUCHAMP

C. Puig Vidal

PL. DES PORTIXÓ

C. Ses Flores

C. del Forn

C. les Cols

C. del Palau

Portitxó

Badia de Cadaqués

Passeig

C. de la Riba-Nemesí Llorens

Es Portal

C. Palau

C. Miquel Rosset

PL. DE FREDERIC RAHOLA

C. Cotxe

C. del Sol de l'Engrol

$

C. Bretxa

PL. DR TRÉMOLS

C. de la Riba-Nemesí Llorens

C. del Vigilant

Super Avui

C. del Vigilant

Riera de Sant Vicens

C. des Call

SA PLAÇA

C. Silvi Rahola

C. Dr. Callís

C. de Caritat Serinyana

Sa Rierassa

Centre d'Art Perrot Moore

C. de Bellaire

R. de la Front

C. Curro

C. Curos

C. E. Meifren

C. Lluís Tassis

C. Unió

Riera de Sant Vicens

C. de Santa Margarida

Museu de Cadaqués

C. Narcís Monturiol

C. Quima Jaume

Portal d'Amunt

Santa Maria

Carretera a Roses i Figueres

C. de la Font Vella

C. de Sa Figuera

C. Guillem Bruguera

C. Nou

C. de la Horta Vella

C. Tina

C. Llampec

C. des Tro

Bus Station (SARFA)

C. Nou

C. de la Pruna

C. de Santa Bárbara

C. Solitari

Cadaqués

▲ ACCOMODATIONS
Hostal Cristina, 5
Hostal Vehi, 1

● MUSEUMS AND SIGHTS
Museu de Cadaqués, 4

● FOOD
Al Gianni, 9
Can Shelabi, 8
Casa Anita, 11
Es Fornet, 10

🍴 NIGHTLIFE
Bar Galeón, 6
Casino, 2
L'Hostal, 7
La Frontera, 12

DAYTRIPS

Casa Anita, C. Miquel Roset, 16 (☎972 25 84 71). The charming, antique interior serves timeless, perfectly cooked cuisine from fish soups and anchovy platters to lobster and whole fish served skin, head, and all. Plates €6-25. Open daily 1:30-3:15pm and 8:15-10:30pm. Reservations recommended. MC/V. ❸

Es Fornet, C. Caritat Serinyana, 12 (☎972 15 91 13). This sleek bakery serves up delicious pastries, the perfect accompaniment to an early morning *café con leche* (€1.50). Try one of the delicious *magdalenas,* which come in chocolate or apple and cream (€1.70), or snack on *bocadillos* (€3) and pizza (€1.80). Open daily 7:30am-10pm. Cash only. ❶

🖸 SIGHTS

🖾**CASA-MUSEU SALVADOR DALÍ.** This is the house where Dalí and his wife Gala lived until her death in 1982. The house is actually seven fishermen's houses that Dalí bought and transformed one by one. While lacking in original Dalí paintings, the house overflows with esoteric trinkets like a stuffed bear and lip-shaped sofas. The pool—inspired by the Alhambra—is inexplicably guarded by a plastic Michelin Man. *(In Port Lligat. Follow the signs at C. Miranda or take the trolley that leaves from Pl. Frederic Rahola for the scenic 10km route to Port Lligat. (45min.; 5 per day 11am-6pm; €7.50, children €5.50). ☎972 25 10 15. Open from mid-June to mid-Sept. daily 9:30am-9pm, last entry 8:10pm; from mid-Sept. to Jan. and mid-Mar. to mid-June Tu-Su 10:30am-6pm, last entry 5:10pm. Mandatory supervised visits with limited space. It's highly recommended to call and reserve 4-5 days in advance. €10, students and seniors €8, under 9 free.)* **Boat rides** in Dalí's own *Gala* depart from the dock in front of the house on the hour for a 55min. trip to Cap de Creus. *(☎617 46 57 57. Open daily 11am-8pm, depending on weather. Min. 2 people. €10, children €5.)*

🖺 NIGHTLIFE

Nightlife in Cadaqués is vibrant in summer but limited to weekends in winter, and centers around Passeig and C. Miquel Rosset, both just off of Pl. Frederic Rahola. Make sure you've got a firm idea of where your lodgings are (or a map) before you go out at night, as you might have some trouble navigating the winding, unpatterned streets after dark, especially after a few beers.

Café Tropical, C. Miquel Rosset, 19 (☎972 25 88 01). Attracts locals and internationals of all ages with mouth-watering mojitos and dancing in a jungle-like atmosphere. Plants hang from the ceiling and the terrace roof is made of tree branches. Beer €4. Mixed drinks €8. Open July-Sept. M-Th and Su 10:30pm-2:30am, F-Sa 10:30pm-3am; Oct.-June F-Sa 10:30pm-3am. MC/V.

La Frontera, C. Miquel Rosset, 22. Stucco interior and a tree-filled terrace make this a good place to chill and nod along to electronica. Billiards (€2) in the back room. Beer €3.50. Open daily 10pm-3am. Cash only.

L'Hostal, Passeig, 8. (☎972 25 80 00), right by the plaça. Features a Dalí-designed logo, walls lined with Surrealist sketches, and a delicious tequila sunrise (€10). 36 years of burning candles have created the massive wax statues by the bar. In summer, daily live music ranges from rumba to rock (midnight-2am). Open daily May-Dec. 10pm-5am; Jan.-Apr. F-Sa 10pm-5am. Cash only.

Bar Galeón, Passeig, 13. A tasteful sea theme with cerulean walls and climbing greenery. Attracts a vibrant crowd for evening drinks to its terrace, which overlooks the town center. Beer €1.70. Open M-Th 8:30pm-2:30am, F-Sa 8:30pm-3am. Cash only.

Casino, Pl. Doctor Trèmols. (☎972 25 81 37). The oldest bar in town. Expect a crowd to converge here early on in the night, loitering inside and outside, beer in hand. Besides beer (€3.10), sangria (€4), and a variety of mixed drinks, also serves *bocadillos* (€3-5) and offers internet (€1 per 15min.). Open M-Th 6am-1am, F-Sa 6am-2:30am. Cash only.

⚠ OUTDOOR ACTIVITIES

Diving Center Cadaqués, C. de la Miranda (☎652 31 77 97; www.divingccadaques.com, info@divingccadaques.com), offers 45min. dives for €45 (including tank, air, and weights). Certain routes depend on wind direction and weather: call for information on special offers. Reservations suggested (Open July-Aug. daily, 9am-8pm; Sept.-June weekends 9am-8pm). The first weekend in September brings dozens of old-fashioned sailboats to the harbor for the renowned **Trobada de Barques de Vela Llatina.**On the weekend before September 11, the **Festa Major d'Estiu** fills the streets with Sardanas, *fútbol,*dances, concerts, and more. December 18 brings more of the same at the **Festa Major d'Hivern.** From late June through August, the **Festival Internacional de Música de Cadaqués** attracts big-name international classical musicians.

PUIGCERDÀ   ☎972

As first your RENFE train and then your bus thread their way skyward through the Catalan Pyrenees, you wouldn't be blamed for asking: what the heck could be all the way up here? The answer: heaven. Puigcerda is a sort of Spanish Vail: a backpacker or ski bum's paradise that—thanks to its art galleries, hot-air ballooning, restaurants, and more—won't disappoint unathletic types. Yet, it's the outdoorsy who will certainly experience Puigcerda at its best—the town's location on both the French and Andorran borders makes it a cheap base for hiking, biking, or skiing in three different countries.

⬛ TRANSPORTATION

Trains: RENFE (☎972 88 01 65; www.renfe.es) trains run from **Barcelona** to **Puigcerda** (3hr., 6 trains per day 5:49am-6:13pm) on the "Cercanias" routes. This can be confusing because "Cercanias" routes are not listed on the RENFE website. Never fear; they do exist and leave from **Sants-Estacio** and **Arc de Triomf.** While there was once and may again someday be a train to Puigcerda, the line is currently undergoing repairs (read: nonexistent) and thus, although travelers can buy a train ticket to Puigcerda, they must get off the train at Ripoll (the last possible stop) so that a bus at no extra cost will take them the rest of the way to Puigcerda.

Buses: Barcelona Nord bus station. **Alsina Graells** (☎902 42 22 42; www.alsa.es) buses run to Puigcerda via **Lleida** (3hr.; M-F 9:15, 11:30am, 4, and 7pm; Sa 11:30am; €15). **Teisa** buses (☎972 20 02 75; www.teisa-bus.com) run between **Girona** (3½hr., M-F leave Girona at 4:15pm and Puigcerda at 6:05am, €18) and Puigcerda. In Puigcerda, buses leave from Pl. Barcelona and then stop outside the train station; buy tickets onboard. Schedules are in Pl. Barcelona, in the station and at Bar Estacio.

Taxis: (☎972 88 00 11). At the train station or on Pl. Cabrinetty.

⬛⬛ ORIENTATION AND PRACTICAL INFORMATION

Puigcerdà's center is at the top of a hill. The train station is at the foot of the western slope. Buses stop at the train station and then at Pl. Barcelona; get off at the second stop if you wish to arrive within the town itself. To reach **Plaça Ajuntament** from the **train station,** walk up the stairs immediately opposite the station itself. To save your legs, take the free **cable car,** which leaves from the top of these stairs (5:30am-midnight, July and Aug. 5:30am-1am). At the top, take the elevator (in front of you and to the left), up to Pl. Ajuntament. From the plaça, walk one block on C. Alfons I to **Carrer Major.** Turn left on C. Major to reach **Plaça Santa María.** You can get to **Plaça Barcelona** through the **Plaça dels**

Herois, which is the end of Pl. Santa María farthest from the bell tower. Between September and July, note that most services and stores shut down on Monday and Sunday.

Tourist Offices: C. Querol, 1 (☎972 88 05 42 or 14 15 22), off Pl. Ajuntament, to the right as you step off the elevator. English, Spanish, and French are spoken. Open Tu-Sa 10am-1pm and 4-7pm. **Regional Comarcal tourist office** (☎972 14 06 65), on the junction of the N-152 and N-160, about a 10min. walk down the highway toward Barcelona from the train station. Turn right as you exit the station. Walk this route with caution, especially during times of heavy traffic, as parts of the road have no sidewalk. Open M-Sa 9am-1pm and 4-7pm, Su 10am-1pm.

Bank: Banco Santander Central Hispano, Pl. Cabrinetty, 15, has a **24hr. ATM.** Open M-F 8:30am-2pm, Sa 8:30am-1pm.

Police: Municipal police, Pl. Ajuntament, 1 (☎972 88 19 72).

Hospital: Hospital de Puigcerdàin, Pl. Santa María (☎972 88 01 50/54), behind the bell tower.

Library: Pg. 10 d'Ábril, 2 (☎972 88 03 04; www.bibgirona.net/puigcerda), next to Eglésia de Sant Domènech, around the back of the building. The building—once a convent—has been converted into a modern, steel-and-glass library. Free internet and Wi-Fi on the 1st fl. Lots of helpful tourist info. Open M 3:30-8:30pm, Tu 10am-1:30pm, W 3:30-8:30pm, Th 10am-1:30pm and 3:30-8:30pm, F 3:30-8:30pm, Sa 10am-1:30pm.

Internet Access: Locutorio Corami, Pl. Cabrinetty, 10 (☎972 14 01 14). Open daily 10:30am-1pm and 5-10:30pm. €2 per hr. There are 2 other *locutorios* in town: **Locutorio del Lac,** on the lefthand side of C. Pons i Gasch, just off Pl. Barcelona, and **Online Informatica,** C. d'Espanya, 32. Both open Tu-Sa 10am-1pm and 5-8pm.

Post Office: Av. Coronel Molera, 11 (☎972 88 08 14), 1 block down from Pl. Barcelona. Open M-F 8:30am-2:30pm, Sa 9:30am-1pm. **Postal Code:** 17520.

ACCOMMODATIONS AND CAMPING

Many *pensiones* are located around Pl. Santa María in the old town.

Hostal Cerdanya, C. Ramon Cosp, 7 (☎972 88 00 10). Basic rooms with all the essentials, including small TVs. Singles €25-50. Cash only. ❶

Camping Stel (☎972 88 23 61; www.stel.es), 2km from Puigcerdà on the road to Llivia. Full-service camping with a chalet-style restaurant, bar, and lounge as well as a supermarket. Bungalows available for month-long stays during winter; check website. Open May 29-Sept. 27. Single bungalows €6.40; site with tent €12, with car €24; 5-person bungalows €108, with car €116. MC/V. ❶

FOOD

Buy cheap produce at the weekly **farmer's market** at Pl. 10 d'Ábril (open Su 6am-2pm) or grab groceries at **Bonpreu,** Av. Coronel Molera, 12, diagonally across from the post office (open M-Sa 9am-9pm, Su 10am-2:30pm; MC/V).

Central, Pl. Santa Maria, 6 (☎972 88 25 53). The name rings true, and this is the place to meet the town's ski-bum chic 20-somethings. Great selection of tapas, crepes, salads, and pizzas. Entrees €8-10. Free Wi-Fi. Open daily 10am-2am. MC/V over €36. ❷

La Maison de Foie Gras, C. Escolas Pies, 3 (☎972 88 11 22). Chef Thierry Motger is a 4th-generation French chef—and you can tell. Red-striped tablecloths and napkins complement the artfully prepared and presented *foie gras*. Perfect wine pairings. Motger has been known to serve a plate of his *foie gras* under a bird cage, lit by a crackling sparkler. Homemade sangria €2. Though not cheap, considering the quality of this food, it's a steal. *Menùs* €12-20. Open in summer daily 10am-midnight; in winter F-Su 10am-midnight. ❸

◎ 🎿 SIGHTS AND SLOPES

ART GALLERIES. Within town, art enthusiasts will be pleased to find two galleries, both named **Galeria Puigcerda, Sala d'Art,** C. Major, 21 and Pl. Barcelona, in the Casino. *(Open Tu-Th 4:30-8:30pm, F-Sa 10am-2pm and 4:30-8:30pm, Su 10am-2pm.)*

PARC SCHIERBECK. This park offers a calm respite, as swans glide over reflections of the snow-covered mountains. *(Just above the Pl. Barcelona. Follow the C. Pons i Gash.)*

SLOPES. **Cercle Aventura** offers a formidable list of outdoor activities in the summer and winter. (☎902 17 05 93; www.cercleaventure.com. Archery €15. Canyoneering €45-55. Rock climbing €65. Paintball €30. Canoe Rental €40. Snowshoe rental €10. Spelunking €30. Bike rental €12 per ½-day, €20 per day. Open daily 9am-2pm and 4-8pm.) **Ski** in your country of choice (Spain, France, or Andorra) at one of 19 ski areas within a 50km radius. The closest on the Spanish side is **Alp 2500,** a conglomerate of **La Molina** (☎972 89 20 31, ski school 978 89 21 57; www.lamolina.cat) and nearby **Masella** (☎972 14 40 00; www.masella.com), which offers the longest run in the eastern Pyrenees. For cross-country skiing, a close site is **Guils-Fontanera** (☎972 19 70 47; www.guils.com). Also try **Lles** (☎973 29 30 49, ski school 973 29 30 49; www.lles.net) or **Aránsa** (☎973 29 30 51). In the spring and summer, the Puigcerdà area is also popular for **biking;** the tourist office has a map detailing several routes. The town of **Llívia,** a Spanish enclave surrounded by France, can make for a pleasant pastoral afternoon excursion. Some travelers also stop by **Rìgolisa** on the way back for a view of the wheat fields at sunset. **Sports Iris,** Av. de França, 16, rents bikes and skis. (☎972 88 23 98; iris.gpscerdanya.info/about. Bike rental €15 per ½-day, €20 per day. Open daily 9am-2pm and 4:30-8pm.) For horseback riding, call **Hípica Sant Marc** (C. de Sant Marc; ☎972 88 00 07). Try piloting or ballooning at **Globus de Pirineu** (☎972 14 08 52; www.globospi.com) or **Cerdanya Globus** (☎609 83 29 74; www.osonaglobus.com). Other adventure sports such as 4X4 and motorbike rental can be arranged with La Molina or Alp 2500 Viatges (☎972 89 20 29) and at **Turing Cerdanya,** Escoles Pies 19 (☎972 88 06 02; www.turingcerdanya.com). Those who prefer their sports less extreme can golf at the **Club Golf Sant Marc** (☎972 88 34 11; www.golfpuigcerda.com).

APPENDIX

CLIMATE

Avg. temperature, precipitation	JANUARY			APRIL			JULY			OCTOBER		
	°C	°F	mm	°C	°F	mm	°C	°F	mm	°C	°F	mm
	6-13	43-55	31	11-18	52-64	43	21-28	70-82	27	15-21	59-70	86

To convert from degrees Fahrenheit to degrees Celsius, subtract 32 and multiply by 5/9. To convert from Celsius to Fahrenheit, multiply by 9/5 and add 32.

CELSIUS	-5	0	5	10	15	20	25	30	35	40
FAHRENHEIT	23	32	41	50	59	68	77	86	95	104

MEASUREMENTS

Like the rest of the rational world, Spain uses the metric system. The basic unit of length is the meter (m), which is divided into 100 centimeters (cm) or 1000 millimeters (mm). One thousand meters make up one kilometer (km). Fluids are measured in liters (L), each divided into 1000 milliliters (mL). A liter of pure water weighs one kilogram (kg), which is divided into 1000 grams (g). One metric ton is 1000kg.

MEASUREMENT CONVERSIONS	
1 inch (in.) = 25.4mm	1 millimeter (mm) = 0.039 in.
1 foot (ft.) = 0.305m	1 meter (m) = 3.28 ft.
1 yard (yd.) = 0.914m	1 meter (m) = 1.094 yd.
1 mile (mi.) = 1.609km	1 kilometer (km) = 0.621 mi.
1 ounce (oz.) = 28.35g	1 gram (g) = 0.035 oz.
1 pound (lb.) = 0.454kg	1 kilogram (kg) = 2.205 lb.
1 fluid ounce (fl. oz.) = 29.57mL	1 milliliter (mL) = 0.034 fl. oz.
1 gallon (gal.) = 3.785L	1 liter (L) = 0.264 gal.

SPANISH

Each vowel has only one pronunciation: *a* ("ah" in "father"); *e* ("eh" in "pet"); *i* ("ee" in "eat"); *o* ("oh" in "oat"); *u* ("oo" in "boot"); (by itself, *y* is pronounced the same as the Spanish i, "ee"). Most consonants are the same as in English. Important exceptions are: *j* ("h" in "hello"); *ll* ("y" in "yes"); *ñ* ("ny" in "canyon"); and *r* at the beginning of a word or *rr* anywhere in a word (trilled). *H* is always silent. *G* before *e* or *i* is pronounced like the "h" in "hen;" elsewhere, it is pronounced like the "g" in "gate." *X* has a bewildering variety of pronunciations: depending on dialect and word position, it can sound like the English "h," "s," "sh," or "x." *B* and *v* have similar pronunciations. Spanish words receive stress on the syllable marked with an accent. In the absence of an accent mark, words that end in vowels, *n*, or *s* receive stress on the penultimate syllable. For words ending in all other consonants, stress falls on the last syllable. The Spanish language has masculine and feminine nouns, and gives a gender to all adjectives. Masculine words generally end with an *o*, feminine words generally end with an *a*. Pay close attention—slight changes in word ending can have drastic changes in meaning. For instance, when receiving directions, mind the distinction between *derecho* (straight; more commonly *recto*) and *derecha* (right). Sentences that end in ? or ! are also preceded by the same punctuation upside-down: *¿Cómo estás? ¡Muy bien, gracias!*

ESSENTIAL PHRASES

ENGLISH	SPANISH	PRONUNCIATION
Hello.	Hola.	OH-la
How are you?	¿Cómo está?	KOH-mo es-TA
Good, thanks.	Muy bien, gracias.	MWEE bee-en, GRA-see-ahs
Goodbye.	Adiós.	ah-dee-OHS
Yes/No	Sí/No	SEE/NO
Please.	Por favor.	POHR fa-VOHR
Thank you.	Gracias.	GRA-see-ahs
You're welcome.	De nada.	DAY NAH-dah
Do you speak English?	¿Habla inglés?	AH-blah een-GLAYCE
I don't speak Spanish.	No hablo español.	NO AH-bloh ehs-pahn-YOHL
Excuse me.	Perdón.	pehr-DOHN
I don't know.	No sé.	NO SAY
Can you repeat that?	¿Puede repetirlo?	PWEH-day reh-peh-TEER-lo
Let's dance.	Bailamos.	by-lah-MOHS

ON ARRIVAL

ENGLISH	SPANISH	ENGLISH	SPANISH
I am from (the US/Europe).	Soy de (los Estados Unidos/Europa).	What's the problem, sir/madam?	¿Cuál es el problema, señor/señora?
Here is my passport.	Aquí está mi pasaporte.	I lost my passport.	Perdí mi pasaporte.
I will be here for less than six months.	Estaré aquí por menos de seis meses.	I have nothing to declare.	No tengo nada para declarar.
Where is customs?	¿Dónde está la aduana?	Where do I claim my luggage?	¿Dónde puedo reclamar mi equipaje?
I don't know where that came from.	No sé de donde vino eso.	Please do not detain me.	Por favor no me detenga.

DIRECTIONS

ENGLISH	SPANISH	ENGLISH	SPANISH
(to the) right/left	(a la) derecha/izquierda	across from	enfrente de/frente a
next to	al lado de/junto a	near/far	cerca/lejos
straight ahead	derecho	turn (command)	doble
on top of/above	encima de/arriba	beneath/below	bajo de/abajo
traffic light	semáforo	corner	esquina
street	calle/avenida	block	cuadra

SURVIVAL SPANISH

ENGLISH	SPANISH	ENGLISH	SPANISH
How can you get to...?	¿Cómo se puede llegar a...?	Is there anything cheaper?	¿Hay algo más barato/ económico?
Does this bus go to (Italy)?	¿Va este autobús a (Italia)?	I'm in a hurry!	¡Tengo prisa!
Where is (Azorín) street?	¿Dónde está la calle (Azorín)?	What bus line goes to..?	¿Qué línea de buses tiene servicio a...?
When does the bus leave?	¿Cuándo sale el bús?	From where does the bus leave?	¿De dónde sale el bús?
I'm getting off at...	Bajo en...	I have to go now.	Tengo que ir ahora.
Can I buy a ticket?	¿Podría comprar un boleto?	How far is...?	¿Qué tan lejos está...?
How long does the trip take?	¿Cuántas horas dura el viaje?	Please let me off at the zoo/hostel.	Por favor, déjeme en el zoológico/hostal
I am going to the airport.	Voy al aeropuerto.	The flight is delayed/ cancelled.	El vuelo está atrasado/ cancelado.
Where is the bathroom?	¿Dónde está el baño?	Is it safe to hitchhike?	¿Es seguro pedir aventón?
I lost my baggage.	Perdí mi equipaje.	I'm lost.	Estoy perdido(a).
How much does it cost per day/week?	¿Cuánto cuesta por día/ semana?	Does it have (heating/ air-conditioning)?	¿Tiene (calefacción/aire acondicionado)?
Where can I buy a cell-phone?	¿Dónde puedo comprar un teléfono celular?	Where can I check e-mail?	¿Dónde se puede chequear el email?
Could you tell me what time it is?	¿Podría decirme qué hora es?	Are there student discounts available?	¿Hay descuentos para estudiantes?

ACCOMMODATIONS

ENGLISH	SPANISH	ENGLISH	SPANISH
Is there a cheap hotel around here?	¿Hay un hotel económico por aquí?	Are there rooms with windows?	¿Hay habitaciones con ventanas?
Do you have rooms available?	¿Tiene habitaciones libres?	I am going to stay for (four) days.	Me voy a quedar (cuatro) días.
I would like to reserve a room.	Quisiera reservar una habitación.	Are there cheaper rooms?	¿Hay habitaciones más baratas?
Can I see a room?	¿Podría ver una habit-ación?	Do they come with private baths?	¿Vienen con baño privado?
Do you have any singles/ doubles?	¿Tiene habitaciones sencillas/dobles?	Does it have (heating/ A/C)?	¿Tiene (calefacción/aire acondicionado)?
I'll take it.	Lo tomo.	Who's there?	¿Quién es?
I need another key/ towel/pillow.	Necesito otra llave/ toalla/almohada.	The shower/sink/toilet is broken.	La ducha/la pila/el servicio no funciona.

EMERGENCY

ENGLISH	SPANISH	ENGLISH	SPANISH
Help!	¡Socorro!/¡Ayúdeme!	Call the police!	¡Llame a la policía!
I am hurt.	Estoy herido(a).	Leave me alone!	¡Déjame en paz!
It's an emergency!	¡Es una emergencia!	He/They robbed me!	¡Me ha/han robado!
Fire!	¡Fuego!/¡Incendio!	He/They went that way!	¡Fue/Fueron en esa dirección!
Call a clinic/ambu-lance/doctor/priest!	¡Llame a una clínica/una ambulancia/un médico/ un padre!	I will only speak in the presence of a lawyer.	Sólo hablaré en presencia de un abogado(a).
I need to contact my embassy.	Necesito contactar mi embajada.	Don't touch me!	¡No me toque!

MEDICAL

ENGLISH	SPANISH	ENGLISH	SPANISH
I feel bad/better/fine/worse.	Me siento mal/mejor/bien/peor.	What is this medicine for?	¿Para qué es esta medicina?
I'm sick/ill.	Estoy enfermo(a).	Where is the nearest hospital/doctor?	¿Dónde está el hospital/doctor más cercano?
I'm allergic to...	Soy alérgico(a) a...	Here is my prescription.	Aquí está la receta médica.
I have a cold/a fever/diarrhea/nausea	Tengo gripe/una calentura/diarrea/náusea.	Call a doctor, please.	Llame a un médico, por favor

OUTDOORS AND RECREATION

ENGLISH	SPANISH	ENGLISH	SPANISH
Is it safe to swim here?	¿Es seguro nadar aquí?	Do you have sunscreen?	¿Tiene crema solar?
What time is high/low tide?	¿A qué hora es marea alta/baja?	Is there a strong current?	¿Hay una corriente fuerte?
Where can I rent a surfboard/bike?	¿Dónde puedo alquilar un planeador de mar/bicicleta?	Where is the trail?	¿Dónde está el rastro?
Do I need a guide?	¿Necesito una guía?	Can I camp here?	¿Puedo acampar aquí?

OUT TO LUNCH

ENGLISH	SPANISH	ENGLISH	SPANISH
Do you have anything vegetarian/without meat?	¿Hay algún plato vegetariano/sin carne?	Can I see the menu?	¿Podría ver la carta/el menú?
I would like to order (the eel).	Quisiera (el congrio).	Table for (one), please.	Mesa para (uno), por favor.
Check, please.	¡La cuenta, por favor!	Do you take credit cards?	¿Aceptan tarjetas de crédito?
Where is a good restaurant?	¿Dónde está un restaurante bueno?	Delicious!	¡Qué rico!

NUMBERS, DAYS, AND MONTHS

ENGLISH	SPANISH	ENGLISH	SPANISH	ENGLISH	SPANISH
0	cero	20	veinte	last night	anoche
1	uno	21	veintiuno	weekend	(el) fin de semana
2	dos	22	veintidos	morning	(la) mañana
3	tres	30	treinta	afternoon	(la) tarde
4	cuatro	40	cuarenta	night	(la) noche
5	cinco	50	cincuenta	month	(el) mes
6	seis	100	cien	year	(el) año
7	siete	1000	mil	early/late	temprano/tarde
8	ocho	1 million	un millón	January	enero
9	nueve	Monday	lunes	February	febrero
10	diez	Tuesday	martes	March	marzo
11	once	Wednesday	miércoles	April	abril
12	doce	Thursday	jueves	May	mayo
13	trece	Friday	viernes	June	junio
14	catorce	Saturday	sábado	July	julio

15	quince	**Sunday**	domingo	**August**	agosto
16	dieciseis	**today**	hoy	**September**	septiembre
17	diecisiete	**tomorrow**	mañana	**October**	octubre
18	dieciocho	**day after tomorrow**	pasado mañana	**November**	noviembre
19	diecinueve	**yesterday**	ayer	**December**	diciembre

CATALAN

Did we mention that Barcelona doesn't speak Spanish? (**Discover,** p. 1) Catalan originated in the AD 8th century. Beginning in the Middle Ages, Catalan became the language of Barcelona's writers and poets and of official legal documents. Shortly after Franco's death, Catalan became the official language of Catalunya in 1980. The Romance language is also spoken in the Alghero, Italy; Andorra; the Balearic Islands; Roussillon, France; and Valencia. The table and glossary below include some basic Catalan phrases and vocabulary.

ESSENTIAL PHRASES

ENGLISH	CATALAN		
Hello.	Hola.	**Where is...?**	On és...?
Goodbye.	Adéu.	**Could you please show me where... consulate is?**	Pot indicar-me on és... el consolat de?
See you soon.	Fins aviat.	**How do I get to the post office, please?**	Per anar a correus, sisplau?
Yes/No.	Sí/No.	**Where is the nearest police station, please?**	On és la comissaria de policia més pròxima, sisplau?
Help!	Ajuda!	**Where is the nearest telephone booth, please?**	On hi ha una cabina telefònica, sisplau?
Please.	Si us plau.	**How are you?**	Com està?
Thank you.	Gràcies.	**Who/What/When/Why**	quem/que/quando/ porque
You're welcome.	De res.	**What time is it, please?**	Quina hora és, sisplau?
Do you speak English?	Parles anglès?	**How do I get to (Madrid)?**	Com puc arribar a (Madrid)?
I don't understand.	No ho entenc.	**Have a nice trip.**	Bon viatge.
Excuse me.	Perdoni.	**Do you have any rooms available?**	Teniu alguna habitació disponible?
I don't know.	No sé.	**Where can I change money, please?**	On puc canviar moneda, sisplau?
Can you repeat that?	Pot repetir?	**Could you bring me the menu, please?**	Em pot portar la carta, sisplau?
Speak slowly, please.	Parli més a poc a poc, sisplau.	**What is your name?/ My name is...**	Com et dius?/Em dic...

NUMBERS

1	u/una	20	vint
2	dos/dues	30	trenta
3	tres	40	quaranta
4	quatre	50	cinquanta
5	cinc	60	seixanta

APPENDIX

6	sis	70	setanta
7	set	80	vuitanta
8	vuit	90	noranta
9	nou	100	cent
10	deu	1000	mil

SPANISH/CATALAN GLOSSARY

TRAVELING

abierto/obert (C): open
albergue/alberg (C): youth hostel
arena: sand
autobús/autocar (C): bus
autopista (C): highway
avenida/avinguda (C): avenue
ayuntamiento/ajuntament (C): city hall
bahía/badia (C): bay
bandera azul: blue flag, EU award for clean beaches
baño/bany (C): bath
barcelonés: of Barcelona
barrio viejo: old quarter
biblioteca: library
billete/boleto/bitllet (C): ticket
bosc (C): forest
botiga: shop
buceo: scuba diving
cabo: cape
cajero automático/ caixer automàtic (C): ATM
calle/carrer (C): street
cambio: currency exchange
capilla/capella (C): chapel
castillo/castell (C): castle
catedral: cathedral
carretera: highway
casco antiguo/viejo: old city
cerrado: closed
chocolate: chocolate or hash
ciudad vieja/ciutat vella (C): old city
consigna: luggage storage
Correos/Correus (C): post office
corrida: bullfight
cripta: crypt
cuarto: room
entrada: entrance
ermita: hermitage
estación/estació (C): station
estany (C): lake
feria: outdoor market, fair
ferrocarriles: trains

fiesta: holiday or festival
fuente/font (C): fountain
gitano: gypsy
glorieta: rotary
iglesia/església (C): church
IVA: value-added tax
jardín público: public garden
judería: Jewish quarter
librería: bookstore
lista de correos/ llista de correus (C): poste restante
litera: sleeping car (in trains)
llegada: arrival
madrugada: early morning
mercado/mercat (C): market
mezquita/mesquita (C): mosque
mirador: lookout point
monestir (C): monastery
monte/muntanya (C): mountain
mozárabe: Christian art style
mudéjar: Muslim architectural style
muelle/moll (C): wharf, pier
murallas: walls
museo/museu (C): museum
oficina: office
palacio/palau (C): palace
parador nacional: state-owned hotel
parte viejo: old town
paseo, Po./passeig, Pg. (C): promenade
pico: peak
playa/platja (C): beach
plaza/plaça, Pl. (C): square, plaza
puente/pont (C): bridge
quiosco: newsstand
rastro: flea market
real/reial (C): royal
REAJ: Spanish youth hostel network
refugio/refugi (C): shelter, refuge
reina/rey, rei (C): queen/king
río/riu (C): river
sacristía: part of the church where sacred objects are kept
sala: room, hall
salida/sortida (C): exit, departure
selva: forest
sepulcro/tomba (C): tomb
seu (C): cathedral

APPENDIX

sierra/serra (C): mountain range
Siglo de Oro: Golden Age
sillería: choir stalls
submarinisme (C): scuba diving
tienda: shop, tent
torre: tower
universidad/universitat (C): university
v.o.: versión original, a foreign-language film subtitled in Spanish
valle/vall (C): valley
zarzuela: Spanish light opera

FOOD AND DRINK

a la plancha/a la brasa (C): grilled
aceite: oil
aceituna: olive
adabo: battered
agua: water
aguacate/alvocat (C): avocado
aguardiente: firewater
ahumado/a: smoked
ajo/all (C): garlic
al horno/al forn (C): baked
albóndigas: meatballs
alioli: Catalan garlic sauce
almejas: clams
almendra/ametlla (C): almonds
almuerzo: midday meal
anchoa/anxova: anchovy
ànec (C): duck
anguila: eel
arroz/arròs (C): rice
arroz con leche: rice pudding
asado: roasted
atún: tuna
bacalao/bacallà (C): salted cod
bistec: steak
bocadillo: sandwich
bodega: wine cellar
bollo: bread roll
brasa: chargrilled
cacahuete/cacauet (C): peanut
café con leche: coffee w/milk
café solo: black coffee
calabacín/carabassó (C): zucchini
calamares/calamar (C): calamari, squid
caldereta/cuinat (C): stew
calimocho: red wine and cola
callos: tripe
camarones: shrimp
caña: beer in a small glass
cangrejo/cranc (C): crab
caracoles: snails

carne/carn (C): meat
cava (C): a sparkling white wine
cebolla/ceba (C): onion
cena: dinner
cerdo: pig, pork
cereza/cirera (C): cherry
cervecería: beer bar
cerveza/cervesa (C): beer
champiñones: mushrooms
choco: cuttlefish
chorizo: spicy red sausage
chuleta/costella (C): chop, cutlet
chupito: shot
churros: fried dough sticks
cigró (C): chickpea
cloïssa (C): clam
cocido: cooked, stew
cogombre (C): cucumber
conejo/conill (C): rabbit
coñac/conyac (C): brandy
copas/copes (C): drinks
cordero: lamb
cortado: coffee with little milk
croquetas: fried croquettes
crudo/cru (C): raw
cuchara/cullera (C): spoon
cuchillo: knife
cuenta: the bill/check
desayuno: breakfast
empanada: meat/fish pastry
enciam (C): lettuce
entremeses: hors d'oeuvres
escabeche: pickled fish
esmorzar (C): breakfast
espagueti/espaguetis (C): spaghetti
espárragos/espàrrec (C): asparagus
espinacas/espinacs (C): spinach
fabada asturiana: bean soup with sausage and ham
formatge (C): cheese
forquilla (C): fork
frambuesa: raspberry
fresa: strawberry
frito/a: fried
galleta/galeta (C): cookie
gambas: prawns
ganivet (C): knife
gelat (C): ice cream
ginebra: gin
glaç (C): ice
guisantes: peas
helado: ice cream
hielo: ice
horchata: sweet almond drink

horneado: baked
huevo: egg
jamón serrano: cured ham
jerez: sherry
langosta/llagosta (C): lobster
langostino: large prawn
leche/llet (C): milk
lechuga: lettuce
lenguado: sole
llobarro (C): sea bass
lomo: pork loin
maduixa (C): strawberry
mandonguilles (C): meatballs
manzana: apple
mayonesa/maionesa (C): mayonnaise
mejillones: mussels
melocotón: peach
menestra de verduras: vegetable mix
menú: full meal with bread, drink, and side dish
merienda: tea/snack
merluza: hake
migas: fried breadcrumb dish
mojito: white rum and club soda with mint and sugar
morcilla: blood sausage
muy hecho/molt fet (C): well-done (steak)
naranja: orange
navajas: razor clams
oli (C): oil
oliva (C): olive
ou (C): egg
paella: rice and seafood dish
pan/pa (C): bread
pasa/pansa (C): raisin
pastanaga (C): carrot
pastas: small sweet cakes
pastel/pasta (C): pastry
patatas bravas/patates braves (C): potatoes w/ spicy tomato sauce and mayo
patatas fritas/patates frites (C): French fries
pato: duck
pavo: turkey
pechuga: chicken breast
pepino: cucumber
picante/picant (C): spicy
pimienta (negra)/pebre (C): (black) pepper
pimiento (rojo)/pebrot (C): (red) pepper
piña/pinya (C): pineapple
plancha: grill

plato del día: daily special **plato combinado:** entree and side dish
pollo/pollastre (C): chicken
poma (C): apple
pulpo/polp (C): octopus
queso: cheese
rabo de toro: bull's tail
ración: small dish
raïm: grape
rebozado: battered and fried
refrescos: soft drinks
relleno/a: stuffed
rostit (C): roasted
sal: salt
salchicha/salsitxa (C): pork sausage
sangria: red wine punch
seco: dried
servilleta: napkin
sesos: brains
setas: wild mushrooms
sidra: (alcoholic) cider
solomillo: sirloin
sopa: soup
sopar (C): dinner
taberna: tapas bar
tapa: bite-sized snack
taronja (C): orange
tenedor: fork
ternera: beef, veal
terraza/terrassa (C): patio seating
tinto: red (wine)
tocino: (Canadian) bacon
tomate/tomàquet (C): tomato
tonyina (C): tuna
tortilla española: potato fritatta
tortilla francesa: omelette
tostada: toast
tovalló (C): napkin
trucha/truita (C): trout
trufas: truffles
tubo: tall glass of beer
uva: grape
vaca, carne de: beef
vaso: glass
verduras: green vegetables
vino/vi (C): wine
vino blanco/vi blanc (C): white wine
vino tinto/vi negre (C): red wine
xai (C): lamb
xampanyería (C): champagne bar
xampinyó (C): mushrooms
xerès (C): sherry
xoriço (C): spicy red sausage
yema: candied egg yolk

APPENDIX

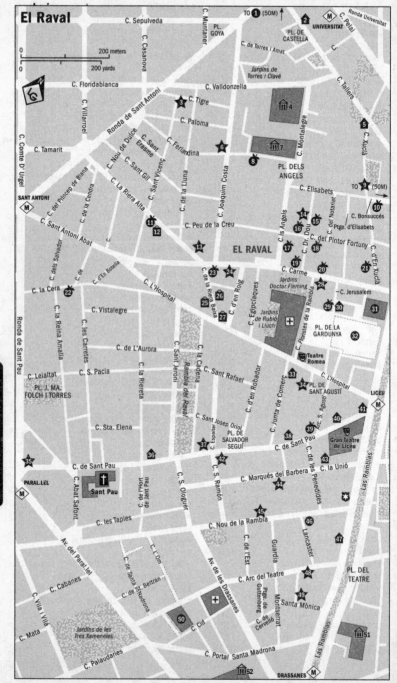

El Raval

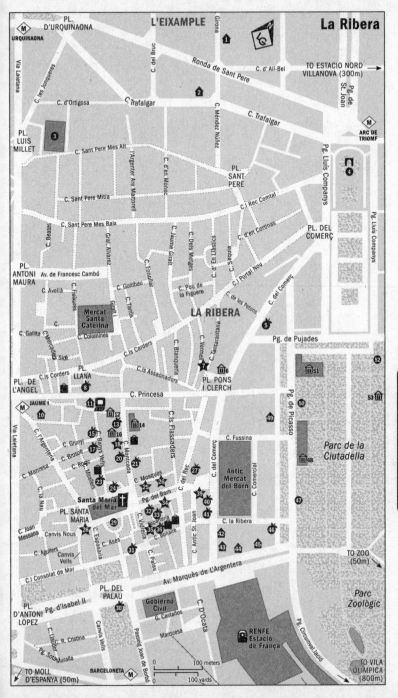

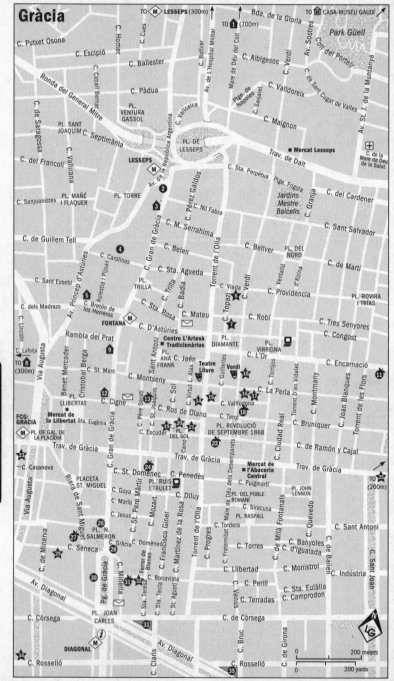

Gràcia

TO Ⓜ **LESSEPS** (300m)

Bda. de la Gloria

TO 🏛 **CASA-MUSEU GAUDÍ**

TO 1 (700m)

C. Putxet Osona

C. Cues

C. Homer

C. Escipió

C. Ballester

Av. de l'Hospital Militar

Mare de Déu del Coll

C. Bolívar

C. Aibigesos

Av. Sostres

Coll del Portell

Park Güell

C. Verdí

C. de Sant Cugat de Valles

Ronda del General Mitre

C. Caball Bernat

C. Pàdua

Pge. de Napoleó

C. Valldoreix

Av. St. J. de la Muntanya

PL. VENTURA GASSOL

C. Vallcalca

C. Sadjalet

C. Maignon

C. de Saragossa

C. de Vallirana

PL. SANT JOAQUIM

C. Septimània

Av. de la República Argentina

PL. DE LESSEPS

Trav. de Dalt

■ Mercat Lessseps

C. de la Mare de Déu de la Salut

C. del Francolí

LESSEPS

Ⓜ

2

Sta. Perpètua

Pge. Frigola

Jardins Mestre Balcells

C. del Cardener

C. Sanjoanistes

PL. MAÑÉ I FLAQUER

PL. TORRE

3

C. Pérez Galdós

C. Nil Fabra

C. Granja

C. Sant Salvador

C. de Guillem Tell

4

C. Gran de Gràcia

C. M. Serrahima

C. Belen

C. Bellver

PL. DEL NORD

C. de Martí

C. Carolines

C. Sta. Agueda

Torrent de l'Olla

C. Viada

C. Verdí

Ventalló

PL. ROVIRA I TRÍAS

C. Sant Eusebi

Av. Princep d'Astúries

Aulestia i Pijoan

PL. TRILLA

C. Trilla

C. Badia

C. Topazi

d'Atzina

C. Providència

C. dels Madrazo

5

C. Bretón de los Herreros

C. Sta. Rosa

C. Mateu

C. Robí

C. Tres Senyores

C. Lincoln

FONTANA

Ⓜ

C. D'Astúries

PL. DIAMANTE

C. L'Or

C. Congost

C. Laforja

Rambla del Prat

Centre L'Artesà ■ Tradicionàrius

PL. VIRREINA

C. Encarnació

TO 8 (300m)

9

Benet Mercader

Cristobal Berga

C. St. Marc

Sant Antoni

PL. ANA FRANK

C. Jaén

Teatre Lliure

C. Guilleries

C. Torrijos

11

Via Augusta

C. Montseny

C. Sol

C. Virtut

C. Alas

Verdi 18

10

C. La Perla

Torrent d'en Vidalet

C. Montmany

C. Joan Blanques

Torrent de les Flors

12

C. Cigne

13

C. Ros de Olano

15

C. Vallfogona

16

C. Terol

C. Bruniquer

FCG: GRACIA

Ⓜ

PL. LLIBERTAT

Mercat de la Llibertat

C. Pere Serafí

C. St. Joaquim

Sta. Eugènia

C. Escuder

PL. DEL SOL

Camp

PL. REVOLUCIÓ DE SEPTEMBRE 1868

22

C. Ciudad Real

PL. DE GAL. DE LA PLACÍDIA

Ⓜ

Trav. de Gràcia

C. Gran de Gràcia

Mercat de l'Abaceria Central ■

C. de Ramón y Cajal

Trav. de Gràcia

23

C. Casanova

PLACETA ST. MIGUEL

24

C. St. Domènec

C. Penedès

Trav. de Gràcia

Mare de Déu del Desemparats

C. Puigmartí

PL. JOHN LENNON

TO (200m)

Riera de Sant Miquel

C. Goya

PL. RUIS I TAULET

C. Diluy

Torrent de l'Olla

PL. DEL POBLE ROMANÍ

C. Siracusa

PL. RASPALL

C. Sant Antoni

C. de Minerva

C. María

C. Jesus

26

PL. N. SALMERON

C. St. Pere Màrtir

C. Mozart

C. Francisco Giner

C. Martínez de la Rosa

C. Progres

C. Fraternitat

C. Tordera

C. de Milà Fontanals

C. Quevedo

C. Sant Antoni

C. de Bailèn

C. Indústria

27

C. Sèneca

28

C. Gràcia

C. Domènech

C. Torres

C. Banyoles

C. d'Igualada

29

Av. Diagonal

30

Pg. de Gràcia

31

C. Bonavista

C. Llibertat

C. Monistrol

C. Sta. Eulàlia

C. Camprodon

C. Còrsega

PL. JOAN CARLES

C. Sta. Teresa

C. Sta. Tecla

C. St. Agustí

C. Perill

C. Terradas

C. de Còrsega

33

DIAGONAL

Ⓜ

i

Av. Diagonal

C. Bruc

C. de Girona

N

0   200 meters

C. Claris

C. Rosselló

C. Rosselló

35

C. de Sant Joan

0   200 yards

El Raval

ACCOMMODATIONS
Barcelona Mar
  Youth Hostel, **36**
Hostal Benidorm, **47**
Hostal Opera, **40**
Hostal La Palmera, **30**
Hostal La Terrassa, **33**
Hotel Peninsular, **38**
Ideal Youth Hostel, **43**
Mare Nostrum, **41**
Pensión 45, **5**
Pensión L'Isard, **2**

FOOD
Bar Ra, **29**

Bar Restaurante Los
  Toreros, **21**
Bar Restaurante Romesco, **39**
Buenas Migas, **10**
Carmelitas, **19**
Colibri, **11**
Dos Trece, **20**
L'Hortet, **16**
Mamacafé, **15**
Pla dels Angels, **8**
Restaurante Biocenter, **18**
Restaurante Can Lluís, **22**
Shalimar, **23**
Silenus, **17**

SHOPPING
Discos Edison's, **26**

Gl Joes Surplus, **27**
Mies & Felj, **25**
Zeus, **12**

MUSEUMS
Centre de Cultura
  Contemporània, **4**
Museu d'Art Contemporani, **7**
Museu de Cera, **51**
Museu Marítim, **52**

SIGHTS
Mercat de la Boqueria, **32**
Mercat de Deu del Carme, **50**
Palau Güell, **46**
Palau de la Virreina, **31**
Universitat de Barcelona, **1**

NIGHTLIFE
El Cafe que pone
  Muebles Navarro, **13**
Casa Almirall, **6**
La Confiteria, **35**
London Bar, **45**
Lupino, **28**
Marsella Bar, **42**
Moog, **48**
Muy Buenas, **24**
La Paloma, **3**
Pastis, **49**
La Oveja Negra, **9**
The Quiet Man, **44**
Raval-Bar, **14**
Rita Blue, **34**
Sant Pau 68, **37**

La Ribera

ACCOMMODATIONS
Gothic Point Youth Hostal, **10**
Hostal de Ribagorza, **2**
Hostal Nuevo Colón, **45**
Hostal Orleans, **44**
Hotel Triunfo, **49**
Pensión Ciutadella, **43**
Pensión Lourdes, **11**
Pensión Port-bou, **42**
Pensión Rondas, **1**

FOOD
Barcelónia, **41**
Bodega la Tinaja, **33**
Café del Born, **40**
Cal Pep, **31**
La Cocotte, **32**
Euskal Etxea, **21**
Gades, **36**
La Habana Vieja, **15**

El Pebre Blau, **24**
Restaurant 7 Portes, **30**
Sandwich and Friends, **27**
Suborn, **46**
Taira, **5**
Tèxtil Café, **13**
Tomate, **24**
Txirimiri, **8**
Va de Vi, **17**
Xampanyet, **20**

SHOPPING
0,925 Argenters, **19**
Arlequí Máscares, **9**
Farcells, **22**
Las 40 Ladronas, **38**
Outlet del Born, **37**

MUSEUMS
Museu Barbier-Mueller, **16**
Museu d'Art Modern, **53**
Museu de Geologia, **48**
Museu de la Xocolata, **6**

Museu de Zoologia, **51**
Museu Picasso, **14**
Museu Textil i d'Indumentària, **12**

SIGHTS
Arc de Triomf, **4**
Cascade Fountains, **52**
El Fossar de les Moreres, **29**
Hivernacle, **50**
Palau de la Música Catalana, **3**
Umbracle, **47**

NIGHTLIFE
El Born, **34**
El Copetin, **26**
Mudanzas, **35**
Palau Dalmase, **18**
Pitin Bar, **39**
Plàstic Café, **26**
Upiaywasi, **7**
La Vinya del Senyor, **28**

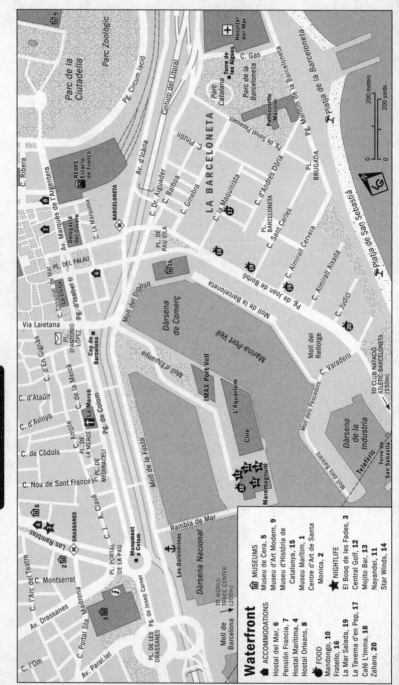

Parc de la Ciutadella

Parc Zoològic

Pg. Circumlació

Cinturó del Litoral

Hospital del Mar

C. Gas

Torre de les Aigües

Parc Catalana

Parc de la Barceloneta

Platja de la Barceloneta

200 meters
200 yards

C. Ribera

RENFE Estació de França

Av. d'Icària

Pg. Marítim de la Barceloneta

LA BARCELONETA

Poliesportiu Marítim

Pg. de Salvat Papasseit

C. Marquès de l'Argentera

8

7

BARCELONETA

Delegació del Govern

Av. Marquès de l'Argentera

C. La Marquesa

C. Dr. Aiguader

C. Balboa

C. Ginebra

C. Pinzón

C. d'Andrés Dòria

C. la Maquinista

17

PL BARCELONETA

C. Sant Carles

C. Almirall Cervera

Platja de Sant Sebastià

BRUGADA

PL DEL PALAU

6

C. Consolat de Mar

Pg. d'Isabel II

PL. DE PAU VILA

15

Moll del Dipòsit

16

18

C. Almirall Aixada

19

C. Almirall Cervera

C. Judici

20

Via Laietana

C. d'En Giglas

PL D'ANTONIO LÓPEZ

Cap de Barcelona

Pg. d'Espanya

Dàrsena de Comerç

Pg. de Joan de Borbó

Marina-Port Vell

Moll del Rellotge

C. Varadero

C. d'Ataülf

C. de la Mercè

La Mercè

Pg. de Colom

Moll de la Barceloneta

IMAX Port Vell

Moll dels Pescadors

TO CLUB NATACIÓ ATLÈTIC-BARCELONETA (150m)

C. d'Avinyó

PL DE LA MERCÈ

L'Aquàrium

Dàrsena de la Indústria

Torre de Sant Sebastià

C. de Còdols

PL DE MEDINACELI

Cine

Teleferic

C. Nou de Sant Francesc

C. A. Clavé

Moll de la Fusta

Maremagnum

10

5

DRASSANES

Las Ramblas

DRASSANES

Rambla de Mar

PL PORTAL DE LA PAU

Monument a Colom

Dàrsena Nacional

2

C. l'Arc del Teatre

C. Montserrat

i

Las Golondrinas

TO WORLD TRADE CENTER (200m)

C. l'Arc del Teatre

Av. Drassanes

1

Moll de Barcelona

C. Portal Sta. Madrona

Pg. de Josep Carner

PL DE LES DRASSANES

C. l'Om

Av. Paral·lel

Waterfront

♦ **ACCOMMODATIONS**
Hostal del Mar, **6**
Pensión Francia, **7**
Hostal Marítima, **4**
Hostal Orleans, **8**

♦ **FOOD**
Mandongo, **10**
Fratello, **16**
La Mar Salada, **19**
La Taverna d'en Pep, **17**
Café L'Imma, **18**
Zahara, **20**

🏛 **MUSEUMS**
Museu de Cera, **5**
Museu d'Art Modern, **9**
Museu d'Història de Catalunya, **15**
Museu Marítim, **1**
Centre d'Art de Santa Monica, **2**

🎭 **NIGHTLIFE**
El Bosq de les Fades, **3**
Central Golf, **12**
Mojito Bar, **13**
Nayandei, **11**
Star Winds, **14**

APPENDIX

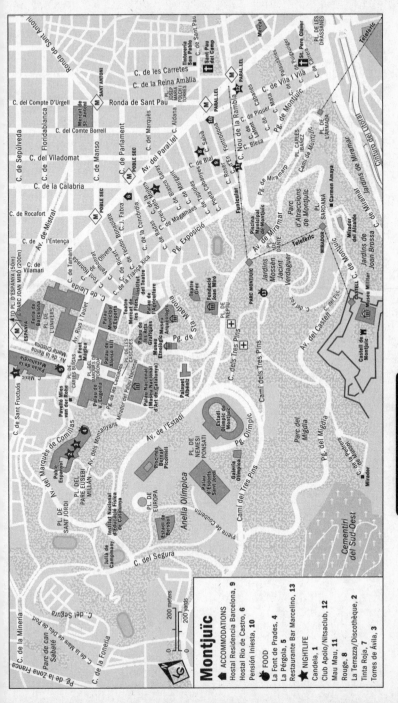

Montjuïc

▲ ACCOMMODATIONS
Hostal Residència Barcelona, 9
Hostal Río de Castro, 6
Pensión Iniesta, 10

🍴 FOOD
La Font de Prades, 4
La Pérgola, 5
Restaurante Bar Marcelino, 13

🎵 NIGHTLIFE
Candela, 1
Club Apolo/Nitsaclub, 12
Mau Mau, 11
Rouge, 8
La Terrazza/Discothèque, 2
Tinta Roja, 7
Torres de Ávila, 3

200 meters
200 yards
0

APPENDIX

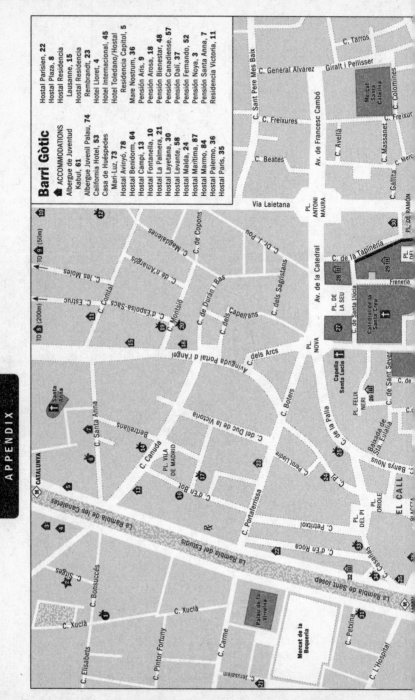

Barri Gòtic

🛏 ACCOMMODATIONS
Albergue de Juventud
  Kabul, 61
Albergue Juvenil Palau, 74
California Hotel, 53
Casa de Huéspedes
  Mari-Luz, 73
Hostal Avinyó, 78
Hostal Benidorm, 64
Hostal Campi, 13
Hostal Fontanella, 10
Hostal La Palmera, 21
Hostal Layetana, 30
Hostal Levante, 58
Hostal Malda, 24
Hostal Marítima, 87
Hostal Marmo, 84
Hostal Palermo, 36
Hostal Paris, 35

Hostal Parisien, 22
Hostal Plaza, 8
Hostal Residencia
  Lausanne, 15
Hostal Residencia
  Rembrandt, 23
Hotel Lloret, 4
Hotel Internacional, 45
Hotel Toledano/Hostal
  Residencia Capitol, 5
Mare Nostrum, 36
Pensión Aris, 9
Pensión Arosa, 18
Pensión Bienestar, 48
Pensión Canadiense, 57
Pensión Dalí, 37
Pensión Fernando, 52
Pensión Noya, 3
Pensión Santa Anna, 7
Residencia Victoria, 11

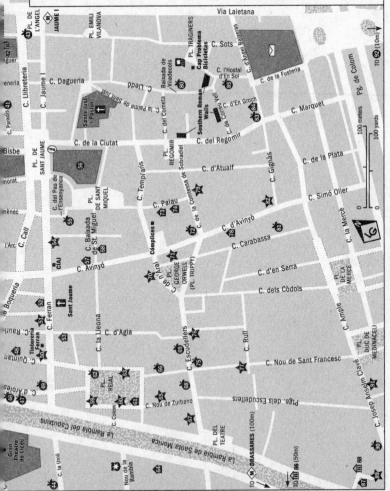

FOOD
L'Antic Bocoi del Gòtic, **80**
Arc Café, **81**
The Bagel Shop, **14**
Bar Ra, **44**
Betawi, **20**
Buenas Migas, **1**
Buen Bocado, **68**
Café de l'Opera, **47**
Los Caracoles, **75**
La Colmena, **43**
Escribà, **31**
Govinda, **17**
Irati, **33**
Italiano's, **46**
Juicy Jones, **34**
Kamasawa, **69**
Il Mercante Di Venezia, **90**
Maoz Falafel, **49**
Mi Burrito y Yo, **55**
Oolong, **83**
Els Quatre Gats, **19**
Les Quinze Nits, **62**
Restaurante Self
Naturista, **6**
El Salón, **85**
Terrablava, **12**
Thiossan, **66**
Venus Delicatessen, **72**
Xaloc, **25**

Museu de Cera, **88**
Museu de l'Eròtica, **32**
Museu d'Història de la
Ciutat, **42**
Museu Diocesà, **28**
Museu Frederic Marès, **29**

● **SIGHTS**
Ajuntament, **56**
Cap de Barcelona, **92**
Casa de l'Ardiaca, **27**
Hebrew Plaque, **39**
Palau de la Generalitat, **40**
Roman Tombs, **16**
Temple of Augustus, **41**

★ **NIGHTLIFE**
Barcelona Pipa Club, **59**
El Bosq de les Fades, **89**
Café Royale, **65**
Casa El Agüelo, **82**
Dot Light Club, **77**
Fonfone, **76**
Glaciar Bar, **63**
Harlem Jazz Club, **79**
Jamboree, **60**
Bar Ovisos, **70**
Margarita Blue, **91**
Molly's Fair City, **50**
New York, **67**
La Oveja Negra, **2**
Schilling, **51**
La Verónica, **71**
Vildsvin, **54**

🏛 **MUSEUMS**
Centre d'Art de Santa
Monica, **86**
Museu del Calçat, **26**

APPENDIX

L'Eixample

Travessera de Gràcia

C. Granada del Penedès

C. Lluis Arigaez

C. Buenos Aires

TO ⭐ (300m) & ⭐ (500m)
TO 🏛 5
(100m)

C. Londres

TO 🟡8
(30m)

C. Paris

Av. Diagonal

Via Augusta

Riera Sant Miquel

Gran de Gràcia

C. Maspons

C. St. Pere Martir

C. Penedès

C. Goya   C. Diluvi

C. Puigmarti

C. Siracusa

C. de Torde

C. Sèneca

Casablanca

C. Mozart

C. F. Giner

C. M. de la Rosa

C. del Torrent de l'Olla

C. Bonavista

C. Torres

C. de la Libert.

C. del Perill

L'EIXAMPLE ESQUERRA

C. Còrsega

🟡9

PL. JOAN
CARLES I
ℹ

🟡10

🟡28

🟡29

Av. Diago

C. Muntaner

🟡12 C. Enrique Granados

🟡13

C. Rosselló

🟡14 C. Aribau

C. Balmes

🟡15

🟡16

C. Provença

🟡17

🟡18

🟡19

C. Mallorca

🟡20

🟡38

C. València

🟡39

DIAGONAL M

🟡21

🟡22

🟡23

🟡24

🟡25

🟡30

Rambla de Catalunya

Pg. de Gràcia

🟡27

🟡26

🟡31

🟡32

🟡44

🟡45

🟡54 🏛 🟡57 🟡58

🟡53 🟡55 🟡56

🟡52

🟡46 🏛

PASSEIG
DE GRÀCIA

🟡59 🟡60

C. de Roger de Llúria

🟡61

C. Bruc

PL. DOCTOR
LETAMENDI

🟡42

🟡43

M

🟡47

🟡48

🟡49 🏛

🟡50

✉ 🟡51

🟡62

🟡40 🟡41

🟡65

🟡66

✉ 🟡67

C. Diputació

Universitat
de Barcelona

🟡71

🟡72

🟡73 🟡74

🟡77

🟡75 🟡76

🟡78

C. de Pau Claris

🟡79

🟡80

🟡81

GI

TO 🟡68 (300m),
🟡69 & 🟡70 (800m)
PL. DE LA
UNIVERSITAT

Av. Gran Via de les Corts Catalanes

M UNIVERSITAT

M

PASSEIG DE
GRÀCIA

ℹ

TO 🟡84
(100m)

Ronda de Sant Antoni

PL. DE
CASTELLA

C. Tallers

🟡85

Ronda Universitat

✉ 🟡86

🟡87

🟡90

C. de Casp

🟡91

C. Valldonzella

🚌 Bus Stop
for Airport
& Bus Turistic

M
CATALUNYA

PL. DE
CATALUNYA

El Corte
Inglés

ℹ

C. Fontanella

🟡93

🟡89

M
URQUINAONA

URQUINAONA

PL.
URQUINAONA

🟡94

🟡95

Ronda St.

C. Trafalgar

🟡32

Barcelona Allotjament ■

🟡88

INDEX

MAP INDEX

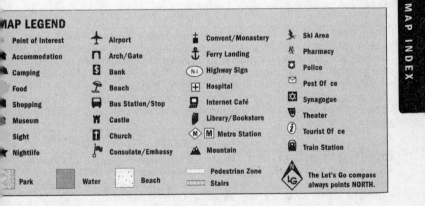

MAP LEGEND

Point of Interest	✈ Airport	♱ Convent/Monastery
Accommodation	⋒ Arch/Gate	⚓ Ferry Landing
Camping	$ Bank	(N-I) Highway Sign
Food	Beach	⊞ Hospital
Shopping	Bus Station/Stop	Internet Café
Museum	Castle	Library/Bookstore
Sight	Church	Ⓜ M Metro Station
Nightlife	Consulate/Embassy	Mountain

⚡ Ski Area		
℞ Pharmacy		
Police		
✉ Post Office		
Synagogue		
Theater		
ⓘ Tourist Office		
Train Station		

Park   Water   Beach

- - - - Pedestrian Zone
▭▭▭▭ Stairs

The Let's Go compass always points NORTH.

LET'S GO. If you want to share your discoveries, suggestions, or cor-
drop us a line. We appreciate every piece of correspondence, whether
ɔage email, or a coconut. Visit Let's Go at **http://www.letsgo.com,** or

ɔsgo.com, subject: "Let's Go Barcelona"

ɔ mail to:

Let's Go Barcelona, 67 Mount Auburn St., Cambridge, MA 02138, USA

In addition to the invaluable travel advice our readers share with us, many are kind enough to
offer their services as researchers or editors. Unfortunately, our charter enables us to employ
only currently enrolled Harvard students.

Maps by Let's Go copyright © 2010 by Let's Go, Inc.

Distributed by Publishers Group West.
Printed in Canada by Friesens Corp.

ISBN-13: 978-1-59880-307-5
ISBN-10: 1-59880-307-7
Fourth edition
10 9 8 7 6 5 4 3 2 1

Let's Go Barcelona is written by Let's Go Publications, 67 Mount Auburn St., Cambridge, MA 02138, USA.

Let's Go® and the LG logo are trademarks of Let's Go, Inc.